Madrid

Damien Simonis

LONELY PLANET PUBLICATIONS
Melbourne • Oakland • London • Paris

Madrid
1st edition – October 2000

Published by
Lonely Planet Publications Pty Ltd ABN 36 005 607 983
90 Maribyrnong St, Footscray, Victoria 3011, Australia

Lonely Planet Offices
Australia Locked Bag 1, Footscray, Victoria 3011
USA 150 Linden St, Oakland, CA 94607
UK 10a Spring Place, London NW5 3BH
France 1 rue du Dahomey, 75011 Paris

Photographs
All of the images in this guide are available for licensing from
Lonely Planet Images.
email: lpi@lonelyplanet.com.au

Front cover photograph
The Tio Pepe sign towers over the busy Puerto del Sol
(Damien Simonis)

ISBN 1 86450 123 5

**Although the authors
and Lonely Planet try
to make the informa-
tion as accurate as
possible, we accept
no responsibility for
any loss, injury or
inconvenience sus-
tained by anyone
using this book.**

Contents

1

2 Contents

PLACES TO STAY 130

PLACES TO EAT 136

ENTERTAINMENT 150

NIGHTLIFE 155

SHOPPING 167

EXCURSIONS 173

LANGUAGE 197

GLOSSARY 204

INDEX 213

MAP SECTION 217

MAP LEGEND back page

METRIC CONVERSION inside back cover

actually got on fairly well with the Christian kingdoms. The relationship with Arab- and Berber-dominated Córdoba was rather less cordial, as the ferocity of a muwallad revolt in the Middle March against Muhammad I testifies. The emir won this battle and managed to retain a degree of control over his testy subjects.

Until well into the 10th century, Magerit remained little more than a fortified garrison. With the exception of a stretch of the city wall below the modern Catedral de Nuestra Señora de la Almudena, nothing survives from it. To get an idea of its situation, head for the Palacio Real. In its place stood the *al-qasr*, or fortress (hence the Spanish word *alcázar*). Immediately to its south was a tiny tangle of lanes huddled behind citadel walls and known as the *al-mudayna* (hence Almudena) in which the soldiery and, with time, their families and hangers-on lived. To the south a stream ran along what is now Calle de Segovia to the Manzanares, which itself served as a first line of defence. To the north of the alcázar, roughly along what is now the Cuesta de San Vicente, ran another stream.

If you walk down to the entrance to the Campo del Moro west of the Palacio Real, you can see that the position's height made it virtually impregnable from the north, west and south. Starting with Ramiro II of Castile in 932 and up until Franco between 1936 and 1939, Magerit/Madrid's assailants have generally found the city impossible to take from this side. The eastern side (where Plaza de Oriente is now) was the weak link and had to be more heavily fortified.

Under the rule of Abderahman III, Magerit grew. South, across what is now Calle de Segovia in the Vistillas area, emerged the busiest of the *arrabales* (suburbs beyond the city walls). A bridge was thrown over the stream to connect the two hills. To this day the warren of streets around Vistillas is known as the *morería*, or Moorish quarter. The main mosque was built on what is now the corner of Calle Mayor and Calle de Bailén (nothing remains of it).

When in 1008 the emirate of Córdoba broke up into a series of smaller kingdoms called *taifas*, Magerit ended up attached to the taifa of Toledo. It became the taifa's primary defensive outpost against increasingly aggressive Christian forces in the north. Fernando I of Castile tried and failed to take Magerit in 1047 and for a while the taifa paid tribute to the Castilian and Leonese rulers in return for peace. Then, in 1085, King Alfonso VI of Castile was virtually handed the taifa. It appears the latter's ruler preferred Valencia and, in return for Alfonso's help in taking it, he abandoned Toledo and its territory. At the time of Alfonso's entry into the town, its population is thought to have numbered as many as 12,000 souls.

In the opening years of the following century, the North African Almoravids swept across much of Spain in support of the Muslim taifas and Madrid came close to falling – it was the last time the Muslims came seriously close to retaking the town.

Medieval Christian Madrid

Threats to Madrid came not only from the Muslims to the south. The Castilian Crown's control over cities in the Middle Ages was not unlimited and cities frequently ran their own affairs. Madrid found neighbours such as Segovia encroaching on its agricultural hinterland and establishing new settlements. It had to appeal repeatedly to the king to intervene and establish stable frontiers.

Madrid long remained a second-rate town. While other Castilian cities received generous *fueros* (self-rule ordinances), Madrid had to content itself with fairly offhand royal rulings laid down in 1118 and 1202. By that time a small number of local families had concentrated municipal power in their hands and were furnishing the members of the town council, the Consejo de Madrid.

In 1348, the horrors of Black Death struck Madrid with as much fury as the rest of urban Europe, and in that same year the king began to name *regidores* (governors) of Madrid and other cities in an attempt to tighten central control over them.

The same families (the Luzón, Vargas and others) ended up monopolising power as regidores and ruled as petty oligarchs. Less favoured families and the lower classes continually protested to the Crown over abuses of power, but although occasionally a *corregidor* (royally appointed co-governor) was sent in to bring the regidores to heel, in practice the latter continued to do as they liked. In Madrid as in other Castilian towns there emerged a basically feudal system of government, the Comunidad de Villa y Tierra, in which the town *(villa)* lorded it over the peasants who worked the surrounding land *(tierra)*.

In 1309, the Cortes (royal court and parliament) sat in Madrid for the first time. Between then and 1561, when Felipe II made the town the permanent seat of the court, Madrid hosted this event 10 times. Madrid (or rather the alcázar) was a popular residence with some of the Castilian monarchs, particularly Enrique IV. They found it a relaxing base from which to set off on hunting expeditions, especially for bears in the El Pardo district.

Although trade was brisk in medieval Madrid, it was on a small scale and the town remained comparatively poor throughout the Middle Ages. The few reports from travellers to the town that survive to this day indicate it had little to offer. One 15th-century observer wrote that 'in Madrid there is nothing except what you bring with you'.

Meanwhile, across Spain great things were happening. In 1474 Isabel was crowned queen of Castile; she subsequently married Fernando in an alliance that united the Castilian and Aragonese Crowns. Together the Reyes Católicos (Catholic Monarchs) completed the Reconquista (Christian reconquest) of Spanish territory, taking the last Muslim stronghold, Granada, in 1492. That same year Columbus bumped into America in the first step of a process that would bring Spain unheard-of wealth.

Isabel died in 1504 and Fernando seemed to do his best to complicate local and European politics, marrying off his offspring to regal houses across Europe. It gets a little complex but the outcome left their grandson, Carlos, as king of Spain in 1516.

Carlos I succeeded to the Habsburg throne three years later and so became Carlos V, Holy Roman Emperor. His territories stretched from Austria to Holland, and from Spain to the American colonies. He spent only 16 years of his 40-year reign in Spain and managed to alienate the Spanish nobility to such an extent that it revolted, carrying many cities with it. In March 1520 Toledo rose and Madrid closely followed. The fight lasted a year but Carlos won.

The nobles lost more than a battle. From then on power was increasingly concentrated in the hands of the monarch. Carlos used much of that power and the wealth pouring in from the Americas on endless wars throughout Europe and against the Turks. All Spain would eventually pay for such short-sighted 'investments'.

A Crummy Capital

Carlos had considered establishing a permanent court in Toledo, but in the end rejected the idea. It would be left to his son and successor, Felipe II, who ascended the Spanish throne (which included the American possessions and the Low Countries) in 1556.

It was in 1561 that he made the decision that must have knocked the socks off all his retinue. He would finally abandon the Castilian habit of the moveable court and put down roots. So far so good, but who would have guessed that he would choose the humble town of Madrid?

It was like writing on a clean slate. To the north, south and east there was endless space for expansion. As a town with only 12,000 inhabitants and a comparatively nondescript history, no-one much would be able to object to grand new building projects. Unlike Toledo, the seat of the Church in Spain, local interests were distinctly small fry and could pose little challenge to royal authority.

Between the grander churches, the alcázar and noble residences, the bulk of the town was made up of precarious houses that amounted to little more than mud huts.

They lined chaotic, ill-defined and, for the most part, unpaved lanes and alleys. By the time Felipe II implanted himself here, this messy sprawl was spreading east to what is now Paseo del Prado. In 1566 he extended the 'walls' (actually little more than a municipal customs barrier) to take in the present-day Plaza de Antón Martín, part of the Santa Ana area and Carrera de San Jerónimo up to where the street starts to descend towards Paseo del Prado. The wall then wound north, and where it crossed the Calle de Alcalá is where the first Puerta de Alcalá stood.

More concerned with the business of empire and building his monastic retreat at San Lorenzo de El Escorial, Felipe II had done little to improve the state of his capital by the time he expired in 1598. That the bulk of the city continued to be something of a cesspit for its inhabitants seems clear from the map drawn of Madrid by Pedro Texeiro in 1656 (the year in which Felipe IV created the fifth and last of the city walls). A scale model designed in 1830 reveals that Madrid continued to consist largely of poor single-storey housing even in the 19th century.

Madrid suffered several handicaps compared with more illustrious capitals elsewhere in Europe. It was about the only capital not to be located on a substantial and navigable river or port. Highways to other parts of the country, let alone over the Pyrenees to the rest of Europe, were poor and dangerous, making trade and communications difficult at best. Not exactly blessed with the richest of agricultural hinterlands, Madrid was not playing with a great set of cards.

Other factors only made things worse. Carlos I and Felipe II presided over the apogee and collapse of Spanish power. Their innumerable wars bled the country dry, in spite of the river of precious metals shipped in from the Americas. Felipe II's successors, Felipe III and Felipe IV, gradually lost control of events. Indeed, they tended to hand management over to a trusted noble rather than take it on themselves. The most notable of these was the Count-Duke of Olivares, who did what he

could to arrest the rapid decline of Spanish power, to little avail.

In the years between the death of Felipe II and Felipe IV's own demise in 1665, royal Madrid paradoxically reached the height of sumptuousness as the court retreated increasingly from the nasty reality that surrounded it. The Palacio del Buen Retiro in the east of the city was completed in 1630 and replaced the alcázar as the prime royal residence (the Museo del Ejército building and Casón del Buen Retiro are all that now remains of the palace). Countless grand churches and convents also sprang up under royal patronage, and the aristocracy pumped increasing sums into building fine mansions. Most of this architectural grandiloquence was raised along an axis between the Palacio del Buen Retiro and the alcázar. Along this route, grand royal entrances and processions occasionally took place. They were designed to impress all and sundry with the magnificence of royal power and had the side effect of costing Madrid's town authorities and better-lined guilds considerable sums of money.

But Madrid was fantasy land. Amid the squalor in which the bulk of its people toiled, royalty and the aristocracy gave themselves over to sickening displays of wealth and cavorted happily in their make-believe world of royal splendour. The national economy, especially in Castile, was collapsing, and plebs poured into Madrid in the hope of eking out a living. But if you took away the court, the city amounted to nothing. In 1601 Felipe III, tired of Madrid, *did* move the court to Valladolid. The move lasted only five years but in that time the population of Madrid halved. '*Sólo Madrid es Corte*' (roughly, 'Only Madrid can be home to the court'), it was said, however, and the good king moved back.

In 1598 Madrid was home to 60,000 inhabitants, more than double the number when Felipe II decided to make it capital. This set the pattern – Madrid would largely remain a city of immigrants. By 1656 the numbers had swollen to 150,000. The need of the court and its followers to exude an image of power and wealth created employment for all sorts of specialists and tradespeople, who streamed in from all corners of the country.

Nobles of every possible rank, and many a son of well-educated families with no title, flocked to Madrid in the hope of gaining patronage or a post in the burgeoning machinery of government. The gentry and Church, who were exempt from taxation and entitled to a tithe on production of their rural holdings, led a rather nice, if generally futile, life.

Felipe IV's successor, the sickly Carlos II, passed on to the hereafter in 1700. Thus the Habsburg dynasty, and Madrid de los Austrias, came to a whimpering end. In a little more than 150 years, what had briefly risen to be the greatest empire in Europe had crumbled into a rotten heap.

The Count-Duke of Olivares could see the true state of the empire but many could not. This was the golden age of art in Spain (while the people starved, the aristocracy patronised artists). Velázquez, El Greco, José de Ribera, Zurbarán, Murillo and Coello were all active in this period.

The Bourbons

Carlos II's big underachievement was to leave Spain without an heir. Felipe V, grandson of Louis XIV of France and Maria Teresa (who was a daughter of Felipe IV), took over, but by 1702 all Europe was warring over the Spanish Succession. After 12 years of debilitating conflict, Felipe V kept Spain (his family, the Bourbons, remain at the head of the Spanish State today) but lost many of its territories. The country was in worse shape than ever.

Felipe set about with some diligence putting things right. He centralised State control and attempted (with little success) land reform. Madrid must still have left a lot to be desired, since the king had a royal retreat built at La Granja (see Around Segovia in the Excursions chapter) and preferred to live there than in the capital. When in 1734 the alcázar was destroyed in a fire, the king laid down plans for a magnificent new Palacio Real (Royal Palace) to take its place.

Felipe V began pushing up daisies in 1746 and was succeeded by Fernando VI. He in turn was followed by Carlos III in 1759. Between them, they gave Madrid and Spain a period of comparatively commonsense government. Carlos (with the big nose – his equestrian statue dominates the Puerta del Sol) in particular came to be known as the best mayor Madrid had ever had. He not only cleaned up the city (it still had a reputation for being among the filthiest in Europe) but also completed the Palacio Real, inaugurated the Jardín Botánico (botanical gardens) and carried out numerous other public works.

An out-and-out centralist who brooked little opposition, Carlos was nevertheless an enlightened ruler who also did much to foster the intellectual life of the city. What is today the Museo del Prado started off as a quite unique (for the times) initiative on the part of the king: he had ordered construction of the neoclassical Palacio de Villanueva (finished in 1785) to house a natural sciences museum. Carlos enticed the likes of Tiepolo across from Italy to paint for the court, and Goya, still a relative unknown, first started working in Madrid towards the end of Carlos' long reign.

The *rey-alcalde* (king-mayor) did occasionally run into trouble with the restive populace of Madrid. His unpopular Italian minister, Squillace, at one point declared long capes illegal in an attempt to reduce crime. He argued that, since the street cleaning had been improved, the capes were no longer necessary for keeping muck off other garments. He further claimed that the average *majo* (spivvy) used the capes to hide weapons. The *madrileños* (people born and bred in Madrid) would have none of it and after long riots the measure was repealed (it was later reintroduced peacefully under a less controversial minister).

In all, by the time Carlos III died in 1788, Spain and its capital were in better shape than they had been for a while. He had expelled the backward-looking Jesuits in 1767 and embarked on a major road-building program. His attempts at land reform were less successful and Spain remained, for all the improvements, an essentially poor country with a big-spending royal court.

A year later the French Revolution set all Europe in a state of fevered panic. Carlos III's successor, Carlos IV, proved in no way equal to the challenge. He and his self-seeking minister, Manuel Godoy, contrived to bring upon Spain the wrath not only of revolutionary France but also, as they cravenly switched sides, Britain.

Napoleonic Interlude

Godoy's machinations could not have done more damage. Allied with France, Spain was crushed by Nelson in the epic Battle of Trafalgar in 1805. The tragedy (from the Spanish point of view) was brilliantly portrayed in a novel in the *Episodes Nacionales* series by Benito Pérez Galdós. Spain never recovered from this blow, which set the stage for the loss of its American colonies in the course of the century.

Next, Napoleon convinced Godoy to allow in his troops so that France and Spain could devour Portugal. It soon became evident that the diminutive Corsican had other things on his mind. By 1808 the French presence had become an occupation and Napoleon's brother, Joseph Bonaparte, had been crowned king of Spain.

Early that year, a French detachment under the command of Murat took control of the city. General Tomás de Morla's bands of hearty but unruly armed citizenry were no match for Napoleon's war machine and were quickly overwhelmed.

An uneasy calm descended on the city, but tension built in April and on the morning of 2 May townspeople attacked French troops around the Palacio Real and what is now Plaza del Dos de Mayo. Murat moved quickly and by the end of the day it was all over. The uprising marked the beginning of the Guerra de la Independencia (War of Independence, or Peninsular War), a long and nasty guerrilla campaign to oust the French. British (and to a lesser extent Portuguese) forces played a key role in the campaign, finally evicting the French in the Battle of Vitoria (in the Basque Country) in 1813. The war left Madrid exhausted. In 1812, 30,000 madrileños perished from hunger alone.

The 19th Century

Fernando VII, whom the madrileños had proclaimed king when they could see where Carlos IV and Godoy were taking them, returned to Spain in 1814. Madrid had become a political backwater in the years of French occupation and a liberal-dominated Cortes called in Cádiz in 1812 had proclaimed a new constitution largely inspired by the French revolutionary and American models. This, Fernando wasted no time in abrogating. Indeed he soon proved to be the most absolutist of monarchs in Spanish history. He also called a halt to just about every civic initiative launched by Joseph Bonaparte. Bonaparte had ordered the destruction of various churches and convents to create public squares, had widened streets, improved sanitation and moved cemeteries to the outskirts of the city – all necessary measures, later observers concurred, but at the time resented.

If madrileños were hoping for more enlightened rule from Fernando, they were to be sorely disappointed. He had the occasional moment of inspiration, opening part of the renewed Parque del Buen Retiro (it had been largely destroyed during the war) to the public and founding an art gallery in the Prado.

Such tokens were clearly insufficient. In 1820, liberal elements in the army revolted and imposed a return to constitutional rule. This lasted all of three years. In 1824, defeat in Peru left Spain bereft of most of its American colonies. At the same time, in what must have seemed bitter irony to most Spaniards, French troops arrived to help maintain Fernando on his throne. When he died in 1833, he left Spain a three-year-old daughter, a recipe for civil war and an economy in tatters.

War & Piecemeal Progress

What Spain and Madrid desperately needed was a long spell of stability. What they got was a civil war. Isabel II, at three, was not yet quite up to running the country, and so began the long years of the regency of her mother, María Cristina. Fernando's brother Don Carlos and his conservative supporters disputed Isabel's right to the throne and this sparked the Carlist wars. María Cristina was obliged to turn to the liberals for help.

Absolutism was over but Madrid society was a strange animal in comparison with that of other European capitals. Although they were in increasing financial difficulties, high society was still dominated by a class of landed aristocrats. A burgeoning middle class only really began to make itself felt from 1837 onwards. In that year, the government ordered the expropriation *(desamortización)* of Church property. The decision came in the wake of bloody riots and the assassination of clergy by furious mobs during a cholera epidemic in July 1834 – the lower classes continued to live in misery and blamed the Church more than anyone for their troubles. No-one raised a finger in defence of the Church when expropriation came three years later. It is reckoned it lost some 1600 properties in Madrid in the first four decades of the 19th century alone.

This move, which would have art historians of later generations in tears, created an unprecedented property boom. Churches and convents were razed and any halfway enterprising businesspeople with some spare pesetas set about buying up the land and building on it (mostly housing of often indifferent quality). The proceeds went into the government's coffers. The winners in this speculative free-for-all would form the basis of the new middle class that in the latter half of the century, finally, would help breathe a little life into the city's economy.

Miraculous development was not the order of the day, however. As late as 1860 a full quarter of Madrid's working populace were employed as servants in aristocratic households – a staggering indication of economic inactivity. Hundreds of small workshops beavered away to supply a local market, but factories in the modern sense were few and far between.

Plan after ambitious plan to guide urban expansion beyond the then limits of the city remained on the drawing board. But talk

was abundant. The sensation of freedom was palpable after Fernando VII's death, and the intellectual life of the city flourished. Madrid continued to be a city of immigrants. Statistics show that, while the bulk of the middle-class traders came from the north of the country, Andalucía supplied an inordinate proportion of lawyers, politicians and scribblers.

Political upheaval remained part of the city's daily diet, characterised above all by alternating coups between conservative and liberal wings of the army. One came in 1840, another in 1843 (the year in which Isabel began to rule in her own right). In 1848, as revolution swept across Europe, a liberal rebellion shook Madrid. In the following 20 years until the revolt that sent Isabel into exile in France, you could just about have set your clock by the regular coups and riots that had become an integral part of the city's life.

Not all was bad news. In 1851, the first railway line, between Madrid and Aranjuez, was opened. It was followed in 1858 by the Canal de Isabel II that would supply the city with water from the Sierra de Guadarrama. National roads radiating from the capital were improved. Public works, ranging from the reorganisation of the Puerta del Sol to the building of the Teatro Real, Biblioteca Nacional and Congreso de los Diputados (lower house of parliament), were carried out. Street paving, the sewage system and garbage collection were improved, and gas lighting was introduced. More importantly still, foreign (mostly French) capital was beginning to fill the investment vacuum. Madrid was finally showing signs of becoming a finance and communications centre.

In the 1860s, the first timid moves to create an *ensanche*, or extension of the city, were undertaken. The initial building spurt arose around Calle de Serrano, where the enterprising Marqués de Salamanca bought up land and built high-class housing aimed at both old and new money. Poor old Salamanca was a little ahead of his time and managed to lose everything in his speculative gamble. By the time the area came

Hoping to get into the Prado?

A song for San Isidro, Madrid's patron saint

Kids at Puerta del Sol, the very centre of Spain

Music is fundamental to Madrid's festivals.

Dancing in Plaza Mayor in vibrant costume

Madrileños in traditional dress

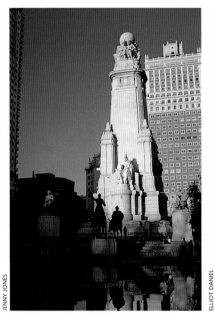

Striking views over the Plaza España

Modern architecture on the bustling Gran Via

A palace? A museum? No, it's the Palacio de Comunicaciones at the Plaza de Cibeles.

good (as he had foreseen), he had already gone to Jesus.

From Restoration to Republic

The six years following Isabel's flight in 1868 were followed by more turmoil. Government was handed to an Italian prince, Amedeo di Savoia. He soon found the task beyond him and in 1873 a republic was called. Matters didn't improve and the army finally decided to restore the Bourbon monarchy, putting Alfonso XII, Isabel's son, on the throne. A period of relative tranquillity ensued.

Building of the ensanche gathered momentum. The city's big train stations were constructed and the foundation stones of a cathedral (Madrid's first) were laid – it would take more than a century to finish! Another kind of cathedral, the Banco de España, was completed with greater alacrity and opened its doors in 1891.

The country ended the century with a rather unpleasant shock. Manoeuvred into a brief and hopeless war with the US, Spain managed in 1898 not only to lose its last colonies, especially the Philippines and Cuba, but saw its entire navy sunk in two ignominious clashes with the new industrial giant of North America.

The trials and tribulations of Spain's European neighbours between 1914 and 1918 initially constituted a boon to Madrid. Until late 1916 money poured in as the western Allies bought up goods in neutral Spain.

Even before the outbreak of WWI things were already moving on more quickly in Madrid. In the year of the 'disaster', 1898, the first city tramlines were electrified. In 1910 work began on the Gran Vía (finished in 1929) and nine years later the first metro line started operation. Inward migration would double the city's population from half a million at the turn of the century to almost one million in 1931, when the second republic was called.

By 1931, Madrid's politics had been radicalised. A militant typographer, Pablo Iglesias, had founded the country's first socialist party in 1879 (see the boxed text 'Pablo Iglesias & the Birth of Spanish So-

cialism' over the page), and for the first time a left-wing coalition, made up of socialists and republicans, won municipal elections in 1910 in spite of vote-rigging.

King Alfonso XIII was becoming increasingly unpopular and the 1906 bomb attack on his wedding parade in Calle Mayor was only the most spectacular of several failed attempts on his life. Calls for constitutional reform grew, as did tension in Madrid, Barcelona and the countryside. While socialists led the way in Madrid under the Partido Socialista Obrera Español (PSOE; Spanish Socialist Workers' Party) and the Unión General de Trabajadores (UGT; General Workers' Union), the bulk of poor farmers around the country and industrial workers in Barcelona were attracted by the anarchist movement, embodied in the Confederación Nacional de Trabajo (CNT; National Confederation of Labour).

The rapid growth in population fuelled tensions. Construction of housing continued in the ensanche (comprising the neighbourhood of Salamanca, the area around Argüelles, and Chamberí) and in the so-called Extrarradio (areas such as Cuatro Caminos, which at the time lay some distance from the city), but the housing shortage for the poorest (and most numerous) classes remained acute. Descriptions of blocks in Lavapiés and other neighbourhoods *(barrios)* south of the Puerta del Sol in the early decades of the 20th century make depressing reading.

Above all else, the drop in exports to the by-now exhausted combatants in WWI brought on an economic crisis in 1917 that would help precipitate events in Madrid. That year a general strike was called across the country. In the following four years several assassinations rocked Madrid, followed by the humiliating defeat of a Spanish army stuck in the morass of a seemingly endless colonial war in northern Morocco. Blame for this latest shambles abroad was laid squarely at the feet of the king, and in 1923 the captain-general of Catalunya, General Miguel Primo de Rivera, launched a coup that would lead to a six-year dictatorship.

Pablo Iglesias & the Birth of Spanish Socialism

Madrid, for hundreds of years the political nerve centre of Spain and its one-time empire, has produced surprisingly few of the country's leading political figures. Kings and queens were almost always from somewhere else and, in more recent times, Franco came from Galicia, while the long-running socialist prime minister until 1996, Felipe González, is from Andalucía.

The founder of González's party, however, was a local boy. Well, almost. Born in Franco's home town of O Ferrol in 1850, Pablo Iglesias was brought to Madrid in his infancy and there he remained. A printer by trade, he began trade-union activities at the age of 20. One year later he got a workers' paper, *La Emancipación*, off the ground. With the rise of Marxist ideas across Europe, in 1879 Iglesias was elected president of a new association that constituted Spain's first clandestine workers' party.

Two years later, the Partido Socialista Obrero Español (PSOE; Spanish Socialist Workers' Party) went public. Its advances were rapid. Within seven years it had branches across the country and Iglesias was running its mouthpiece, *El Socialista*. The Unión General de Trabajadores (UGT; General Workers' Union) was organised thereafter, with strong PSOE influence. By the turn of the century socialist candidates were winning seats in local government.

Iglesias himself was elected several times to the Cortes (national parliament) from 1910 to 1916. By then ailing and increasingly shy of the limelight, Iglesias had become a working-class myth. Even in the wake of the general strike called in 1917 by the UGT, which was suppressed without any ceremony, Iglesias was left in peace. He remained president of the PSOE and UGT, albeit in a largely honorary fashion, until his death in 1925.

A statue raised in his honour in the Parque del Oeste was buried there by republicans during the Civil War to protect it from the nationalists. Problem is, no one knows exactly where. Many years after the war ended, the head was accidentally dug up – the rest has never been found.

Primo de Rivera clamped down on republican and other opposition voices. The CNT was forced underground and the UGT's activities were curtailed. The dictator was not inactive, and promoted the growth of industry and road-building and so on. It was not enough. In Madrid his repression of dissent, which weighed heavily on the university, provoked student strikes and helped swell the ranks of the UGT, PSOE and republican groups. He could do little to combat the impact of the Wall Street Crash that hit Spain as hard as anywhere else. Alfonso XIII, who had done little to challenge the general, finally had him removed in 1930.

Madrid greeted the decision with joyful demonstrations. Municipal elections were called around the country and on 12 April 1931 a coalition of republicans and socialists carried the day. Three days later the second republic was proclaimed and Alfonso XIII fled. The republican government opened up the Casa de Campo – until then a private royal playground – to the people of Madrid and passed a law specifically recognising Madrid as the capital of the Spanish state. Other measures contained in the new constitution of December 1931, ranging from greater autonomy for Catalunya, attempts at land reform and dropping Catholicism as the State religion, mostly served to add to the sensation of political confrontation. The conservative right and extreme left, especially the anarchists who had been virtually excluded from government, whipped up street violence.

Divisions on the left helped a right-wing coalition into power in 1933. This in turn fuelled calls for revolution from the anarchists and the fledgling Communist Party. Strikes were called and a miners' revolt in the northern region of Asturias in 1934 was bloodily put down by Foreign Legion troops under General Francisco Franco.

In February 1936 the left-wing Frente

Popular (Popular Front) just beat the right's Frente Nacional (National Front) into power. One of its first moves was to move suspect generals out of the way – Franco was sent to the Canary Islands. One way or another, a violent face-off appeared inevitable. Either the army would move first in a coup or the extreme left would have its revolution.

The Civil War
In the end the army moved first. In July 1936, garrisons in North Africa revolted, quickly followed by others on the mainland. There followed three years of bloody warfare, characterised by horrendous atrocities carried out by both the republican and nationalist sides.

Having stopped nationalist troops advancing from the north, Madrid came under threat from Franco's forces moving up from the south. By early November 1936 they were in the Casa de Campo. The government fled to Valencia, but the resolve of the city's defenders, a mix of hastily assembled recruits, sympathisers from the ranks of the army and airforce, the International Brigades (which started arriving on 9 November) and Soviet advisers, held firm. Fighting was heaviest in the north-west of the city, around Argüelles, but Franco's frontal assault failed – until 28 March 1939, that is, by which time Franco had most of the country in his hands, and Madrid finally surrendered.

In the two and a half years of siege, madrileños lived in a bizarre reality. People went about their business, caught the metro to work and got on with things as best they could while skirmishes continued around Argüelles and nationalist artillery intermittently shelled the city from the Casa de Campo.

The Franco Years
A deathly silence fell over the city as the new dictator made himself at home. He had at first considered shifting the capital south to the more amenable Seville, but decided instead to convert Madrid into a capital worthy of its new masters.

General Francisco Franco, Spain's dictator from 1939 to 1975

In those dark years, as Western Europe was again tearing itself apart in a world war and Franco and his right-wing Falangist Party maintained a heavy-handed repression, Madrid's problems remained acute.

The 1940s and 1950s proved the most trying. These were the years of *autarquía* (economic self-reliance, largely induced by Spain's international isolation after the end of WWII) or, more simply, for most Spaniards, the *años de hambre* – the years of hunger. Only in 1955 did the average wage again reach the level of 1934!

Repression was at its harshest throughout the 1940s. Many thousands of suspects, ranging from supporters of the Frente Popular through to union members, were harassed, imprisoned, employed in forced labour (such as housing projects from which private enterprise made enormous profits or the construction of the nationalist Valle de los Caídos monument), tortured and shot. Prior to 1945, thousands of political prisoners were shipped off to Nazi concentration camps – few returned.

The government of Madrid, as in all municipalities, was put in the hands of a mayor directly named by a *gobernador civil* (civil governor), who represented the State. In

Madrid more than anywhere this effectively meant that local government was in central State hands.

Hundreds of thousands of starving *campesinos* (peasants) flocked to the capital in the hope of finding work, increasing the already enormous pressure for housing. In the 10 years from 1950 alone, more than 600,000 arrived. Most contented themselves with erecting *chabolas* (shanty towns) on the outskirts of town. Ugly satellite suburbs began to grow and the private sector seemed to specialise in building cheap, poor-quality housing en masse and with little regard for planning rules. As early as the 1950s, discontent began to express itself openly in Madrid. It began in the universities and, perhaps surprisingly for some, in new Catholic youth and workers organisations set up to fight the official line towed by government-sponsored trade unions.

Franco might not have liked communists much, but he and Spain could thank their lucky stars for the existence of the Soviet Union. In 1953, the USA decided to change tack and grant economic aid to Franco's Spain in exchange for the use of Spanish air and naval bases. By the early 1960s, when Franco had largely replaced Falangist ideologues in government with conservative technocrats, industry was taking off in and around Madrid. Foreign investment poured in (factories of the American Chrysler motor company were Madrid's single biggest employers in the 1960s) and the services and banking sector boomed. It was now that Paseo de la Castellana took on much of its present aspect. Fine old palaces were routinely demolished and replaced by such buildings as the Torres de Colón. These were the boom years of Spain's 'economic miracle', in part guided by the government's 1959 economic Stabilisation Plan.

The boom years brought greater prosperity and buying power to madrileños. In 1960 fewer than 70,000 cars were on the road in Madrid. Ten years later more than half a million clogged the capital's streets. Bread alone doesn't do the trick though and, from 1965 onwards, opposition to Franco's regime became steadily more vocal. Again,

the universities were repeatedly the scene of confrontation, but clandestine trade unions, such as Comisiones Obreras (Workers Commissions) and the outlawed UGT, began to make themselves heard again too.

The waves of protest were not restricted to Madrid. In the Basque Country the terrorist group Euskadi Ta Askatasuna (ETA; 'Basques and Freedom') began to fight for Basque independence. Their first important action was the assassination in Madrid in 1973 of Admiral Carrero Blanco, Franco's prime minister and designated successor. At that time ETA would have been applauded by a broad range of Spaniards. That it still occasionally assassinates public figures in the streets of Madrid today has rendered it vile in the eyes of virtually all madrileños and even most Basques.

In 1974 Franco fell ill. His agony was prolonged and he did not finally abandon this mortal coil until 20 November 1975. In the meantime, Spanish politics went on the boil.

Return to Democracy

The PSOE (socialists), Partido Comunista de España (PCE; Spanish Communist Party), trade unions and a wide range of opposition groups and figures emerged from hiding and exile in the months before and after Franco's death. No-one was entirely sure what turn events would take, but King Juan Carlos I, of the Bourbon family that had left the Spanish political stage with the flight of Alfonso XIII in 1931, surprised everyone.

The king entrusted Adolfo Suárez, a former Francoist, with government in July 1976 and he quickly rammed a raft of changes through parliament. By 1977, when elections were called, opposition parties and trade unions had been legalised. Suárez and his centre-right coalition won the elections and set about writing a new constitution in collaboration with the opposition. It provided for a parliamentary monarchy with no State religion and guaranteed a large degree of devolution to the 17 regions into which the country was now divided.

Spaniards got a fright in 1981 when a pistol-brandishing, low-ranking Guardia

Civil (Civil Guard) officer, Antonio Tejero Molina, marched into the Cortes with an armed detachment and held parliament captive for 24 hours. The king made it clear he did not back Tejero and the coup finally fizzled out. A year later Felipe González's PSOE won the national elections. González remained in power until 1996, when the Partido Popular (PP; Popular Party), a right-of-centre party, picked up the baton that it has held to this day.

The first free municipal elections were held in Madrid in 1979, and Enrique Tierno Galván became mayor of a left-wing council. A charismatic leader, he was in charge of the city until his death in 1986. His successor, Juan Barranco, kept power in socialist hands until 1991, when the PP's José María Alvarez del Manzano won an absolute majority. He is still mayor today.

In the little more than 20 years since Tierno Galván first became mayor, Madrid has changed remarkably. He encouraged a flourishing of artistic and cultural activity in the city, the restoration and improvement of much of the old centre, and improved public transport and public housing. The *movida*, that explosion of zesty nightlife that marked Madrid in the late 70s and most of the 80s, was in keeping with a policy of turning Madrid into an open, fashionable city.

The movida has now lost much of its oomph and the present mayor is more sympathetic to residents' desires for peace and quiet than he is concerned about Madrid's image as a centre for endless nocturnal diversion. That said, he continues policies of urban renewal and improvement.

As the national economy embarked on a renewed phase of confident growth in the late 1990s, Madrid has felt the not-always-positive side effects. Housing prices are skyrocketing ahead of wages' growth. Parts of the city remain dirty and even squalid. And while ambitious expansion programs for the metro and airport go ahead, the problems of the urban poor remain all too apparent. Madrid in 2000 is, despite its rocky history and continuing problems, a remarkably lively, happening city. The murky days of the crummy capital seem long gone.

GEOGRAPHY
The City

Madrid lies at the epicentre of the country on comparatively high, flat ground, which ranges from just over 600m above sea level at its lowest points to more than 700m above sea level at Plaza de Castilla. Little opposes the continuing spread of suburban construction in any direction. Historically, the narrow trickle that is the Río Manzanares, which runs roughly north to south, formed the natural western boundary of the city. Phalanxes of high-rise apartment blocks have long swamped the river in a seemingly endless westwards sprawl.

The steepest bit of terrain in the whole city is the ridge along which the original Islamic fortress town (the alcázar) was raised. From the Palacio Real, the Catedral de Nuestra Señora de la Almudena and Vistillas, the land falls away into parks towards the Manzanares. A tributary once raced down what is now Calle de Segovia.

To the east, the heart of old Madrid rises almost imperceptibly before dropping down again to the great north–south boulevard, the Paseo de la Castellana (which changes name several times in its long journey), which itself was laid in a former river bed. To the east of the Castellana is one of the city's principal green lungs, the Parque del Buen Retiro. The other, the much more extensive and unkempt Casa de Campo, stretches away west of the Manzanares.

The city is pushing its way out in all directions. Its peripheral ringroad was long the M-30 until it was swallowed up by development; the much wider M-40 was completed in the 1990s. Seeing that even this will be breached, another ringroad, the M-50, is planned.

The city continues to consume neighbouring towns and municipalities. Places such as Leganés and Getafe, to the south, are now barely distinguishable from the municipality of Madrid itself.

Comunidad de Madrid

The city lies at the heart of a single-province autonomous region (the Comunidad de Madrid) in the rough shape of a triangle. It covers 8028 sq km (less than 2% of Spanish territory) on a high continental plateau some 650m above sea level. The north-western boundary is closed off by a series of mountain ranges known collectively as the Sierra. They take in ranges of the Somosierra, the Sierra de Guadarrama and the Sierra de Gredos (all of which Madrid shares with the autonomous region of Castilla y León). They run from the north-east to the south-west for 140km and are part of the longer chain known as the Cordillera Central, which runs across much of central Spain.

The main route north out of Madrid passes through the Puerto de Somosierra pass (1864m). The highest point in the north is the Peña Cebollera (2129m). From the Puerto de Somosierra, the Sierra de Guadarrama stretches south-west to the Alberche depression. Its highest peak (the highest in the whole Madrid chain) is Peñalara (2430m). From the Alberche depression rise the first peaks of the Sierra de Gredos, which continues beyond Madrid's territory into the province of Ávila.

The eastern and southern boundaries of the region are shared with the Castilla-La Mancha region. To the east a series of minor rivers and hilly country separate the Comunidad de Madrid from Castilla-La Mancha. Heading south, the land is made up of flat plains (*vegas*) and low hill country (*campiñas*).

Quite a few rivers crisscross Madrid's territory, most of them beginning and ending elsewhere. The most important is the Río Tajo, which in its course from the Sistema Ibérico mountain range to the east crosses the Comunidad de Madrid for 70km before flowing gradually south-west to empty into the Atlantic at Lisbon. The Río Manzanares rises in the Sierra de Guadarrama and passes through Madrid on its meandering way south.

CLIMATE

Madrid 'enjoys' a continental climate – scorching in summer, cold in winter and dry. Madrileños sum up their feelings on the subject with the neat phrase: '*Nueve meses de invierno y tres de infierno*' ('Nine months of winter and three of hell'). This is a trifle

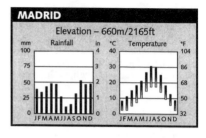

overstated, but it gets the message across that, at its worst, Madrid can be nastily cold and infernally hot.

July is the hottest month, with August running a close second. Average highs hover above 30°C, but the maximum is frequently in excess of 35°C and sometimes nudges 40°C. At 4 am you can still be gasping for air. Air-con in your room is a godsend at this time of year.

The coldest months are December and January, when daily average highs are below 10°C. At night it can get close to freezing, although snow in Madrid is a rarity. This may not seem a big deal but, if you bear in mind that many older houses have no central heating and that icy winds frequently blow in off the snow-capped Sierra, you soon realise that a Madrid winter is a short but rather sharp shock to the system. February is oddly often rather pleasant, with blue skies and daytime temperatures reaching the high teens.

The heaviest rainfall (such as it is) comes in spring and autumn, with more than 50mm quite common in October. March can be unpredictable. In Spain they say that '*cuando en marzo mayea, en mayo marzea*'. In other words, if you get nice, warm and dry days in March (weather more typical of May), you'll be wiping that grin off your face in May, when the wet spells you missed earlier catch up with you! April too can be capricious. They say that '*mes de abril, aguas mil*', which indicates that it rains a lot in this spring month.

ECOLOGY & ENVIRONMENT

Problems of air pollution in Madrid are typical of a comparatively crowded and busy city. Although restrictions apply to parking and driving through the centre of town, the city is generally full to bursting. Cars jostle about the place and the air is none too clean.

The disposal of garbage remains a fairly unecological affair. True, large brightly coloured containers have been scattered about the city for the separated collection of paper, glass and cans – but use of them depends entirely on the citizenry. Discouragingly, it is not unusual to see mounds of rubbish piling up around these and other general refuse containers – the stuff is eventually hauled off, but it is hard to escape the feeling that it is not a big priority.

Madrid is justly acclaimed for its nightlife. But this brings with it dubious pleasures for anyone trying to get some shuteye. For more on this see the boxed text 'A Booming Trade'.

Noise pollution is a big problem throughout the city. Rowdy traffic, late-night garbage collection, lusty use of sirens by the emergency services and trigger-happiness with car horns all help to keep nerves well jangled. To live in many streets in central Madrid is to invite insomnia. The general hubbub of bar-goers, cars and scooters starting up and passing by can go on until 4 am or even later. If you're unlucky enough to live above a general store, you will often have delivery trucks, engines turning over, parked outside your place by 7 am. And two hours later the intense traffic that is a call sign of downtown Madrid will have

A Booming Trade

A report issued in March 2000 claimed that almost all of central Madrid was seriously affected by noise pollution, about half from traffic and the other half caused by the high concentration of bars and their vociferous patrons. Residents have often protested to the city government – *Silencio Por Favor* is their cry.

And in the zone around Plaza de Santa Ana and Calle de las Huertas it appeared in early 2000 that these cries of distress may not have fallen on deaf ears (as it were). The conservative mayor, José María Álvarez del Manzano, declared that not only would no new licences for bars be issued in the area (enclosed roughly by Calle de Espoz y Mina, Calle de Atocha, Paseo del Prado and Carrera de San Jerónimo) but that some places might have to close.

And the municipality also intends to impose earlier closing hours (under a recently passed regional law that gives local municipalities room to decide as they see fit). At the time of writing most bars were licensed to remain trading until 3.30 am. More often than not they stay open longer and simply collect fines (ranging up to one million ptas) they have no intention of ever paying.

The mayor's latest moves provoked an outcry from the small bars (around 200 of them) in the affected area, convinced that the moves disguise attempts by the big clubs here and elsewhere throughout town to monopolise nightlife. The clubs responded that, by allowing punters to dance until the wee hours in bars, the latter were taking business away from clubs with higher overheads and taxes to pay.

Many bars chose to vent their discontent by staying open until 6 am on Saturday nights in March 2000. This battle (or 'drinks rebellion' as bar-owners themselves called it) was, they cried, one over citizens' rights to eat, drink and be merry at any hour they might choose. The mayor's response was to send in police armed with noise meters to register the decibels pumped out by the night spots. Any move to impose earlier closing times, the bars claimed, would be unconstitutional. At the time of writing nothing had been resolved either way.

To the British, such protests must seem vaguely amusing. In London, a city that rather smugly considers itself the hippest place in the Western world, most punters find themselves turfed out of pubs by 11.30 pm – an hour when most madrileños are thinking about their first course at dinner.

swept away any last chance you might have had to snooze. Long live double glazing.

GOVERNMENT & POLITICS

Three governments rule from Madrid. The national government has its home in the Cortes (parliament), which is divided into two houses, the Congreso de los Diputados (lower house) on Carrera de San Jerónimo, and the Senado (senate), off Plaza de España.

The city government, or *ayuntamiento*, is led by the mayor *(alcalde)*, who at the moment is the right-wing Partido Popular's (PP's) José María Álvarez del Manzano. He and his councillors operate out of the Ayuntamiento (City Hall) on Plaza de la Villa in the heart of the old city. In the 1999 municipal elections the PP actually came off considerably worse than four years before, dropping two seats to 28, while the main opposition, Partido Socialista Obrera Español (PSOE; Spanish Socialist Workers' Party), went from 16 to 20. The remaining five seats went to the left-wing grouping Izquierda Unida (IU; United Left).

In early 2000 Álvarez del Manzano saw himself at the centre of a storm over potential misuse of public funds. Money from a restricted account over which he has complete control was used, the opposition claimed, to pay for his wife's travel abroad, and to pay speeding fines and donations to religious institutions.

Permanent seat of Spain's ruling royal house since the latter half of the 16th century, Madrid got a promotion in 1833 when it was decided to create a province around it. The Castilian provinces surrounding Madrid (in particular Segovia, Toledo and Guadalajara) all lost territory to make way for the newcomer. The decision was taken in part to bring most (but not all) of the royal estates *(reales sitios)* of El Pardo, Aranjuez and San Lorenzo de El Escorial under the direct administration of the capital. In addition, it was hoped that the creation of the province would lend the capital greater dignity and weight.

Until the fall of Franco, the province of Madrid remained a part of Castilla La

Nueva (New Castile), the predecessor of the modern region of Castilla-La Mancha. With devolution in 1983, the province of Madrid became a separate autonomous region *(comunidad autónoma)*. The new autonomous regions of Castilla y León and Castilla-La Mancha refused to take in the province, fearing Madrid would siphon off funds and attention from more far-flung corners of their respective regions.

The Comunidad de Madrid is governed by a government council *(consejo de gobierno)*, whose actions are controlled by the regional parliament, or Asamblea de Madrid. At the head of the government is a president, at the moment Alberto Ruiz-Gallardón. Like his mayoral counterpart he is a PP man. With 55 of a total 102 seats, he governs with a fairly comfortable majority and enjoys a considerably better reputation than Álvarez del Manzano.

Elections to the city and regional governments take place every four years (the last were in 1999). They are free and by direct universal suffrage. The members of each house thus elected then vote to appoint the president of the province and the mayor.

For administrative purposes Madrid is divided into 21 districts, each with its own local council *(junta municipal)*.

ECONOMY

The city and its surrounding region are home to a fairly wide range of farming and industry. Principal crops include wheat, barley, corn, potatoes, alfalfa, melons, lettuce, garlic and grapes. That said, the province's share of national agricultural output is small. Livestock and dairy holdings are also scattered about the region. Principal industries include metallurgy, chemicals, textiles, tobacco, paper and some foodstuffs. The city itself is largely given over to services.

Average pay in Madrid is only marginally higher than elsewhere in the country, even though costs such as rent are considerably higher. While a blue-collar worker or secretary may earn about 175,000 ptas a month, better-qualified professionals average as much as 300,000 ptas.

According to figures published in early

A Bear in There

Every city has its symbols and Madrid is no different. Initially the town's coat of arms was more of a slogan than anything else: *'Fui sobre agua edificada, mis muros de fuego son'* ('I was built on water and my walls are of fire'). The explanation is simple enough. Madrid was rich in fresh-water streams (now mostly covered up) and the flinty stone used to build its walls was excellent for sparking and so lighting fires.

JANE SMITH

Later on a new symbol developed that would eventually result in the present emblem of the city: a she-bear nuzzling a *madroño*, or strawberry tree (because its fruit looks similar to strawberries). This is bordered by a frame bearing seven five-point stars and topped by a crown.

The story of the bear, madroño and stars is more than a trifle complicated.

When Alfonso VI took Madrid in 1085, Madrid was symbolically seen by some as the first of a long line of conquests that would take the Christians south. Thus Madrid became an example of things to come, or a north point. Another popular explanation for the stars is that Madrid, like Rome, was built on seven hills. As it happens, a group of seven stars that lies close to the North Star in the northern hemisphere form a shape known as the Ursa Minor, or small she-bear.

Thus the bear and seven stars came to symbolise Madrid. The fact that in medieval times bears roamed the El Pardo area just north of Madrid in some abundance adds a more prosaic (and, dare we say, likely) spin to the explanation of the origins of the animal element. The madroño was also once common around Madrid.

The bears have long since gone, but the madroño can still be seen. The city government has planted some in the Puerta del Sol and indeed they can be found right around the country, from Galicia, where it is known as *erbedo* or *bedreiro*, through to the Basque Country, where they call it *kurrkuz* or *animania*.

Above the frame is a crown. They say that Carlos I allowed the city of Madrid to use the symbol of the imperial crown in its coat of arms after he successfully cured a fever using madroño leaves (a popular medicinal herb in those days).

The five points of the stars represent the five provinces that surround the Comunidad de Madrid (Segovia, Ávila, Toledo, Cuenca and Guadalajara).

This coat of arms appears on a deep-violet background to form the city's flag. When the Comunidad de Madrid was created as a region under the Autonomies Statute of the late 1970s, the town fathers had to come up with a flag for it. They chose to put the seven stars on to a red background, which symbolises the territories of Castile from which the new province was carved.

2000, Madrid received more visitors than any other Spanish city in 1999, with 4.6 million registered in the city's hotels. Of course they weren't all tourists, but tourism makes a fair contribution to the city's coffers.

POPULATION & PEOPLE

The city of Madrid is Spain's biggest, with a population of 3.1 million. The surrounding region, the Comunidad de Madrid, counts a further two million, making it the most densely populated part of the country (whose total population is 39.8 million), with 12.8% of the country's inhabitants in an area that covers less than 2% of the territory. In absolute terms the Comunidad de Madrid ranks third behind Andalucía (18.2%) and Catalunya (15.4%), both of them much larger territories.

Some 150,000 migrants in Madrid have residence permits but many others live here illegally as *clandestinos*. In the working-class neighbourhoods of Lavapiés and around you will encounter North Africans rubbing shoulders with smaller groups of Pakistanis, black Africans, Latin Americans and others. Others live in the poorer outer dormitory suburbs.

EDUCATION

Each region in Spain administers its own education system, although overall guide-

---

Dyed in the Wool

Especially around the Fiestas de San Isidro, the *chulapos* and *manolas* of Madrid come out of the woodwork. The gents dress in their traditional short jackets and berets and the women in *mantones de Manila*, and put their best feet forward in a lively *chotis*.

What is all this? The *mantón de Manila* is an embroidered silk shawl, which few people now wear except during fiestas. The *chotis* is a traditional working-class dance not unlike a polka. One of the most common versions involves a quick three-step to the left, the same to the right, and is topped off with a brisk twirl. Only a small portion of the really *castizo* (true-blue) madrileños bother with this any more, but those who do so do it with a certain pride.

The *chulapo* – or dyed-in-the-wool, born-and-bred madrileño – is now more commonly known as a *chulo*. Now this is a word to beware of. It generally implies a degree of bravado and even arrogance of character, although in the eyes of madrileños this is no bad thing. As an adjective it can simply mean 'cool' (usually in reference to an object). But to many people (especially beyond Madrid) the word bears quite negative qualities – brash, showy. The word can also mean 'pimp', so you'd want to be sure of your company and context before bandying it around too much. The fast-talking, hard-living Madrid version of James Dean is also typecast as a *macarra*, which at its worst also means a spiv.

These breezy types, especially the kind you'd come across in the inner working-class neighbourhoods such as Lavapiés, were also once generally referred to as *manolos* (Manolo is a common first name). So it stands to reason that their girls should be known as *manolas*!

An edible castizo phenomenon is the *barquillo*. You may stumble across chaps in black-and-white-chequered waistcoats and berets hauling heavy, red cylindrical containers around the Parque del Buon Retiro and other strategic points in town. They are selling an old Madrid favourite – basically a lightly sweetened pastry made of the same ingredients as an ice-cream cone. They come in various flavours, including vanilla and cinnamon, and cost around 150 ptas. Locals love them.

To complete the picture, full-blooded madrileños are also known to the rest of Spain as *gatos*, or cats – a nice image to reflect their city savvy. The term quite appeals to the locals, as it has come to reflect their tendency to be crawling around the city like cats till all hours. They say the term was coined as one of Alfonso VI's soldiers artfully scaled Muslim Magerit's formidable walls in 1085. 'Look,' cried his comrades, 'he moves like a cat!'

Much as London cockneys or streetwise Parisians, gatos have their own colourful language, called *cheli* by some, that is full of fast-witted word play. The outsider can sometimes wonder how much Spanish they ever really learned when confronted with this snappy repartee.

They say a true gato is not only born and bred in Madrid but has parents and grandparents who can make the same boast. Since the capital has always been a magnet for Spaniards from around the country, the specimen is rare. That said, plenty of madrileños with less 'pedigree' feel themselves swept up by the city and thus become 'honorary' gatos.

lines are similar throughout the country. In the Comunidad de Madrid a total of 970,000 people are enrolled in some kind of school, from pre-school to secondary education.

At tertiary level, there are six State universities or other institutes and five private ones. About 250,000 students are enrolled in some form of tertiary education. The lion's share (almost half) attend the city's main university, the Complutense.

Illiteracy is still a minor issue in Madrid, as throughout the country. The national average is 3.9%, but in Madrid it is less than half at 1.57%. Since the bulk of these people are in older age groups, it is to be supposed that the problem will gradually diminish.

ARTS
Architecture
Spain is a unique repository of European architecture. Phoenicia, Carthage, Greece, Rome and the Visigoths all left their mark, only to be subsequently overshadowed by the brilliance of the Muslims. At the same time, all the great European movements – from Romanesque to Gothic, from Baroque to neoclassicism and Art Nouveau – seeped into Spain, although usually later than elsewhere and often altered to suit local tastes.

As a latecomer to the stage, Madrid is bereft of signs of the earlier phases in Spain's architectural history. A tendency to destroy and replace with new structures has contributed to the loss of precious clues to the city's past. Little of even the oldest quarters of the city predates the 18th century.

When Felipe II decided to make Madrid imperial capital, he decided that pretty much all of the modest medieval town had to go to make way for fine new buildings worthy of its new status. Then in the 19th century waves of confiscations hit the Church and a great many of the city's churches and convents were destroyed. The Civil War and postwar construction, characterised by an almost boisterous disregard for the capital's past, did the rest. We are all much poorer as a result, and medieval Madrid exists only in the mind's eye of the specialist historian.

Fortunately, you can compensate for this by making a series of day trips to cities around Madrid. You can thus give yourselves a taste of everything from the Muslim magnificence of Córdoba through to the Gothic grandeur of Toledo's cathedral. Searching further back in time, you can also admire traces of Visigothic handiwork in Toledo and Roman genius in Segovia's giant aqueduct. See the Excursions chapter later in the book for more details.

The Ancients Celts and Greeks left behind remnants of their ancient settlements, although none of them are anywhere close to Madrid. The Roman legacy in Spain is not as great as in some other of the empire's former provinces. One spectacular exception is the huge and extraordinary aqueduct in Segovia.

Visigoths & Pre-Romanesque Filling the vacuum left by the departing Romans, the Visigoths employed a more humble but remarkably attractive style, which survives in a handful of small churches well beyond Madrid. You can get a taste of the style in Toledo. The disarming simplicity of pre-Romanesque construction is something you will only really experience if you travel in the north of the country.

Muslim Architecture Meanwhile, the Muslims were settling in for a long occupation: they would remain for almost 800 years in their longest-lasting enclave, Granada. Córdoba was the centre of Muslim political power and culture for the first 300 years and, after Granada, is one of the best places in Spain to immerse yourself in the country's Muslim past.

The Syrian Omayyad dynasty that set up shop here brought with it architects imbued with ideas and experience won in Damascus. This was soon put to use in the construction of the mosque (mezquita) in Córdoba, whose style was echoed across Muslim Spain. Easily recognisable features which are comparable with buildings raised in Damascus include horseshoe-shaped and lobed arches; the use of exquisite tiles –

mostly with calligraphy (usually verses from the Qur'an) and floral motifs – in the decoration; peaceful inner courtyards; complex stucco work; and stalactite ceiling adornments.

Closer to home, the visible leftovers of Muslim rule are scarce. A small mosque, the Mezquita de la Luz, is Toledo's main reminder of its pre-Reconquista past. In Madrid itself, virtually nothing remains of the modest Islamic outpost of Magerit, except a stretch of the town wall below the Catedral de Nuestra Señora de la Almudena.

Mozarabic & Mudéjar In much the same way, little is left to remind us of the presence of *mozarabs* (Christians in Muslim territory) or the *mudéjares* (Muslims who remained behind in reconquered Christian territory) in Madrid.

The skills of the latter were found to be priceless (but cheap) and throughout Spain their influence is evident. One unmistakable *mudéjar* feature is the preponderance of brick: castles, churches and mansions all over the country were built of this material. Another tell-tale feature can be seen in the ceilings. Extravagantly decorated timber creations, often ornately carved, are a mark of the mudéjar hand. Several different types get constant mention. The term *armadura* refers to any of these wooden ceilings, especially when they have the appearance of an inverted boat.

The single biggest mudéjar feast you are likely to lay your eyes on during a stay in Madrid is Toledo. Segovia's Romanesque churches tend be accompanied by mudéjar bell towers. All that remains of this style in Madrid are the bell towers of the San Pedro and San Nicolás churches.

Romanesque As the Muslim tide was turned back and the Reconquista gathered momentum, the first great medieval European movement in design began to take hold in Spain, spreading from Italy and France. From about the 11th century, churches, monasteries, bridges, pilgrims' hospices and other buildings in the Romanesque style mushroomed in the north.

Nothing in this style survives in Madrid, although the city was well in Christian hands by the time Romanesque took hold. Although the pickings are not as rich as in northern Spain, you can get some idea of the characteristics of the style during your day trips to Ávila and Segovia. The Basílica de San Vicente in the former and a series of less significant churches in the latter are the main Romanesque attractions.

Romanesque is easily identified by a few basic characteristics. The exterior of most edifices bears little decoration and structures tend to be simple and angular. In the case of churches in particular, the concession to curves comes with the semicilindrical apse or, in many cases, triple apse. The single most striking element of decoration is the semicircular arch or arches that grace doorways, windows, cloisters and naves.

The Transition During the 12th century, modifications in the Romanesque recipe became apparent. The pointed arch and ribbed vault of various kinds are clear precursors of the Gothic revolution to come. A good example close to home is the cathedral in Ávila.

Gothic Starting in France and rapidly spreading across northern Europe, a spectacular new style of building resulted in the creation of towering cathedrals that had parishioners gasping. These were made possible by the use of flying buttresses and other technical innovations.

The idea caught on later in Spain and one of several great Spanish Gothic cathedrals was built in Toledo in the 13th century. The Spaniards introduced some novel elements. The huge decorative altarpieces *(retablos)* towering over the high altar were one such innovation. And although not an exclusively Spanish touch, the placing of the choirstalls *(coro)* in the centre of the nave became a rule rather than the exception in Spanish Gothic.

The main structural novelty was star-vaulting (a method of weight distribution in the roof in which ribbed vaults project outwards from a series of centre points), while a clearly Hispanic touch is the cloister and gardens.

A problem with identifying to what style a monument belongs is that often it will belong to several. Many great buildings begun at the height of Romanesque glory were only completed long after Gothic had gained the upper hand. In many cases, these Gothic or Romanesque-Gothic buildings received a plateresque or Baroque overlay at a later date. Mudéjar influences abound. Toledo is covered in Gothic-Mudéjar combinations.

Finally, the so-called Isabelline style was a late addition to the cocktail. Taking some decorative cues from the more curvaceous traits of Islamic design, it was in some ways an indirect precursor to plateresque. Perhaps its ultimate expression is Toledo's San Juan de los Reyes, originally destined to be the final resting place of the Catholic Monarchs.

The 16th century saw a revival of pure Gothic and the Segovia cathedral was about the last Gothic house of worship to be constructed in Spain.

Madrid, again, is a poor runner-up compared with the cities that surround it. Apart from the much-interfered-with late-Gothic Casa de Cisneros, precious little survives in the capital from this period.

Renaissance The Renaissance in Spain can be roughly divided into three distinct styles. First was the Italian-influenced special flavour of plateresque, best appreciated in Salamanca, west of Madrid and beyond the scope of this book (see Lonely Planet's *Spain*). One of the main exponents of plateresque, Alonso de Covarrubias (1488–1570), was busy in his home city of Toledo (he designed the alcázar). Another more purist form of Renaissance building under the likes of Diego Siloé developed in Andalucía.

Finally, Juan de Herrera (1530–97) is the last and perhaps greatest figure of the Spanish Renaissance. A student of Juan Bautista de Toledo (died 1567), who was also at work in Madrid, Herrera developed a style that bears almost no resemblance to anything else of the period. His austere masterpiece

was the palace-monastery complex of San Lorenzo de El Escorial.

Baroque The heady frills and spills of Baroque can be seen all over Spain, but usually in the form of additions rather than complete buildings. Three loose phases can be identified in Spain, starting with a sober Baroque still heavily influenced by Herrera, followed by a period of greater architectural exuberance (some would say, a sickening amount) and finally running into a mixture of Baroque with the beginnings of neoclassicism.

Even after his death, Herrera's style lived on in Madrid. The sternness of his Renaissance style fused with a timid approach to the kind of voluptuous ornament that was inherent in the Baroque. Together they formed a characteristic style that to some has come to be known as *barroco madrileño*.

The facades of the Real Casa de la Panadería, the Palacio del Duque de Uceda (now the Capitanía General), the Ayuntamiento and the Convento de la Encarnación loosely fall into this category. The last two were designed by Juan Gómez de Mora (1586–1648), while his uncle Francisco de Mora (1560–1610) had a hand in the Palacio del Duque de Uceda. Gómez de Mora was also behind the royal prisons facing Plaza de la Santa Cruz, now the Ministerio de Asuntos Exteriores (Foreign Ministry).

The Basílica de San Isidro, completed in the 1660s, is another example of restrained Baroque, although it clearly moves a little closer to the gaudier style of Franco-Italian influence with which most are more familiar. A good example of the latter is the Transparente in Toledo's cathedral. In Madrid one of the few clear tastes of the style is the main entrance of what is now the Museo Municipal.

One of Madrid's foremost architects of the latter half of the 18th century was Ventura Rodríguez (1717–85). He designed the new interior of the Convento de la Encarnación and the Palacio de Liria. His style was controlled and clearly heading towards neoclassicism. His main competitor was the

Italian Francesco Sabatini (1722–97), who finished the Palacio Real and raised the Puerta de Alcalá. In favour with Carlos III, his star faded after the king's death, as his Italianate Baroque fell from fashion.

Neoclassicism Juan de Villanueva (1739–1811) picked up the baton from Rodríguez in the late 18th century. He designed the building that would bear his name and eventually house the Prado, as well as numerous outbuildings of the royal residences such as San Lorenzo de El Escorial.

The 19th Century As Madrid emerged from the chaos of the first half of the century, something of a building boom got under way. The use of iron and glass became common and it is in this period that the Palacio de Cristal in the Parque del Buen Retiro was built, along with the viaduct across Calle de Segovia, train stations and numerous other buildings. Two styles looking to the past were neo-Gothic and neo-mudéjar. Bullrings in particular were built in the latter style, in Madrid and beyond, well into the 20th century. The ring at Las Ventas, finished in 1934, is a prime example. Although it took a while to finish, the most obvious case of neo-Gothic in Madrid is the Catedral de Nuestra Señora de la Almudena.

Finally, as the century came to a close, a more grandiose style that some call 'eclecticism' emerged. The Banco de España and Ministerio de Agricultura are perfect examples.

Modernismo & Art Deco The brief but florid blooming of Modernismo, the local version of Art Nouveau construction, in Barcelona towards the end of the 19th century was a purely regional affair that left most of Spain as untouched as it was unmoved. Gaudí and co had few counterparts outside Catalunya, and just one seriously sinewy mansion in the style was raised in Madrid, the Sociedad General de Autores y Editores building in Malasaña.

In the 1920s, the newly created Gran Vía provided a perfect opportunity for new building, and a number of Art Deco caprices raised then still line the boulevard today. More overwhelming (and of questionable taste) is the Palacio de Comunicaciones (or post office to some) on Plaza de la Cibeles.

Modern As the Jam would have it, this is a modern world, and Madrid is a modern city. Much of what you see today has been built in the last 100 years or so, from the sprawling high-rise suburbs through to the chic districts of Salamanca and Goya.

The modern architecture buff will dig up several pieces of interest in Madrid, although relatively few edifices display the truly imaginative sparkle of the kind one witnesses in truly 20th-century metropolises such as New York or Hong Kong, or even rival capitals such as London and Paris.

From the Franco era the Edificio de España in the square of the same name is an extraordinary piece of what we might call dictatorial architecture. It would not look at all out of place in Soviet Moscow.

Much of what is new and skyscrapery in Madrid has gone up along the city's main axis, Paseo de la Castellana, especially in the Nuevos Ministerios area. Capping the boulevard to the north are the strange leaning Torres Puerta Europa on Plaza de Castilla

Painting & Sculpture

Madrid's role as a centre of artistic production did not really begin until Felipe II decided to settle the imperial court here in 1561. Even from that point onwards, the bulk of notable artists who lived and worked in Madrid came from the provinces.

Out of the Limelight Apart from the odd Roman mosaic fragment and small portions of the Muslim town wall, virtually nothing of artistic or even architectural interest has survived as a testimony to human creativity in pre-Christian Madrid. We can only guess at what the Islamic decoration of buildings (such as the main mosque) might have been like.

Even after the arrival of the Christians in

1085, Madrid remained in the shadows of its powerful neighbours, Toledo and Segovia, until Felipe II made his move in 1561. Until then serious artists had little incentive to so much as acknowledge the town's existence. In any case, the focal point of much of Spain's best medieval art lay in the north-east (Catalunya, Aragón and Valencia, for instance).

By the 15th century Castile was humming with artistic activity, but most of it was happening outside Madrid. Pedro Berruguete (1438–1504) and his son Alonso (1488–1561), from Paredes de Nava, were among the outstanding painters and sculptors respectively of the time. Both studied in Urbino, Italy, and their work appears mainly in towns such as Toledo, Ávila and Salamanca.

Perhaps the most extraordinary, and temperamental, of the 'Spanish' artists of the 16th century was the Cretan-born Domenikos Theotokopoulos (1541–1614), known as El Greco (literally 'the Greek'). On arriving from Italy, where he had trained, he decided that Toledo, Spain's ecclesiastic capital, would be the most lucrative place to ply his trade.

El Greco and Spanish artists in general had a hard time raising interest in their material at the court of Felipe II, who above all preferred Titian and a series of lesser Italian Mannerists. Holding up the Spanish side to a certain extent was Logroño-born El Mudo ('the Mute'), Juan Navarrete (1526–79), who became one of Spain's first practitioners of tenebrism, a fashion that largely aped Caravaggio's chiaroscuro style.

Velázquez & the Golden Age None of the towering figures of the Golden Age of Spanish art hailed from Madrid, but some need to be mentioned, if only because you will come across their works in the capital.

Across the Mediterranean in Italy, the Valencian José (Jusepe) de Ribera (1591–1652) came under the influence of Caravaggio and produced fine chiaroscuro works, an extensive collection of which you can see in the Prado.

The star, however, was Seville-born Diego Rodríguez de Silva Velázquez (1599–1660), who moved to Madrid as court painter and stayed put for life. Velázquez stands in a class of his own. He composed scenes that owe their life not only to his photographic eye for light and contrast but to a compulsive interest, not unlike Ribera's, in the humanity of his subjects. With him any trace of the idealised stiffness that characterised a by now spiritless Mannerism fell by the wayside. Realism became a key, and the majesty of his royal subjects springs from a capacity to capture the essence of the person – king or *infanta* – and the detail of their finery. Between commissions he'd take just as sympathetic a view of less fortunate members of the royal menagerie, such as court jesters and dwarfs.

His masterpieces include *Las Meninas* and *La Rendición de Breda* (The Surrender of Breda), both on view in the Prado, and a portrait of Pope Innocent X he carried out while in Rome in 1650.

A less exalted contemporary and close friend of Velázquez, Francisco de Zurbarán (1598–1664) moved *to* Seville as an official painter. Probably of Basque origin but born in Extremadura, he is best remembered for the startling clarity and light in his portraits of monks. He died in poverty in Madrid. A series of his paintings of monks is on display in the Real Academia de Bellas Artes de San Fernando. A room of the Prado is also dedicated to him.

Bartolomé Esteban Murillo (1618–82) lived and painted for most of his life in his native Seville. His opus enjoyed enormous success in his lifetime, and a good collection hangs in the Prado.

Madrid School A parade of late-Baroque artists working over the course of the 17th century have been loosely lumped together as the Madrid School, some of them actually born and raised in Madrid.

Among their number, a few names stand out. Antonio de Pereda (1608–78), born in Valladolid, started off decorating the Palacio del Buen Retiro in Madrid but fell out of royal favour and spent most of his working life in the employ of the clergy. His *El Sueño del Caballero* is in the Real Academia de Bellas Artes de San Fernando.

The monk Fray Juan Rizi (1600–81), son of an Italian immigrant painter, was born in Madrid but ended his days in the country of his ancestors. He did most of his work for Benedictine monasteries across the length and breadth of Castile, including Madrid's Convento de San Martín. Today some of his works can be seen in the Real Academia de Bellas Artes de San Fernando.

Francisco Rizi (1614–85), the monk's younger brother, worked in the monasteries and churches of Madrid and Toledo but was above all a successful set painter for theatre pieces given in the Palacio del Buen Retiro for the capital's elite.

A student of Velázquez and for some critics the most important exponent of the Madrid School was the Asturian Juan Carreño de Miranda (1614–85), who became the official painter at the royal court. His successor at court and, for many, the last of the Madrid School was the madrileño Claudio Coello (1642–93). He specialised in the big picture, literally. Some of his enormous decorative canvases adorn the complex at San Lorenzo de El Escorial, among them his magnum opus, *La Sagrada Forma*.

The 18th Century The Bourbon kings had little interest in sponsoring Spanish talent, being obsessed, rather, with all things French and, to a lesser extent, Italian. Carlos III had Anton Raphael Mengs (1728–79) brought from Bohemia as court painter, and the latter became the maker and breaker of rising artists. Aided by Zaragoza-born Francisco Bayeu (1734–95), he was a gifted if unexciting portraitist. Madrid-born artists patronised by the court at this time included Luis Paret y Alcázar (1746–99) and José del Castillo (1737–93).

Goya Mengs could spot talent. He encouraged Francisco José de Goya y Lucientes (1746–1828), a provincial hick from Fuendetodos in Aragón, as a cartoonist in the Real Fábrica de Tapices in Madrid. Here began the long and varied career of Spain's

JANE SMITH

Goya's merciless and visionary paintings changed the course of European art.

only truly great artist of the 18th (and, indeed, even the 19th) century.

In the early stages of his rise, Goya's portrayals of everyday scenes recall something of the candour of Hogarth and in some cases betray the influence of Tiepolo, whom Carlos III attracted to Spain to work on the Palacio Real.

In 1776 Goya began designing for the tapestry factory and by 1799 was appointed Carlos IV's court painter. Illness in 1792 left him deaf. This perhaps affected his style, which was increasingly unshackled by convention and often merciless.

Several distinct series and individual paintings mark the progress of his life and work. In the last years of the century he painted such enigmatic masterpieces as *La Maja Vestida* and *La Maja Desnuda*, identical portraits but for the lack of clothes in the latter. At about the same time he executed the frescoes in Madrid's Ermita de San Antonio de la Florida and *Los Caprichos* (The Caprices), a biting series of 80 etchings lambasting the follies of court life and ignorant clergy.

The arrival of the French and war in 1808 had a profound impact on him. Unforgiving portrayals of the brutality of war are *El Dos de Mayo* (The Second of May) and, more dramatically, *El Tres de Mayo* (The Third of May). The latter depicts the execution of Madrid rebels by French troops.

With the return of Fernando VII, Goya's position became more tenuous. After he retired to the Quinta del Sordo (Deaf Man's House), as he called his modest lodgings west of the Manzanares in Madrid, age and perhaps bitterness prompted the creation of his most extraordinary paintings, the nightmarish *Pinturas Negras* (Black Paintings). Executed on the walls of the house, they were later removed and now hang in the Prado. *Saturno Devorando a Su Hijo* (Saturn Devouring his Son) is emblematic of the hallucinatory horror of these works. He spent the last years of his life in voluntary exile in France, where he continued to paint until his death.

It is difficult to do justice to Goya's role in the evolution of European painting. An obvious precursor to many subsequent strands of modern art, he was an island of grandeur in a sea of mediocrity in Spain.

The Late 19th Century Although no-one of the stature of Goya can be cited, new trends were noticeable in the latter decades of the century. For a time the focus shifted to Valencia. Joaquín Sorolla (1863–1923) flew in the face of the French impressionist style that influenced many lesser Spanish artists at this time, preferring the blinding sunlight of the Valencian coast to the muted tones favoured in Paris. His work can be studied in Madrid's Museo de Sorolla.

Leading the way into the 20th century was Madrid's José Gutiérrez Solana (1886–1945). Typical of his disturbing and avant-garde approach to painting are sombre colours, low lighting and the deathly pale figures who people his works.

Juan Gris & Cubism Picasso dabbled in it but Madrid-born Juan Gris (1887–1927) remained true to the cubist mode of artistic expression to the end of his days. You can see a nice set of his canvases in the Centro de Arte Reina Sofía.

Picasso & Dalí in Madrid Discussing Spanish art without mentioning Málaga-born Pablo Ruiz Picasso (1881–1973) seems unthinkable, but Picasso's links with the capital amount to little. One of the grand masters of 20th-century art, Picasso arrived in Madrid in 1897 at the behest of his father for a year's study at the Escuela de Bellas Artes de San Fernando. But the precocious Picasso was already bored with school and instead took himself to the Prado to learn from the masters and to the streets to depict life as he saw it.

Picasso went on to become the master of cubism and sundry other faces of 20th-century art. One of the best known of his works is *Guernica*, a complex painting portraying the horror of war. It was inspired by the German aerial bombing of the Basque town Gernika in 1937 and now hangs in the Centro de Arte Reina Sofía in Madrid.

In 1922, Salvador Dalí (1904–89) arrived in Madrid from Catalunya. He no more liked studying at the Escuela de Bellas Artes de San Fernando than Picasso before him, but his time in the capital was important for other reasons. Here he met the Andalucian poet Federico García Lorca and future film director Luis Buñuel. With the latter he created some of the earliest strips of serious (if barely comprehensible) Spanish cinema, such as *Un Chien Andalou*.

Dalí, one of the whackiest of contemporary artists and a consummately eccentric, self-promoting showman, had little time for Madrid and less still after Franco installed himself as dictator in 1939. A few of his hallucinatory works can be seen in the Centro de Arte Reina Sofía.

From the 1920s to the 1960s Other madrileños at work in the 1920s and 1930s included Francisco Bores (1898–1972), Rosario de Velasco (1904–91) and Roberto Fernández Balbuena (1891–1966).

Toledo-born Alberto Sánchez (1895–1962) was one of the few outstanding sculptors to come out of Spain in the middle decades of the 20th century. He spent his last years in Moscow. Another sculptor to produce interesting work was Ángel Ferrant (1890–1961).

In the postwar years, Palencia-born Juan Manuel Diaz Caneja (1905–88) set new trends in landscape painting, suffusing it with vivid Spanish sunlight. He ended up in Madrid. In portraiture, Luis Castellanos (1915–46) was a leading figure. More abstract was Gerardo Rueda (1926–96), of the collective Equipo 57.

Contemporary Art Huesca-born Antonio Saura (born 1930) was swept up in the surrealist movement during a stint of several years in Paris in the 1950s. On his return to Francoist Spain, he headed for Madrid and joined a group of artists in founding an art revue, *El Paso* (which lasted from 1957 to 1960). His painting, influenced by De Kooning and full of verve, frequently addresses the contradictions and absurdities of modern society.

Pablo Palazuelo (born 1916 in Madrid) has produced a steady flow of paintings and sculptural works in iron.

The art of Madrid's Eduardo Arroyo (born 1937) is steeped in the radical spirit that kept him in exile from Spain for 15 years from 1962. His paintings tend in part to pop art, brimming with ironic sociopolitical comment. His work has taken him into various worlds – in 2000 he did the sets for a fresh new version of *Aida* directed by Riccardo Chailly in Amsterdam. Others of Arroyo's generation include Alfredo Alcaín (born 1936) and Elena Asins (born 1940).

The Spanish contemporary art scene is busy if sometimes a little spotty. Madrid is crawling with art galleries of every possible category and plenty of interesting local and foreign talent gets an airing. Some madrileños worth keeping an eye out for include painters Alberto Capón Medina (born 1968), Diana Larrea Gimeno (born 1972), Gonzalo Mayoral Corral (born 1967), Manuel Saro Romero-Gion (born 1970) and José Manuel Vela Caballero (born 1968). Promising sculptors are Beatriz Barral León (born 1968), David Gamella González (born 1971) and Esther Pizarro Juanas (born 1967)

Literature

Rise of Spanish Given Madrid's late start as a city of any importance, it is hardly surprising that before the 16th century little of mention was happening in the fortress town's literary circles.

Spanish as a literary vehicle had first emerged as early as the 10th century. Since the arrival of the Muslims in Spain two centuries earlier, a great amount of the literary and learned output in the peninsula had been predominantly in Latin (in the north), Arabic and Hebrew. Provençal troubadours brought their tongue to northern Spain with their songs of courtly love. Alfonso X, king of Castile and León (1252–84) and known as El Sabio ('the Learned'), did much to encourage the use of Castilian as a language of learning and literature, himself writing on diverse subjects.

Of all the works produced in Spanish in the Middle Ages, the *Poema de Mio Cid*, which has survived in a version penned in 1307 (although first written in 1140), is surely the best known. It is the epic tale of El Cid Campeador, or Rodrigo Díaz, the warrior whose exploits culminated in his mastery over Valencia.

El Siglo de Oro The completion of the Reconquista in 1492 seemed to galvanise the entire peninsula, and it was in the 16th century that Spanish letters began to take off. The Toledo-born Garcilaso de la Vega (1501–36), steeped in Italian literary sensibilities and *au fait* with the likes of Ariosto and Bembo, left behind sonnets and eclogues of unparalleled beauty.

His successor and perhaps the greatest of all Spanish poets was Luis de Góngora (1561–1627), born in Córdoba in the year Felipe II decided to make Madrid his capital. Unconcerned by theories, morals or high-minded sentiments, Góngora manipulated words with a majesty that has largely defied attempts at critical 'explanation'; his verses are above all intended as a source of sensuous pleasure.

With Góngora begins El Siglo de Oro, 'the Golden Century' of Spanish literature that would continue well into the 17th century. And it was very much Madrid's century. The greatest scribblers of the epoch were either born or spent much of their time in the young capital.

The advent of the *comedia* in early-17th-century Madrid produced some of the country's greatest playwrights. Lope de Vega (1562–1635), also an outstanding lyric poet, was perhaps the most prolific: more than 300 of the 800 plays and poems attributed to him remain. He explored the falseness of court life and roamed political subjects with his imaginary historical plays. Less playful and perhaps of greater substance is the work of Tirso de Molina (1581–1648), in whose *El Burlador de Sevilla* (The Seducer of Seville) we meet the immortal character of Don Juan, a likeable seducer who meets an unhappy end.

Yet another illustrious name of the period is Pedro Calderón de la Barca (1600–81). The beauty of this grand stage-master's works lies in his agile language and inventive techniques as a dramatist. The themes and storylines of his work were, however, comparatively run-of-the-mill. His more powerful pieces are *La Vida es Sueño* (Life's a Dream) and *El Alcalde de Zalamea* (The Mayor of Zalamea); in both, Calderón upholds an idea of righteousness and justice irrespective of class and caste.

Also noteworthy is Francisco de Quevedo (1580–1645), an accomplished poet working in almost diametric opposition to Góngora. He is perhaps best known today for his prose – a sparkling virtuoso game of metaphor and wordplay, but often laden with a heavy dose of bitter and unforgiving social commentary. His *La Historia de la Vida del Buscón Llamado Don Pablos*, tracing the none too elevating life of an antihero, El Buscón, is laced with especial venom for the lower classes.

Cervantes & the Novel Even had he been born in Barcelona, Cervantes would have to appear in this march past of Madrid writers. As it happens he was born in the not-too-distant Alcalá de Henares and ended his tumultuous days in Madrid.

His life something of a jumbled obstacle course of trials, tribulations and peregrinations, Miguel de Cervantes Saavedra (1547–1616) had little success with his forays into theatre and verse. Today he is commonly thought of as the man who gave modern literature a new genre: the novel.

El Ingenioso Hidalgo Don Quijote de la Mancha (known in English simply as Don Quixote) started life as a short story, designed to make a quick peseta, but Cervantes found himself turning it into an epic tale by the time it appeared in 1605. The ruined *ancien régime* knight and his equally impoverished companion, Sancho Panza, embark on a trail through the foibles of his era – a journey whose timelessness and universality marked the work out for greatness.

The 18th & 19th Centuries The years following El Siglo de Oro were less than inspiring in Spain. The decline and impoverishment of the nation found its reflection in literature, and few names of even passing interest appeared in Madrid.

The age of the Romantics touched Spain less than much of Europe. The Lord Byron of Spain, Badajoz-born José de Espronceda (1808–42), was a rare exception. A tormented revolutionary who found himself often in either jail or exile, he spent much of his time in Madrid, where he died. The apex of his poetic creativity was the unfinished *El Diablo Mundo,* the story of a man who incites people to feverish life in the face of the enigma of existence and death. There is not a little of the writer in his character.

One novelist towers above the rest through to the end of the 19th century. Benito Pérez Galdós (1843–1920) is the closest Spain produced to a Dickens or a Balzac. Born in the Canary Islands, he spent virtually all his adult life in Madrid. His novels and short stories ranged from social critique to the simple depiction of society through the lives of its many players. His more mature works, such as *Fortunata y Jacinta* (Fortunata and Jacinta), display a bent towards naturalism and, in the early 20th century, even symbolism.

The Franco Years The censors of fascist Spain kept a lid, albeit far from watertight, on literary development in Spain, and Madrid was no exception. Much of what was good in Spanish writing was penned by writers in exile.

To the Present Lorenzo Silva (born 1936) tells a good tale, including *El Aquimista Impaciente* (The Impatient Alchemist), in which a Guardia Civil officer sets about investigating a murder, a process in which we learn much more about the victim than the murderer. Manuel Rico (born 1952) has several novels to his credit, including *La Mujer Muerta* (The Dead Woman).

One of the country's leading poets is the Valencia-born Francisco Brines (born 1932), who has lived much of his life in Madrid.

José Luis Cebrian (born 1944) recently published *La Agonía del Dragón* (The Agony of the Dragon), which recounts the last tortured episodes of the dying days of Franco's Spain.

A promising new writer is Nuria Barrios (born 1962), whose second book, *El Zoo Sentimental*, came out in 2000. In a series of stories she uses animals to reflect human beings and their conflicts.

Younger still is Marcos Giralt Torrente (born 1968), whose first novel, *París*, won critical accolades. His second, *Nada Sucede Solo* (Nothing Happens Alone), tells of a couple who leave the rat race to do up a mill, only to have the wife's sister arrive and send things awry.

Music & Dance

Classical & Opera If Spain in general has been noticeable mostly by its absence from the world of great classical music and opera, Madrid has been even less blessed. The country's few composers of note (such as Isaac Albéniz, Enrique Granados, Joaquín Rodrigo and Manuel de Falla) all came from other parts of the country.

The single obvious exception to the rule is Plácido Domingo (born 1934), the country's leading opera tenor and born *gato* (full-blooded madrileño). Birth and early childhood was where the charming singer's relationship with Madrid more or less ended, as his parents, zarzuela performers, moved to Mexico, where he made his singing debut years later.

Flamenco The musical and dance form most readily identified with all Spain is rooted in the *cante hondo* (deep song) of the *gitanos* (Roma people) of Andalucía and is probably influenced by North African rhythms (or, indeed, the music of Al-Andalus).

The melancholy cante hondo is performed by a singer, who may be male *(cantaor)* or female *(cantaora)*, to the accompaniment of a blood-rush of guitar from the *tocador* (player). Although in its pure, traditional form this is sometimes a little hard for the uninitiated to deal with, it is difficult not to be moved by the very physical experience. The accompanying dance is performed by one or more *bailaores* (flamenco dancers).

It is impossible here to delve into the intricacies of the various orthodox schools of flamenco that have emerged over the past century (schools of Cádiz, Seville, Jerez, Córdoba and so on) or of the different kinds of song and music (ranging from the most anguished *siguiriyas* and *soleás* to the more lively *bulerías, boleros, fandangos, alegrías* and *farrucas*). Suffice to say that there is more to it than meets the eye.

The gitanos had settled in Andalucía early in the 15th century, and by the end of the 18th century several centres of cante hondo (also known as *cante jondo*) had emerged, among them Cádiz, Jerez de la Frontera and the Triana area of Seville. This does not make it the exclusive preserve of the south. Indeed, quite the opposite. Madrid has long attracted migrants from the south and they brought with them their music. Since the mid-19th century at least, the best performers of flamenco have turned up at one time or another in Madrid – and many were born there. At first, the gitanos and Andalucians were concentrated in the area around Calle de Toledo. The novelist Benito Pérez Galdós found no fewer than

88 Andalucian taverns along that street towards the end of the 19th century.

The flamenco singer and businessman Silverio Franconetti (1831–89) is credited with winning a madrileño audience for the fiery music of the gitanos. By the 1850s several stars of the genre were living in the capital. The scene shifted in the early 20th century to Plaza de Santa Ana, where the singer Antonio Chacón (1869–1929) performed in Los Gabrieles and the Villa Rosa (see the Entertainment chapter for both). In those days the creme de la creme of Madrid society, including King Alfonso XIII, used to hang out late into the night drinking in flamenco magic.

The genre flourished in the 1920s but with the Civil War things went downhill. Not until the 1950s did flamenco come to life again. In those dark years of austere dictatorship, even fun was considered suspect and so the hidden world of smoky cabarets and *tablaos* (flamenco shows) was born. These shows, now often geared to tourists, usually lack the genuine emotion of real flamenco, although a few are worth seeing if you have no alternative. Many of the original places have disappeared, but some, such as the Corral de la Morería and Café de Chinitas, are still in business today. See the Entertainment chapter for these and other places where you can enjoy flamenco in Madrid.

Performers Past & Present Flamenco's real golden age may well be opening up before us. Never has it been so popular both in Spain and abroad, and never has there been such a degree of innovation. Strangely, among the most successful proponents of modern flamenco (or flamenco-style) music are the Gipsy Kings, who are from southern France, not Spain.

Paco de Lucía (born 1947) is doubtless the best-known flamenco guitarist internationally. He has a virtuosity few would dare claim they can match and is the personification of *duende*, that indefinable capacity to transmit the power of flamenco. There is a wealth of albums to choose from; the double album *Paco de Lucía Antología* is a good introduction to his work, ranging from 1967 to 1990.

Paco de Lucía spends more time abroad than in Spain, but plenty of other good musicians fill the gap at home. The list of fine flamenco guitarists is long, among them the Montoya family (some of whom are better known by the sobriquet of 'los Habichuela'), especially Juan (born 1933) and Pepe (born 1944). Other artists to watch for include El Tomatito (born 1947), Manolo Sanlúcar (born 1943) and Moraíto Chico (born 1956).

Paco de Lucía's friend El Camarón de la Isla (1950–92) was, until his death, the leading light of contemporary cante hondo; plenty of flamenco singers today try to emulate him. Another who has reached the level of cult figure is Enrique Morente (born 1942), referred to by a Madrid paper as 'the last bohemian'. Among other leading vocalists figure such greats as Carmen Linares (born 1951), from the province of Jaén, and the Sevillano José Menese (born 1941). Other topnotch singers include, among women, Remedios Amaya and Aurora Vargas (born 1956), and, among men, Juan Peña Fernández 'El Lebrijano' (born 1941), Calixto Sánchez (born 1946), Chano Lobato (born 1927) and Vicente Soto 'El Sordera' (born 1927). El Camarón's younger successors include Antonio Vargas (known as 'El Potito'), Juan Cortés Duquende and Miguel Poveda (born 1973). Rising female vocalists include Aurora (born 1972).

Of Spain's flamenco dancers and choreographers, the greatest name this century is with little doubt Antonio Ruiz Soler (1921–96). One of the great all-time bailaoras was the fiery Barcelona-born Carmen Amaya (1913–63). Leading contemporary figures include Joaquín Cortés (born 1969) and Antonio Canales (born 1962), who is more of a flamenco purist. Traditionalists dislike fashionable attempts to mix flamenco dance with ballet and other forms. One of the great traditional bailaores, Farruco (1936–97) was a wild gitano soul who argued that performers such as Cortés don't dance flamenco. The only *'puro masculino'* bailaor these days, Farruco used to say, was his teenage grandson Farruquito (born 1983). And indeed 'little Farruco' is today on the verge of becoming a major star of flamenco dance.

Manuela Vargas (born 1941), Antonio Gades (born 1936), Cristina Hoyos (born 1946), Miguel Peña Vargas 'El Funi' (born 1939) and Sara Baras (born 1971) are other excellent dancers, some with their own successful companies.

Nuevo Flamenco & Fusion Possibly the most exciting developments in flamenco have taken it to other musical shores. Two of the best-known groups that have experimented with flamenco-rock fusion since the 1980s are Ketama and Pata Negra, whose music is labelled by some as Gypsy rock. One of Ketama's best albums is *Canciones Hondas*, while Pata Negra's seventh, *Como Una Vara Verde*, is a good choice. A former member of Pata Negra, Raimundo Amador (born 1960), has gone his own way and in 1996 made a CD with the American blues master BB King.

In the early 1990s, Radio Tarifa emerged with a mesmerising mix of flamenco, North African and medieval sounds. The first CD, *Rumba Argelina*, was a great hit. A more traditional flamenco performer, El Lebrijano (see under Performers Past & Present earlier in the chapter) has created some equally appealing combinations with classical Moroccan music. His CD *Encuentros*, recorded with the Andalucian Orchestra of Tangier, is a good sample.

Perhaps most astonishing was Enrique Morente's 1996 collaboration with the Granada technopunks Lagartija Nick on *Omega*, an interpretation of Lorca's poetry collection *Poeta en Nueva York* (Poet in New York) along with songs by the Lorca-influenced Leonard Cohen.

Contemporary Dance In the eyes of most, Barcelona has the liveliest contemporary dance scene, but Madrid is not inactive. Nacho Duato, head and principal dancer of the Madrid-based Compañía Nacional de Baile since 1990, transformed it from a low-profile classical company into one of the world's most technically dazzling and accomplished contemporary dance groups. The Ballet Nacional de España, founded in 1978, mixes classical ballet with Spanish dance.

Contemporary Music The Spanish music scene is busy indeed, although comparatively little of what goes down in Madrid reaches the export markets.

Since the days of the movida in the late 70s and early 80s, Madrid's home-grown rock scene has been vibrant, at least in terms of quantity if perhaps not always in quality. Seguridad Social is a good old-fashioned hard-rock group that was a constant force throughout much of the 1990s. Another legend of the Madrid rock scene is Rosendo, who started off with the group Leño in the late 1970s, at the height of the movida, and hasn't stopped since.

Huevos Canos is a loose association of musos from the area around Calle de Hortaleza. The songs they perform display a mix of styles and are full of social critique.

Madrid-born Antonio Vega was one of the sensations of the mid-1990s but seems to have faded a little into the background in the past couple of years.

Cinema

Although Madrid is the uncontested capital of the nation's film industry, comparatively few madrileños actually make the flicks.

Madrid's most senior cinematic bard is probably Juan Antonio Bardem (born 1922). He wrote the script for Luis García Berlanga's 1952 classic, *Bienvenido Mr Marshall* (Welcome Mr Marshall), and followed himself in 1955 with *Muerte de un Ciclista* (Death of a Cyclist). His best film was perhaps *Nunca Pasa Nada* (Nothing Ever Happens, 1963). It looked at the stultifying life of the provinces through the eyes of failures, but it bombed at the box office. Much of the stuff he has done since has been mediocre.

Fernando Trueba (born 1955) has signed some fine Spanish films, the best of which was his 1992 *Belle Epoque*, which examines the melancholy underside to bliss through the story of four sisters' pursuit of a young chap. It is one of only three Spanish films to have taken an Oscar.

Pedro Almodóvar (born 1951) repeated the trick in 2000 with his 1999 hit, *Todo Sobre mi Madre* (All About My Mother). The capital might like to think of Almodóvar as one of its own. He lived the years of the movida in the capital, but was born and raised in the south of Castilla-La Mancha. Still, it seems churlish not to mention Spain's best-known cinema-directing export. He has won many fans with such quirkily comic looks at modern Spain as *Mujeres al Borde de un Ataque de Nervios* (Women on the Edge of a Nervous Breakdown, 1988) and *Átame* (Tie Me Up, Tie Me Down, 1990). Darker sentiments are explored in productions such as *Matador* (1986), where the blood lust of the *corrida* (bullfight) and the lust of the bed are closely tied together.

Fernando Colomo (born 1946), after developing a name as a popular director of often pretty trashy comedy, has in the past few years come up with some more interesting efforts, such as *Alegre Ma Non Troppo* (1994) and *El Efecto Mariposa* (The Butterfly Effect, 1995).

An astounding line-up of some of Spain's best actresses comes from Madrid. They include: Victoria Abril (born 1959), Ana Belén (born 1950), Penelope Cruz (born 1974), Carmen Maura (born 1945), Silke (born 1974), and Maribel Verdú (born 1970).

SOCIETY & CULTURE

Spaniards can be economical with etiquette and thank-yous but this does not signify unfriendliness. One way in which you may notice people expressing their fellow feeling is the general '*Buenos días*' they often utter to all present when they enter a small shop or bar, and the '*Adiós*' when they leave.

Madrileños are true urban animals and are not necessarily waiting about to meet you just because you have blown in from abroad. On the other hand, as big cities go it can be surprisingly friendly. Meeting lo-

cals in bars – especially if you have some mastery of Spanish – is a lot easier than in towns such as London. Don't expect lifelong friendship however. The kind of contact such 'blow ins' are likely to come across is more superficially social and tied to the moment than anything truly lasting. Invitations to Spanish homes are rare enough to be a mark of true friendship.

Day, Night & Time

The Spanish attitude to time *is* more relaxed than that of most western cultures. But things that need a fixed time – trains, buses, cinemas, football matches – get one and it's generally stuck to. Things that need to get done, get done. Waiters may not always be in a hurry, but they come before too long.

What's different is the daily timetable. The Spanish *tarde* (afternoon) doesn't really start until 4 pm or so and goes on until 9 pm or later. Shops and offices close from around 2 to 5 pm, then mostly open again until around 8 pm. In hot summer months people stay outside late, enjoying the coolness. And, of course, Friday and Saturday nights, all year round, barely begin until midnight for those doing the rounds of bars and clubs.

Siesta Contrary to popular opinion, most Spaniards do not have a sleep in the afternoon. The siesta is generally devoted to a long, leisurely lunch and lingering conversation. But then again, if you've stayed out until 6 am and gone straight to work from the club...

Dos & Don'ts

The standard form of greeting between men and women (even when meeting for the first time) and between women is a kiss on each cheek, right then left. Now we're not talking about big sloppy ones – a light brushing of cheeks is perfectly sufficient. Men seem to be able to take or leave handshakes on informal occasions, but they are pretty much standard in a business context.

In some older bars it is quite the norm to chuck your rubbish – paper, toothpicks, cigarette butts and so on – onto the floor. At the end of the day it will all be swept up. This does not apply everywhere, so don't start indulging your deeply buried urges to be a litterbug unless you are quite sure you are in a sufficiently grungy bar. A quick inspection of the floor and of other customers' behaviour should clue you in.

Treatment of Animals

Those who cannot help but see the bullfight as a cruel sport can contact the following organisations for information and suggested action:

People for the Ethical Treatment of Animals (PETA)
Britain: (☎ 020-7388 4922, fax 7388 4925)
PO Box 3169, London NW1 2JF
USA: (☎ 757-622 7382, fax 622 1078)
501 Front St, Norfolk, VA 23510
Web site: www.peta.org
World Society for the Protection of Animals (WSPA)
Britain: (☎ 020-7793 0540, fax 7793 0208,
✉ wspahq@gn.apc.org)
2 Langley Lane, London SW8 1TJ
USA: (☎ 617-522 7000, fax 522 7077,
✉ wspa@world.std.com)
PO Box 190, Boston, MA 02130
Canada: (☎ 416-369 0044, fax 369 0147,
✉ 102232.3627@compuserve.com)
44 Victoria St, Suite 1310, Toronto, Ontario M5C 1Y2
Web site: www.wspa.org.uk

See also the special section 'The Bullfight' after the Facts for the Visitor chapter.

RELIGION

Madrid, like the rest of Spain, is largely Catholic, at least in name. As much of the rest of the country, it has known the presence of the three great monotheistic faiths, the Jewish, Muslim and Christian religions. The completion of the Reconquista in 1492 and subsequent expulsions of Muslims and Jews radicalised religion in Spain and set the stage for the Inquisition and the military-style Jesuit order.

According to Pope Pius XII, Spain is 'God's chosen country', but it has paid heavily for its faith. In the year 2000 the Spanish

Church repeated a claim before a Vatican commission that some 10,000 Spaniards had died martyrs in the 20th century. Almost 7000 of those who died for the faith fell in the Civil War and most of the rest in the years immediately preceding the conflict.

Under Franco, Catholicism was again made a State religion and the Church played a major role in society.

The wealth of the Church fuelled the violent anticlericalism of the 19th century that saw countless churches and convents expropriated and destroyed in Madrid. The ill-feeling continued into the 20th century, and it was hardly surprising that the Church should align itself with Franco. In doing so it won itself many bitter enemies. It is pointless to speculate whether or not so many priests and other clergy would have lost their lives between 1936 and 1939 had the Church chosen not to take sides.

Nowadays, many Spanish theologians, much as their counterparts elsewhere in Europe and the USA, criticise the Church for its conservatism on issues of sex, abortion, divorce and the like, warning that it will lose even more ground with Spaniards if it does not 'modernise'.

And yet, as in the rest of Spain, the visible religiosity of madrileños remains strong. Great Easter processions, in which penitents of religious fraternities dress up in strange habits, put on conical masks (capilotes) and march solemnly around the city bearing crosses and beating drums, still attract enormous crowds of people who otherwise might rarely set foot in a church.

LANGUAGE

Spanish, more appropriately known as castellano (Castilian), is the language of the city. While you will find madrileños, especially younger people and employees in some hotels and restaurants, who understand some English, you cannot bank on it at every occasion. Learning some Spanish before you arrive is a worthwhile investment. See the Language chapter for some of the basics.

Facts for the Visitor

WHEN TO GO

As in much of Spain, spring is the best time to be in Madrid. The weather is generally agreeable (although April can be very wet), the city has a fresh feel to it and it isn't too much overrun with tourists.

From late June until the first weeks of September the heat can be appalling, making the place quite unpleasant unless you happen to enjoy feeling like you're inside a pressure cooker. Locals who don't escape (and the city becomes eerily quiet in August) keep themselves amused by staying out all night long in the squares, *terrazas* (pavement cafes) and other watering holes. A series of local fiestas from July to August also keeps *madrileños* (natives of Madrid) distracted from the oven-like conditions.

Winter is an odd thing here. It gets bitterly cold, especially when winds blow in off the Sierra de Guadarrama. That said, February can be a surprisingly good month – regularly giving a taster of spring with crisp blue days and temperatures around 17°C. In some respects it's ideal.

ORIENTATION

One of the most striking aspects of Madrid's layout is the absence of water (if you exclude the fine public fountains). The pathetic dribble that constitutes the Río Manzanares doesn't flow through the city centre like the Thames, Seine or Tiber – indeed, it barely flows at all – and most visitors to Madrid leave blissfully unaware that there is a 'river' here.

Madrid is also surprisingly compact. The main north–south artery, Paseo de la Castellana (which becomes Paseo de los Recoletos and Paseo del Prado at its southern end), lies in a shallow depression (once a stream) and connects the city's two main train stations, Chamartín and Atocha.

The area around the southern portion of this promenade monopolises the interest of out-of-towners. The core of the city's oldest quarters is squeezed in between Paseo del Prado to the east and the Palacio Real to the west. Roughly halfway between them is the Puerta del Sol, once a city gate but long since the point from which distances to all corners of the country are measured.

The majestic Plaza Mayor lies a short stroll west of the Puerta del Sol, surrounded by a warren of captivating back streets. South-east of Sol, the old *barrios* (districts) are a happening, dynamic mix of seemingly endless restaurants, bars and cafes. The tangle of lanes spills southwards into the equally fascinating working-class barrio of Lavapiés. This is perhaps one of the last quarters with a real feeling of local community, where the people, a mix of *gatos* (natives of Madrid, literally 'cats'), *gitanos* (Romany people) and migrants (many from North Africa and the Middle East), live cheek by jowl. In the heat of the long summer nights, families jostle with revellers for space in the streets in a voluble but good-natured competition to fill the air with an energy rarely wasted on sleep – except in the hot, languid afternoons of the siesta.

Moving westwards to the area around Calle de Toledo you enter a slightly more polished version of Lavapiés, La Latina. On the way to the Palacio Real it in turn feeds into one of the oldest parts of the city, once known as the *morería*, or Moorish quarter.

Madrid's great art galleries – the must-sees on everyone's list – are clustered about the Paseo del Prado. Not far from the gallery of the same name spreads out one of the city's green lungs, the elegant Parque del Buen Retiro ('El Retiro' for short). Once the preserve of royals and dandies, it now throws open its gates to all those in search of respite from the city's hectic atmosphere.

The densest concentrations of accommodation can be found in a couple of zones. The area around Puerta del Sol and Plaza de Santa Ana is saturated with little *pensiones* (guesthouses) and *hostales* (cheap hotels). Similarly blessed are the barrios of Malasaña and

Getting Addressed

You might think that, if you have the address of a hotel, office or cafe, you should have little trouble locating it. But if the Pensión España should turn out to be at C/ Madrid 2ºD Int, not far from Gta Atocha and just round the corner from Pº del Prado, you could be forgiven for being a little confused. Here's a key to common abbreviations used in addresses:

Almd	Alameda
Av or Avda	Avenida
C/	Calle
Cllj	Callejón
Cno	Camino
Cril	Carril
Ctra or Ca	Carretera
Gta	Glorieta (major roundabout)
Pº or Po	Paseo
Pje	Pasaje
Pl, Pza or Pª	Plaza
Pllo	Pasillo
Pte	Puente
Rda	Ronda
s/n	sin número (without number)
Urb	Urbanización

MICK WELDON

The following are used where there are several flats, hostales, offices etc in a building. They're often used in conjunction, eg 2ºC or 3ºI Int:

2º	2nd floor
3º	3rd floor
4º	4th floor
C	centro (middle)
D or dcha	derecha (right-hand side)
I or izq	izquierda (left-hand side)
Int	interior (a flat or office too far inside a building to look onto any street – the opposite is Ext, exterior)

If someone's address is Apartado de Correos 206 (which might be shortened to Apdo Correos 206 or even just Apdo 206), don't bother going looking for it at all. An *apartado de correos* is a post-office box.

Note also that the word 'de' is often omitted: Calle de Madrid (literally 'Street of Madrid') may be truncated to C/ Madrid. In fact it's not uncommon for streets to be referred to by their names alone: Calle de Alfonso Rodríguez will just as likely be referred to as Alfonso Rodríguez.

Chueca, just north of Gran Vía, which itself is lined with hotels of varying quality.

Main Transport Terminals

Buses arrive at numerous points throughout the city, depending on their origin. However, the main bus station is Estación Sur de Autobuses, south-west of the Atocha train station. Pretty much everything south of Madrid (and much that is not) is served by buses from this station. Airport buses terminate at Plaza de Colón.

euro currency converter 1000 ptas = €6.01

Chamartín train station, where all international trains arrive, lies in the north of the city, while Atocha (which is the more important of the two stations) lies just south of the old centre of town. All these transport termini (and the airport) are linked to the city's metro system. See the Getting Around chapter for further details.

MAPS

The free maps at tourist offices are sufficient, but better ones are available for sale. The *Michelin Madrid* map N1042, which comes with a complete street directory and costs 880 ptas, is one of the best foldout maps of the city.

If you want something more comprehensive you have several choices. *Madrid*, published by Vía XXI Ediciones, is a good colour product with a street index and costs 2950 ptas. Less complete but adequate for most people is the *Guía Urbana de Madrid* published by GeoPlaneta. It costs 1700 ptas.

A handy one that will fit into your back pocket is Neguri Editorial's *Plano y Guía de Madrid* (2200 ptas).

All these are available in La Casa del Libro bookshop (see the Shopping chapter).

TOURIST OFFICES
Local Tourist Offices

The main tourist office (Map 7; Oficina de Turismo; ☎ 91 429 49 51) is at Calle del Duque de Medinaceli 2. It is open from 9 am to 7 pm Monday to Friday and 9 am to 1 pm on Saturday. The office at Chamartín train station (☎ 91 315 99 76) opens from 8 am to 8 pm Monday to Friday and 8 am to 1 pm on Saturday. The one at Barajas airport (Aeropuerto de Barajas; ☎ 91 305 86 56) is on the ground floor in Terminal T1 and opens the same hours.

Another Oficina de Turismo (Map 7; ☎ 91 364 18 76), Ronda de Toledo 1, is in the Centro Comercial de la Puerta de Toledo. It is open from 9 am to 7 pm Monday to Friday and 9.30 am to 1.30 pm on Saturday.

The Patronato Municipal de Turismo (Map 7; ☎ 91 588 29 06), Plaza Mayor 3, specialises in the city. It is open from 10 am to 8 pm Monday to Friday, 10 am to 2 pm and 3 to 8 pm on Saturday and 10 am to 3 pm on Sunday.

The city's general information line (dealing with everything from public transport to shows) is on ☎ 010. It operates from 8.30 am to 9.30 pm Monday to Friday. You can also try the Comunidad de Madrid's regional information line on ☎ 012.

Finally, there is a nationwide tourist information line in several languages, which might come in handy if you are calling from elsewhere in Spain. Call ☎ 901 30 06 00 from 9 am to 6 pm any day for basic information in Spanish, English and French.

Tourist Offices Abroad

Information on Madrid is available from the following branches of the Oficina Española de Turismo abroad:

Belgium (☎ 02-280 19 26, @ bruselas@tourspain.es) Ave des Arts 21, B-1040 Brussels
Canada (☎ 416-961 3131, @ toronto@tourspain.es) 2 Bloor St W, 34th Floor, Toronto M4W 3E2
Denmark (☎ 33 15 11 65, @ copenhague@tourspain.es) NY Ostergade 34, 1, DK-1101 Copenhagen
France (☎ 01 45 03 82 57, @ paris@tourspain.es) 43 rue Decamps, 75784 Paris, Cedex 16
Germany (☎ 030-882 6036, @ berlin@tourspain.es) Kurfürstendamm 180, D-10707 Berlin
Branches in Düsseldorf, Frankfurt am Main and Munich
Italy (☎ 06-678 31 06, @ roma@tourspain.es) Via del Mortaro 19, Interno 5, 00187 Rome
Japan (☎ 03-34 32 61 41, @ tokio@tourspain.es) Daini Toranomon Denki Bldg 4f, 3-1-10 Toranomon, Minato-Ku
Netherlands (☎ 070-346 59 00, @ lahaya@tourspain.es) Laan Van Meerdervoort 8a, 2517 The Hague
Portugal (☎ 01-357 1992, @ lisboa@tourspain.es) Avenida Sidónio Pais 28 3° Dto, 1050 Lisbon
UK (☎ 020-7486 8077, brochure request 0891 669920 at 50p a minute, @ londres@tourspain.es) 22-23 Manchester Square, London W1M 5AP

euro currency converter € 1 = 166 ptas

USA (☎ 212-265 8822, ✉ oetny@tourspain.es)
666 Fifth Ave, 35th Floor, New York,
NY 10103
Branches in Chicago, Los Angeles and Miami

TRAVEL AGENCIES

Madrid is not the ideal place for bargain-basement flights. That said, it is possible to get reasonable deals to major destinations and in some cases – such as London – steals.

One agency with a reputation for getting the best available deals is Viajes Zeppelin (☎ 91 542 51 54), Plaza de Santo Domingo 2 (Map 5; metro: Santo Domingo). Zeppelin also has offices at Calle de la Infanta Mercedes 62 (Map 1; ☎ 91 571 82 58) and Calle de la Hermosilla 92 (Map 2; ☎ 91 431 40 36).

One of the country's biggest agencies is Halcón. It is reliable and has 68 offices spread right across Madrid. Their national phone reservation number is ☎ 902 30 06 00.

Students and young people can try looking around several other agencies. Juventus Viajes (Map 5; ☎ 91 319 41 35), Calle de Fernando VI 9; and Cadimar Viajes (Map 5; ☎ 91 542 59 05), on the corner of Calle de San Leonardo de Dios and Plaza de España, are both worth a look. USIT Unlimited (Map 5; ☎ 902 25 25 75), Plaza del Callao 3, is a specialised youth and student travel agency. You could also try TIVE (see Hostel Cards under Documents immediately below).

DOCUMENTS
Visas

Spain is one of 15 countries that have signed the Schengen Convention, an agreement whereby all EU (European Union) member countries (except the UK and Ireland) plus Iceland and Norway have agreed to abolish checks at internal borders by the end of 2000. The other EU countries are Austria, Belgium, Denmark, Finland, France, Germany, Greece, Italy, Luxembourg, the Netherlands, Portugal and Sweden. Legal residents of one Schengen country do not require a visa for another Schengen country. In addition, nationals of a number of other countries, including the UK, Canada, Ireland, Japan, New Zealand and Switzerland do not require visas for tourist visits of up to 90 days to any Schengen country.

Various other nationals not covered by the Schengen exemption can also spend up to 90 days in Spain without a visa. These include Australian, Israeli and US citizens. However, all non-EU nationals entering Spain for any reason other than tourism (such as study or work) should contact a Spanish consulate as they may need a specific visa. If you are a citizen of a country not mentioned in this section, you should check with a Spanish consulate whether you need a visa.

The standard tourist visa issued by Spanish consulates is the Schengen visa, valid for up to 90 days. A Schengen visa issued by one Schengen country is generally valid for travel in all other Schengen countries. However, individual Schengen countries may impose additional restrictions on certain nationalities. It is therefore worth checking visa regulations with the consulate of each Schengen country you plan to visit.

Those needing a visa must apply *in person* at the consulate. Postal applications are not accepted. In the UK you will be required to produce a UK residence permit, proof of sufficient funds, an itinerary, return tickets and a letter of recommendation. Finally, the visa does *not* guarantee entry.

You can apply for no more than two visas in any 12-month period and they are not renewable once you are in Spain. Options include 30-day and 90-day single-entry visas (in London these cost UK£17.75 and UK£21.30 respectively), 90-day multiple-entry visas (UK£24.85) and various transit visas. Schengen visas are free for spouses and children of EU nationals.

You *could* avoid the visa if you are willing to gamble. Travelling from the UK by boat or train there is a chance your passport will not be checked on entering France or Belgium. From there you could travel overland with some hope (but no certainty) of not having your passport checked. Travelling by air, however, you have no chance.

Take this seriously, as travellers have been bundled onto planes back to the country they flew from.

Visa Extensions & Residence Schengen visas cannot be extended. Nationals of EU countries, Norway and Iceland can virtually (if not technically) enter and leave Spain at will. Those wanting to stay in Spain longer than 90 days are supposed to apply during their first month for a residence card *(tarjeta de residencia)*. This is a lengthy bureaucratic procedure – if you intend to subject yourself to it, consult a Spanish consulate before you go to Spain as you will need to take certain documents with you.

People of other nationalities who want to stay in Spain longer than 90 days are also supposed to get a residence card, and for them it's a truly nightmarish process, starting with a residence visa issued by a Spanish consulate in your country of residence. Start the process aeons in advance.

Non-EU spouses of EU citizens resident in Spain can apply for residence too. The process is lengthy and those needing to travel in and out of the country in the meantime could ask for an *exención de visado* – a visa exemption. In most cases, the spouse is obliged to make the formal application in their country of residence. A real pain.

Travel Insurance
Medical costs might already be covered through reciprocal healthcare agreements (see Health later in this chapter) but you'll still need cover for theft or loss and for unexpected changes in travel plans (ticket cancellation etc). Check what's already covered by your local insurance policies and credit card – you might not need separate travel insurance. In most cases, however, this secondary type of cover is limited and its small print is laced with loopholes. For peace of mind, nothing beats straight travel insurance at the highest level you can afford.

Driving Licence & Permits
EU member states' pink-and-green driving licences are recognised in Spain. If you hold a licence from other countries you are supposed to obtain an International Driving Permit (IDP) too.

Hostel Cards
A valid HI (Hostelling International) card or youth hostel card from your home country is required at most HI youth hostels in Spain, including those in Madrid. If you don't have one, you can get an HI Card, valid until 31 December of the year you buy it, at most HI hostels in Spain. You pay for the card in instalments of 300 ptas each night you spend in a hostel, up to the total of 1800 ptas (people legally resident in Spain for at least a year can get a Spanish hostel card for 1000 ptas).

Another place to buy a card is the Oficina de Turismo Juvenil (TIVE; Map 2; ☎ 91 543 74 12, fax 91 544 00 62) at Calle de Fernando El Católico 88, open from 9 am to 2 pm Monday to Friday and 9 am to noon on Saturday. You can also buy one at the Centro Regional de Información y Documentación Juvenil (CRIDJ; Map 5; ☎ 91 580 42 42) at Gran Vía 10. It is open from 9 am to 2 pm and 5 to 8 pm Monday to Friday.

Student, Teacher & Youth Cards
These cards can get you worthwhile discounts on travel, and reduced prices at some museums, sights and entertainments.

The International Student Identity Card (ISIC), for full-time students (700 ptas in Spain), and the International Teacher Identity Card (ITIC), for full-time teachers and academics (1000 ptas), are issued by more than 5000 organisations around the world – mainly student-travel-related organisations that often sell student air, train and bus tickets too. They include:

Australia
STA Travel (☎ 03-9349 2411) 222 Faraday St, Carlton, Melbourne, Victoria 3053
   (☎ 02-9360 1822) 9 Oxford Street, Paddington, Sydney, NSW 2021
Canada
Travel CUTS (☎ 416-979 2406) 187 College St, Toronto

FACTS FOR THE VISITOR

Voyages Campus (☎ 514-398 0647) Université McGill, 3480 rue McTavish, Montreal

UK

Cards are best obtained from STA Travel and USIT Campus offices (see The UK under Air in the Getting There & Away chapter).

USA

Council Travel (☎ 212-822 2700) 205 East 42nd St, New York, NY 10017
(☎ 310-208 3551) 10904 Lindbrook Drive, Los Angeles, CA 90024
(☎ 415-421 3473) 530 Bush St, San Francisco, CA 94108

In Madrid you can get them at the TIVE office (see Hostel Cards earlier in this section).

Anyone aged under 26 can get a GO25 card or a Euro<26 card. Both these give similar discounts to the ISIC and are issued by most of the same organisations. The Euro<26 has a variety of names, including the Under 26 Card in England and Wales and the Carnet Joven Europeo in Spain. For information you can contact USIT Campus (see The UK under Air in the Getting There & Away chapter). In Spain, the Euro<26 is issued by various youth organisations, including Madrid's TIVE office, CRIDJ (see Hostel Cards earlier in this section) or at USIT Unlimited (see Travel Agencies earlier in this chapter).

As an example of the sorts of discounts you can expect in Spain, the better things on offer for Euro<26 card holders include 20% or 25% off most 2nd-class train fares; 10% or 20% off many Trasmediterránea ferries and some bus fares; good discounts at some museums; and discounts of up to 20% at some youth hostels.

Other Documents

If you intend to look for work in Madrid (see also Visas earlier in this section and Work towards the end of this chapter), you should bring along any paperwork that might help. English teachers, for instance, will need certificates demonstrating qualifications, and references from previous employers. Increasingly there is cross-recognition of degrees and other tertiary qualifications, so it may be worthwhile bringing proof of these as well. Translations validated by the Spanish embassy in your country wouldn't hurt either.

Copies

All important documents (passport data page and visa page, credit cards, travel insurance policy, air/bus/train tickets, driving licence etc) should be photocopied before you leave home. Leave one copy with someone at home and keep another with you, separate from the originals.

There is another option for storing details of your vital travel documents before you leave – Lonely Planet's online Travel Vault. Storing details of your important documents in the vault is safer than carrying photocopies. It's the best option if you travel in a country with easy Internet access. Your password-protected Travel Vault is accessible online at any time. You can create your own Travel Vault for free at www.ekno.lonelyplanet.com.

EMBASSIES & CONSULATES
Your Own Embassy

It's important to realise what your own embassy – the embassy of the country of which you are a citizen – can and can't do to help you if you get into trouble. Generally speaking, it won't be much help in emergencies if the trouble you're in is remotely your own fault. You are bound by the laws of the country you are in.

In genuine emergencies you might get some assistance, but only if other channels have been exhausted. For example, if you need to get home urgently, a free ticket home is exceedingly unlikely – the embassy would expect you to have insurance. If you have all your money and documents stolen, it might assist with getting a new passport, but a loan for onward travel is out of the question.

Spanish Embassies & Consulates

Here is a list of Spanish embassies and consulates in a selection of countries throughout the world:

Andorra (☎ 82 00 13) Carrer Prat de la Creu 34, Andorra la Vella
Australia (☎ 02-6273 3555,

@ embespau@mail.mae.es) 15 Arkana St, Yarralumla, Canberra, ACT 2600
Consulates in Brisbane (☎ 07-3221 8571), Melbourne (☎ 03-9347 1966), Perth (☎ 09-9322 4522) and Sydney (☎ 02-9261 2433)

Canada (☎ 613-747-2252, @ spain@ docuweb.ca) 74 Stanley Ave, Ottawa, Ontario K1M 1P4
Consulates in Toronto (☎ 416-977 1661) and Montreal (☎ 514-935 5235)

France (☎ 01 44 43 18 00, @ ambespfr@ mail.mae.es) 22 ave Marceau, 75008 Paris, Cedex 08

Germany (☎ 030-261 60 81, @ embesde@ mail.mae.es) Lichtensteinallee 1, 10787 Berlin
Consulates in Düsseldorf (☎ 0211-43 90 80), Frankfurt am Main (☎ 069-959 16 60) and Munich (☎ 089-98 50 27)

Ireland (☎ 01-269 1640) 17A Merlyn Park, Ballsbridge, Dublin 4

Japan (☎ 03-3583 8533, @ embesjpj@mail.mae .es) 1-3-29 Roppongi Minato-Ku, Tokyo 106

Morocco (☎ 07-26 80 00,@ embesjpj@mail .mae.es) 3 Zankat Madnine, Rabat
Consulates in Rabat (☎ 07-70 41 47), Casablanca (☎ 02-22 07 52) and Tangier (☎ 09-93 70 00)

Netherlands (☎ 070-364 38 14, @ embespnl@ mail.mae.es) Lange Voorhout 50, 2514 EG The Hague

New Zealand See Australia

Portugal (☎ 01-347 2381, @ embesppt@ mail.mae.es) Rua do Salitre 1, 1250 Lisbon

UK (☎ 020-7235 5555, @ espemblon@ espemblon.freeserve.co.uk) 39 Chesham Place, London SW1X 8SB
Consulates in London (☎ 020-7589 8989, 20 Draycott Place, London SW3 2RZ), Manchester (☎ 0161-236 1233) and Edinburgh (☎ 0131-220 1843)

USA (☎ 202-452 0100) 2375 Pennsylvania Ave NW, Washington, DC 20037
Consulates in Boston (☎ 617-536 2506), Chicago (☎ 312-782 4588), Houston (☎ 713-783 6200), Los Angeles (☎ 213-938 0158), Miami (☎ 305-446 5511), New Orleans (☎ 504-525 4951), New York (☎ 212-355 4080) and San Francisco (☎ 415-922 2995)

Embassies in Madrid

Embassies (*embajadas* in the phonebook) in Madrid include:

Australia (Map 3; ☎ 91 441 93 00) Plaza del Descubridor Diego de Ordás 3–2, Edificio Santa Engrácia 120

Canada (Map 6; ☎ 91 431 43 00) Calle de Núñez de Balboa 35

France (Map 6; ☎ 91 435 55 60) Salustiano Olózaga 9

Germany (Map 6; ☎ 91 319 91 00) Calle de Fortuny 8

Ireland (Map 4; ☎ 91 436 40 95) Paseo de la Castellana 46

Morocco (Map 1; ☎ 91 563 10 90) Calle de Serrano 179
Consulate: (Map 1; ☎ 91 561 21 45) Calle de Leizaran 31

Netherlands (Map 1; ☎ 91 350 32 36) Avenida del Comandante Franco 32

New Zealand (Map 9; ☎ 91 523 02 26, 91 531 09 97) Plaza de la Lealtad 2

Portugal (Map 4; ☎ 91 561 78 00/08) Calle del Pinar 1
Consulate: (Map 6; ☎ 91 577 35 38) Calle Lagasca 88

Tunisia (Map 5; ☎ 91 447 35 16) Plaza de Alonso Martínez 3

UK (Map 6; ☎ 91 700 82 72) Calle de Fernando el Santo 16
Consulate: (Map 6; ☎ 91 308 53 00) Calle del Marqués Ensenada 16

USA (Map 4; ☎ 91 577 40 00) Calle de Serrano 75

CUSTOMS

People entering Spain from outside the EU are allowed to bring in duty-free one bottle of spirits, one bottle of wine, 50 mL of perfume and 200 cigarettes.

Duty-free allowances for travel between EU countries were abolished in 1999. For *duty-paid* items bought at normal shops in one EU country and taken into another, the allowances are 90L of wine, 10L of spirits, unlimited quantities of perfume and 800 cigarettes.

MONEY

A combination of travellers cheques and credit or cash cards is the best way to carry your money.

Currency

Until the euro notes and coins are in circulation, Spain's currency will remain the peseta (pta). It comes in coins of 5, 10, 25, 50, 100, 200 and 500 ptas, and notes of 1000, 2000, 5000 and 10,000 ptas.

A 5 ptas coin is widely known as a *duro*

euro currency converter € 1 = 166 ptas

FACTS FOR THE VISITOR

Introducing the Euro

On 1 January 1999 a new currency, the euro, was introduced in Europe. Along with national border controls, the currencies of various European Union (EU) members are being phased out. Not all EU members have adopted the euro. Denmark, Sweden and the UK rejected or postponed participation, and Greece has so far failed to satisfy the requirements for adhesion. The 11 countries participating from the start are: Austria, Belgium, Finland, France, Germany, Ireland, Italy, Luxembourg, the Netherlands, Portugal and Spain.

The timetable for the introduction of the euro runs as follows:

• On 1 January 1999 the exchange rates of the participating countries were fixed to the euro. In Spain, the value of one euro was set at 166.4 ptas. The euro came into force for 'paper' accounting and prices could be displayed in local currency and in euros.
• On 1 January 2002 euro banknotes and coins will be introduced. They will circulate alongside the local currency for two months.
• On 1 March 2002 local currencies in the 11 countries will be withdrawn. Only euro notes and coins will remain in circulation as legal tender.

The €5 note in France is the same €5 note you will use in Italy and Portugal. There will be seven euro notes, in denominations of €500, €200, €100, €50, €20, €10 and €5. The eight euro coins will be in denominations of €2 and €1, then 50, 20, 10, 5, 2 and 1 cents. On the reverse side of the coins each participating state will be able to display their own designs, but all euro coins can be used anywhere that accepts euros.

Before the introduction of banknotes and coins it is somewhat uncertain exactly what practices will be adopted. Travellers may find varying degrees of 'euro-readiness' between different countries, between different towns in the same country, or between different establishments in the same town. If you pay in cash or by credit/debit card you are unlikely to need to think in terms of euros until 2002.

Euro cheque accounts and travellers cheques are available but their acceptance by individual establishments is uneven.

Once euro cash is in circulation, travellers should check bills carefully to make sure that the correct conversion rate from local currency is applied. The most confusing period will probably be between January 2002 and March 2002, when there will be two sets of notes and coins.

The euro should eventually make things easier for the traveller. Prices in the countries of what has been dubbed Euroland will be directly comparable, avoiding all those tedious calculations. And once euro notes and coins are issued, you won't need to change money at all when travelling within Euroland. Banks may still charge a handling fee (yet to be decided) for travellers cheques, but they won't be able to profit by buying the currency from you at one rate and selling it back to you at another, as they do now. Even EU countries not participating may price goods in euros and accept euros over shop counters.

Most of the many euro Web sites are devoted to its legal implications and business issues, with little of use to the traveller. The Lonely Planet Web site at www.lonelyplanet.com has a link to a currency converter and up-to-date news on the integration process. At the time of going to press, exchange rates were:

Australia	A$1	=	€0.6145	New Zealand	NZ$1	=	€0.4914
Canada	C$1	=	€0.7202	United Kingdom	UK£1	=	€1.6051
Japan	¥100	=	€0.989	United States	US$1	=	€1.0737

euro currency converter 1000 ptas = €6.01

JULIET COOMBE

Traditional painted tiles near the Plaza Mayor

JENNY JONES

Beautiful tiles adorn the inside of a church.

JULIET COOMBE

Art of a different sort covers some of Madrid's walls.

The tile decoration outside and inside Villa Rosa makes this club unique.

These hand-painted tiles show a society scene...

...while graffiti makes a political comment.

and it's fairly common for small sums to be quoted in duros: *dos duros* for 10 ptas, *cinco duros* for 25 ptas, even *veinte duros* for 100 ptas.

Exchange Rates

At the time of going to press, exchange rates were:

country	unit		ptas
Australia	A$1	=	102
Canada	C$1	=	120
France	1FF	=	25
Germany	DM1	=	85
Japan	¥100	=	165
New Zealand	NZ$1	=	82
United Kingdom	UK£1	=	267
USA	US$1	=	179

Exchanging Money

You can change cash or travellers cheques at virtually any bank or exchange office, at bus and train stations and at the airport. The main-road border crossings also usually have exchange facilities. Banks tend to offer the best rates, with minor differences between them. They're mostly open from 8.30 am to 2 pm Monday to Friday and 9 am to 1 pm on Saturday – although some don't bother with Saturday opening in summer. Many banks have ATMs (automated teller machines). Madrid is swarming with banks.

Exchange offices (you'll see many around Puerta del Sol and along Gran Vía), usually indicated by the word *cambio* (exchange), generally offer longer opening hours and quicker service than banks but have poorer exchange rates.

Travellers cheques usually bring a slightly better exchange rate than cash but often attract higher commissions than cash exchange.

Wherever you change your money, ask about commissions first and confirm that exchange rates are as posted (in other words, that they haven't changed since the sign was last updated). Also, make sure that the exchange rate posted is for buying pesetas, not for selling them. Commissions vary from bank to bank, may be different for travellers cheques and cash, and may depend on how many cheques, or how much in total, you're cashing. A typical commis-

sion is 3%, with a minimum of 300 to 500 ptas, but there are places that charge a minimum commission of 1000 or even 2000 ptas. Places that advertise 'no commission' may offer poor exchange rates to start with.

Remember that there should be no commission payable on exchanges between currencies that have signed up for the euro, or for changing euro travellers cheques into cash pesetas. To be sure of this, go to the Banco de España (Map 5) on Plaza de la Cibeles.

American Express (Amex; Map 7; 24 hours ☎ 91 527 03 03) is at Plaza de las Cortes 2. It's open from 9 am to 5.30 pm Monday to Friday and 9 am to noon on Saturday. They also have a branch (☎ 91 393 82 15) at Barajas airport.

Cash Don't bring wads of cash from home – travellers cheques and plastic are much safer. If you wander around with pounds and dollars in your pockets you are just inviting rubber fingers to make you instantly poor. It is, however, an idea to keep an emergency stash separate from other valuables in case you should lose your travellers cheques and credit cards.

You will, of course, need pesetas in cash for many day-to-day transactions (many small pensiones, eateries and shops take cash only). Try not to carry around more than you need at any one time – in much the same way as you try to avoid doing so at home!

Travellers Cheques These protect your money because they can be replaced if they are lost or stolen. They can be cashed at most banks and exchange offices. Amex and Thomas Cook are widely accepted brands. For Amex travellers cheque refunds you can call ☎ 900 99 44 26 from anywhere in Spain.

It doesn't really matter whether your cheques are in pesetas or in the currency of the country you buy them in – Spanish exchange outlets will change most non-obscure currencies. Get most of your cheques in fairly large denominations (the equivalent of 10,000 ptas or more) to reduce the number of per-cheque commission charges you pay.

It's vital to keep your initial receipt, and a record of your cheque numbers and the ones you have used, separate from the cheques themselves.

Take your passport when you go to cash travellers cheques.

Credit/Debit Cards You can use plastic to pay for many purchases (including meals and rooms at many establishments, especially from the middle price range up, and long-distance trains), and obviously you can use it to withdraw cash pesetas from banks and ATMs. Among the most widely accepted cards are Visa, MasterCard, Eurocard, Amex, Cirrus, Plus, Diners Club and JCB.

On the exchange-rate front you also generally get a better deal than with cash and cheques, even taking into account any charges levied on foreign transactions and cash advances (usually around 1.5%).

A high proportion of Spanish banks, even in small towns and villages, have an ATM (*cajero automático*) that will dispense cash pesetas any time (and no queues!) if you have the right piece of plastic to slot into it. Some stop accepting foreign cards at midnight.

Check with your card's issuer before leaving home on how widely usable your card will be, on how to report and replace a lost card, on withdrawal/spending limits, and on whether your personal identification number (PIN) will be acceptable (some European ATMs don't accept PINs of more than four digits).

Always report a lost card straight away. Amex are among the easiest cards to replace – you can call ☎ 902 37 56 37 or ☎ 91 572 03 03 (in Madrid) at any time. For Visa cards call ☎ 900 97 44 45; for Master-Card/Eurocard ☎ 900 97 12 31; and for Diners Club ☎ 91 547 40 00.

TravelMoney Visa TravelMoney comes in the form of a prepaid disposable credit card which you buy from selected banks or travel agencies for amounts from UK£100 to UK£5000. It works for ATM withdrawals wherever the Visa sign is displayed. Inquire at Thomas Cook (☎ 01733-318900 in the UK) or call Visa before you travel.

International Transfers To have money transferred from another country, you need to organise someone to send it to you (through a bank at home or a money-transfer service such as Western Union or Money-Gram) and a bank (or Western Union or MoneyGram office) in Madrid at which to collect it. If there's money in your bank account back at home, you may be able to instruct the bank yourself.

For information on Western Union services and branches, call ☎ 900 63 36 33 free from anywhere in Spain. For MoneyGram call ☎ 900 20 10 10; there's an office on Plaza de España (Map 5).

A bank-to-bank telegraphic transfer typically costs the equivalent of about 3000 or 4000 ptas and should take about a week. Western Union and MoneyGram can supposedly hand money over to the recipient within 10 minutes of its being sent. The sender pays a fee in proportion to the amount sent. It's also possible to have money sent through Amex.

Security

Keep only a limited amount of cash, with the bulk of your money in more easily replaceable forms such as travellers cheques or plastic. If your accommodation has a safe, use it. If you have to leave money in your room, divide it into several stashes and hide them in different places.

For carrying money on the street the safest thing is a shoulder wallet or under-the-clothes money belt. An external money belt attracts rather than deflects attention.

Costs

Being the capital, Madrid is inevitably expensive by Spanish standards, but northern Europeans generally find it reasonable. Travellers from beyond the EU (such as the USA and Australia) tend to find anywhere in Europe pricey. Costs of accommodation, eating out and transport are considerably lower than in Britain or France. If you are particularly frugal, it's just about possible to scrape by on 4000 to 5000 ptas a day. This would involve staying in the cheapest possible accommodation, not eating in restaurants or going to museums or bars, and not moving around too much.

A more comfortable budget would be 7000 ptas a day. This could allow you around 2500 ptas for accommodation; 700 ptas for breakfast (coffee, juice and a pastry); 1000 to 1400 ptas for a set lunch; 300 ptas for public transport (two metro or bus rides); 500 ptas a day for museums; and 1500 ptas for a simple dinner, with a bit over for a drink or two.

With 25,000 ptas a day you can stay in excellent accommodation, splurge in Madrid's better restaurants and even hire a car for a few days' touring outside town.

Ways to Save Two people can travel more cheaply (per person) than one by sharing rooms. You'll also save money by avoiding the peak tourist seasons (Christmas, Easter and summer), when room prices can go up. A student or youth card, or a document such as a passport proving you're aged over 60, brings worthwhile savings on some travel costs and admission to some museums and sights (see Documents earlier in this chapter). Some museums and sights have free days now and then, and a few are cheaper for EU passport holders.

Prolific letter-writers can save a few pesetas on long-distance mail by sending aerograms instead of standard letters or postcards (this does not apply to letters under 20g posted to European countries).

Tipping & Bargaining
In restaurants, the law requires that menu prices include service charges, so tipping is a matter of personal choice – most people leave some small change if they're satisfied and 5% is usually plenty. It's common to leave small change at bar and cafe tables. Hotel porters will generally be happy with 200 ptas and most won't turn their noses up at 100 ptas.

In pensiones and hotels it can be worth asking about discounts for prolonged stays.

Taxes & Refunds
Value-added tax (VAT) is known as IVA ('EE-ba', *impuesto sobre el valor añadido*). On accommodation and restaurant prices, IVA is 7% and is usually – but not always – included in quoted prices. On retail goods IVA is 16%. On vehicle hire it seems to fluctuate between 7% and 16%. To check whether a price includes IVA, you can ask *'?Está incluido el IVA?'* ('Is IVA included?').

Visitors are entitled to a refund of the 16% IVA on purchases costing more than 15,000 ptas, from any shop, if they take the goods out of the EU within three months. Ask the shop for a Cashback refund form showing the price and IVA paid for each item and identifying the vendor and purchaser. Then present the form at the customs booth for IVA refunds when you depart from Spain (or elsewhere from the EU). You will need your passport and a boarding card that shows you are leaving the EU. The officer will stamp the invoice and you hand it in at a bank at the departure point for the reimbursement.

At Barajas airport, go to the Argentaria or Amex branches on the 1st floor in T1 with your Cashback refund form for an immediate refund. If you don't have such a form, you will need to present the goods, receipts and so on to the customs (*aduana*) desk between check-in desks 31 and 32 in T1. They will stamp the receipts, which you will then need to mail to the vendor (with your address) to have a refund sent to you. It is possible to have the tax paid back to your credit card or by cheque.

POST & COMMUNICATIONS
Post
Stamps are sold at most *estancos* (tobacconist shops with *'Tabacos'* in yellow letters on a maroon background), as well as post offices *(correos y telégrafos)*.

The main post office is in the ornate Palacio de Comunicaciones on Plaza de la Cibeles (Map 6). *Lista de correos* (poste restante) is at windows 78–80. Take your passport with you. To send big parcels, head for Puerta N on the southern side of the post office on Calle de Montalbán – they even offer a reasonably priced packing service. The office is open from 8 am to 9.30 pm Monday to Friday and 8.30 am to 2 pm on Saturday.

Rates A postcard or letter weighing up to 20g costs 70 ptas to other European countries, 115 ptas to North America, and 185 ptas to Australasia or Asia. Three A4 sheets in an air-mail envelope weigh between 15g and 20g. An aerogram costs 85 ptas to anywhere in the world.

Certificado (registered mail) costs an extra 175 ptas for international mail. *Urgente* service, which means your letter may arrive two or three days quicker, costs an extra 230 ptas for international mail. You can send mail both urgente and certificado (which costs 240 ptas when added to urgente).

A day or two quicker than the urgente service – but a lot more expensive – is Postal Exprés, sometimes called Express Mail Service (EMS). This uses courier companies for international deliveries. Packages weighing up to 1kg cost 4100 ptas to anywhere in Europe, 7000 ptas to North America, and 8000 ptas to Australia or New Zealand.

Sending Mail It's quite safe to post your mail in the yellow street postboxes *(buzones)* as well as at post offices. Ordinary mail to other western European countries normally takes up to a week; to North America up to 10 days; and to Australia or New Zealand up to two weeks.

Receiving Mail Delivery times are similar to those for outbound mail. Using the Spanish five-digit postcode (which goes *before* the name of the city) will speed up the process.

Poste restante mail will be delivered to the main post office unless another one is specified. Take your passport when you go to pick up mail. A letter addressed to poste restante in central Madrid should look like this:

> Jenny JONES
> Lista de Correos
> 28080 Madrid
> Spain

Amex card or travellers cheque holders can use the free client mail-holding service at its main office in Madrid (see Exchanging Money under Money earlier in this chapter).

Couriers Most international courier services have reps in Madrid, including United Parcel Service (UPS; ☎ 900 10 24 10) and DHL (☎ 902 12 24 24). Simply call them to pick up or deliver.

Telephone

The ubiquitous blue payphones are easy to use for international and domestic calls. They accept coins, phonecards issued by the national phone company Telefónica *(tarjetas telefónicas)* and, in some cases, various credit cards. Tarjetas telefónicas come in 1000 and 2000 ptas denominations (the latter usually have 2100 ptas worth of call time as an enticement) and, like postage stamps, are sold at post offices and tobacconists.

Public phones inside bars and cafes, and phones in hotel rooms, are nearly always a good deal more expensive than street payphones.

The main Telefónica office *(locutorio;* Map 5), Gran Vía 30, is open from 9.30 am to midnight daily. It has telephone cabins, telex services and phone directories for the whole country.

Mobile Phones Spain uses GSM 900/1800, which is compatible with the rest of Europe and Australia but not with the North American GSM 1900 or the totally different system in Japan (although some North Americans have GSM 1900/900 phones that do work here). If you have a GSM phone, check with your service provider about using it in Spain, and beware of calls being routed internationally (very expensive for a 'local' call).

You can organise to rent a mobile phone by calling Phonerent on ☎ 91 541 07 00 or ☎ 608 42 10 55. You may be just as well off buying one. You can get decent phones that operate with prepaid cards for about 10,000 ptas, with 4000 ptas of calls thrown in.

Costs As elsewhere in Europe, the cost of making a phonecall is slowly falling in Spain. Within Spain you can make three types of call: *metropolitana* (local), *provincial* (a call within the same province) and *interprovincial* (national). Note that calls from payphones cost about 35% more than calls from private phones.

The cost of a call depends on when you make it. Three cost bands operate. *Punta* is the dearest and runs from 8 am to 5 pm Monday to Friday and 8 am to 2 pm on Saturday. *Normal* operates from 5 to 10 pm Monday to Friday. The rest of the time is *reducida* rate, the cheapest band.

A payphone call lasting three-minutes costs around 25 ptas within your local area, 65 ptas to other places within the same province, and 110 ptas to other provinces in Spain.

For international calls, two bands operate, normal and reducida – the latter is the same as for national calls. A three-minute payphone call at normal rate to Australia will cost 820 ptas. To the USA you pay 280 ptas. Calls to the rest of Europe cost 230 ptas for about three minutes.

Calls to Spanish numbers starting 900 are free. Calls to numbers starting 902 cost around 75 ptas for three minutes. Calls to mobile phones – numbers starting with 6 – cost 230 ptas for three minutes.

Cut-Rate Phonecards Lonely Planet's eKno Communication Card is aimed specifically at independent travellers and provides budget international calls, a range of messaging services, free email and travel information – but for local calls, you're usually better off with a local card. You can join online at www.ekno.lonelyplanet.com.

To use eKno once in Spain dial ☎ 900 93 19 51 or ☎ 900 97 15 37.

If you're arriving from the USA or the UK, you are probably already acquainted with the idea of buying cut-price phonecards. You buy the card, dial a toll-free number and then follow the instructions – they can bring savings on international calls if you are calling from a payphone, but nothing to get too excited about. Compare rates (where possible, before buying). Cut-rate cards can be bought from estancos and newsstands in central Madrid.

Private phone companies specialising in cut-rate overseas calls are beginning to appear in Madrid. One is Sol Telecom (Map 8), Puerta del Sol 6. It is open from 8 am to 11 pm daily and claims to undercut Telefónica by up to 60%. Another is the VIC locutorio (Map 5) at Calle de los Reyes (one of several branches), just off Plaza de España.

Domestic Calls There are no area codes in Spain. All numbers have nine digits and you just dial that nine-digit number. Older signs still give the first two digits as an area code (the 91 with which all Madrid numbers start was, until early 1998, a two-digit area code).

Dial ☎ 1009 to speak to a domestic operator, including for a domestic reverse-charge (collect) call *(una llamada por cobro revertido)*. For directory inquiries dial ☎ 1003; calls cost about 45 ptas from a private phone.

International Calls The access code for international calls is 00. To make an international call dial the access code, wait for a new dialling tone, then dial the country code, area code and number you want.

International collect calls are simple: dial 900 followed by a code for the country you're calling: Australia (99 00 61), Belgium (99 00 32), Canada (99 00 15), Denmark (99 00 45), France (99 00 33), Germany (99 00 49), Ireland (99 03 53), Israel (99 09 72), Italy (99 03 91), Japan (98 09 81, 98 08 11, 98 08 12), Netherlands (99 00 31), New Zealand (99 00 64), Portugal

FACTS FOR THE VISITOR

(99 03 51), UK (99 00 44 for BT, 99 09 44 for Cable & Wireless) and USA (99 00 11 for AT&T, 99 00 13 for Sprint, 99 00 14 for MCI, 99 00 17 for Worldcom). Codes for other countries are sometimes posted up in payphones. You'll get straight through to an operator in the country you're calling. The same numbers can be used with direct-dial calling cards.

If for some reason the above information doesn't work for you, in most places you can get an English-speaking Spanish international operator on ☎ 1008 (for calls within Europe) or ☎ 1005 (rest of the world).

For international directory inquiries dial ☎ 025.

Calling Madrid from Abroad Spain's country code is ☎ 34. Follow this with the full nine-digit number you are calling.

Fax

Most main post offices have a fax service: sending one page costs about 350 ptas within Spain, 1115 ptas to elsewhere in Europe, and 2100 to 2500 ptas to other countries. However, you'll often find cheaper rates at shops or offices with 'Fax Público' signs.

Email & Internet Access

Travelling with a portable computer is a great way to stay in touch with life back home, but unless you know what you're doing it's fraught with potential problems. If you plan to carry your notebook or palm-top computer invest in a universal AC adapter, which will enable you to plug in your computer anywhere without frying the innards. You'll also need a plug adapter for Spain – the standard European two-round-pin variety. This is easier to buy before you leave home.

Also, your PC-card modem may or may not work once you leave your home country – and you won't know for sure until you try. The safest option is to buy a reputable 'global' modem before you leave home, or buy a local PC-card modem if you're spending an extended time in Spain.

Spanish phone sockets have for the most part been standardised to the US RJ-11 type.

For more information on travelling with a portable computer, check out the Web sites at www.teleadapt.com or www.warrior.com.

Major Internet service providers such as AOL (www.aol.com) and CompuServe (www.compuserve.com) have dial-in nodes in Spain; it's best to download a list of the dial-in numbers before you leave home. If you access your Internet email account at home through a smaller ISP or your office or school network, your best option is either to open an account with a global ISP, such as those mentioned above, or to rely on cybercafes and other public access points to read your mail.

If you do intend to rely on cybercafes, you'll need three pieces of information to access your Internet mail account: your incoming (POP or IMAP) mail server name, your account name and your password. Your ISP or network supervisor will be able to give you this information, which should enable you to access your Internet mail account from any Net-connected machine in the world, provided it runs some kind of email software. It pays to become familiar with the process for doing this before you leave home.

A final option to collect mail through cybercafes is to open a free Web-based email account such as HotMail (www.hotmail.com) or Yahoo! Mail (www.mail.yahoo.com). You can then access your mail from anywhere in the world from any Net-connected machine running a standard Web browser.

Cybercafes It's taken a while, but Madrid seems to have discovered the Internet and embraced the cybercafe idea. Prices can vary quite dramatically, so shop around. The following should be regarded as a taster, as new places seem to emerge every day.

Aroba52 (Map 5; ☎ 91 758 13 90) Calle de los Reyes. This is one of a number of dirt-cheap places immediately around Plaza de España. It charges 300 ptas an hour on computers connected by ISDN line, or you can buy 10 hours for 2500 ptas (to use when you want).

Cervecería El Alama (Map 5) Calle del Alamo 7. Again, here you pay 300 ptas an hour. It is open until midnight Monday to Saturday.

Connection Room (Map 2; ☎ 91 399 34 39) Calle de Cea Bermúdez 66. It opens from 8 am to midnight daily. One hour online costs 700 ptas.

La Casa de Internet (Map 3; ☎ 91 446 55 41) Calle de Luchana 20. Here you pay 900 ptas per hour online (700 ptas for students). They also do international phone calls via the Internet and will even sell you a computer if they can. They open from 10 am (4 pm at the weekend) to midnight daily.

Nevada 2000 (Map 5; ☎ 91 531 15 13) Calle de los Reyes 7. This is a gaming parlour where you can go online for 300 ptas.

Open Nautas (Map 5; ☎ 91 444 00 69) Calle de San Hermenegildo 4. This place is open from 10 am (noon at the weekend) to midnight daily. Going online costs 700 ptas an hour.

WWW2.Call.Home (Map 7; ☎ 91 354 01 04) Plaza Puerta de Moros 2. Here you can make cheap phone calls, send and receive faxes, muck around on Photoshop and so on. Oh, and you can go online for 500 ptas an hour. It opens from 10 am (11 am on Saturday and noon on Sunday) to 11 pm daily.

Xnet Café (Map 5; ☎ 91 594 09 99) Calle de San Bernardo 81. They have an original approach here – you buy a drink for 500 ptas and they'll let you sit down for 45 minutes' Net time.

INTERNET RESOURCES

Scouring the Net for a few hours can lead you to some interesting tips about most aspects of the city, including a lot of practical information such as event listings and public transport details. Many of the sites are multilingual (eg Castilian, English and French). Some initial sites you might like to surf include:

All About Spain A varied site with information on everything from fiestas to hotels, and a yellow pages guide to tour operators around the world that offer trips in Spain.
www.red2000.com

Cities.Com Search for Madrid on this site and it takes you to a list of other potentially interesting sites, some of which appear in this list.
www.cities.com

Ciudad Hoy This is one of the better sites (in Spanish). Search for Madrid and you are transferred to Madridhoy.net, a comprehensive site with broad listings, general news, links to white and yellow pages sites and more.
www.ciudadhoy.com

Comunidad de Madrid Lots of background information about the region around Madrid, and links to government offices.
www.comadrid.es

Consorcio de Transportes de Madrid This is the umbrella organisation for public transport throughout Madrid and the surrounding region. You can get information on anything from the metro to night buses.
www.ctm-madrid.es

Excite Travel Excite's travel Web pages, with farefinder and bookings plus links to metro maps, restaurant tips and the like.
www.excite.com/travel/countries/spain/madrid

Internet Cafe Guide At this site you can get a list of Internet cafes in Madrid (and around Spain). It's not as up to date as you might expect, but it is a start (see also Cybercafes earlier in this chapter).
www.netcafeguide.com

Interocio This is not a bad site (in Spanish) in which to search for new ideas on restaurants, bars and clubs in Madrid.
www.interocio.es

Madrid City Council The Ayuntamiento's English-language site, but it's not particularly detailed.
www.munimadrid.es/ayuntamiento/htmling/indice.html

Renfe This site offers timetables, tickets and special offers on Spain's national rail network.
www.renfe.es

TuCiudad.Com Pick a city (in this case Madrid) on this Spanish site and you will end up in a fairly good listings site.
www.tuciudad.com

Turismo, Cultura y Ocio The Ayuntamiento de Madrid's information site on Madrid, with limited listings. It's not bad if you are searching for a particular address such as a consulate, but fails to give you an easily accessible global look at what the city offers.
www.munimadrid.es/ayuntamiento/html/turismo.html

BOOKS

Most books are published in different editions by different publishers in different countries. As a result, a book might be a hard-cover rarity in one country and readily available in paperback in another. Fortunately, bookshops and libraries search by title or author, so your local bookshop or library is best placed to advise you on the availability of the following recommendations.

Bookshops Abroad

In London several good bookshops specialise in the business of travel. For guidebooks and maps, Stanfords bookshop (☎ 020-7836 2121), 12–14 Long Acre, London WC2E 9LP, is acknowledged as one of the better first ports of call. A well-stocked source of travel literature is Daunts Books for Travellers (☎ 020-7224 2295), 83 Marylebone High St, London W1M 4AL. For books in Spanish, one of the best options is Grant & Cutler (☎ 020-7734 2012), 55–57 Great Marlborough St, London W1V 2AY.

Still in the UK, Books on Spain (☎ 020-8898 7789, fax 8898 8812, ✉ keith harris@books-on-spain.com), PO Box 207, Twickenham TW2 5BQ, can send you mail-order catalogues of hundreds of old and new titles on Spain. See the Web site at www.books-on-spain.com.

In Australia, the Travel Bookshop (☎ 020-9261 8200), 3/175 Liverpool St, Sydney, is worth a browse. In the USA, try Book Passage (☎ 415-927-0960), 51 Tamal Vista Blvd, Corte Madera, California, and The Complete Traveler Bookstore (☎ 212-685 9007), 199 Madison Ave, New York. In France, L'Astrolabe rive gauche (☎ 01 46 33 80 06), 14 rue Serpente, Paris, is recommended.

Lonely Planet

If you're planning to travel extensively from Madrid, check out Lonely Planet's companion titles, including *Barcelona*, *Spain*, *Walking in Spain*, *Andalucía* and *France*.

World Food Spain by Richard Sterling is a trip into Spain's culinary soul, from tapas to *postres* and the *menú del día* to the *carta de vinos*, with a comprehensive culinary dictionary. The *Spanish Phrasebook* will enable you to fill some of the gaps between *¡hola!* and *adiós*.

History & People

Spain For a thorough but colourful and not over-long survey of Spanish history,

The Story of Spain by Mark Williams is hard to beat. Also concise and worthwhile is Juan Lalaguna's *A Traveller's History of Spain*.

Gerald Brenan's *The Spanish Labyrinth* (1943) is an in-depth but readable unravelling of the tangle of political and social movements in the half-century or so before the Civil War.

If you are looking for a more detailed and somewhat academic exploration of Spanish history, the series *A History of Spain*, edited by John Lynch, covers the subject in more than a dozen separate volumes by various authors.

The Spanish Civil War by Hugh Thomas is probably the classic account of the conflict in any language, long and dense with detail, yet readable, even-handed and humane. Paul Preston's *Franco* is the big biography of one of history's little dictators.

Contemporary Spain To put things in context, you may want to read a little more widely about Spain. One of the best overall introductions to modern Spain is *The New Spaniards* by John Hooper, a former Madrid correspondent for the *Guardian*.

Madrid If you read Spanish, a comprehensive and limpid survey of the city's history is *Madrid: Historia de una Capital* by Santos Juliá, David Ringrose and Cristina Segura.

Less of a tome is *Historia Breve de Madrid* by Fidel Revilla, Ramón Hidalgo and Rosalía Ramos.

The definitive guide to street names and their history is Pedro de Répide's *Las Calles de Madrid*.

Art & Architecture

If you want a reasonable introduction to the collection of the Prado you could do worse than *A Basic Guide to the Prado*, by J Rogelio Buendía, which has been translated into several languages.

Jonathon Brown's *Velázquez: Painter and Courtier* is an in-depth evaluation of one of Spain's greatest painters and leading light in the imperial court. Pierre Gassier delivers, in *Goya, a Witness of his Times*, an equally complete account of another of the nation's foremost painters.

Hemingway & the Bullfight

Ernest Hemingway's *Death in the Afternoon* is his definitive book on bullfighting. It can be a little turgid but in all it gives you a deep insight into the whys, hows and wherefores of this strange blood sport.

Cuisine

A general introduction to Spanish cooking in English is Robert Carrier's *Great Dishes of Spain*.

For a Madrid slant on cooking, several possibilities in Spanish suggest themselves. *La Cocina Típica de Madrid* by Manuel Martínez Llopis and Simone Ortega mixes in recipes with general information and anecdote on the subject of cooking in the capital. Victor Alperi's *Cocina y Gastronomía de Madrid* is a fairly exhaustive recipe book, or you could try *Cocina Madrileña*, part of the Cocina Regional series published by Susaeta.

You can find all these in Madrid's La Casa del Libro bookshop (see the Shopping chapter).

FILMS

Madrid has not attracted a great deal of foreign film interest. John Malkovich's decision to shoot some of his first feature film (as director) in the Spanish capital in 2000 might inject a little more interest into the place as a set for non-Spanish directors.

If you want to give yourself a general introduction to the best of flamenco, try to see Carlos Saura's 1995 flick, *Flamenco*. A double-CD set of the music is also available.

See Cinema under Arts in the Facts about Madrid chapter for a discussion of the city's cinematic history.

CD-ROMS

There are some interesting CD-ROMs available on subjects related to Madrid and/or Spain, but most of them have text and any voice-over in Spanish only and could be hard to come by outside Spain. The other problem is that most seem to

come and go. Among those available at the time of writing were:

Flamenco Biblioteca Multimedia's fairly basic guide to the wonders of flamenco song and dance (4950 ptas).

História de España Lectus Vergara publishes the introductory survey of the history of Spain (9990 ptas).

História de España: De la Monarquía Totalitaria a la Monarquía Absoluta Published by the Encyclopedia Universal del Saber, this disk takes you through Spanish history from the Catholic Monarchs to Empire and then the Bourbon kings (9990 ptas).

Miguel de Cervantes Saavedra: Obras Completas The complete works of the genius who gave us Don Quijote. It is published by the Centro de Estudios Cervantes (6950 ptas).

Toledo A tour of this medieval city 'of the three cultures' produced by Nazarí Multimedia (4995 ptas).

Velázquez A selection of the grand master's works from the Prado, published by Abibi and presented in English and Spanish (4995 ptas).

NEWSPAPERS & MAGAZINES

You can easily find a wide selection of national daily newspapers from around Europe and the UK at newsstands all over central Madrid, especially along Gran Vía and around Puerta del Sol. The *International Herald Tribune*, *Time*, *The Economist*, *Le Monde*, *Der Spiegel* and a host of other international magazines are also available.

Spanish National Press

The main Spanish dailies can be identified along roughly political lines, with the old-fashioned paper *ABC* representing the conservative right, *El País* identified with the Partido Socialista Obrero Español (PSOE; Spain's centre-left socialist party) and *El Mundo,* a more radicalised left-wing paper that prides itself on breaking political scandals. For a good spread of national and international news, *El País* is the pick. One of the best-selling dailies is *Marca*, devoted exclusively to sport.

Local Press

El País contains a central section devoted to the goings-on in Madrid and the Comunidad.

Since February 2000 a limited-circulation free newspaper, *Madrid y Mas*, has been distributed at metro stations and other key rush-hour points around the city.

Useful Publications

Madrid's entertainment bible is the weekly magazine *Guía del Ocio* (125 ptas), which comes out on Thursday and lists almost everything that's on in the way of music, film, exhibitions, theatre and more. You can pick it up at most newsstands. An alternative is the free *En Cartel*, which you can find in many bars and bookshops. It is not nearly as complete as the *Guía del Ocio*.

The free monthly English-language *In Madrid* is a handy newspaper-format rag with articles on the local scene and classifieds that will lead you to English-speaking doctors, dentists, baby-sitters and other useful information. It's aimed at long-term residents. You can pick it up at various bars (especially Irish pubs and the like), restaurants and shops all over town, as well as at several consulates, schools (such as International House; see Language Courses in the Things to See & Do chapter) and occasionally at the tourist offices. Otherwise, call ☎ 91 364 16 97 to find out where you can get it. Another handy publication is the *Broadsheet*, an expat rag.

For long listings of upcoming flamenco performances and ads for flamenco tuition, see the free monthly magazine *Alma 100*. It mainly concentrates on Andalucían venues, however. Another monthly flamenco mag is *El Olivo*.

RADIO

You can pick up BBC World Service broadcasts on a variety of frequencies. Broadcasts are directed at western Europe on, among others, 648, 9410 and 12,095 kHz (short wave).

Voice of America (VOA) can be found on various short-wave frequencies, including 9700, 9760 and 15,205 kHz, depending on the time of day. The BBC and VOA broadcast round the clock, but the quality of reception varies considerably and you may

have to do a lot of dial twiddling (for instance from midnight to 5 am).

The Spanish national network Radio Nacional de España (RNE) has several stations: RNE 1 (88.2 FM in Madrid) has general interest and current affairs programs; RNE 5 (90.3 FM) concentrates on sport and entertainment; and RNE 3 (93.2 FM) presents a decent range of pop and rock music. For classical music you can tune into Sinfo Radio (104.3 FM). Among the most listened-to rock and pop stations are 40 Principales (93.9 FM), Onda Cero (98 FM) and Cadena 100 (99.5 FM).

TV

Most TVs receive seven channels: two from Spain's state-run Televisión Española (TVE1 and La 2), three independent (Antena 3, Tele 5 and Canal Plus) and the regional Telemadrid station. More than 20 tiny local stations scattered about the Comunidad de Madrid struggle to survive. A couple you may pick up include Canal 7 and TvL.

News programs are generally decent and you can occasionally catch an interesting documentary or film (look out for the occasional English-language classic late at night on La 2). Otherwise, the main fare is a rather nauseating diet of soaps (many from Latin America), endless talk shows and almost vaudevillian variety shows (with plenty of glitz and tits). Canal Plus is a pay channel dedicated mainly to movies: you need a decoder and subscription to see the movies, but anyone can watch the other programs.

Many private homes and better hotels have satellite TV. Foreign channels you may come across include BBC World (mainly news and travel), BBC Prime (other BBC programs), CNN, Eurosport, Sky News, Sky Sports, Sky Sports 2, Sky Movies and the German SAT 1.

VIDEO SYSTEMS

If you want to record or buy video tapes to play back home, you won't get a picture if the image registration systems are different. TVs and nearly all pre-recorded videos on sale in Spain use the PAL (phase alternation line) system common to most of western Europe and Australia, incompatible with France's SECAM system or the NTSC system used in North America and Japan. PAL videos can't be played back on a machine that lacks PAL capability.

PHOTOGRAPHY & VIDEO
Film & Equipment
Most main brands of film are widely available and processing is fast and generally efficient.

A roll of print film (36 exposures, ISO 100) costs around 650 ptas and can be processed for around 1250 ptas (more for same-day service), although there are often better deals if you have two or three rolls developed together. The equivalent in slide *(diapositiva)* film is around 850 ptas plus 800 ptas for processing.

You can have film developed all over the city. Photo Express (Map 5; ☎ 91 542 83 90) at Gran Vía 84, right on Plaza de España, is reliable. Another one is Image Center (Map 8; ☎ 91 522 76 66) at Plaza de Santa Ana 1.

Technical Tips
The bright middle-of-the-day sun in Spain tends to bleach out your shots. You will get more colour and contrast earlier or later in the day whether you are using still or video film.

Restrictions
Some museums and galleries ban photography, or at least flash, and soldiers can be touchy about it. Video is also often not allowed.

Photographing People
It's common courtesy to ask – at least by gesture – when you want to photograph people unless, perhaps, they're in some kind of public event such as a procession.

Airport Security
Your camera and film will be passed routinely through airport X-ray machines. These shouldn't damage film but you can ask for inspection by hand if you're worried. Lead pouches for film, available in some specialised camera stores, are another solution.

TIME
Spain (and hence Madrid) is on GMT/UTC plus one hour during winter, and GMT/UTC plus two hours during the daylight-saving period from the last Sunday in March to the last Sunday in October. Most other western European countries have the same time as Spain year round, the major exceptions being Britain, Ireland and Portugal, which are an hour behind.

When it's noon in Madrid, it's 11 am in London, 6 am in New York and Toronto, 3 am in San Francisco, 9 pm in Sydney and 11 pm in Auckland. Note that there is usually a couple of weeks' difference between the changeover to/from daylight saving in Europe and in North America and Australasia.

ELECTRICITY
Electric current in Madrid is 220V, 50Hz, as in the rest of Continental Europe. Several countries outside Europe (such as the USA and Canada) use 60Hz supplies, which means that appliances that have electric motors (such as some CD and tape players) from those countries may perform poorly. It is always safest to use a transformer.

Plugs have two round pins, again as in the rest of Continental Europe.

WEIGHTS & MEASURES
The metric system is used in Spain. Like other Continental Europeans, the Spanish indicate decimals with commas and thousands with points. You will sometimes see years written thus: 1.998.

LAUNDRY
Well-placed coin-operated laundrettes in central Madrid include: Lavandería Alba (Map 5), Calle del Barco 26; Lavomatique (Map 8) on Calle de Cervantes, open from 9 am to 8 pm Monday to Friday and 10 am to 2 pm on Saturday (400 ptas to wash a load and 100 ptas to dry); and Lavandería España (Map 8) on Calle del Infante.

euro currency converter € 1 = 166 ptas

TOILETS

Public toilets are not particularly common in Madrid but it's OK to wander into most bars and cafes to use their toilet, even if you're not a customer (although this writer prefers to do them the courtesy of having a quick coffee). It's worth carrying some loo paper with you, though, as many toilets don't have it. If there's a bin beside the loo, it's there because the local sewerage system couldn't cope otherwise, so put paper etc in it.

HEALTH

You should encounter no particular health problems in Madrid. Your main risks are likely to be sunburn, dehydration or mild gut problems at first if you're not used to a lot of olive oil. Most travellers experience no problems.

Spain has reciprocal health agreements with other EU countries. Citizens of those countries need to get hold of an E111 form from their national health bodies (in the UK and Ireland, get one at the local post office). If you should require medical help you will need to present this, plus photocopies of the form, and your national health card. This is only valid for Spanish public healthcare.

Travel insurance is still a good idea, however. You should really get it to cover you for theft, loss and unexpected travel cancellations anyway, so you will be covered for the cost of private healthcare as well.

No vaccinations are required for Spain unless you are coming from an infected area (this generally relates to yellow fever – you may be asked for proof of vaccination).

For minor health problems you can head to your local *farmacia* (pharmacy), where pharmaceuticals tend to be sold more freely without prescription than in places such as the USA, Australia or UK.

Condoms are available in pharmacies and some supermarkets. Other contraceptives are available in pharmacies only.

Medical Services

If you have medical problems, pop into the nearest Insalud clinic – often marked 'Centro de Salud'. Make sure you have all your insurance details with you (including your E111 if you are an EU citizen). A handy such clinic in the city centre is at Calle de las Navas de Tolosa 10 (Map 5).

If you don't have medical insurance or an E111, your best bet is probably to head to the Hospital General Gregorio Marañón (Map 2; ☎ 91 586 80 00; metro: Ibiza), Calle del Doctor Esquerdo. In emergencies they will treat you regardless.

You can also get help at the Anglo-American Medical Unit (Map 6; ☎ 91 435 18 23; metro: Retiro), Calle del Conde de Aranda 1. Staff speak Spanish and English and the unit is open from 9 am to 8 pm Monday to Friday.

At least one pharmacy is open 24 hours a day in each district of Madrid. They mostly operate on a rota and details appear daily in *El País* and other papers. One that offers this service permanently is the Farmacia del Globo (Map 8; ☎ 91 369 20 00), Plaza de Antón Martín 46. Another is the Real Farmacia de la Reina Madre (Map 7; ☎ 91 548 00 14) at Calle Mayor 15. Otherwise you can call ☎ 098 or ☎ 010. Note that at some late-night pharmacies you have to knock at a small shutter for service. Often they will only fill prescriptions or deal with urgent problems outside normal business hours – this is not the time to buy your shampoo.

Emergency

For an ambulance call the Cruz Roja on ☎ 91 522 22 22 or ☎ 91 335 45 45, Insalud on ☎ 061, or the general emergency number ☎ 112.

Apart from hospital casualty departments, there are five first-aid stations *(urgencias)* scattered around Madrid to help with medical emergencies (open 24 hours). The handiest is Centro (Map 5; ☎ 91 521 00 25), Calle de las Navas de Tolosa 10; another such centre (open 8 am to 9 pm) is Tetuán (Map 1; ☎ 91 588 66 69), Calle de Bravo Murillo 357.

HIV & AIDS

Although the reported spread of AIDS/HIV (SIDA/VIH in Spanish) has slowed since the peak years of 1994–6, it remains a big problem in Spain. Madrid is no exception. If you are, or fear you may be, HIV positive you can seek advice at the Fundación Anti-Sida de España (Map 1; ☎ 900 11 10 00; metro: Cuatro Caminos) at Calle de Juan Montalvo 6. It is open from 10 am to 8 pm Monday to Friday. You can get tested for HIV at the Centro Sanitario Sandoval (Map 3; ☎ 91 445 23 28) at Calle de Sandoval 7. It opens from 9 am to noon Monday to Friday.

WOMEN TRAVELLERS

As visitors have flooded into Madrid, the fascination of the local boys with foreign women has tended to diminish. In general terms, therefore, harassment is unlikely to be much more apparent here than in any other European metropole, and in some cases probably less so.

Since the death of Franco, women have surged into the workforce and become far more assertive, but the truisms that apply elsewhere in the world apply here too. More often than not women are paid less than their male counterparts and glass ceilings are well in place. Household duties still tend to fall onto the shoulders of women (even among younger people) and in many cases working women find themselves doing most of the family raising too.

These days in the swimming pools you'll see just as many women with bikini tops off as on.

Organisations

The Asociación de Asistencia a Mujeres Violadas (Association for Assistance to Raped Women; Map 2; ☎ 91 574 01 10), Calle de O'Donnell 42, offers advice and help to rape victims and can refer you to similar centres in other cities, though only limited English may be spoken. The phone line is open from 10 am to 2 pm and 4 to 7 pm Monday to Friday; there's a recorded message in Spanish at other times.

On the subject of assault, the nationwide Comisión de Investigación de Malos Tratos a Mujeres (Commission of Investigation into the Abuse of Women) has a free 24-hour national emergency line for victims of physical abuse: ☎ 900 10 00 09.

The Centro de la Mujer (Map 5; ☎ 91 319 36 89) is one of several women's and lesbian groups based in the same address, Calle de Barquillo 44. Many other women's organisations are listed on the Web site www.secociti.org/mujer/mujer.htm.

Recommended reading is the *Handbook for Women Travellers* by M & G Moss.

GAY & LESBIAN TRAVELLERS

Gay and lesbian sex are both legal in Spain and the age of consent is 16 years, the same as for heterosexuals. A bill proposing the recognition of de facto gay and lesbian couples has been held up for several years in the Cortes by the ruling conservative Partido Popular (PP) and it is unlikely to move while that party remains in power. The PP-run government of the Comunidad de Madrid did, however, sponsor a move in early 2000 to set up a regional information and support office for gays, lesbians and transsexuals, while rejecting out of hand an opposition call to allow gay weddings.

An international gay guide worth tracking down is the *Spartacus Guide for Gay Men* (the Spartacus list also includes the comprehensive *Spartacus National Edition España*, in English and German), published by Bruno Gmünder Verlag, Mail Order, PO Box 61 01 04, D-10921 Berlin. It is not always terribly up to date, but it's a good start. Lesbians might try *Places for Women*, published by Ferrari Publications, Phoenix, AZ, USA.

There are a few Spanish queer sites on the Web. You could start with the site put up by the Fundación Triángulo (see the following Organisations section) at www .redestb.es/triangulo. The Barcelona-based Coordinadora Gai-Lesbiana has a good site with nationwide links at www.pangea.org/org/cgl. Here you can zero in on information ranging from bar, sauna and hotel listings through to contacts pages.

The heart of gay Madrid is the zone around Chueca, within the broader area of Malasaña. If the new bars and discos opening up here are anything to go by, the gay scene is full of life and getting better all the time. Madrid's gays claim that their city has the second greatest concentration of gays in Europe, and some even say they total one million (which, given the city population of 3.1 million, seems a trifle unlikely)!

Entiendes, a gay magazine, sells for 500 ptas. *Mensual* (500 ptas) is a monthly gay guys' listings magazine with bars, hotels, saunas and so on listed for all Spain. Yet another one you can find in Madrid is *Shangay*, available in gay bookshops. *Nosotras* is a bi-monthly lesbian review (600 ptas), available at the Librería de Mujeres (see the Shopping chapter).

The *Mapa Gaya de Madrid* lists gay bars, discos, saunas and other places of specific gay and lesbian interest in the city. You can pick up a copy in the Berkana bookstore in Chueca (see Books in the Shopping chapter).

Madrid's gay and lesbian pride march is held on the last Saturday in June.

Organisations

The Colectivo de Gais y Lesbianas de Madrid (Cogam; Map 5; ☎/fax 91 532 45 17) has an information office and social centre (Urania's Café) at Calle de Fuencarral 37. Its information line (☎ 91 523 00 70) is open from 5 to 9 pm daily.

Fundación Triángulo (Map 3; ☎/fax 91 593 05 40), Calle de Eloy Gonzalo 25, is another source of information on gay issues.

Rosa Que Te Quiero Rosa (☎ 91 394 28 28), based at the Universidad Complutense Somosaguas campus, is an exclusively lesbian organisation.

The women's squat Eskalera Karakola (Map 7), at Calle de los Embajadores 40, puts on activities for women during the week and runs a bar on Friday evening.

Nexus (☎ 91 522 16 86) can help with AIDS counselling for gay people.

DISABLED TRAVELLERS

Madrid is not particularly geared to the needs of the disabled. Just getting around the streets is a problem. Few bus and metro lines are equipped to deal with wheelchairs,

although it is possible to get wheelchair-adapted taxis.

Some Spanish tourist offices in other countries can provide a basic information sheet with some useful addresses for disabled travellers and give details of accessible accommodation in specific places.

Organisations

The UK-based Royal Association for Disability and Rehabilitation (RADAR) publishes a useful guide called *European Holidays & Travel Abroad: A Guide for Disabled People*, which provides a good overview of facilities available to disabled travellers throughout Europe. Contact RADAR (☎ 020-7250 3222), Unit 12, City Forum, 250 City Rd, London EC1V 8AS, or look at their Web site at www.radar.org.uk.

Another organisation worth calling is Holiday Care (☎ 01293-774535), 2nd Floor, Imperial Buildings, Victoria Rd, Horley, Surrey RH6 7PZ. They produce an information pack on Spain for disabled people and others with special needs. Tips range from hotels with disabled access through to where you can hire equipment and tour operators dealing with the disabled.

INSERSO (☎ 91 347 88 88), Calle de Ginzo de Limia 58, 28029 Madrid, is the Spanish government department for the disabled, with branches in all 50 provinces. ONCE (☎ 91 577 37 56), Calle de José Ortega y Gasset 18, 28001 Madrid, is the Spanish association for the blind.

The Ayuntamiento de Madrid publishes a *Guía de Accesibilidad* which contains information on disabled access to everything from the city's cinemas through to its public service buildings. It is really designed for disabled residents rather than visitors.

SENIOR TRAVELLERS

People aged over 65 can get free or half-price admission to many museums and other attractions in Madrid. For more details see the Things to See & Do chapter.

Reductions are possible on some long-distance transport, mainly trains. You usually need to provide proof of age. It is always worth asking.

You should also seek information in your own country on travel packages and discounts for senior travellers, through seniors' organisations and travel agencies.

MADRID FOR CHILDREN

Although Spain is generally a child-friendly country, Madrid is, after all, a busy capital. That said, you will usually have no problem in restaurants, hotels, cafes and the like, although few locals are inclined to take their *peques* (little ones) out for a night at a disco.

Kids can nevertheless open doors where adults alone never would. This is especially so where a language barrier impedes communication – cute kids doing the cute things that cute kids sometimes do can be a great ice-breaker.

Madrileños have fewer qualms about keeping their children up late than people from more northerly climes. In summer especially, you'll see them at the local fiestas until the wee hours. Taking children to cafes or snack bars with outdoor tables (preferably in pedestrian zones) is no problem at all. Of course your wee bairn's body clock may not quite be up to it.

What to Do with Anklebiters

Details of all of these attractions are in the Things to See & Do chapter unless stated.

The little darlings are likely to tire sooner rather than later of the Prado and other art galleries, so why not reward them with a wander in the Parque del Buen Retiro? At the weekend especially there are often activities and kids' shows. At any rate it is rarely a boring place to be. You could even take them rowing on the little lake.

Swimming pools, especially outdoor ones in the heat of summer, are a sure winner.

If you are feeling particularly indulgent you could allow yourself to be hauled around the Parque de Atracciones, Madrid's version of Luna Park. Not far away is the town Zoo and Aquarium. Another one for the kids could be the Museo de Cera (Wax Museum).

Another attraction with a reasonable chance of keeping the darlings sweet is the Cosmocaixa interactive science museum in Alcobendas (see the Excursions chapter). On the subject of excursions, heading out to some of the towns around the capital might help mollify the kiddies too.

Madrid is full of other galleries and museums, some too obscure to go into. Among the better ones that might interest small persons (depending on their age) as well as their elders are the Museo Arqueológico Nacional, Museo del Ejército, Museo del Ferrocarril and Museo del Libro. You might maintain their interest in the Templo de Debod too.

Before You Go

There are no particular health precautions you need to take, although kids tend to be more affected than adults by unaccustomed heat, changes in diet and sleeping patterns, and just being in a strange place. Nappies, creams, lotions, baby foods and so on are all easily available in Madrid, but if there's some particular brand you swear by it's best to bring it with you. Calpol, for instance, isn't easily found.

Lonely Planet's *Travel with Children* has lots of practical advice on the subject and first-hand stories from many Lonely Planet authors, and others, who have done it.

Finally, even the most adventurous of children will at times feel nostalgia for toys back home. Bring a couple of favourites to keep them occupied in dull moments or when you're just trying to kick back yourself.

USEFUL ORGANISATIONS

The Instituto Cervantes, with branches in over 30 cities around the world, exists to promote the Spanish language and the cultures of Spain and other Spanish-speaking countries. It's mainly involved in Spanish teaching and in library and information services. The library at the London branch (☎ 020-7235 0353), 102 Eaton Square, London SW1 W9AN, has a wide range of reference books, books on history and the arts, periodicals, over 1000 videos including feature films, language-teaching material, electronic databases and music CDs. In New York, the institute (☎ 212-689 4232) is at

122 East 42nd St, Suite 807, New York, NY 10168. You can find more addresses on the institute's Web site at www.cervantes.es.

UNIVERSITIES

Throughout the territory of the Comunidad de Madrid are 11 universities, five of them private. Together they account for more then 250,000 students. Of the foreign students following courses here, most come either from Latin America or from elsewhere in Europe. In the latter case most of the students are on one-year programs under the Erasmus scheme, as part of their undergraduate studies. You need to approach the Socrates and Erasmus council in your country for more information.

Of the universities, the most important is the Universidad Complutense de Madrid (☎ 91 394 10 00), Avenida de Séneca 2, 28040 Madrid. Their Web site is at www.ucm.es. It has faculty buildings spread out all over the city, although the main concentration is in the Ciudad Universitaria just north of Argüelles. Degree subjects range from philosophy to physics, covering a broad range of the sciences and humanities.

Among the other institutions are:

Universidad Autónoma de Madrid (☎ 91 397 50 00, fax 91 397 41 23) Ciudad Universitaria de Cantoblanco, 28049 Madrid. Languages, art history, law, medicine and several sciences figure among the faculties, which are spread around in and beyond the city.
Web site: www.uam.es

Universidad Carlos III de Madrid (☎ 91 624 94 31, 91 624 95 00, 91 856 12 00) Calle de Madrid 126, 28903 Getafe, Madrid. This university, which opened in 1989, has campuses dotted about the periphery of the city in Getafe, Leganés and Colmenarejo. Degrees awarded include law, economics, business studies and humanities.
Web site: www.uc3m.es.

Universidad de Alcalá (☎ 91 885 40 21, fax 91 885 40 95) Antiguo Colegio de San Pedro y San Pablo, Plaza de San Diego s/n, 28801 Alcalá de Henares. This institution has had seven centuries of very uneven history. From its glory days in the 16th and 17th centuries to its virtual shutdown in the 19th, it has been brought back to life in the years since the demise of Franco.

Degrees are in a range of humanities and science subjects and the town is about a half-hour from central Madrid by train.
Web site: www.alcala.es

For general information on studying in Madrid and some clues as to what to choose, a first port of call could be the Centro de Información y Asesoramiento Universitario (Map 6; ☎ 91 580 45 88, fax 91 580 45 81), Calle de Alcalá 32, 28014 Madrid.

CULTURAL CENTRES

If you're yearning for a whiff of home, you might consider wandering into one of the foreign cultural centres. They all have libraries, and they organise film nights and other activities.

France
  Institut Français (Map 6; ☎ 91 308 49 50) Calle del Marqués de la Ensenada 12
  Alliance Française (Map 4; ☎ 91 435 15 32) Calle de Velázquez 94
Germany
  Goethe Institut (Map 6; ☎ 91 391 39 44) Calle de Zurbarán 21
Italy
  Istituto Italiano di Cultura (Map 7; ☎ 91 547 52 04) Calle Mayor 86
UK
  British Council (Map 3; ☎ 91 337 35 00) Paseo del General Martínez Campos 31
USA
  Washington Irving Center (Map 4; ☎ 91 564 55 15) Paseo de la Castellana 52

DANGERS & ANNOYANCES

Madrid is a fairly safe city, although petty crime (in particular theft) is a problem, and its victims are often new to town.

Before You Leave Home

You can take a few precautions before you even arrive in Madrid. Inscribe your name, address and telephone number *inside* your luggage, and take photocopies of the important pages of your passport, travel tickets and other important documents. Keep the copies separate from the originals and ideally leave one set of copies at home. These steps will make things easier if you do suffer a loss or theft.

Travel insurance against theft and loss is another very good idea. See also Copies and Travel Insurance under Documents earlier in this chapter.

Theft & Loss

Prevention...is better than a cure! Only walk around with the amount of cash you intend to spend that day or evening. Hidden money belts or pouches are a good idea. The popular 'bum bags' and external belt pouches people wear around their tummies are like shining beacons to hawks on the lookout for targets. You may as well wear a neon sign saying, 'Pick Me: I'm a Tourist.'

You need to keep an eye out for pickpockets and bagsnatchers in the most heavily touristed parts of town, especially Plaza Mayor, the Puerta del Sol and the Prado. Lavapiés has become particularly problematic recently. At night you need to be aware of your surroundings in the Malasaña, Huertas and Plaza de Santa Ana areas when bar-hopping.

As a rule, dark, empty streets are to be avoided. They may be perfectly OK, but who wants to be the one to find out that they are not? Luckily, Madrid's most lively nocturnal areas are generally busy with crowds having a good time – and there is definitely safety in numbers.

Never leave anything visible in your car and preferably leave nothing in it at all. Temptation usually leads to smashed windows at least. Foreign and hire cars are especially vulnerable.

In hotels, hostels etc, use the safe if there is one. Try not to leave valuables in your room. If you must, then bury them deep in your luggage.

If anything does get lost or stolen, you need to report it to the police and get a written statement from them if you intend to claim on insurance. If your ID or passport disappears, you must also contact your nearest consulate, as early as possible, to arrange for a replacement.

Parts of the Parque del Oeste are given over to prostitution by night and are not ideal for a late-evening stroll. Paseo de Camoens y Valero and Paseo de Ruperto Chapi are where most of the tricks are done. The Casa de Campo is also swarming with ladies of the night, pimps and junkies. Some of the city's biggest traffic snarls occur here in the wee hours!

The area around Calle de la Luna, near Gran Vía, is similar. Most of the time you will have no problems, but it is as well to be aware of what you are walking into.

The area behind the Templo de Debod is a popular summertime cruising patch. In El Retiro the same activity is conducted in the south-western corner around La Chopera. This may not appeal to all tastes.

Lost & Found

The Negociado de Objetos Perdidos (☎ 91 588 43 46), Plaza de Legazpi 7 (metro: Legazpi), is open from 9 am to 2 pm. If you leave something in a taxi you need to call ☎ 91 588 43 44.

EMERGENCIES

The general EU standard emergency number is ☎ 112. You can reach all emergency services on this number and occasionally even get multi-lingual operators.

Otherwise you can call the Policía Nacional on ☎ 091, the Policía Municipal on ☎ 092 or the Guardia Civil on ☎ 062. The main police station (Map 5; ☎ 91 541 71 60) is at Calle de los Madrazo 9. For the fire brigade call ☎ 080. See also Emergency under Health earlier in this chapter.

LEGAL MATTERS

If you're arrested you will be allotted the free services of a duty solicitor (*abogado de oficio*), who may speak only Spanish. You're also entitled to make a phone call. If you phone your embassy or consulate, it will probably be able to do no more than refer you to a lawyer who speaks your language. If you end up in court, the authorities are obliged to provide a translator.

Drugs

Spain's liberal drug laws were severely tightened in 1992. The only legal drug cannabis, and then only if it's for personal use – which means very small amounts.

La Policía – Who's Who

Spanish police are on the whole more of a help than a threat to the average law-abiding traveller. Most are certainly friendly enough to be approached for directions on the street. Highway police can be hard on locals but tend to steer clear of foreign vehicles unless they stop to give help (but see the Getting Around chapter for the list of documents and equipment you should carry in your vehicle). Unpleasant events such as random drug searches do occur, but not with great frequency.

There are three main types of *policía*: the Policía Nacional, the Policía Municipal and the Guardia Civil.

Guardia Civil

Most numerous are the green-uniformed members of the Guardia Civil. Their main areas of responsibility are roads, the countryside, villages, prisons, international borders and some environmental protection. These are the guys who used to wear those alarming winged helmets, which still resurface on some ceremonial occasions.

The Guardia Civil was set up in the 19th century to quell banditry, but soon came to be regarded as a politically repressive force that clamped down on any challenge to established privilege. Although its image has softened since responsibility for the force has been switched from the defence ministry to the interior ministry, it's still a military body in some ways: most officers have attended military academy and members qualify for military decorations.

Policía Nacional

This force covers cities and bigger towns, and is the main crime-fighting body because most crime happens on its patch. Those who wear uniforms are in blue. There is also a large contingent in plain clothes, some of whom form special squads dealing with drugs, terrorism and the like. Most of them can be found in large bunker-like police stations called *comisarías*, shuffling masses of paper and dealing with things such as issuing passports, DNIs (*documentos nacionales de identidad*, or national identity cards) and residence cards for foreigners who like Spain enough to opt for long-term entanglement with its bureaucracy.

Policía Municipal

The Policía Municipal is controlled by the *ayuntamiento* (city government) and deals mainly with minor matters such as parking, traffic and bylaws. They wear blue-and-white uniforms.

Public consumption of any drug is apparently illegal, yet you may still come across the occasional bar where people smoke joints openly. Most, however, will ask you to step outside if you light up. In short, be discreet if you use cannabis. There is a reasonable degree of tolerance when it comes to people having a smoke in their own home, but it would be unwise to do so in hotel rooms or guesthouses, and could be risky in even the coolest of public places.

Travellers entering Spain from Morocco should be ready for intensive drug searches, especially if they have a vehicle.

BUSINESS HOURS

Generally, people work Monday to Friday from about 9 am to 2 pm and then again from 4.30 or 5 pm for another three hours. Shops and travel agencies are usually open for these hours on Saturday too, although some may skip the evening session. Big supermarkets and department stores such as El Corte Inglés often stay open all day Monday to Saturday, from about 9 am to 9 pm. A handful of shops are open on Sunday. Many government offices don't bother with afternoon opening any day of the year.

Museums all have their own unique opening hours. Major museums tend to open for something like normal Spanish business hours (with or without the afternoon break), but often have their weekly closing day on Monday, not Sunday.

See Exchanging Money under Money, and Post under Post & Communications earlier in this chapter for bank and post office opening hours.

PUBLIC HOLIDAYS & SPECIAL EVENTS
Vacation Periods

The two main periods when madrileños go on holiday are Semana Santa (the week leading up to Easter Sunday) and, more noticeably, the month of August. At Easter, the number of incoming tourists makes up for the leaving locals, but in August the city is like a ghost town, even though in recent years the tendency has been to stagger departures and returns in two-week chunks over July and August.

Public Holidays

In Madrid, as in the rest of Spain, there are 14 official holidays a year – some observed nationwide, some local. When a holiday falls close to a weekend, people like to make a *puente* (bridge) – meaning they take the intervening day off too. On the odd occasion when a couple of holidays fall close, they make an *acueducto* (aqueduct)!

The 12 holidays celebrated at national and/or regional level are:

Año Nuevo (New Year's Day)
1 January – plenty of parties in the discos and clubs on New Year's Eve (Noche Vieja). Expect to pay higher than usual prices. As the clock strikes midnight you are expected to eat a grape for each chime. Traditionally madrileños gather in Puerta del Sol at this time of night, grapes in hand.

Epifanía (Epiphany) or Día de los Reyes Magos (Three Kings' Day)
6 January – when children traditionally receive presents (generally they get little or nothing at Christmas). A parade with floats winds its way around the city to the delight of the kiddies.

Jueves Santo (Good Thursday)
March/April – this day kicks off the official holiday period known in Spain as Semana Santa (Holy Week). For many madrileños it means a chance to get away from the city for a few

days' rest and recreation. Nevertheless, local *cofradías* (lay fraternities) organise religious processions on this day and throughout the Easter period.

Viernes Santo (Good Friday)
Good Friday and Easter in general are celebrated with greater enthusiasm in some of the surrounding towns. Chinchón, in particular, is known for its lavish Easter processions.

Fiesta del Trabajo (Labour Day)
1 May – you'll probably hardly notice it's a holiday except for all the closed offices, banks and shops.

Fiesta de la Comunidad de Madrid
2 May – commemorating the events of El Dos de Mayo, when Napoleon's troops put down an uprising in Madrid (see the boxed text 'El Dos de Mayo' later in this chapter), the day is an opportunity for much festivity, especially in the area around the square of the same name in Malasaña, which was where resistance lasted longest. Celebrations kick off with a speech by a local personality from the balcony of the Casa de Correos in the Puerta del Sol. The Comunidad de Madrid organises a host of cultural events around this period, which can last as long as two weeks.

La Asunción (Feast of the Assumption)
15 August – also known as the Fiesta de la Virgen de la Paloma.

Día de la Hispanidad (Spanish National Day)
12 October – a fairly sober occasion.

Todos los Santos (All Saints' Day)
1 November

Día de la Constitución (Constitution Day)
6 December

La Inmaculada Concepción (Feast of the Immaculate Conception)
8 December

Navidad (Christmas)
25 December – this is a family time. Many celebrate with a big midday meal, although some prefer to eat on Christmas Eve *(nochebuena)*. Some of the oddest things about Christmas are the nativity scenes. An exposition of these cribs is held in the Plaza Mayor.

In addition to these holidays, each *municipio* (municipality) celebrates two more. This means that what is a holiday in the city of Madrid is not necessarily so in a nearby town, let alone all over Spain.

Fiestas de San Isidro
May 15 – this is Madrid's big holiday, when the city celebrates the feast day of its patron saint. It kicks off with the *pregón*, a speech delivered by

FACTS FOR THE VISITOR

some VIP, and is the starting signal for a week of cultural events around the city. The country's most prestigious *feria*, or bullfighting season, also begins now and continues for a month, at the Plaza de Toros Monumental de las Ventas.

Día de la Virgen de la Almudena

9 November – the *castizos* (true-blue madrileños) of Madrid gather in Plaza Mayor to hear Mass on this the feast day of the city's female patron saint.

Festivals
February/March
Carnavales (Carnival)

Several days of fancy-dress parades and merry-making in many places across the Comunidad de Madrid, usually ending on the Tuesday 47 days before Easter Sunday. It is not as big in Madrid as in other Spanish cities, with celebrations tending to be a fairly localised affair in several districts. Still, it is a good excuse (if one were needed) for festive drinking and general carry-on. The celebrations culminate in the Entierro de la Sardina (Burial of the Fish), a procession in which an effigy of a sardine is paraded to the Paseo de la Florida and there interred. It is a ritual that accompanies Carnavales across much of a Spain but its origins are rather obscure. You can see Goya's take on it in a painting hanging in the Real Academia de Bellas Artes de San Fernando (see the Things to See & Do chapter for details).

June
Día del Orgullo de Gays, Lesbianas y Transexuales

The city's gay and lesbian pride festival and parade take place on the last Saturday of the month.

24 June
Día de San Juan

Celebrated in other parts of Spain with considerable gusto, this holiday is a minor affair in the Madrid area. It's traditionally marked with fireworks and bonfires (particularly in Catalunya and the Balearic Islands) and a few towns in the Comunidad de Madrid make an effort. The fiery stuff and accompanying merry-making happen the night before. In the case of Madrid the action is in the Parque del Buen Retiro.

June–July
Local Fiestas

Just about every district in Madrid celebrates the feast day of one saint or another. If you are in Madrid in this period, ask the tourist office for details of where and when these local knees-ups take place.

27 July–15 August
Fiestas de San Lorenzo, San Cayetano & La Virgen de la Paloma

Not all of Madrid leaves town in the heat of mid-summer, and not all those who stay behind remain in a sun-stroke-induced torpor. These three local patron saints' festivities (which revolve around La Latina, Plaza de Lavapiés and Calle de Calatrava in La Latina respectively) keep the central districts of Madrid busy for the best part of the three weeks.

September
Local Fiestas

Several local councils organise fiestas in the first and second weeks of September. They include Fuencarral-El Pardo, Vallecas, Arganzuela, Barajas, Moncloa-Aravaca and Usera. In the last week of the month you can check out the Fiesta de Otoño in Chamartín. These are very local affairs and provide a rare insight into barrio life of the average madrileño.

Fiesta del PCE

In mid-September the Partido Comunista de España (Spanish Communist Party) holds its annual fund-raiser in the Casa de Campo. This mixed bag of regional-food pavilions, rock concerts and political soap boxing lasts all weekend.

Arts & Music Festivals
Madrid plays host to several arts-oriented festivals in the course of the year. Among the more important are:

February
Festival Flamenco

This is a yearly event that has been gaining in prestige since it was first staged in the early 1990s. A combination of big names and rising talent get together for five days of fine flamenco music in one of the city's theatres – in 2000 it was held at the Teatro Albéniz.

Arco

Staged in the Parque Ferial Juan Carlos I exhibition centre out near Barajas, this is one of Europe's single biggest homages to modern art. Known also as the Feria Internacional de Arte Contemporánea, it brings together galleries and exhibitors from all over the world and is a wonderful occasion for the general public to get clued up to what is happening in art across the globe, apart from being a major forum for the art-business bods themselves.

April
Artemanía

The Feria de Arte y Antigüedades is the nation's top date for the antique lover. Dealers from all over Spain pack their best material and converge on the Palacio de Congresos y Exposiciones on Paseo de la Castellana. You can admire anything from Picasso lithographs to ebony furniture items or even ancient pottery.

May/June
Festimad
This is Madrid's big contribution to Spain's year-round circuit of major music festivals. In this case bands from all over the country and beyond converge on the city for an orgy of gigs in bars, halls and on open-air stages. It has been going on since the mid-90s, but in 2000 organisers decided to take a breather for a year because they feared it was becoming too commercial. Their avowed aim is to promote emerging Spanish talent, not well-established

bands. The organisers promised Festimad would return in full strength in 2001.

July–August
Veranos de la Villa
For those poor sods who have to hang about Spain in the high heat through these months, the town authorities stage a series of cultural events, shows and expositions throughout Madrid. The name translates roughly as 'Summers in the City'.

October–December
Festival de Otoño
Since the early 1980s the city has thrown off the torpor of summer with a busy calendar of musical and theatrical activity right up to the approach to Christmas. The nature and scope of

El Dos de Mayo

In early 1808, the French army marched into Madrid, amid much confusion in the wake of the voluntary and cowardly abdications of Carlos IV and Fernando VII. General Tomás de Morla, who had armed the citizens to help defend the city, soon found he could not control his unruly forces, and they were quickly overwhelmed by Napoleon's troopers. Morla's decision to surrender probably saved the city from the wholesale destruction promised by the French emperor in the event of continued resistance.

But the madrileños were not to be so easily pacified. In the last days of April, men began to converge on Madrid from the neighbouring countryside. Pamphlets exhorting the populace to revolt were circulated and tension grew. On the morning of 2 May, the blood-letting began, with isolated troops coming under attack from armed townspeople, starting near the Palacio Real and around what is now Plaza del Dos de Mayo.

The French commander, Murat, soon ordered his units, which were camped outside Madrid, to move in. The 'mob', as he saw it, was concentrated at various points throughout the city, but those in the centre, at the Puerta del Sol, have gone down in history as a symbol of Spanish patriotism. Murat sent in Polish infantry and Mameluke cavalry – a fearsome unit brought to Europe from Egypt for precisely this kind of occasion.

The motley band of madrileños, gathered at the Puerta del Sol, fought with whatever came to hand – rifles, knives, bricks. As the Mamelukes charged into the crowds, sabres cutting into the rebels, local women joined in the fight, stabbing at the Mamelukes' horses and bombarding them with household items from the houses above. As the imperial forces gained the upper hand, the rebels were pushed into Calle Mayor, where some commandeered houses to subject the troops to a bloody crossfire.

All was in vain. By the end of the day the streets, here and elsewhere in the city, had been cleared. Some of the rebels were rounded up to be shot the next day, and road blocks around the city cut off all chance of escape.

Goya immortalised the events of this day and the shootings of the following day in his grim paintings *El Dos de Mayo* and *El Tres de Mayo*, which now hang in the Prado. And *el dos de Mayo* (2 May) went into the annals of Spanish history as the quintessence of the country's patriotic fervour. It also marked the beginning of the Guerra de la Independencia (War of Independence), which to the British, who ultimately tipped the balance and forced Napoleon out of Spain five years later, came to be known simply as the Peninsular War.

the program changes greatly from year to year (and depends in no small measure on budget constraints).

November
International Jazz Festival
This is the best time of the year to hear good jazz in Madrid, with groups from far and wide playing in venues around the city.

DOING BUSINESS
Although Barcelona does its best to promote itself as an alternative, more 'European' destination, Madrid is with little doubt the nation's business capital. The city is promoting itself as the prime direct gateway into Europe for Latin American companies, and hence the prime hub for Latin American–European business.

Useful Contacts Abroad
People wishing to make the first moves towards expanding their business into Spain should get in touch with their own country's Department of Trade (such as the DTI in the UK). The trade office of the Spanish embassy in your country should also have information – at least on red tape.

In the UK a good initial point of contact is the Export Market Information Centre (☎ 020-7215 5444, @ emic@xpd3.dt.gov.uk) at Kingsgate House, 66–74 Victoria St, London SW1E 6SW. Alternatively, you could try one of the DTI's Business Link offices, which are spread across the country. To find the one nearest you call ☎ 0345 567765.

Useful Contacts in Madrid
The trade office of your embassy may be able to provide tips and contacts. Otherwise, your first port of call should be the Oficina de Congresos de Madrid (or Madrid Convention Bureau). It is housed in the Patronato de Turismo office (Map 7; ☎ 91 588 29 00, fax 91 588 29 30), at Calle Mayor 69, and opens from 9 am to 2 pm Monday to Friday. They publish the *Guía de Congresos e Incentivos*, in Spanish and English, which can be helpful for those interested in organising meetings or conventions. It also details hotels (of which there are about 40)

with potentially useful business services. For more specific help or pointers, you will need to call ahead and make an appointment.

The Cámara Oficial de Comercio e Industria de Madrid, the city's chamber of commerce (Map 6; ☎ 91 538 35 00, fax 91 538 37 18), is at Plaza de la Independencia 1, 28001 Madrid. They offer advisory services on most aspects of doing or setting up business in Madrid, as well as video-conferencing facilities and an accessible business database.

Business Services in Madrid
A GSM mobile phone and a good laptop computer will probably be all you need to do business in Madrid. Some of the top hotels have business centres or secretarial assistance for guests.

The Chamber of Commerce has an office (☎ 91 305 88 07, fax 91 305 88 08) in terminal T1 (arrivals hall) at Barajas airport. They provide an information service for arriving business people, and fax, phone and photocopy facilities and a small meeting area (up to 10 people) are available for 5000 ptas (plus IVA) an hour. The office is open from 8 am to 9 pm daily.

Several companies can provide you with a postal and/or email address, phones and someone to take messages – for a fee. Most such companies have multi-lingual secretaries and some provide translators and interpreters. For contact details of such companies, try asking at the Oficina de Congresos.

Exhibitions & Conferences
Madrid's main trade-fair centre is the IFEMA, or Feria de Madrid (☎ 91 722 80 00, fax 91 722 57 99), located at the Parque Ferial Juan Carlos I in Campo de las Naciones (metro: Campo de las Naciones), just one metro stop from the airport. It hosts all sorts of events throughout the year, from the Fitur tourism fair through to the Arco arts show. Work on expansion of the trade-fair complex means that by 2001 it will boast 10 pavilions and in total 150,000 sq m of exhibition space.

Another important trade-fair centre is the Palacio de Congresos y Exposiciones (Map 1; ☎ 91 337 81 00, fax 91 597 10 94) at Paseo de la Castellana 99. The auditorium can seat 2000 and there are smaller meeting rooms, with technical support and secretarial services.

The Palacio Municipal de Congresos (☎ 91 722 04 00, fax 91 721 06 07), also in the Campo de las Naciones area, is yet another big conference centre. It has various auditoriums equipped with all the technical facilities you are likely to need (videoconferencing, simultaneous translators and so on).

You can review the month's upcoming trade fairs in the free *En Madrid* booklet available at tourist offices.

If you need to organise something a little more modest, contact the Oficina de Congresos, as its staff can help arrange events in such elegant settings as the Círculo de Bellas Artes and the Castillo de Manzanares El Real.

WORK

Although unemployment fell steeply in the second half of the 1990s, it still outstrips EU averages. Spain is therefore hardly the ideal place to look for work, but there are a few ways of earning your keep (or almost) while you're here.

Bureaucracy

Nationals of EU countries, Norway and Iceland may work in Spain without a visa, but for stays of more than three months they are supposed to apply within the first month for a residence card (for information on this laborious process, see Documents earlier in this chapter). If you are offered a contract, your employer will usually steer you through the labyrinth.

Virtually everyone else is supposed to obtain, from a Spanish consulate in their country of residence, a work permit and, if they plan to stay more than 90 days, a residence visa. These procedures are well-nigh impossible unless you have a job contract lined up before you begin them; in any case you should start the process a long time before you aim to arrive in Madrid. That said, quite a few people do work, discreetly, without bothering to tangle with the bureaucracy.

Opportunities

Language Teaching This is the obvious option, for which language-teaching qualifications are a big help (and are often indispensable). Madrid is loaded with language schools, although many fall into the 'cowboy outfit' category – they tend to pay badly and often aren't overly concerned about quality. Still, the only way you'll find out is by hunting around. Schools are listed under 'Academias de Idiomas' in the yellow pages. Rates rarely exceed 3000 ptas per teaching hour.

Getting a job in a school is harder if you're not an EU citizen. Some schools do employ people without work papers, usually at lower than normal rates. Giving private lessons is another worthwhile avenue, but unlikely to bring you a living wage straight away.

Sources of information on possible teaching work – school or private – include foreign cultural centres (such as the British Council), foreign-language bookshops (such as Booksellers) and universities and language schools (such as International House). Many of these have notice boards where you may find work opportunities, or where you can advertise your own services.

THE BULLFIGHT

The low-lying sun floods the arena with heavy summer light from the west. There is a buzz as places fill. Families jostle for space with older, beret-wearing enthusiasts, their faces creased by years of farm toil, and bright young things sporting sky-blue sunglasses. Some clutch plastic cups of beer; others swig red wine from animal-hide *botas* (wine bottles). All but those who have paid for the comfort of real seats in the shade have brought some kind of cushion: after a while, bare concrete or wooden slats can be uncomfortable for unprotected behinds. Many have chosen to huddle on the cheap benches facing the unforgiving midsummer sun. At one end of the ring, high up in the top rows, a brass band strikes up a stirring *pasodoble*, while on the opposite side the president of the fight and his adjutants await the arrival of the *toros* (bulls).

The *corrida* (bullfight) is a spectacle with a long history. It is not, as some suggest, simply a ghoulish alternative to the slaughterhouse (itself no pretty sight). Aficionados say the bull is better off dying at the hands of a *matador* (killer) than in the *matadero* (abattoir). The corrida is about many things – death, bravery, performance. No doubt, the fight is bloody and cruel. To witness it is not necessarily to understand it, but doing so might give an insight into some of the thought and tradition behind it. Many Spaniards loathe the bullfight, but there is no doubting its overall popularity. If on a bar-room TV there is football on one channel and a corrida on another, the chances are high that football fever will cede to the fascination of the fiesta.

Contests of strength, skill and bravery between man and beast are no recent phenomenon. The ancient Etruscans liked a good bullfight, and the Romans caught on. Of course things got a little kinky under the Romans and half the time there was no fight at all, merely the merciless butchery of Christians and other criminal fodder.

La lidia, as the art of bullfighting is also known, really took off in an organised fashion in Spain in the mid-18th century. In the 1830s, Pedro Romero, the greatest *torero* (bullfighter) of the time, was at the age of 77 appointed director of the Escuela de Tauromaquia de Sevilla, the country's first bullfighters' college. It was around this time too that breeders succeeded in creating the first reliable breeds of *toro bravo*, or fighting bull.

El Matador & la Cuadrilla

Traditionally, young men have aspired to the ring in the hope of fame and fortune, much as boxers have done. Most attain neither one nor the other. Only champion matadors make good money, and some make a loss. For the matador must rent or buy his outfit and equipment, pay for the right to fight a bull and also pay his *cuadrilla* (team).

If you see a major fight, you will notice this team is made up of quite a few people. Firstly there are several *peones*, junior bullfighters under the orders of the main torero, who is the matador. The peones come out to distract the bull with great capes, manoeuvre him into the desired position and so on.

View over the Río Guadalquivir, Córdoba

Toledo almost beat Madrid to be Spain's capital.

Segovia is packed with monuments and attractions, not least the striking Gothic cathedral.

Holy Week in Avila

Traditional ceramics for sale in Córdoba

The magnificent Mezquita in Córdoba – well worth a trip from Madrid

Christian Monarchs, began as a palace and fort for Alfonso X in the 13th century. Its extensive gardens, full of fishponds, fountains, orange trees, flowers and topiary, are among the most beautiful in Andalucía. It opens from 10 am to 2 pm and 6 to 8 pm Tuesday to Saturday (4.30 to 6.30 pm from October to April), and 9.30 am to 3 pm on Sunday and holidays. Admission costs 300 ptas (free on Friday).

Río Guadalquivir & Torre de la Calahorra Just south of the Mezquita, the Guadalquivir is crossed by the much restored **Puente Romano** (Roman Bridge).

At its southern end is the **Torre de la Calahorra**, a 14th-century tower housing a museum containing, among other items, good models of the Mezquita and Granada's Alhambra. It's open from 10 am to 2 pm and 4.30 to 8.30 pm daily (10 am to 6 pm from October to April). Admission costs 500 ptas.

Museo Arqueológico Córdoba's Archaeological Museum, in a Renaissance mansion on Plaza de Jerónimo Páez, has an extensive collection ranging from Palaeolithic to Islamic times. It is open from 3 to 8 pm on Tuesday, 9 am to 8 pm Wednesday to Saturday, and 9 am to 3 pm on Sunday and holidays. Admission costs 250 ptas (free for EU citizens).

Plaza del Potro Traders, adventurers and all sorts used to meet in this pretty square east of the Mezquita in the 16th and 17th centuries. The former Hospital de la Caridad houses the **Museo de Bellas Artes**, with a collection of paintings by mainly Córdoban artists (opening hours and admission as for the Museo Arqueológico); and the **Museo Julio Romero de Torres**, which includes a wonderful collection of sensual portraits of Córdoban women by Romero de Torres (1880–1930). It is open from 10 am to 2 pm and 6 to 8 pm Tuesday to Saturday (4.30 to 6.30 pm from October to April), and 9.30 am to 2.30 pm on Sunday and holidays. Admission costs 450 ptas (free on Friday).

Palacio de Viana This Renaissance palace, at Plaza de Don Gome 2, has 12 beautiful patios and a garden, along with a rich collection of antique furniture, art and crafts. It opens from 9 am to 2 pm Monday to Saturday, June to September; and 10 am to 1 pm and 4 to 6 pm Monday to Friday, and 10 am to 1 pm on Saturday, the rest of the year. Admission costs 500 ptas.

Special Events Semana Santa is one of Córdoba's major festivals, with big processions every evening from Palm Sunday to Good Friday. The Feria de Nuestra Señora de la Salud in late May/early June means 10 days of partying, while the Festival Internacional de Guitarra in late June/early July is a two-week celebration of the guitar with live performances of classical, flamenco, rock, blues and more in the Alcázar gardens.

Places to Eat Córdoba prides itself on its *tabernas* (taverns), busy bars where you can usually also sit down to eat. Some tabernas have been going over 100 years and have entered city folklore.

The basic and tiny ***Bar Santos*** *(Calle Magistral González Francés 3)*, facing the eastern side of the Mezquita, is a fine stop for *bocadillos* (snacks; 200 to 300 ptas), tapas (150 ptas) and raciones (500 ptas). ***El Caballo Rojo*** *(Calle Cardenal Herrero 28)* specialises in Mozarabic food from caliphal times. The *menú* is a hefty 2950 ptas plus IVA, but you're guaranteed something different from the usual fare.

The Judería is good hunting ground. ***Casa Pepe de la Judería*** *(Calle Romero 1)* serves tasty tapas (200 to 350 ptas) and raciones in its bar and at tables in rooms around its little patio. A few doors up the street, ***Restaurante El Rincón de Carmen*** *(Calle Romero 4)* has a patio with a *menú* costing 1600 ptas.

One of Córdoba's best restaurants is ***El Churrasco*** *(☎ 957 29 08 19, Calle Romero 16)*. The food is rich, the portions generous and the service attentive, with prices to match. The *menú* costs 3500 ptas; most mains are 2000 ptas plus.

If you head east of the Mezquita, you'll

EXCURSIONS

EXCURSIONS

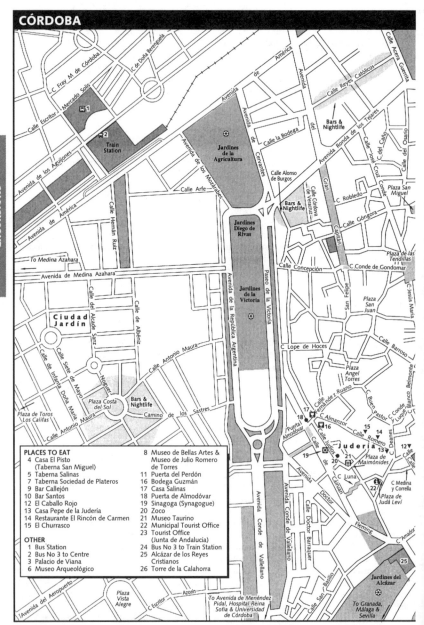

CÓRDOBA

PLACES TO EAT
4 Casa El Pisto
  (Taberna San Miguel)
5 Taberna Salinas
7 Taberna Sociedad de Plateros
9 Bar Callejón
10 Bar Santos
12 El Caballo Rojo
13 Casa Pepe de la Judería
14 Restaurante El Rincón de Carmen
15 El Churrasco

OTHER
1 Bus Station
2 Bus No 3 to Centre
3 Palacio de Viana
6 Museo Arqueológico

8 Museo de Bellas Artes &
  Museo de Julio Romero
  de Torres
11 Puerta del Perdón
16 Bodega Guzmán
17 Casa Salinas
18 Puerta de Almodóvar
19 Sinagoga (Synagogue)
20 Zoco
21 Museo Taurino
22 Municipal Tourist Office
23 Tourist Office
  (Junta de Andalucía)
24 Bus No 3 to Train Station
25 Alcázar de los Reyes
  Cristianos
26 Torre de la Calahorra

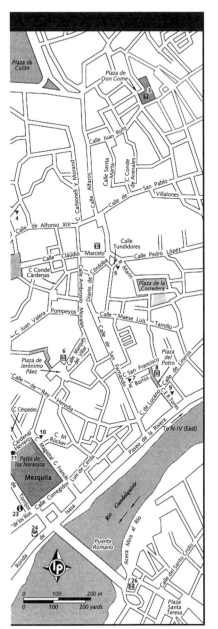

find **Taberna Sociedad de Plateros** *(Calle San Francisco 6)*, a popular tavern serving reasonably priced tapas. It is closed on Monday.

On pedestrianised Calle Enrique Romero de Torres, **Bar Callejón** has outside tables looking up to Plaza del Potro. Omelettes and many meat and fish dishes cost 500 to 800 ptas, and a three-course *menú* with a drink costs 1200 ptas.

The homely **Taberna Salinas** *(Calle Tundidores 3)* serves good, inexpensive Cordoban fare – the *bacalao* (cod) with bitter oranges makes an interesting change. It is closed on Sunday.

Just north of Plaza de las Tendillas, **Casa El Pisto**, officially **Taberna San Miguel** *(Plaza San Miguel 1)*, is one of Córdoba's most popular and atmospheric tabernas. Here you'll find a good range of tapas (250 to 275 ptas), media-raciones (500 to 1000 ptas) and raciones, and inexpensive Moriles wine standing ready in jugs on the bar. El Pisto has been going since 1880 and some of the bullfight photos and press cuttings on the walls are almost as old. It is closed on Sunday.

Entertainment Most bars in the medieval city close by midnight. **Bodega Guzmán** *(Calle Judíos 7)* is an atmospheric local favourite, with wines from the barrel and decor devoted to bullfighting and Córdoba's May feria. **Casa Salinas**, round the corner on Calle Fernández Ruano, is a cosier alternative.

For those who decide to stay overnight, the real action takes place beyond the old city. One lively street is Calle Reyes Católicos, off Plaza de Colón, and there are more bars in Calle Cordova de Veracruz and Calle Alonso de Burgos, south of Avenida Ronda de los Tejares. A third nightlife area is the Ciudad Jardín suburb around Plaza Costa del Sol, 350m west of Avenida de la República Argentina.

Getting There & Away The bus station is behind the train station, and from here you can make bus connections all over Andalucía. Long-distance buses also run to

euro currency converter € 1 = 166 ptas

destinations as far off as Barcelona. Buses to Madrid (1580 ptas; at least six daily) are run by Secorbus.

The train station is on Avenida de América, 1km north-west of Plaza Tendillas. About 20 trains daily run to/from Sevilla. Several others go to Granada, Málaga and other destinations in southern Spain.

The only sensible way to make Córdoba a day trip from Madrid is to take the high-speed AVE train (1¾ hours). It costs 6100 to 7200 ptas.

Getting Around Bus No 3 (115 ptas), from the street between the train and bus stations, runs to Plaza de las Tendillas and down Calle de San Fernando, 300m east of the Mezquita. For the return trip you can pick it up on Ronda de Isasa, just south of the Mezquita, or on Avenida Doctor Fleming.

Language

Spanish, or castellano (Castilian) as it is more correctly known, is one of the world's major languages. Taking some time to learn a little will not only make your stay in Madrid more enjoyable, it will be a worthwhile investment for the traveller heading elsewhere in Spain or to Latin America.

English is widely (if often haltingly) spoken in the bigger hotels and classier restaurants, but you should by no means expect everyone you encounter to speak anything much but Spanish. Young madrileños, especially students, are more likely than their elders to have some grasp of English or other foreign languages, but any attempt on your part to speak the local lingo will ease communication and help break the ice.

Pronunciation
Vowels
Unlike English, each of the vowels has a uniform pronunciation which doesn't vary. For example, the letter 'a' has one pronunciation rather than the numerous ones we find in English, such as in 'cake', 'care', 'cat', 'cart' and 'call'. Many words have a written accent. This acute accent (as in *días*) indicates a stressed syllable; it does not change the sound of the vowel. Vowels are pronounced clearly even if they are in unstressed positions or at the end of a word.

a	as the 'u' in 'nut', or a shorter sound than the 'a' in 'art'
e	as in 'met'
i	between the 'i' in 'marine' and the 'i' in 'flip'
o	similar to the 'o' in 'hot'
u	as the 'oo' in fool'

Consonants
Some consonants are the same as their English counterparts. The pronunciation of other consonants varies according to which vowel follows. The Spanish alphabet also contains the letter ñ, which is not found in the English alphabet. Until recently, the clusters **ch** and **ll** were also officially separate consonants, and you're likely to encounter many situations – eg in lists and dictionaries – in which they are still treated that way.

b	soft, as the 'v' in 'van'; also (less commonly) as in 'book' when word-initial or when preceded by a nasal such as 'm' or 'n'
c	as in 'cat' before 'a', 'o', 'u' or a consonant; as the 'th' in 'thin' before 'e' and 'i' (ie, like a lisp)
ch	as in 'choose'
d	as in 'dog' when word-initial; elsewhere as the 'th' in 'thin'
g	as in 'go' when initial and followed by 'a', 'o' or 'u'; elsewhere it's much softer. Before 'e' or 'i' it's a harsh, breathy sound, a bit like the 'h' in 'hit'.
h	always silent
j	a harsh, guttural sound similar to the 'ch' in Scottish *loch*
ll	between the 'lli' in 'million' and the 'y' in 'yell'
ñ	a nasal sound like the 'ni' in 'onion' or the 'ny' in 'canyon'
q	always followed by a silent 'u' and either 'e' (as in *que*) and 'i' (as in *aquí*); the combined sound of **qu** is like the 'k' in 'kick'
r	a rolled 'r' sound; longer and stronger when word-initial or doubled
s	as in 'send'
v	same sound as Spanish **b**
x	as the 'x' in 'taxi' when between two vowels; as the 's' in 'say' before a consonant
z	as the 'th' in 'thin'

Greetings & Civilities

Hello.	*¡Hola!*
Goodbye.	*¡Adiós!*
Yes.	*Sí.*
No.	*No.*
Please.	*Por favor.*
Thank you.	*Gracias.*
You're welcome.	*De nada.*
Excuse me.	*Perdón/Perdóneme.*
Sorry/Excuse me.	*Lo siento/ Discúlpeme.*

Useful Phrases

Do you speak English?	*¿Habla inglés?*
Does anyone speak English?	*¿Hay alguien que hable inglés?*
I understand.	*Entiendo.*
I don't understand.	*No entiendo.*
Just a minute.	*Un momento.*
Could you write it down, please?	*¿Puede escribirlo, por favor?*
How much is it?	*¿Cuánto cuesta/vale?*

Getting Around

What time does the ... leave/arrive?	*¿A qué hora sale/ llega el ...?*
bus (city)	*autobús/bus*
bus (intercity)	*autocar*
train	*tren*
metro/ underground	*metro*
next	*próximo*
first	*primer*
last	*último*
I'd like a ... ticket.	*Quisiera un billete ...*
one-way	*sencillo*
return	*de ida y vuelta*
1st class	*primera clase*
2nd class	*segunda clase*
Where is the bus stop?	*¿Dónde está la parada de autobús?*
I want to go to ...	*Quiero ir a ...*
Can you show me (on the map)?	*¿Me puede indicar (en el mapa)?*
Go straight ahead.	*Siga/Vaya todo derecho.*

Signs

ENTRADA	ENTRANCE
SALIDA	EXIT
OCUPADO, COMPLETO	FULL, NO VACANCIES
INFORMACIÓN	INFORMATION
ABIERTO	OPEN
CERRADO	CLOSED
PROHIBIDO	PROHIBITED
COMISARÍA	POLICE STATION
HABITACIONES LIBRES	ROOMS AVAILABLE
SERVICIOS/ASEOS	TOILETS
HOMBRES	MEN
MUJERES	WOMEN

Turn left.	*Gire a la izquierda.*
Turn right.	*Gire a la derecha.*
near	*cerca*
far	*lejos*

Around Town

I'm looking for ...	*Estoy buscando ...*
a bank	*un banco*
the city centre	*el centro de la ciudad*
the embassy	*la embajada*
my hotel	*mi hotel*
the market	*el mercado*
the police	*la policía*
the post office	*los correos*
public toilets	*los aseos públicos*
a telephone	*un teléfono*
the tourist office	*la oficina de turismo*
the bridge	*el puente*
the castle	*el castillo*
the cathedral	*la catedral*
the church	*la iglesia*
the hospital	*el hospital*
the main square	*la plaza mayor*
the mosque	*la mezquita*
the old city	*la ciudad antigua*
the palace	*el palacio*
the ruins	*las ruinas*
the square	*la plaza*
the tower	*el torre*
What time does it open/close?	*¿A qué hora abren/cierran?*

Accommodation

Where is a cheap hotel?	*¿Dónde hay un hotel barato?*
What's the address?	*¿Cuál es la dirección?*
Could you write it down, please?	*¿Puede escribirla, por favor?*
Do you have any rooms available?	*¿Tiene habitaciones libres?*

I'd like ...	*Quisiera ...*
a bed	*una cama*
a single room	*una habitación individual*
a double room	*una habitación doble*
a room with a bathroom	*una habitación con baño*
to share a dorm	*compartir un dormitorio*

How much is it ...?	*¿Cuánto cuesta ...?*
per night	*por noche*
per person	*por persona*

May I see it?	*¿Puedo verla?*
Where is the bathroom?	*¿Dónde está el baño?*
Is breakfast included?	*¿Incluye el desayuno?*

Time & Dates

What time is it?	*¿Qué hora es?*
today	*hoy*
tomorrow	*mañana*
yesterday	*ayer*
in the morning	*de la mañana*
in the afternoon	*de la tarde*
in the evening	*de la noche*

Monday	*lunes*
Tuesday	*martes*
Wednesday	*miércoles*
Thursday	*jueves*
Friday	*viernes*
Saturday	*sábado*
Sunday	*domingo*

January	*enero*
February	*febrero*
March	*marzo*
April	*abril*

Emergencies

Help!	*¡Socorro/Auxilio!*
Call a doctor!	*¡Llame a un doctor!*
Call the police!	*¡Llame a la policía!*
Go away!	*¡Vete!*

May	*mayo*
June	*junio*
July	*julio*
August	*agosto*
September	*setiembre/septiembre*
October	*octubre*
November	*noviembre*
December	*diciembre*

Health

I'm ...	*Soy...*
diabetic	*diabético/a*
epileptic	*epiléptico/a*
asthmatic	*asmático/a*

I'm allergic to ...	*Soy alérgico/a a ...*
antibiotics	*los antibióticos*
penicillin	*la penicilina*

antiseptic	*antiséptico*
aspirin	*aspirina*
condoms	*preservativos/ condones*
contraceptive	*anticonceptivo*
diarrhoea	*diarrea*
medicine	*medicamento*
nausea	*náusea*
sunblock cream	*crema protectora contra el sol*
tampons	*tampones*

Numbers

0	*cero*
1	*uno, una*
2	*dos*
3	*tres*
4	*cuatro*
5	*cinco*
6	*seis*
7	*siete*
8	*ocho*
9	*nueve*
10	*diez*

11	once
12	doce
13	trece
14	catorce
15	quince
16	dieciséis
17	diecisiete
18	dieciocho
19	diecinueve
20	veinte
21	veintiuno
22	veintidós
23	veintitrés
30	treinta
31	treinta y uno
40	cuarenta
50	cincuenta
60	sesenta
70	setenta
80	ochenta
90	noventa
100	cien/ciento
1000	mil

one million   *un millón*

FOOD
breakfast	*desayuno*
lunch	*almuerzo/comida*
dinner	*cena*
menu	*carta*
waitress/waiter	*camarera/o*

I'd like the set menu.	*Quisiera el menú del día.*
Is service included in the bill?	*¿El servicio está incluido en la cuenta?*
I'm a vegetarian.	*Soy vegetariano/a*

Food Glossary
Madrid has such a variety of foods and food names that you could spend years here and still find unfamiliar items on almost every menu. The following guide should at least help you sort out what's what.

Basics
botella – bottle
carta – menu
cocina – kitchen

comida – lunch, meal, food
copa – glass, especially a wine glass
cuchara – spoon
cuchillo – knife
cuenta – bill (check)
media-ración – half a *ración*
menú del día – fixed-price set meal
mesa – table
plato – plate
ración – meal-sized serving of a *tapa* dish
taza – cup
tenedor – fork
vaso – glass

aceite (de oliva) – (olive) oil
azúcar – sugar
caliente – hot
confitura – jam
frío/a – cold
hierba buena/menta – mint
mayonesa – mayonnaise
mermelada – jam
miel – honey
picante – hot (spicy)
pimienta – pepper
sal – salt
salsa – sauce
soja – soy
vegetal – vegetable (adjective)
vinagre – vinegar

arroz – rice
bollo – bread roll
empanada – pie
espagueti – spaghetti
fideo – vermicelli noodle
harina – flour
macarrones – macaroni
mollete – soft bread roll
pan – bread
panecillo – bread roll
tostada – toasted roll
trigo – wheat

Cooking Methods & Common Dishes
a la brasa – char-grilled
a la parrilla – grilled
a la plancha – grilled on a hotplate
adobo – a marinade of vinegar, salt, lemon and spices, usually for fish before frying

ahumado/a – smoked
albóndiga – meatball or fishball
aliño – in a vinegar and oil dressing
alioli – garlic mayonnaise
asado/a – roasted
caldereta – stew
caldo – broth, stock
casero/a – home-made
cazuela – casserole
cocido – cooked; also hotpot/stew
croqueta – croquette
crudo – raw
escabeche – a marinade of oil, vinegar and water for pickling perishables, usually fish or seafood
espeto – (roasting) spit
estofado – stew
flamenquín – rolled and crumbed veal or ham, deep fried
frito/a – fried
gratinado/a – au gratin
guiso – stew
horno – oven
horno de asar – roasts
horneado/a – baked
migas – simple dish, basically composed of fried flour and water
olla – pot
paella – rice, seafood and meat dish
pavía – battered fish or seafood
pil pil – garlic sauce usually spiked with chilli
potaje – stew
rebozado/a – battered and fried
relleno/a – stuffed
salado/a – salted, salty
seco/a – dry, dried
tierno/a – tender, fresh
zarzuela – fish stew

Soups, Starters & Snacks – *Sopas, Entremeses & Meriendas*
bocadillo – bread roll with filling
ensalada – salad
gazpacho – cold, blended soup of tomatoes, peppers, cucumber, onions, garlic, lemon and breadcrumbs
montadito – small bread roll with filling, or a small sandwich, or an open sandwich – often toasted

pincho – a tapa-sized portion of food, or a *pinchito* (see Meat & Poultry)
pitufo – small filled baguette or roll
sopa de ajo – garlic soup
tabla – selection of cold meats and cheeses on a board
tapa – snack on a saucer

Fruits – *Frutas*
aceituna – olive
aguacate – avocado
cereza – cherry
chirimoya – custard apple, a tropical fruit
frambuesa – raspberry
fresa – strawberry
granada – pomegranate
higo – fig
lima – lime
limón – lemon
mandarina – tangerine
manzana – apple
manzanilla – camomile (also a type of olive or a type of sherry)
melocotón – peach
melon – melon
naranja – orange
pasa – raisin
piña – pineapple
plátano – banana
sandía – watermelon
uva – grape

Vegetables – *Vegetales/Verduras/ Hortalizas*
ajo – garlic
alcachofa – artichoke
apio – celery
berenjena – aubergine, eggplant
calabacín – courgette, zucchini
calabaza – pumpkin
cebolla – onion
champiñones – mushrooms
col – cabbage
coliflor – cauliflower
espárragos – asparagus
espinacas – spinach
guindilla – chilli pepper
guisante – pea
hongo – wild mushroom
judías blancas – butter beans

judías verdes – green beans
lechuga – lettuce
maíz – sweet corn
patata – potato
patatas a lo pobre – 'poor man's potatoes', a potato dish with peppers and garlic
patatas bravas – spicy fried potatoes
patatas fritas – chips, French fries
pimiento – pepper, capsicum
pipirrana – salad of diced tomatoes and red peppers
puerro – leek
seta – wild mushroom
tomate – tomato
verdura – green vegetable
zanahoria – carrot

Pulses & Nuts – *Legumbres & Nueces*
almendra – almond
alubia – dried bean
anacardo – cashew nut
cacahuete – peanut
garbanzo – chickpea
haba – broad bean
lentejas – lentils
nuez (pl: *nueces*) – nut, walnut
piñón – pine nut
pipa – sunflower seed

Fish – *Pescados*
aguja – swordfish
anchoa – anchovy
atún – tuna
bacalao – salted cod; it's soaked before cooking, prepared many different ways and can be succulent
boquerones – anchovies
caballa – mackerel
cazón – dogfish
chanquetes – whitebait (illegal, but not un-common)
dorada – sea bass
lenguado – sole
merluza – hake
mero – halibut, grouper, sea bass
mojama – cured tuna
pescadilla – whiting
pescaíto frito – small fried fish
pez espada – swordfish
platija – flounder

rape – monkfish
rosada – ocean catfish, wolf-fish
salmón – salmon
salmonete – red mullet
sardina – sardine
trucha – trout

Seafood – *Mariscos*
almejas – clams
calamares – squid
camarón – shrimp
cangrejo – crab
cangrejo de río – crayfish
carabinero – large prawn
chipirón – small squid
choco – cuttlefish
cigala – crayfish
gamba – prawn
langosta – lobster
langostino – large prawn
mejillones – mussels
ostra – oyster
peregrina – scallop
pulpo – octopus
puntillita/o – small squid, fried whole
sepia – cuttlefish
venera – scallop
vieira – scallop

Meat & Poultry – *Carne & Aves*
beicon – bacon (usually thin-sliced and pre-packaged; see *tocino*)
bistek – thin beef steak
butifarra – thick sausage (to be cooked)
cabra – goat
cabrito – kid, baby goat
callos – tripe
caracol – snail
carne de monte – 'mountain meat' such as venison or wild boar
caza – hunt, game
cerdo – pig, pork
chacinas – cured pork meats
charcutería – cured pork meats
chivo – baby goat, kid
chorizo – red sausage
chuleta – chop, cutlet
cochinillo asado – roast suckling pig
codorniz – quail
conejo – rabbit
cordero – lamb

cuchifritos – lamb, tomato and egg cooked in white wine with saffron
embutidos – the many varieties of sausage
faisán – pheasant
filete – fillet
hamburguesa – hamburger
hígado – liver
jabalí – wild boar
jamón (serrano) – (mountain-cured) ham
lengua – tongue
lomo – loin (of pork unless otherwise specified – usually the cheapest meat dish on the menu)
longaniza – dark pork sausage
morcilla – black pudding
paloma – pigeon
pajarito – small bird
pato – duck
pavo – turkey
pechuga – breast, of poultry
perdiz – partridge
picadillo – minced meat
pierna – leg
pinchito – Moroccan-style kebab
pollo – chicken
rabo (de toro) – (ox) tail
riñón – kidney
salchicha – fresh pork sausage
salchichón – cured sausage
sesos – brains
solomillo – sirloin (usually of pork)
ternera – beef, veal
tocino – bacon (usually thick; see *beicon*)
vaca, carne de – beef
venado – venison

Dairy Products & Eggs – *Productos Lácteos & Huevos*
leche – milk
mantequilla – butter
nata – cream
queso – cheese
revuelto de ... – eggs scrambled with ...
tortilla – omelette
tortilla española – potato omelette
yogur – yoghurt

Desserts & Sweet Things – *Postres & Dulces*
churro – long, deep-fried doughnut
galleta – biscuit, cookie

helado – ice cream
natillas – custards
pastel – pastry, cake
tarta – cake
torta – round flat bun, cake
turrón – almond nougat or rich chocolatey sweets that appear at Christmas
yema – sweet made of egg yolk and sugar

DRINKS
Nonalcoholic
water	*agua*
fizzy mineral water	*agua mineral con gas*
plain mineral water	*agua mineral sin gas*
tap water	*agua del grifo*
almond drink	*horchata*
fruit juice	*zumo*
soft drinks	*refrescos*
coffee ...	*café ...*
with liqueur	*carajillo*
with a little milk	*cortado*
with milk	*con leche*
iced coffee	*café helado*
black coffee	*café solo*
long black	*doble*
decaffeinated	*café descafeinado*
tea	*té*

Alcoholic
anise	*anís*
beer	*cerveza*
small beer	*caña*
champagne	*champán/cava*
cider	*sidra*
cocktail	*combinado*
brandy	*coñac*
rum	*ron*
sangría (red wine punch)	*sangría*
sherry	*jerez*
whisky	*güisqui*
a glass of ... wine	*un vino ...*
red	*tinto*
white	*blanco*
rosé	*rosado*
sweet	*dulce*
sparkling	*espumoso*

Glossary

abierto – open
acueducto – aqueduct
aduana – customs
aficionado – enthusiast
albergue juvenil – youth hostel; not to be confused with *hostal*
alcalde – mayor
alcázar – Muslim-era fortress
Almoravid – member of a fanatical people of Berber origin and Islamic faith who founded an empire in North Africa that spread over much of Spain in the 11th century
altar mayor – high altar
apartado de correos – post office box
auto de fe – elaborate execution ceremony staged by the Inquisition
autonomía – autonomous community or region: Spain's 50 *provincias* are grouped into 17 of these
autopista – motorway (with tolls)
autovía – motorway (toll-free)
ayuntamiento – city or town hall; city or town council

bailaores – flamenco dancers
baño completo – full bathroom, with a toilet, shower and/or bath, and basin
barrio – district, quarter (of a town or city)
biblioteca – library
bodega – literally, a cellar (especially a wine cellar); also means a winery, or a traditional wine bar likely to serve wine from the barrel
bomberos – fire brigade
bota – leather wine or sherry bottle
buzón – letter box

cajero automático – automatic teller machine (ATM)
calle – street
callejón – lane
cama – bed
cambio – in general, change; also currency exchange
cantador(a) – flamenco singer
cante hondo – deep song (flamenco)
capilla – chapel

capilla mayor – chapel containing the high altar of a church
carnaval – carnival; a period of fancy-dress parades and merrymaking in many places, usually ending on the Tuesday 47 days before Easter Sunday
carretera – highway
casco – literally, helmet; often used to refer to the old part of a city (more correctly, *casco antiguo/histórico/viejo*)
castillo – castle
castizo – literally 'pure'; refers to people and things distinctly from Madrid
catedral – cathedral
centro de salud – health centre
cercanías – local trains serving big cities' suburbs and nearby towns
cerrado – closed
certificado – registered mail
cervecería – beer bar
chato – glass
churrigueresque – ornate style of Baroque architecture named after the brothers Alberto and José Churriguera
comedor – dining room
comisaría – National Police (Policía Nacional) station
completo – full
comunidad – fixed charge for maintenance of rental accommodation (sometimes included in the rent)
comunidad autónoma – see *autonomía*
Comunidad de Madrid – the province of Madrid
condones – condoms
consejo – council
consigna – left-luggage office or lockers
confradías – lay fraternities
coro – choirstall
correos – post office
corrida de toros – bullfight
Cortes – national parliament
cuesta – lane (usually on a hill)
custodia – monstrance

día del espectador – cut-price ticket day at cinemas (literally 'viewer's day')
diapositiva – slide film

**documentos nacionales de identidad
(DNI)** – national identity cards
ducha – shower
duende – spirit; an indefinable capacity
to transmit the power of flamenco
duro – five peseta coin

embajada – embassy
entrada – entrance
ermita – hermitage or chapel
estación de autobuses – bus station
estanco – tobacconist shop

farmacia – pharmacy
faro – lighthouse
feria – fair; can refer to trade fairs as well
as to city, town or village fairs which are basically several days of merrymaking; can
also mean a bullfight or festival stretching
over days or weeks
ferrocarril – railway
fiesta – festival, public holiday or party
fin de semana – weekend
flamenco – means flamingo and Flemish
as well as flamenco music and dance
fútbol – football (soccer)

gatos – literally 'cats'; also a colloquial
name for *madrileños*
gitanos – the Roma people (formerly
known as the Gypsies)
glorieta – big roundabout

habitaciones libres – literally 'rooms
available'
hostal – commercial establishment providing accommodation in the one to three star
category; not to be confused with *albergue
juvenil*

iglesia – church
infanta – princess
infante – prince
interprovincial – national (call)
IVA – *impuesto sobre el valor añadido*, or
value-added tax

judería – Jewish quarter

lavabo – washbasin
lavandería – laundrette
librería – bookshop

lista de correos – poste restante
litera – couchette
llegada – arrival
locutorio – telephone centre
luz – electricity

macarras – Madrid's rough but (usually)
likeable lads
media-raciónes – a serving of *tapas*,
somewhere between the size of *tapas* and
raciónes
madrileño – a person from Madrid
madrugada – the 'early hours', from
around 3 am to dawn – a pretty lively time
in Madrid!
marcha – action, life, 'the scene'
marisquería – seafood eatery
menú del día – fixed-price meal available
at lunchtime, sometimes in the evening too;
often called just a *menú*
mercado – market
meseta – the high tableland of central
Spain
metropolitana – local (call)
morería – former Islamic quarter in a town
moro – 'Moor' or Muslim (usually in a
medieval context)
movida – similar to *marcha*; a *zona de
movida* is an area of a town where lively
bars and maybe discos are clustered. In
Madrid the movida refers to the halcyon
days of the post-Franco years when the city
plunged into an excess of nightlife – something that doesn't seem to have changed so
much.
Mozarab – Christians who lived in Muslim-
ruled Spain; also refers to their style of
architecture
mudéjar – a Muslim living under Christian
rule in medieval Spain; also refers to their
style of architecture
municipio – municipality, Spain's basic
local administrative unit
muralla – city wall
museo – museum

objetos perdidos – lost and found office
oficina de turismo – tourist office; also
oficina de información turística

Páginas Amarillas – phone directory (the
'Yellow Pages')

parador – hotel in an historic building
pasos – sculpted figures depicting the passion of Christ
peques – children, little ones
peña – a club, usually of flamenco aficionados or Real Madrid football fans; sometimes a dining club
pensión – pension, guest house
piscina – swimming pool
plateresco – plateresque; an ornate architecture style popular in Spain during the 16th century
plaza de toros – bullring
plaza mayor – main square
policía – police
preservativos – condoms
prohibido – prohibited
provincial – (call) within the same province
pueblo – village
puente – bridge

RACE – Real Automóvil Club de España
ración – meal-sized serve of *tapas*
rastro – flea market; car-boot (trunk) sale
retablo – altarpiece
ronda – ring road

salida – exit or departure
Semana Santa – Holy Week, the week leading up to Easter Sunday
servicios – toilets
sevillana – Andalucían folk dance
SIDA – AIDS
sierra – mountain range

sol – shade
sombra – sun

tabernas – taverns
tablao – tourist-oriented flamenco performances
taifa – small Muslim kingdom in medieval Spain
tapas – bar snacks traditionally served on a saucer or lid *(tapa)*
taquilla – ticket window/office
tarde – afternoon
tarjeta de crédito – credit card
tarjeta de residencia – residence card
tarjeta telefónica – phonecard
teleférico – cable car
temporada alta/media/baja – high/mid/ low season
terraza – terrace; often means a cafe's or bar's outdoor tables
tetería – teahouse, usually in Middle Eastern style with low seats round low tables
tienda – shop or tent
tierra – land
tocador – player (of a musical instrument)
toro – bull
torreón – tower
transept – the two wings of a cruciform church at right angles to the nave
turismo – means both tourism and saloon car; *el turismo* can also mean the tourist office

urgencia – first-aid station

VIH – HIV
villa – town

LONELY PLANET

You already know that Lonely Planet publishes more than this one guidebook, but you might not be aware of the other products we have on this region. Here is a selection of titles that you may want to check out as well:

Andalucía
ISBN 1 86450 191 X
US$17.99 • UK£10.99

Barcelona
ISBN 1 86450 143 X
US$14.99 • UK£8.99

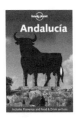

Canary Islands
ISBN 1 86450 310 6
US$15.99 • UK£9.99

Europe on a shoestring
ISBN 1 86450 150 2
US$24.99 • UK£14.99

Mediterranean Europe
ISBN 1 86450 154 5
US$27.99 • UK£15.99

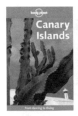

Read This First: Europe
ISBN 1 86450 136 7
US$14.99 • UK£8.99

Spain
ISBN 1 86450 192 8
US$24.99 • UK£14.99

Spanish phrasebook
ISBN 0 86442 475 2
US$5.95 • UK£3.99

Walking in Spain
ISBN 0 86442 543 0
US$17.95 • UK£11.99

Western Europe
ISBN 1 86450 163 4
US$27.99 • UK£15.99

World Food Spain
ISBN 1 86450 025 5
US$12.95 • UK£7.99

Available wherever books are sold.

Lonely Planet Guides by Region

Lonely Planet is known worldwide for publishing practical, reliable and no-nonsense travel information in our guides and on our Web site. The Lonely Planet list covers just about every accessible part of the world. Currently there are 16 series: Travel guides, Shoestring guides, Condensed guides, Phrasebooks, Read This First, Healthy Travel, Walking guides, Cycling guides, Watching Wildlife guides, Pisces Diving & Snorkeling guides, City Maps, Road Atlases, Out to Eat, World Food, Journeys travel literature and Pictorials.

AFRICA Africa on a shoestring • Botswana • Cairo • Cairo City Map • Cape Town • Cape Town City Map • East Africa • Egypt • Egyptian Arabic phrasebook • Ethiopia, Eritrea & Djibouti • Ethiopian Amharic phrasebook • The Gambia & Senegal • Healthy Travel Africa • Kenya • Malawi • Morocco • Moroccan Arabic phrasebook • Mozambique • Namibia • Read This First: Africa • South Africa, Lesotho & Swaziland • Southern Africa • Southern Africa Road Atlas • Swahili phrasebook • Tanzania, Zanzibar & Pemba • Trekking in East Africa • Tunisia • Watching Wildlife East Africa • Watching Wildlife Southern Africa • West Africa • World Food Morocco • Zambia • Zimbabwe, Botswana & Namibia
Travel Literature: Mali Blues: Traveling to an African Beat • The Rainbird: A Central African Journey • Songs to an African Sunset: A Zimbabwean Story

AUSTRALIA & THE PACIFIC Aboriginal Australia & the Torres Strait Islands •Auckland • Australia • Australian phrasebook • Australia Road Atlas • Cycling Australia • Cycling New Zealand • Fiji • Fijian phrasebook • Healthy Travel Australia, NZ & the Pacific • Islands of Australia's Great Barrier Reef • Melbourne • Melbourne City Map • Micronesia • New Caledonia • New South Wales • New Zealand • Northern Territory • Outback Australia • Out to Eat – Melbourne • Out to Eat – Sydney • Papua New Guinea • Pidgin phrasebook • Queensland • Rarotonga & the Cook Islands • Samoa • Solomon Islands • South Australia • South Pacific • South Pacific phrasebook • Sydney • Sydney City Map • Sydney Condensed • Tahiti & French Polynesia • Tasmania • Tonga • Tramping in New Zealand • Vanuatu • Victoria • Walking in Australia • Watching Wildlife Australia • Western Australia
Travel Literature: Islands in the Clouds: Travels in the Highlands of New Guinea • Kiwi Tracks: A New Zealand Journey • Sean & David's Long Drive

CENTRAL AMERICA & THE CARIBBEAN Bahamas, Turks & Caicos • Baja California • Belize, Guatemala & Yucatán • Bermuda • Central America on a shoestring • Costa Rica • Costa Rica Spanish phrasebook • Cuba • Cycling Cuba • Dominican Republic & Haiti • Eastern Caribbean • Guatemala • Havana • Healthy Travel Central & South America • Jamaica • Mexico • Mexico City • Panama • Puerto Rico • Read This First: Central & South America • Virgin Islands • World Food Caribbean • World Food Mexico • Yucatán
Travel Literature: Green Dreams: Travels in Central America

EUROPE Amsterdam • Amsterdam City Map • Amsterdam Condensed • Andalucía • Athens • Austria • Baltic States phrasebook • Barcelona • Barcelona City Map • Belgium & Luxembourg • Berlin • Berlin City Map • Britain • British phrasebook • Brussels, Bruges & Antwerp • Brussels City Map • Budapest • Budapest City Map • Canary Islands • Catalunya & the Costa Brava • Central Europe • Central Europe phrasebook • Copenhagen • Corfu & the Ionians • Corsica • Crete • Crete Condensed • Croatia • Cycling Britain • Cycling France • Cyprus • Czech & Slovak Republics • Czech phrasebook • Denmark • Dublin • Dublin City Map • Dublin Condensed • Eastern Europe • Eastern Europe phrasebook • Edinburgh • Edinburgh City Map • England • Estonia, Latvia & Lithuania • Europe on a shoestring • Europe phrasebook • Finland • Florence • Florence City Map • France • Frankfurt City Map • Frankfurt Condensed • French phrasebook • Georgia, Armenia & Azerbaijan • Germany • German phrasebook • Greece • Greek Islands • Greek phrasebook • Hungary • Iceland, Greenland & the Faroe Islands • Ireland • Italian phrasebook • Italy • Kraków • Lisbon • The Loire • London • London City Map • London Condensed • Madrid • Madrid City Map • Malta • Mediterranean Europe • Milan, Turin & Genoa • Moscow • Munich • Netherlands • Normandy • Norway • Out to Eat – London • Out to Eat – Paris • Paris • Paris City Map • Paris Condensed • Poland • Polish phrasebook • Portugal • Portuguese phrasebook • Prague • Prague City Map • Provence & the Côte d'Azur • Read This First: Europe • Rhodes & the Dodecanese • Romania & Moldova • Rome • Rome City Map • Rome Condensed • Russia, Ukraine & Belarus • Russian phrasebook • Scandinavian & Baltic Europe • Scandinavian phrasebook • Scotland • Sicily • Slovenia • South-West France • Spain • Spanish phrasebook • Stockholm • St Petersburg • St Petersburg City Map • Sweden • Switzerland • Tuscany • Ukrainian phrasebook • Venice • Vienna • Wales • Walking in Britain • Walking in France • Walking in Ireland • Walking in Italy • Walking in Scotland • Walking in Spain • Walking in Switzerland • Western Europe • World Food France • World Food Greece • World Food Ireland • World Food Italy • World Food Spain **Travel Literature:** After Yugoslavia • Love and War in the Apennines • The Olive Grove: Travels in Greece • On the Shores of the Mediterranean • Round Ireland in Low Gear • A Small Place in Italy

Lonely Planet Mail Order

onely Planet products are distributed worldwide. They are also available by mail order from Lonely Planet, so if you have difficulty finding a title please write to us. North and South American residents should write to 150 Linden St, Oakland, CA 94607, USA; European and African residents should write to 10a Spring Place, London NW5 3BH, UK; and residents of other countries to Locked Bag 1, Footscray, Victoria 3011, Australia.

INDIAN SUBCONTINENT & THE INDIAN OCEAN Bangladesh • Bengali phrasebook • Bhutan • Delhi • Goa • Healthy Travel Asia & India • Hindi & Urdu phrasebook • India • India & Bangladesh City Map • Indian Himalaya • Karakoram Highway • Kathmandu City Map • Kerala • Madagascar • Maldives • Mauritius, Réunion & Seychelles • Mumbai (Bombay) • Nepal • Nepali phrasebook • North India • Pakistan • Rajasthan • Read This First: Asia & India • South India • Sri Lanka • Sri Lanka phrasebook • Tibet • Tibetan phrasebook • Trekking in the Indian Himalaya • Trekking in the Karakoram & Hindukush • Trekking in the Nepal Himalaya • World Food India **Travel Literature:** The Age of Kali: Indian Travels and Encounters • Hello Goodnight: A Life of Goa • In Rajasthan • Maverick in Madagascar • A Season in Heaven: True Tales from the Road to Kathmandu • Shopping for Buddhas • A Short Walk in the Hindu Kush • Slowly Down the Ganges

MIDDLE EAST & CENTRAL ASIA Bahrain, Kuwait & Qatar • Central Asia • Central Asia phrasebook • Dubai • Farsi (Persian) phrasebook • Hebrew phrasebook • Iran • Israel & the Palestinian Territories • Istanbul • Istanbul City Map • Istanbul to Cairo • Istanbul to Kathmandu • Jerusalem • Jerusalem City Map • Jordan • Lebanon • Middle East • Oman & the United Arab Emirates • Syria • Turkey • Turkish phrasebook • World Food Turkey • Yemen **Travel Literature:** Black on Black: Iran Revisited • Breaking Ranks: Turbulent Travels in the Promised Land • The Gates of Damascus • Kingdom of the Film Stars: Journey into Jordan

NORTH AMERICA Alaska • Boston • Boston City Map • Boston Condensed • British Columbia • California & Nevada • California Condensed • Canada • Chicago • Chicago City Map • Chicago Condensed • Florida • Georgia & the Carolinas • Great Lakes • Hawaii • Hiking in Alaska • Hiking in the USA • Honolulu & Oahu City Map • Las Vegas • Los Angeles • Los Angeles City Map • Louisiana & the Deep South • Miami • Miami City Map • Montreal • New England • New Orleans • New Orleans City Map • New York City • New York City City Map • New York City Condensed • New York, New Jersey & Pennsylvania • Oahu • Out to Eat – San Francisco • Pacific Northwest • Rocky Mountains • San Diego & Tijuana • San Francisco • San Francisco City Map • Seattle • Seattle City Map • Southwest • Texas • Toronto • USA • USA phrasebook • Vancouver • Vancouver City Map • Virginia & the Capital Region • Washington, DC • Washington, DC City Map • World Food New Orleans **Travel Literature:** Caught Inside: A Surfer's Year on the California Coast • Drive Thru America

NORTH-EAST ASIA Beijing • Beijing City Map • Cantonese phrasebook • China • Hiking in Japan • Hong Kong & Macau • Hong Kong City Map • Hong Kong Condensed • Japan • Japanese phrasebook • Korea • Korean phrasebook • Kyoto • Mandarin phrasebook • Mongolia • Mongolian phrasebook • Seoul • Shanghai • South-West China • Taiwan • Tokyo • Tokyo Condensed • World Food Hong Kong • World Food Japan **Travel Literature:** In Xanadu: A Quest • Lost Japan

SOUTH AMERICA Argentina, Uruguay & Paraguay • Bolivia • Brazil • Brazilian phrasebook • Buenos Aires • Buenos Aires City Map • Chile & Easter Island • Colombia • Ecuador & the Galapagos Islands • Healthy Travel Central & South America • Latin American Spanish phrasebook • Peru • Quechua phrasebook • Read This First: Central & South America • Rio de Janeiro • Rio de Janeiro City Map • Santiago de Chile • South America on a shoestring • Trekking in the Patagonian Andes • Venezuela **Travel Literature:** Full Circle: A South American Journey

SOUTH-EAST ASIA Bali & Lombok • Bangkok • Bangkok City Map • Burmese phrasebook • Cambodia • Cycling Vietnam, Laos & Cambodia • East Timor phrasebook • Hanoi • Healthy Travel Asia & India • Hill Tribes phrasebook • Ho Chi Minh City (Saigon) • Indonesia • Indonesian phrasebook • Indonesia's Eastern Islands • Java • Lao phrasebook • Laos • Malay phrasebook • Malaysia, Singapore & Brunei • Myanmar (Burma) • Philippines • Pilipino (Tagalog) phrasebook • Read This First: Asia & India • Singapore • Singapore City Map • South-East Asia on a shoestring • South-East Asia phrasebook • Thailand • Thailand's Islands & Beaches • Thailand, Vietnam, Laos & Cambodia Road Atlas • Thai phrasebook • Vietnam • Vietnamese phrasebook • World Food Indonesia • World Food Thailand • World Food Vietnam

ALSO AVAILABLE: Antarctica • The Arctic • The Blue Man: Tales of Travel, Love and Coffee • Brief Encounters: Stories of Love, Sex & Travel • Buddhist Stupas in Asia: The Shape of Perfection • Chasing Rickshaws • The Last Grain Race • Lonely Planet ... On the Edge: Adventurous Escapades from Around the World • Lonely Planet Unpacked • Lonely Planet Unpacked Again • Not the Only Planet: Science Fiction Travel Stories • Ports of Call: A Journey by Sea • Sacred India • Travel Photography: A Guide to Taking Better Pictures • Travel with Children • Tuvalu: Portrait of an Island Nation

Index

Text

Boxed Text

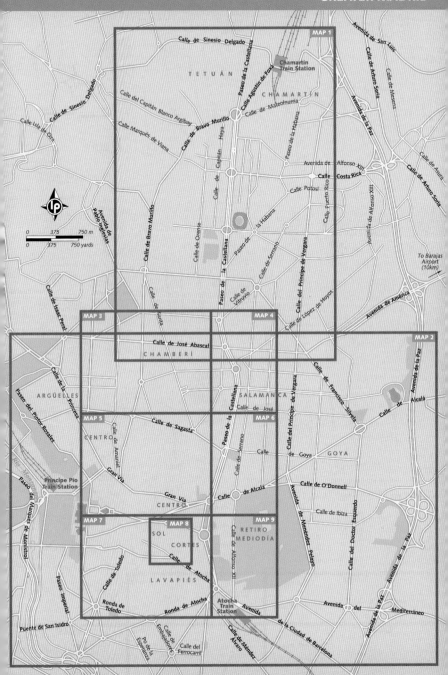

GREATER MADRID

MAP 1 - NORTHERN MADRID

C H A M A R T I N

Avenida de El Ferrol

To
Inerso
(500m)

Calle de Ribadavia

Calle de Sinesio Delgado

Calle de Vía Límite

Calle de Padre Rubio

Calle del General Pintos

Calle de Ciudad Rodrigo

Paseo de la Dirección

Ventilla

TETUAN

Calle de Abascal

Plaza de Castilla

Calle Caston

Calle de la Castellana

Paseo de la Castellana

1
Chamartín
Train Station

Avenida de Pío XII

To
Lufthansa
Airlines
(100m)

200   400m
200   400yd

Plaza Duque

Plaza de Castilla

Murtia

Duque de
Pastrana

Calle Carlos de la
División Azul

To El Bosque (1km)

2

Avda del Comandante
Franco

Valdeacederas

Bravo
Murillo

4

Calle José Castón
Tobeñas

Calle Francisco Suárez

Calle de Jerez

Pío XII

Calle de las Azucenas

Calle de la Infanta Mercedes

Calle Félix Boix

Calle Apolonio Morales

3

Tetuán

8

Calle Rosario del Pino

6

Plaza de
Cuzco

Calle de Francisco Gervás

Cuzco

9

Avenida de Alberto Alcocer

Plaza de la
República
Dominicana

Calle Costa Rica

Calle del General Yagüe

10

11

Estadio
Santiago
Bernabéu

Plaza de la
República
del Ecuador

Calle de Uruguay

Estrecho

Avenida General Perón

12

Plaza de
Lima

Lima

Plaza de
Sagrados
Corazones

14

Calle de San Raimundo

Calle de Teruel

Alvarado

13

15

Avenida de Concha Espina   Avenida de Ramón y Cajal

Calle de Hernani

16

17

Calle de Pradillo

Nuevos
Ministerios

Cuatro
Caminos

25

Calle de Raimundo
Fernández
Villaverde

20

Plaza del Poeta
Manuel del Palacio

Calle de Joaquín Costa

18

24

23 22

21

Ríos Rosas

Calle Carbonero y Sol

Avenida
República
Argentina

19

Cruz del
Reyo

MAP 3   MAP 4
MAP 2   MAP 2

Calle de Ríos Rosas

Plaza San Juan
de la Cruz

Calle Particular

Plaza del
Descubridor
Diego de Ordás

Calle de Espronceda

Avenida de
Cartagena

CHAMBERÍ

Calle de José Abascal

Avenida de
América

MAP 1

PLACES TO EAT
6 Restaurante Sulú
7 China Crown; Viajes Zeppelin
9 Asador La Tahona

OTHER
1 Space of Sound
2 Netherlands Embassy
3 Instalación Deportiva Municipal Chamartín
4 Centro de Salud
5 La Oleoteca
8 El Rastrillo
10 Irish Rover
11 Palacio de Congresos y Exposiciones
12 Moda Shopping
13 Moroccan Embassy
14 Lesen
15 Librería Alemana Auryn
16 Moroccan Consulate
17 Thai Airways International
18 Auditorio Nacional de Música
19 Museo de la Ciudad
20 American Airlines
21 Librería Italiana
22 La Tienda Verde
23 Continental-Auto Bus Station
24 La Tienda Verde
25 Renoir Cinema

JULIET COOOMBE

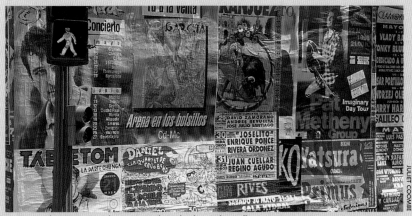

Not sure what to see or where to go? then check out the walls.

Map 2

PLACES TO STAY
29 Hostal Retiro
38 Hotel Ramón de la Cruz

PLACES TO EAT
11 Casa Mingo
15 Prada a Tope
34 Taberna de Daniela
37 Restaurante El Pescador

OTHER
1 Connection Room
2 Museo de América
3 Faro de Madrid
4 TIVE
5 Bus to El Pardo
6 El Corte Inglés
7 Terraza España
8 Teleférico
9 Cementerio de la Florida
10 Ermita de San Antonio de la Florida
12 La Viuda de Cuenllas
13 Templo de Debod
14 Buses to Segovia, La Granja de San Ildefonso, Ávila & Navacerrada
16 Entry to Campo del Moro
17 Museo de los Carruajes
18 Catedral de Nuestra Señora de la Almudena
19 Muralla Arabe
20 Puente de Segovia
21 La Riviera
22 Basílica de San Francisco el Grande
23 Estadio Vicente Calderón
24 Sala Caracol
25 AutoRes Bus Station
26 La Veloz
27 Hospital General Gregorio Marañon
28 Asistencia a Mujeres Violadas
30 Librería Henri Avellan
31 Museo de la Moneda & National Mint
32 Playmon Camera Repairs
33 Viajes Zeppelin
35 Fundación Juan March
36 Regional Airlines
39 Euro Rental
40 Plaza de Toros Monumental de las Ventas & Museo Taurino
41 Intercambiador de Avenida de América (Bus Station)

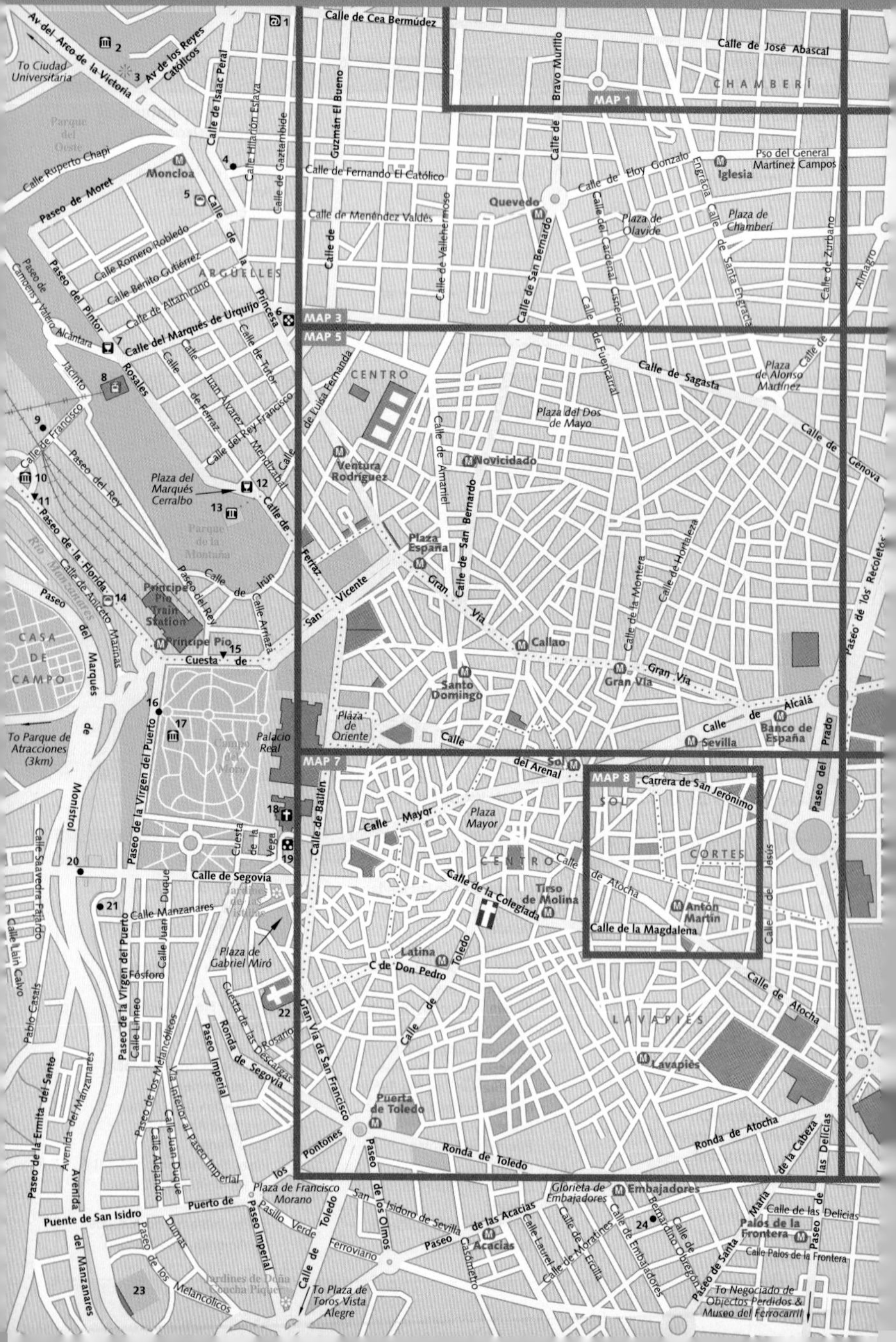

MAP 2

Calle de Cea Bermúdez
Calle de José Abascal
Av del Arco de la Victoria
To Ciudad-Universitaria
Av de los Reyes Católicos
Bravo Murillo
CHAMBERÍ
MAP 1
Calle de Isaac Peral
Calle Hilarión Eslava
Calle de Guzmán El Bueno
Calle de Gaztambide
Calle de Eloy Gonzalo
Pso del General Martínez Campos
Parque del Oeste
Calle Ruperto Chapi
Calle de Fernando El Católico
Iglesia
Moncloa
Calle de Menéndez Valdés
Quevedo
Plaza de Olavide
Plaza de Chamberí
Paseo de Moret
Calle de Vallehermoso
Calle de San Bernardo
Calle de Santa Engracia
Calle de Zurbano
Paseo del Pintor
Paseo de Camoens
Calle Benito Gutiérrez
ARGÜELLES
Calle de Altamirano
Calle del Marqués de Urquijo
MAP 3
MAP 5
Calle de Sagasta
Plaza de Alonso Martínez
Calle de Génova
Rosales
CENTRO
Plaza del Dos de Mayo
Calle de Juan Álvarez de Mendizábal
Ventura Rodríguez
Novidciado
Plaza del Marqués de Cerralbo
Plaza España
Calle de San Bernardo
Paseo de los Recoletos
Plaza de Oriente
Santo Domingo
Gran Vía
Callao
Gran Vía
Alcalá
Banco de España
Sevilla
Príncipe Pío Train Station
Príncipe Pío
Cuesta de
Plaza de Oriente
Palacio Real
Calle
MAP 7
del Arenal
Sol
MAP 8
Carrera de San Jerónimo
CORTES
Calle Mayor
Plaza Mayor
CENTRO
Calle de Atocha
Antón Martín
Calle de la Colegiata
Tirso de Molina
Calle de la Magdalena
Latina
C de Don Pedro
Gran Vía de San Francisco
LAVAPIÉS
Calle de Atocha
Lavapiés
Plaza de Gabriel Miró
Calle de Segovia
Ronda de Segovia
Puerta de Toledo
Ronda de Toledo
Ronda de Atocha
Calle de las Delicias
Plaza de Francisco Morano
Glorieta de Embajadores
Embajadores
Palos de la Frontera
Puente de San Isidro
ACACIAS
Paseo de las Acacias
Calle Palos de la Frontera
To Plaza de Toros Vista Alegre
To Negociado de Objetos Perdidos & Museo del Ferrocarril

MAP 2

Paseo de la Castellana
Calle de
Pedro de Valdivia
Avenida de Cartagena
41
Avenida de América
Calle de María de Molina
MAP 1
Calle de César
Calle Cadarso
Calle de López de Hoyos

Calle de Serrano

Calle del General Oraá
Calle de Diego de León
Calle de César
Calle de Ardemans
Calle del Ereso
Calle de Azcona
Calle Martínez Izquierdo
Calle Luis Cabo
Calle de Brasilia
Calle Virgen de Lourdes
Avenida Donostiarra
Avenida de la Paz

Paseo Eduardo Data
Calle de Juan Bravo
Calle de Francisco Silvela
Calle de Cartagena
Calle de Martínez
Calle Fundación
Avenida de los Toreros
40
El Carmen

Rubén Darío
SALAMANCA
Calle de Castelló
Calle de Vergara
Calle de Padilla
Diego de León
39
Avenida de Francisco Santos
Ventas
Calle de Alcalá
Calle de Londres

35
Plaza del Marqués de Salamanca
José Ortega y Gasset
37
Lista
Calle de Pedro Heredia
Calle del Marqués
Calle Sancho Dávila
Antonio Priale
Calle de Cresto

Núñez de Balboa
36
Don Ramón de la Cruz
Calle de Alcántara
38
Plaza de Manuel Becerra
Manuel Becerra
Calle del Marqués de Mondéjar
Calle de Ricardo Ortiz

Calle del Príncipe de Vergara
General Pardiñas
Ayala
Calle de Alcalá
Paseo del Marqués de Zafra

34
Hermosilla
Goya
33
GOYA
Calle Fuente del Berro
Calle de Peñascales
Calle Ibiza

Plaza de Colón
Serrano
Velázquez
Calle de Goya
Calle de Jorge Juan
32
O'Donnell
Calle de Vinaroz

Jardines del Descubrimiento
Príncipe de Vergara
30
Calle del Duque de Sesto
31
Calle de Vicálvaro

Plaza de la Independencia
Retiro
29
Navarra
Calle de O'Donnell
Calle del Doctor Esquerdo
Calle de Juan Esplandiú

Plaza Maestro Villa
28
Calle del Doctor Castelo
Calle de Menorca
Calle Vaquerías
Calle del Marqués

RETIRO
Ibiza
27
Calle de Ibiza
Calle de Fernán
Paseo de John Lennon
Parque de Roma

MEDIODÍA
Calle del Alcalde Sáinz de Baranda
Sáinz de Baranda
Volador
Calle Alcalde Garrido Juaristi

Real Jardín Botánico
Avenida de Menéndez Pelayo
Calle del Doce de Octubre
Calle de Pío Baroja
Calle Antonio
Calle del Pez Austral
Calle de Sirio
Avenida de la Paz
Calle de Manuel Machado

Calle de Alfonso XII
Parque del Buen Retiro
Calle de Samaria
Estrella
Calle de los Vinateros

Atocha
Paseo de la Reina Cristina
Plaza de Mariano de Cavia
Avenida del Mediterráneo
Conde de Casal
26
25
Avenida del Mediterráneo

Atocha Train Station
Menéndez Pelayo
Pacífico
Plaza del Conde de Casal
Calle de Lira

To Estación Sur de Autobuses & Cine Imax
Calle de Méndez Alvaro
0   200   400 m
0   200   400 yards

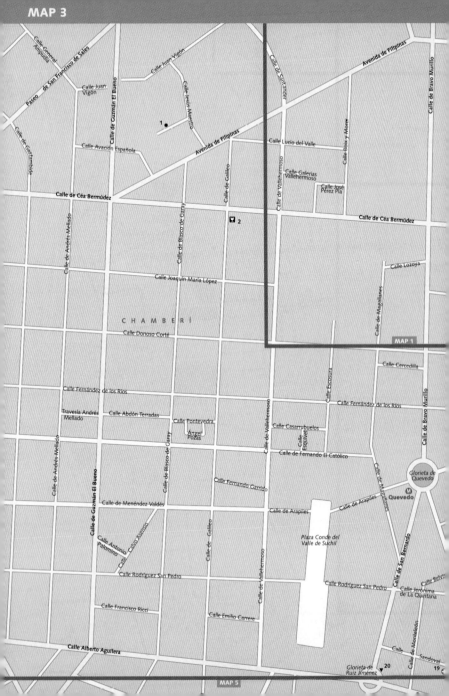

MAP 3

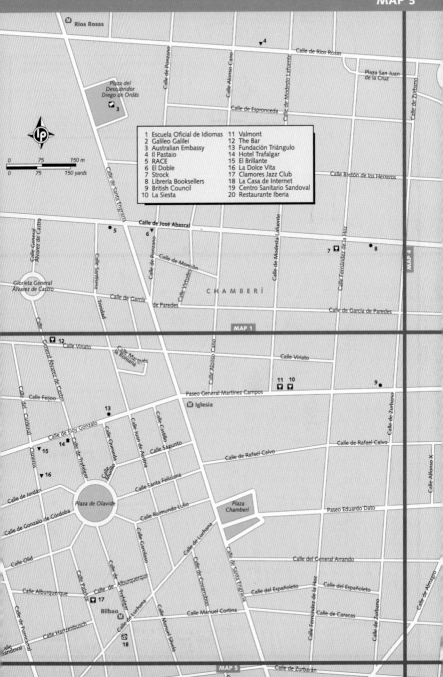

Ⓜ Ríos Rosas

Plaza del Descubridor Diego de Ordás

3

Calle de Ponzano

Calle de Alonso Cano

Calle de Modesto Lafuente

Calle de Zurbano

4

Calle de Ríos Rosas

Plaza San Juan de la Cruz

Calle de Espronceda

1	Escuela Oficial de Idiomas	11	Valmont
2	Galileo Galilei	12	The Bar
3	Australian Embassy	13	Fundación Triángulo
4	Il Pastaio	14	Hotel Trafalgar
5	RACE	15	El Brillante
6	El Doble	16	La Dolce Vita
7	Strock	17	Clamores Jazz Club
8	Librería Booksellers	18	La Casa de Internet
9	British Council	19	Centro Sanitario Sandoval
10	La Siesta	20	Restaurante Iberia

Calle de Bretón de los Herreros

Calle de Santa Engracia

Calle General Álvarez de Castro

Calle de José Abascal

5

6

Calle de Ponzano

Calle de Moreón

Calle Santísima

Calle de Modesto Lafuente

Calle Fernández de la Hoz

7   8

MAP 4

Glorieta General Álvarez de Castro

Calle Trinidad

Calle de García

de Paredes

CHAMBERÍ

Calle de García de Paredes

MAP 1

12   Calle Viriato

Calle General Álvarez de Castro

Calle Marqués de la Romana

Calle Alonso Cano

Calle Viriato

11 10

Paseo General Martínez Campos

9

Calle de Zurbano

Calle Feijoo

Calle del Cardenal

Ⓜ Iglesia

13

Calle de Eloy Gonzalo

14

Calle de Trafalgar

Calle Quevedo

Calle Juan de Austria

Calle Castillo

Calle Sagunto

Calle de Rafael Calvo

Calle de Rafael Calvo

Calle Alfonso X

Claveros

15

16

Calle Murillo

Calle Santa Feliciana

Plaza de Olavide

Calle de Jordán

Calle Raimundo Lulio

Plaza Chamberí

Paseo Eduardo Dato

Calle de Gonzalo de Córdoba

Calle Olid

Calle Alburquerque

Calle Palafox

Calle de Alburquerque

Calle Garellano

Calle de Trafalgar

Calle de Luchana

Calle de Covarrubias

Calle de Santa Engracia

Calle del General Arrando

Calle del Españoleto

Calle Fernández de la Hoz

Calle del Españoleto

Calle de Zurbano

Calle de Almagro

17

Bilbao

Ⓜ

Calle Hartzenbusch

Calle de Luchana

Calle Manuel Silvela

Calle Manuel Cortina

Calle de Caracas

18

Calle de Fuencarral

Calle Sandoval

MAP 5

Calle de Zurbarán

MAP 4

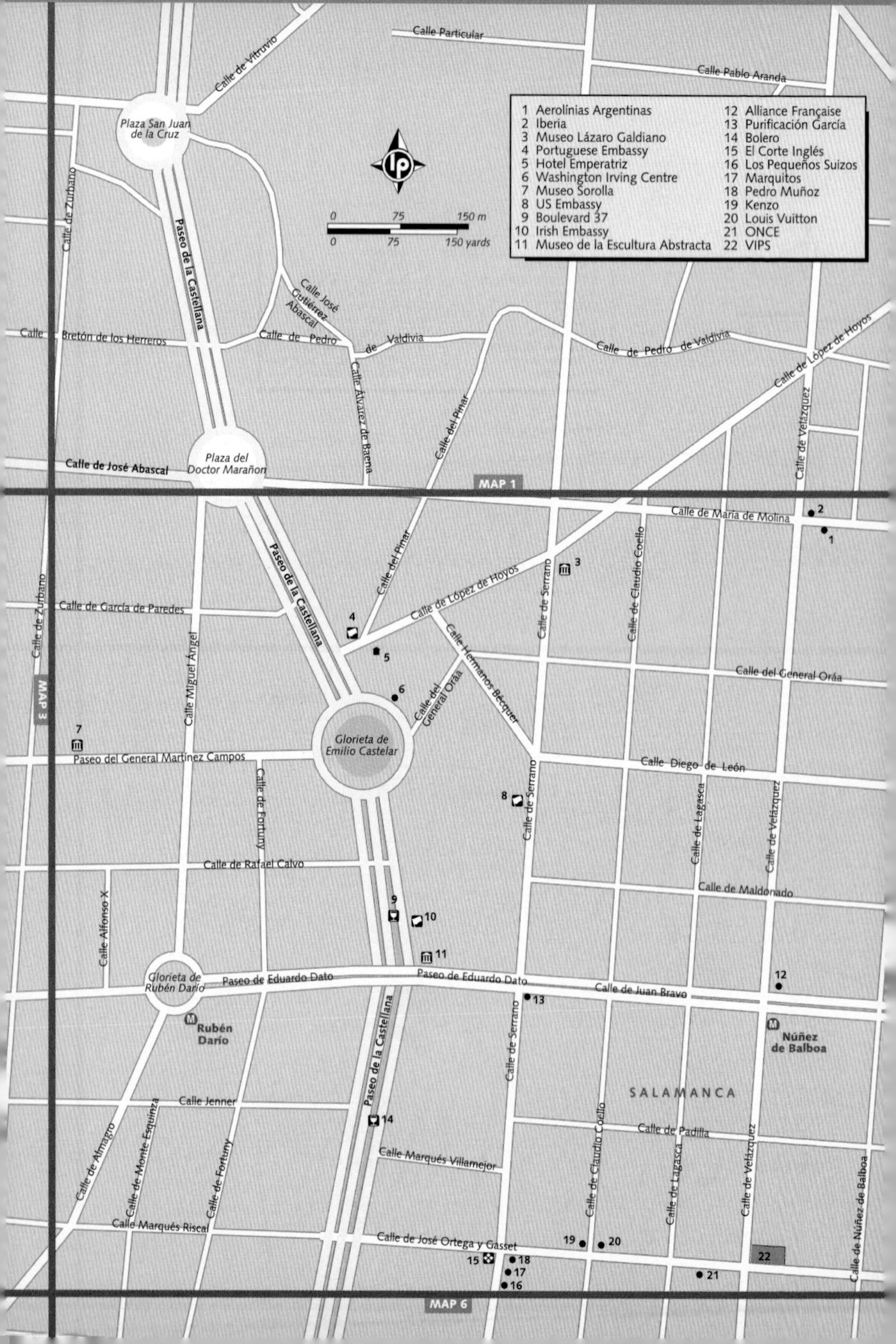

Legend:

1 Aerolínias Argentinas
2 Iberia
3 Museo Lázaro Galdiano
4 Portuguese Embassy
5 Hotel Emperatriz
6 Washington Irving Centre
7 Museo Sorolla
8 US Embassy
9 Boulevard 37
10 Irish Embassy
11 Museo de la Escultura Abstracta
12 Alliance Française
13 Purificación García
14 Bolero
15 El Corte Inglés
16 Los Pequeños Suizos
17 Marquitos
18 Pedro Muñoz
19 Kenzo
20 Louis Vuitton
21 ONCE
22 VIPS

Map labels:

Calle Particular
Calle Pablo Aranda
Plaza San Juan de la Cruz
Calle de Vitruvio
Calle de Zurbano
Paseo de la Castellana
Calle José Gutiérrez Abascal
Calle de Pedro de Valdivia
Calle de Pedro de Valdivia
Calle de López de Hoyos
Calle Bretón de los Herreros
Calle del Pinar
Calle Álvarez de Baena
Plaza del Doctor Marañon
Calle de José Abascal
MAP 1
Calle de María de Molina
Calle de López de Hoyos
Calle del Pintor
Calle de Serrano
Calle de Claudio Coello
Calle de García de Paredes
Calle de Zurbano
MAP 3
Calle Miguel Ángel
Calle Hermanos Bécquer
Calle del General Oráa
Calle del General Oráa
Paseo del General Martínez Campos
Glorieta de Emilio Castelar
Calle del General Oráa
Calle Diego de León
Calle de Fortuny
Calle de Serrano
Calle de Lagasca
Calle de Velázquez
Calle de Rafael Calvo
Calle Alfonso X
Calle de Maldonado
Glorieta de Rubén Darío
Paseo de Eduardo Dato
Paseo de Eduardo Dato
Calle de Juan Bravo
Rubén Darío
Núñez de Balboa
Paseo de la Castellana
SALAMANCA
Calle Jenner
Calle de Almagro
Calle de Monte Esquinza
Calle de Fortuny
Calle de Serrano
Calle de Claudio Coello
Calle de Padilla
Calle Marqués Villamejor
Calle Marqués Riscal
Calle de Lagasca
Calle de Velázquez
Calle de Núñez de Balboa
Calle de José Ortega y Gasset

MAP 5

PLACES TO STAY
1 Albergue Santa Cruz de Marcenado
47 Hotel Los Condes
49 Hostal Besaya
53 Hostal Alcázar Regis
55 Hostal Lamalonga
60 Hotel de Santo Domingo
65 Hotel Tryp Ambassador
69 Hotel California
70 Hostal Andorra
71 Hotel Regente
84 Hostal Ivor
85 Hostal Paz
102 Hostal Sil & Hostal Serranos
110 Hostal Senegal
121 Hostal Medieval
149 Hostal Palacios
151 Hotel Laris
153 Hostal Ginebra
161 Hotel Mónaco
167 Hotel Arosa
174 Hostal Delfina
192 Hotel Regina

PLACES TO EAT
8 Café Isadora
10 Restaurante La Granja
11 Pizzeria Mastropiero
12 Café Manuela
13 Tetería de la Abuela
16 Restaurante de Cañas y Barro
17 Taquería de Birrä
18 La Dama Duende
26 Café Macaluca
27 Café de las Extrellas
34 Restaurante Veracruz
35 Restaurante Bali
36 Restaurante Siam
37 Adrish
62 Taberna La Bola
79 Café de Oriente
80 Taberna del Alabardero
81 Restaurante La Paella Real
86 Casa Parrondo
89 El Locro
90 Fado
94 Café Comercial
122 Café La Sastrería
130 El Mentidero de la Villa
142 La Gastroteca de Stéphane y Arturo
145 Restaurante Momo
147 Restaurante Dame Noire
156 Divina la Cocina
158 Restaurante Extremadura
160 La Carreta
163 Undata
169 Restaurante Integral Artemisa
177 Restaurante La Barraca
178 Restaurante Robata
185 Círculo de Bellas Artes

BARS, PUBS & CLUBS
9 Café Magerit
14 Siroco
15 Café Moderno
19 Midnight
21 Ambigú 16
30 Arena
48 Morocco
74 Ales
87 El Templo del Gato (California Music Bar)
88 Strong
95 Vinos
96 Café del Foro
98 Corripio
101 Pachá
103 La Vía Lactea
104 Maderfaker
105 Triskel
109 Cervecería Bulevar
111 Cervecería de Santa Bárbara
116 Vaiven
118 Bodega de la Ardosa
119 The Quiet Man
124 New Leather
125 Café Belén
128 Big Bamboo
129 Finnegan's
135 Kingston's
136 Rimmel
138 Sierra Ángel
140 Acuarela Café
141 Truco
144 Truck
146 Cruising
152 Ya'sta!
155 Bar La Carmencita
157 Libertad 8
162 Rick's
171 El Sol
172 Museo Chicote
173 Del Diego Bar
176 Cock Bar
179 Star's Dance Café
191 Café Club Mad

SHOPS
5 Mamah Africa
22 VIPS
51 VIPS
52 Cántaro
56 Camper
57 Sefarad
58 VIPS
59 Antigua Casa Talavera
63 Alambique
72 FNAC Store
76 The International Bookshop
78 Librería del Patrimonio Nacional
83 7-Eleven
91 Madrid Rock
93 El Corte Inglés
97 VIPS
108 Patrimonio Cultural Olivarero
112 Ana Benjumea
113 Elvira González
117 Elba Benítez
120 Mercado Fuencarral
126 Centro de la Mujer
127 Galería Juana de Aizpuru
131 Piamonte
132 Ararat (II)
133 Ararat (I)
134 Moriarty
137 Berkana
139 Lenguajes
143 Casa Postales
154 La Maison Folle
159 Adamante
164 Ático Tipo
165 Madrid Rock
168 La Casa del Libro

OTHER
2 Moto Alquiler
3 Palacio de Liria
4 Antiguo Cuartel del Conde Duque
6 Open Nautas
7 Xnet Café
20 RoomMadrid
23 Alphaville Cinema
24 Renoir Cinema
25 Museo de Cerralbo
28 Cinema Princesa
29 Torre de Madrid; Air France; Sabena; Virgin Express
31 Cadimar Viajes
32 Hertz
33 Europcar
38 Nevada 2000
39 Cervecería El Alama
40 Aroba52
41 MoneyGram
42 Photo Express
43 National/Atesa rentacar
44 Telephones (VIC locutorio)
45 Teatro Alfil
46 Teatro Lara
50 Avis
54 KLM
61 Café de Chinitas (Flamenco)
64 Convento de la Encarnación
66 Localidades La Alicantina
67 Carrión Building
68 USIT Unlimited
73 Centro de Salud
75 Viajes Zeppelin
77 Pullmantur
82 Real Cinema
92 Convento de las Descalzas Reales
99 Tunisian Embassy
100 International House
106 Museo Municipal
107 Museo Romántico
114 Juventus Viajes
115 Sociedad General de Autores y Editores
123 Iglesia de San Antón
148 Cogam & Urania's Café
150 Lavandería Alba
166 Telephones
170 Localidades Galicia
175 CRIDJ
180 Casa de las Siete Chimeneas
181 Palacio Buenavista
182 Banco de España
183 Iglesia de San José
184 RENFE Booking Office
186 Teatro de Bellas Artes
187 Main Police Station
188 Centro de Información y Asesoramiento Universitario
189 Edificio Metropolis Building
190 Edificio Grassy
193 Real Academia de Bellas Artes de San Fernando

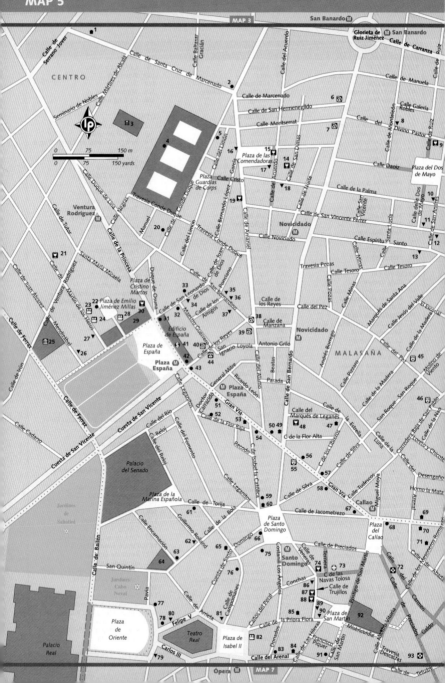

MAP 5

MAP 3

San Banardo Ⓜ

Glorieta de Ruiz Jiménez

San Banardo Ⓜ

CENTRO

Ⓜ Ópera MAP 7

MAP 5

MAP 3

MAP 7

MAP 6

MAP 4

1
2
Calle de Tortuny
Calle de Zurbarán
Calle Blanca de Navarra
Calle Marqués de Villamagna
4
5
6
Calle de Don Ramón de la Cruz
10
11
8
7
9
Calle de Serrano
Calle de Lagasca
Calle de Velázquez
Calle de Núñez de Balboa
3
Calle de Amador de los Ríos
Calle de Fernando El Santo
Calle de Ayala
12
13
Calle de Ayala
14
Calle de Monte Esquinza
Calle Alcalá Galiano
Paseo de la Castellana
15
16
Calle de la Hermosilla
Calle de la Hermosilla
18
Marqués de Zurgena
Calle de Claudio Coello
21
20
Calle de Génova
19
17
22
Colón
Plaza de Colón
26
Calle de Goya
Calle de Goya
García Gutiérrez
Calle del Marqués Ensenada
23
25
24
28
Jardines del Descubrimiento
29
30
Serrano
Velázquez
31
Calle de Serrano
27
33
MAP 5
34
32
Calle de Jorge Juan
Calle de Jorge Juan
35
Calle de Puigcerdá
39
Gurtubay
Calle de Velázquez
Calle de Núñez de Balboa
Tamayo y Baus
37
38
Gil de Santivañes
Calle de Villanueva
Calle del Cid
Paseo de los Recoletos
36
Calle Recoletos
43
42
41
Calle Conde de Aranda
44
45
Calle Columela
40
Calle de Lagasca
Retiro
Calle de Alcalá
Calle de Alcalá
Calle de O'Donnell
Calle Salustiano Olozaga
Villalar
47
Plaza de la Independencia
46
Marqués del Duero
Pedro Muñoz Seca
Calle de Alcalá
Plaza Maestro Villa
48
Plaza de Cibeles
49
Calle Alfonso XI
Calle Valenzuela
Palacio de Comunicaciones
Avenida México
Paseo Bolivia
Paseo de Colombia
Paseo de la República Dominicana
Paseo del Prado
50
Calle de Montalbán
51
Calle de Alfonso XII
Paseo Salón del Estanque

MAP 9

0   75   150 m
0.1   75   150 yards

MAP 6

PLACES TO STAY & EAT
8 Casa Julián
9 Restaurante Oter
15 Hostal Don Diego
16 La Trainera
18 Teatriz
20 Hard Rock Café
32 Thai Gardens
35 Café-Restaurante El Espejo; Pabellón del Espejo
36 Gran Café de Gijón
39 El Amparo
40 Alfredo's Barbacoa

OTHER
1 German Embassy
2 Goethe Institut
3 UK Embassy
4 Lladró
5 Gutiérrez
6 Portuguese Consulate
7 Mallorca
10 Gucci
11 Fundación de la Caixa
12 Terraza de Serrano
13 Bombonería Santa
14 Marks & Spencer
17 Canadian Embassy
19 Max Mara
21 Torres de Colón
22 UK Consulate
23 Institut Français
24 French Embassy
25 Museo de Cera
26 Centro Cultural de la Villa; Café de la Villa
27 Monumento a Colón
28 Airport Bus
29 Monumento al Descubrimiento
30 El Jardín de Serrano
31 Fann
33 Purificación García
34 Biblioteca Nacional & Museo del Libro
37 Museo Arqueológico Nacional
38 Adolfo Dominguez
41 Garamond
42 Anglo-American Medical Unit
43 Farrutx
44 Armani
45 Mallorca
46 Puerta de Alcalá
47 Cámara Oficial de Comercio e Industria de Madrid
48 Palacio de Linares
49 Main Post Office (Palacio de Comunicaciones)
50 Museo Naval
51 Museo de Artes Decorativos

MAP 7

PLACES TO STAY
1 Hostal Cosmopolitan
3 Hostal Riesco
4 Hotel Moderno
20 Hostal Pinariega
23 Hostal Mairu
26 Hostal Montalvo
27 Hostal La Perla Asturiana
28 Hostal Santa Cruz & Hostal Cruz Sol
30 Hostal Madrid
31 Hostal Arcos
40 Hostal La Macarena
86 Hotel París
90 Hotel Palace
92 Hotel Ritz
94 Hostal Sudamericano & Hostal La Coruña

PLACES TO EAT
5 Casa Labra
8 Chocolatería de San Ginés
10 Café del Real
11 Café Vergara
13 La Cruzada
14 Café de los Austrias
22 Marechiaro
37 Restaurante Sobrino de Botín
38 Casa Antonio
39 Casa Paco
49 Casa Ciríaco
58 Taquería de Birrà (II)
59 Restaurante Gure-Etxea
60 El Estragón
66 Oliveros
67 Restaurante Julián de Tolosa
69 Casa Víctor
76 Casa Pepa
80 La Burbuja Que Ríe
99 Maceíra
100 La Vaca Verónica
103 El Brillante
106 Elqui
107 Nuevo Café Barbieri
108 Babilonya
109 Restaurante La Pampa
113 El Granero de Lavapiés
116 Beirut

PUBS, BARS & CLUBS
6 Palacio Gaviria
7 Teatro Joy Eslava
55 Bar Ventorrillo
57 Travesía
62 Café del Nuncio
63 El Madroño
65 Taberna de Antonio Sánchez
68 La Chata
70 Taberna de Cien Vinos
71 Taberna Almendro 13
72 La Soleá
73 Berlin Cabaret
74 Taberna Tempranillo
78 El Viajero
97 Refugio
98 Candela
102 Kapital
112 Eucalipto
114 El Boquerón
115 La Mancha de Madrid

OTHER
2 Casa de Correos
9 Iglesia de San Ginés
12 Real Musical
15 Palacio Real
16 Catedral de Nuestra Señora de la Almudena
17 Iglesia de San Nicolás de los Servitas
18 Berceo
19 Real Farmacia de la Reina Madre
21 Tienda El Flamenco Vive
24 Madrid Rock
25 Real Casa de la Panadería
29 Librería de Mujeres
32 Teatro Albéniz
33 Iglesia de Santa Cruz
34 Palacio de Santa Cruz; Ministerio de Asuntos Exteriores
35 Tourist Office (Patronato Municipal de Turismo)
36 El Arco Artesanía
41 Mercado
42 Basílica de San Miguel
43 Casa de Cisneros
44 Casa de los Lujanes
45 Ayuntamiento
46 Madrid Convention Bureau
47 La Librería
48 Contreras
50 Istituto Italiano di Cultura
51 Garrido Bailén; Site of Iglesia de Santa María de la Almudena
52 Palacio del Duque de Uceda (Capitanía General)
53 Iglesia del Sacramento
54 Former Estudio Público de Humanidades
56 Corral de la Morería
61 Iglesia de San Pedro El Viejo
64 Basílica de San Isidro
75 Iglesia de San Andrés
77 Teatro de la Latina
79 WWW2.Call.Home
81 Tourist Office; Café del Mercado
82 Fotocasión
83 El Rastro Flea Market
84 Eskalera Karakola
85 Mariblanca (White Maria)
87 American Express
88 Museo Thyssen-Bornemisza
89 Main Tourist Office (Oficina de Turismo)
91 VIPS
93 Objetos de Arte Toledano
95 Multicines Ideal
96 Teatro Calderón
101 Centro de Salud
104 Centro de Arte Reina Sofía
105 Galería Helga de Alvear
110 La Corrala
111 Teatro Olimpia

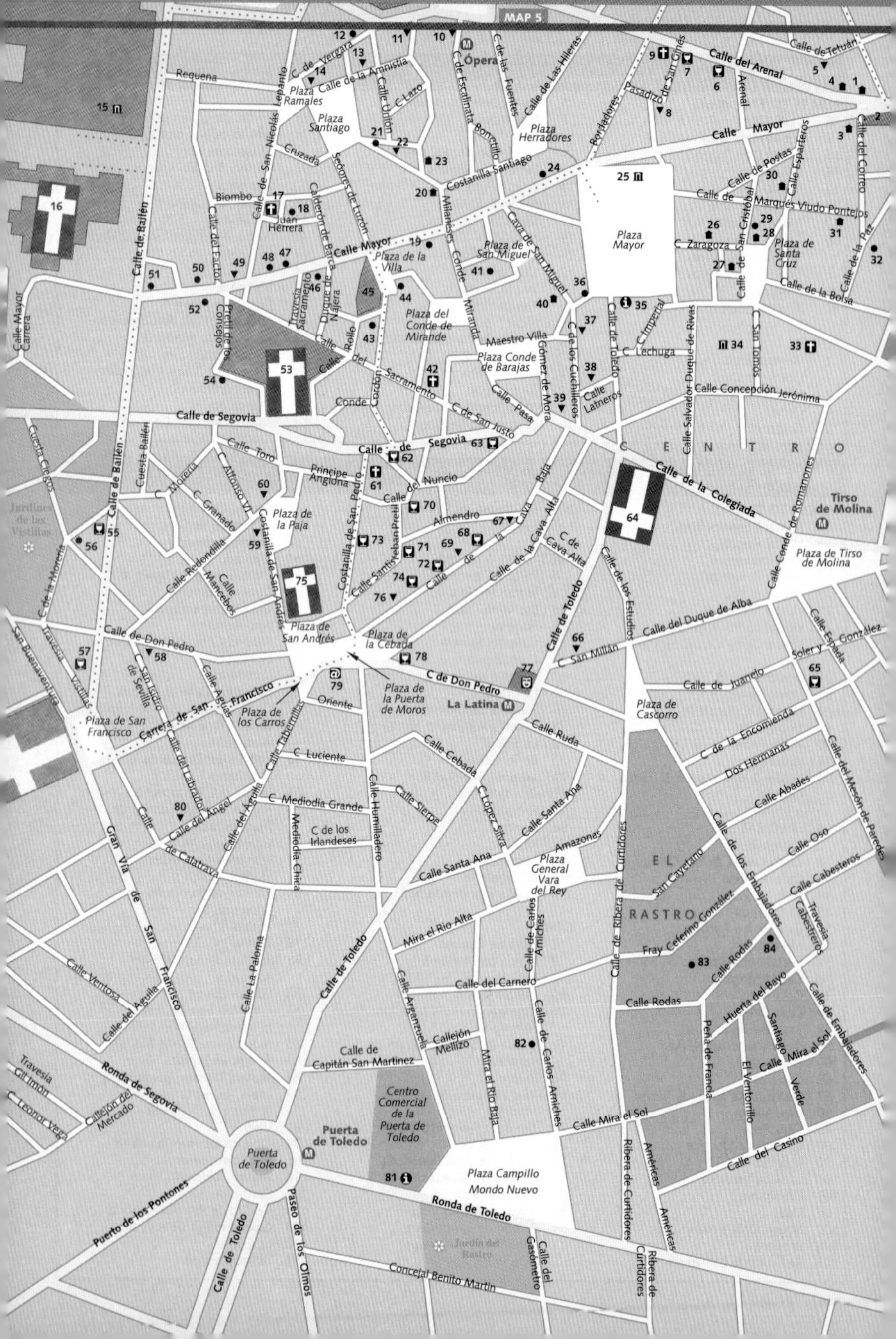

MAP 7

MAP 5

Requena

15

16

Calle de Bailén

Calle Mayor Carrera

51

50

49 48 47 46

52

53

54

Calle de Segovia

Plaza Ramales
Calle de Yerguas
Plaza Calle de la Aronilla
12
13
14
Plaza Santiago
Calle de San Nicolás
Biombo
17
18
Juan Herrera
Calle del Factor
Calle Mayor
21
22
23
20
19
Plaza de la Villa
44
45
43
Plaza del Conde de Miranda
42
Conde
Calle de San Justo

11
10
Ópera
Calle de los Fuentes
Calle de las Hileras
Plaza Herradores
Costanilla Santiago
24
Plaza de San Miguel
41
Maestro Villa
Plaza Conde de Barajas
Sacramento
C. de San Justo

9
7
6
8
Calle del Arenal
Pasadizo
Calle Mayor
25
26
27
Zaragoza
Plaza Mayor
Calle de Postas
30
Marqués Viudo Pontejos
29
28
Plaza de Santa Cruz
Calle de la Bolsa

Calle de Tetuán
5
4
3
1
2
Calle de Cádiz
Calle Espartanos
31
32

36
40
37
35
Lechuga
38
39
34
33

Calle de Segovia
63
Calle
62
61
Nuncio
70
71 72
69 68
67
Plaza de la Paja
59
60
Plaza de San Andrés
73
74
76
75
78
Plaza de la Cebada
Calle de la Cava Alta
C. de Cava Alta
64
Calle de la Colegiada
Tirso de Molina
Plaza de Tirso de Molina

55
56
57
58
Jardín de las Vistillas
Calle de Bailén

Plaza de San Francisco
Carrera de San Francisco
79
Oriente
Plaza de los Carros
La Latina
C de Don Pedro
77
San Millán
66
Calle del Duque de Alba
Plaza de la Puerta de Moros
Plaza de Cascorro
Soler y González
65

80
Gran Vía
Plaza de San Francisco
C. Luciente
C. Mediodía Grande
C. de los Irlandeses
Calle Sierpe
Calle Humilladero
Calle Santa Ana
Calle Santa Ana
Calle Toledo
Calle Ruda
Calle Cebada
Calle de la Encomienda
Dos Hermanas
Calle Abades
Calle Oso
EL RASTRO
San Cayetano
Calle de los Embajadores
Calle de Ribera de Curtidores
Plaza General Vara del Rey
Mira el Río Alta
Calle del Carnero
Fray Ceferino González
83
84
Calle Rodas
Huerta del Bayo
Travesía Cabestreros
Calle Cabestreros

Calle de Toledo
Ronda de Segovia
Travesía Gil Imón
C. Leonor Vega
Puerta de Toledo
Calle de Toledo
Paseo de los Olmos
Puente de los Pontones
Calle de Capitán San Martínez
Callejón Mellizo
82
Centro Comercial de la Puerta de Toledo
Plaza Campillo Mondo Nuevo
81
Ronda de Toledo
Jardín del Rastro
Concejal Benito Martín
Mira el Río Baja
Calle de Carlos Arniches
Calle Mira el Sol
Ribera de Curtidores
Amézfras
Ribera de Curtidores
Calle del Casino
Peña de Francia
El Ventorrillo
Calle Mira el Sol
Santiago Verde

CENTRO

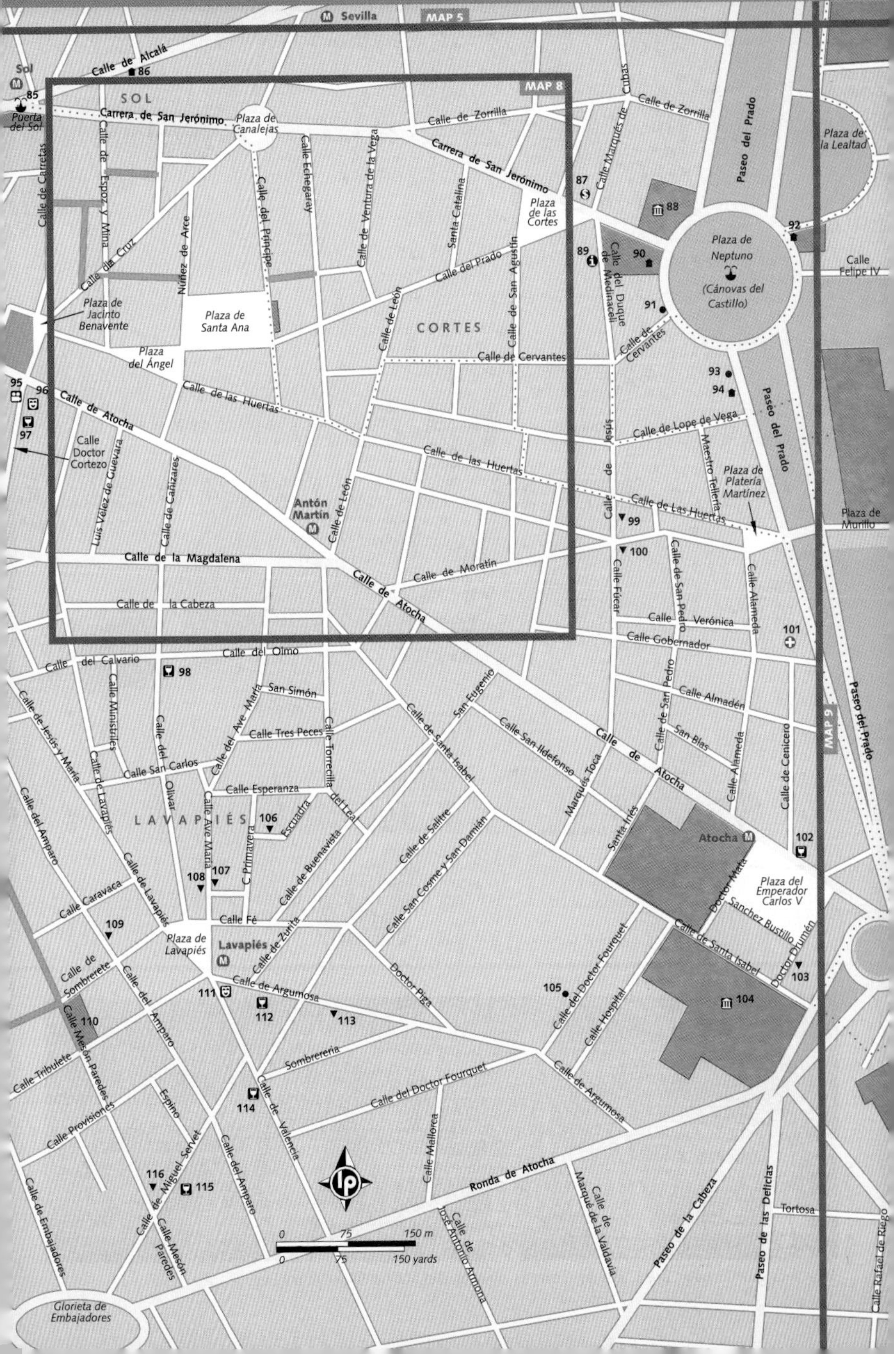
Sevilla
MAP 5
MAP 8
MAP 9
Sol
Puerta del Sol
SOL
CORTES
LAVAPIÉS
Calle de Alcalá
Carrera de San Jerónimo
Plaza de Canalejas
Calle de Zorrilla
Calle Marqués de Cubas
Paseo del Prado
Plaza de la Lealtad
Plaza de las Cortes
Plaza de Neptuno (Cánovas del Castillo)
Calle Felipe IV
Calle del Duque de Medinaceli
Calle de Cervantes
Calle de Carretas
Calle de Espoz y Mina
Calle de la Cruz
Núñez de Arce
Calle del Príncipe
Calle Echegaray
Calle de Ventura de la Vega
Santa Catalina
Calle del Prado
Calle de San Agustín
Calle de León
Plaza de Jacinto Benavente
Plaza de Santa Ana
Plaza del Ángel
Calle de las Huertas
Calle de Lope de Vega
Maestro Tellería
Plaza de Platería Martínez
Plaza de Murillo
Calle de Atocha
Calle Doctor Cortezo
Luis Vélez de Guevara
Calle de Cañizares
Antón Martín
Calle de la Magdalena
Calle de Moratín
Calle de Jesús
Calle Fúcar
Calle de San Pedro
Calle Alameda
Calle de la Cabeza
Calle Verónica
Calle Gobernador
Calle del Olmo
Calle del Calvario
San Simón
Calle Ministriles
Calle del Ave María
Calle Tres Peces
Calle Torrecilla del Leal
Calle de Santa Isabel
San Eugenio
Calle San Ildefonso
Calle Almadén
San Blas
Calle de Cenicero
Calle de Jesús y María
Calle de Lavapiés
Calle del Olivar
Calle San Carlos
Calle Esperanza
Calle Ave María
Escuadra
C Primavera
Calle de Buenavista
Calle de Salitre
Calle San Cosme y San Damián
Marqués Toca
Santa Inés
Atocha
Doctor Mata
Plaza del Emperador Carlos V
Sánchez Bustillo
Doctor Drumén
Calle del Amparo
Calle Caravaca
Calle Fé
Plaza de Lavapiés
Lavapiés
Calle de Zurita
Calle de Sombrerete
Calle de Argumosa
Doctor Piga
Calle del Doctor Fourquet
Calle Hospital
Calle Mesón Paredes
Calle Tribulete
Sombrerería
Calle de Valencia
Calle Provisiones
Espino
Calle Mallorca
Ronda de Atocha
Calle de Miguel Servet
Calle de Embajadores
Calle José Antonio Armona
Calle de Marqués de la Valdavia
Paseo de la Cabeza
Paseo de las Delicias
Tortosa
Calle Rafael de Riego
Glorieta de Embajadores
0 75 150 m
0 75 150 yards
85 86 87 88 89 90 91 92 93 94 95 96 97 98 99 100 101 102 103 104 105 106 107 108 109 110 111 112 113 114 115 116

MAP 8

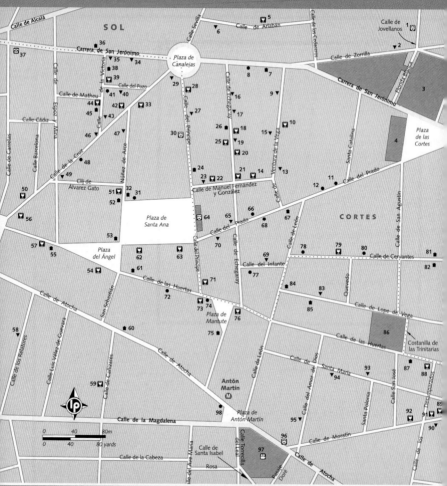

SOL

Calle de Jovellanos

Calle de Alcalá

Calle de Sevilla

Calle de Ariabán

Calle de los Cedaceros

Carrera de San Jerónimo

Plaza de Canalejas

Calle de Zorrilla

Carrera de San Jerónimo

Plaza de las Cortes

Calle de Matheu

Calle del Pozo

Calle de la Victoria

Calle Cádiz

Calle de Carretas

Calle de Barcelona

Espoz y Mina

Calle de la Cruz

Cll de Álvarez Gato

Núñez de Arce

Calle del Príncipe

Plaza de Santa Ana

Plaza del Ángel

Calle de Manuel Fernández y González

Calle de la Gorguera

Calle de Echegaray

Calle del Prado

Calle del Prado

Calle de León

Santa Catalina

Calle del Prado

Calle de San Agustín

CORTES

Ventura de la Vega

Calle de Cervantes

Calle del Infante

Quevedo

Calle de las Huertas

Calle de Atocha

San Sebastián

Calle de Lope de Vega

Plaza de Mantute

Costanilla de las Trinitarias

Calle de los Relatores

Calle Luis Vélez de Guevara

Calle de Cañizares

Calle de León

Calle del Amor de Dios

Calle de Santa María

Santa Polonia

Calle San José

Calle de las Huertas

Antón Martín

Plaza de Antón Martín

Calle de la Magdalena

Calle de Moratín

Calle Torrecilla del Leal

Calle de Santa Isabel

Calle de la Cabeza

Rosa

Calle del Ave María

Paseo del Prado

Calle de Atocha

0   40   80m
0   40   80 yards

DAMIEN SIMONIS

Revelers gather near the Casa de Correos, Puerta del Sol on New Years Eve.

MAP 8

PLACES TO STAY

4	Hotel Villa Real
7	Hostal Aguilar; Hostal Universal; Hostal León; Hostal Mondragón
24	Hostal San Isidro
26	Hotel Inglés
32	Hostal Santa Ana
36	Hostal Cetro Sol
38	Hostal Esmeralda
45	Hostal Tineo & Hostal Gibert
52	Hostal Delvi
53	Gran Hotel Reina Victoria
55	Hostal Persal
60	Hostal Castilla I
61	Hostal Vetusta
67	Hostal Sardinero
75	Hostal Matute
81	Hostal Dulcinea
82	Hostal Gonzalo
84	Hostal Castro
85	Hostal Casanova
87	Hostal López

PLACES TO EAT

2	Restaurante Al Natural
6	La Finca de Susana
9	Restaurante Integral-Artemisa
13	Los Gabrieles Restaurant
15	El Inti de Oro
16	Mesón La Caserola
17	Restaurante Donzoko
19	Aki
23	La Trucha II
27	Prada a Tope
29	Café del Príncipe
34	Lhardy
35	Museo del Jamón
40	Antigua Pastelería del Pozo
43	La Oreja de Oro; Taberna Alhambra
46	La Casa del Abuelo
47	La Trucha
49	Las Bravas
58	El Basha
65	El Tocororo
69	Gula Gula
70	El Cenador del Prado
83	Restaurante Pasadero
90	Champagnería Gala
93	La Farfalla
94	El Café de Sherazade
95	Restaurante La Sanabresa

BARS, PUBS & CLUBS

5	Stella-Wake Club
10	No Se Lo Digas A Nadie
14	Carbones
18	La Venencia
20	Cardamomo
21	Los Gabrieles
22	Viva Madrid
25	El Margai
28	Cuevas de Sésamo
33	Suristán
39	La Fontana de Oro
42	La Cartuja
44	El Son
50	Torero
51	Villa Rosa
54	Café Central
56	Bar Matador
57	España Cañí
59	Casa Patas
62	La Moderna

63	Cervecería Alemana
71	El Parnasillo
73	Casa Alberto
76	Café Populart
79	Oui
88	El Hecho
89	Taberna de los Conspiradores
91	Begin the Beguine
92	El Parnaso

OTHER

1	Teatro de la Zarzuela
3	Congreso de los Diputados
8	Casa Mira
11	Romero
12	Ateneo Científico, Literario y Artístico
30	Teatro de la Comedia
31	Image Center
37	Telephones (Sol Telecom)
41	Bullfight & Football Ticket Offices
48	Capas de Seseña
64	Teatro Español
66	Rolle
68	Brunswick
72	Azteca
74	Mexico
77	Lavandería España & Damasco Salón de Te
78	Lavomatique
80	Casa de Lope de Vega
86	Convento de las Trinitarias
96	Teatro Monumental
97	Cine Doré & Filmoteca Nacional
98	Farmácia del Globo

A new slant on Madrid's greatest square, Plaza Mayor.

JULIET COOMBE

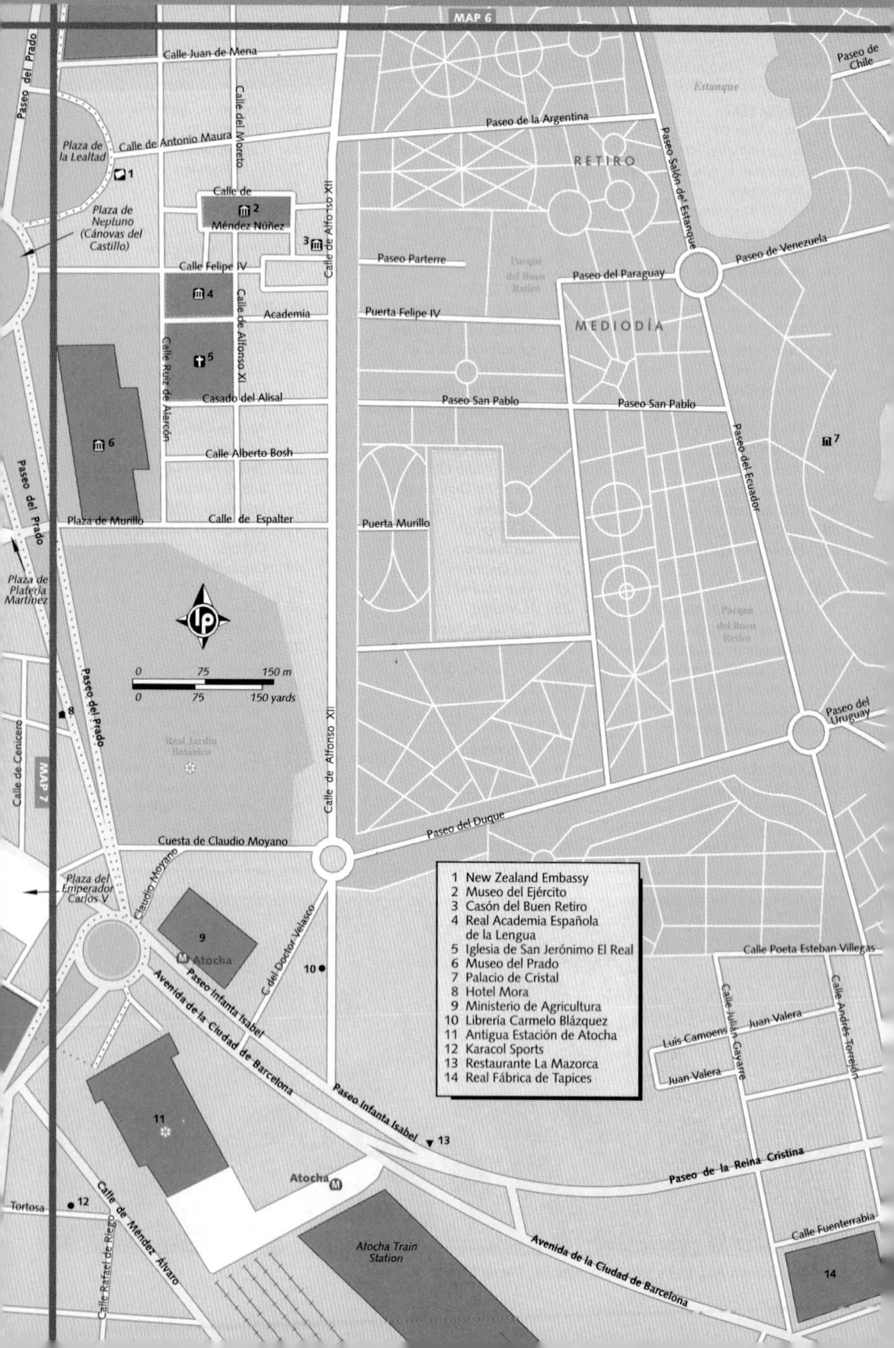

MAP 9

MAP 6

Calle Juan de Mena

Calle del Moreto

Paseo de la Argentina

RETIRO

Estanque

Paseo de Chile

Plaza de
la Lealtad

Calle de Antonio Maura

1

Plaza de
Neptuno
(Cánovas del
Castillo)

Calle de
Méndez Núñez

2

3

Calle Felipe IV

4

Academia

Calle de Alfonso XI

Calle Ruiz de Alarcón

Paseo del Prado

5

Casado del Alisal

6

Calle Alberto Bosh

Plaza de Murillo

Calle de Espalter

Plaza de
Platería
Martínez

Paseo del Prado

8

Real Jardín
Botánico

Calle de Alfonso XII

Paseo Parterre

Parque
del Buen
Retiro

Paseo del Paraguay

Paseo de Venezuela

MEDIODÍA

Puerta Felipe IV

Paseo San Pablo

Paseo San Pablo

7

Paseo del Ecuador

Puerta Murillo

Parque
del Buen
Retiro

Paseo del
Uruguay

Calle de Cenicero

MAP 7

0   75   150 m
0   75   150 yards

Paseo del Duque

Cuesta de Claudio Moyano

Plaza del
Emperador
Carlos V

9

Atocha

10

Paseo Infanta Isabel

C. del Doctor Velasco

Avenida de la Ciudad de Barcelona

11

Atocha

12

Tortosa

Calle de Méndez Álvaro

Calle de Rafael de Riego

Atocha

Paseo Infanta Isabel

13

Atocha Train
Station

Calle Poeta Esteban Villegas

Luis Camoens

Juan Valera

Calle Julia F. Cayarre

Juan Valera

Calle Andrés Torrejón

Paseo de la Reina Cristina

Calle Fuenterrabía

Avenida de la Ciudad de Barcelona

14

1 New Zealand Embassy
2 Museo del Ejército
3 Casón del Buen Retiro
4 Real Academia Española
  de la Lengua
5 Iglesia de San Jerónimo El Real
6 Museo del Prado
7 Palacio de Cristal
8 Hotel Mora
9 Ministerio de Agricultura
10 Librería Carmelo Blázquez
11 Antigua Estación de Atocha
12 Karacol Sports
13 Restaurante La Mazorca
14 Real Fábrica de Tapices

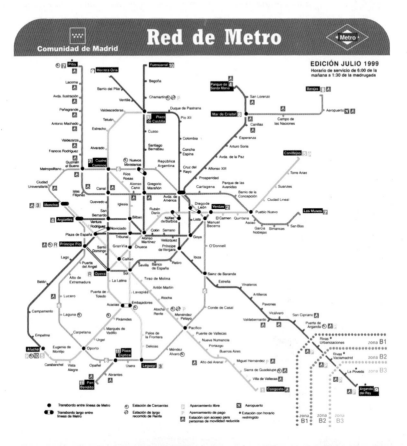

Red de Metro

Comunidad de Madrid

EDICIÓN JULIO 1999
Horario de servicio de 6:00 de la
mañana a 1:30 de la madrugada

Sol

ELLIOT DANIEL

The Metro is a fast, safe and efficient way to get around.

MAP LEGEND

BOUNDARIES

Provincial	

HYDROGRAPHY

Coastline	
River, Creek	
Lake	
Canal	

ROUTES & TRANSPORT

Freeway	
Primary Road	
Secondary Road	
Tertiary Road	
Unsealed Road	
City Freeway	
City Highway	

City Road	
City Street, Lane	
Pedestrian Mall	
Footpath	
Walking Tour	
Train Route & Station	
Cable Car or Chairlift	

AREA FEATURES

Building	
Hotel	
Urban Area	

Park, Gardens	
Cemetery	
Market	

Forest	
Beach	
Rocks	

MAP SYMBOLS

MADRID	City	✈	Airport		Mountain Range
Toledo	Large Town		Ancient or City Wall		Museum
Segovia	Town		Bank		Palacio
			Bus Station, Bus Stop		Parking Area
			Church, Cathedral		Police Station
•	Point of Interest		Cinema		Post Office
			Embassy or Consulate		Ruins
▪	Place to Stay		Fountain		Shopping Centre
	Camp Site		Hospital or Clinic		Synagogue
	Caravan Park		Information		Swimming Pool
	Hut or Chalet		Internet Cafe		Telephone
			Metro Station		Temple
▼	Place to Eat		Mosque		Theatre
	Pub, Bar or Club	▲	Monument		Transport

Note: not all symbols displayed above appear in this book

LONELY PLANET OFFICES

Australia
Locked Bag 1, Footscray, Victoria 3011
☎ 03 8379 8000 fax 03 8379 8111
email: talk2us@lonelyplanet.com.au

USA
150 Linden St, Oakland, CA 94607
☎ 510 893 8555 TOLL FREE: 800 275 8555
fax 510 893 8572
email: info@lonelyplanet.com

UK
10a Spring Place, London NW5 3BH
☎ 020 7428 4800 fax 020 7428 4828
email: go@lonelyplanet.co.uk

France
1 rue du Dahomey, 75011 Paris
☎ 01 55 25 33 00 fax 01 55 25 33 01
email: bip@lonelyplanet.fr
www.lonelyplanet.fr

World Wide Web: www.lonelyplanet.com *or* AOL keyword: lp
Lonely Planet Images: lpi@lonelyplanet.com.au

Facts about Madrid

HISTORY

Measured by the standards of its neighbours, Madrid is something of a parvenue at the table of European capital cities. It has none of the noble legacy of cities, such as London and Paris, founded by the mighty Rome. And even when it was finally selected from rural obscurity to become capital in the second half of the 16th century, it was less significant in imperial Spain than Bonn in postwar Germany. Still, that all soon changed, as we shall see.

The Origins

To imagine the kind of human settlement there might have been in what is now Madrid, wander down to the Río Manzanares. Archaeologists have found abundant material around the river that demonstrates a human presence, probably nomadic, as far back as Palaeolithic times. Neolithic tribesmen brought their flocks to drink at the river and graze but it is uncertain whether they established any permanent settlements here.

Many voices have been raised to affirm the theory that the Romans established a town called Mantua Carpetana here, but proof is non-existent (although isolated villas dating from Roman times were scattered about the countryside). Such claims grew wholly out of a desire on the part of imperial hagiographers to assign the city what they considered a more 'fitting' origin than that accepted by historians today – that of Islamic garrison.

Meanwhile, Across Spain...

Whatever the occasional nomadic group of pastoralists or farmers may have been up to around the Manzanares, events of great moment dot the history of the Iberian Peninsula. Ancient Phoenicians, Greeks and Carthaginians established coastal trading enclaves, while in the interior roamed Celtiberian tribes. The Romans made a concerted effort to bring the peninsula under their control and founded cities such as Toletum (Toledo) and Complutum (near present Alcalá de Henares), but nothing on the site of Madrid.

As the weakening imperial hand relaxed its grip on what it had come to call Hispania, Visigothic hordes marched in during the 5th century AD to fill the vacuum, inheriting the towns, infrastructure and administration left behind by the Romans. But the Visigoths were too small in number and too divided among themselves to resist the next wave of invasion, that of the divinely inspired Muslim armies – part Berber, part Arab – that swept ashore at Gibraltar under the command of Tariq ibn Ziyad in 711. As had been the case before in the Middle East and North Africa, the Islamic blitzkrieg rolled out with apparent unstoppable force. The invaders were only brought to a halt at Poitiers, in France, in 732.

In 756 the emirate of Córdoba was established in the south of what the Muslims called Al-Andalus, which covered most of the peninsula until the beginning of the 9th century.

Muslim Frontier Town

The 15th-century Arab historian Ibn Khaldun traced the foundation of Madrid to the 9th century. Convention has it that Muhammad I, emir (prince) of Córdoba, established a fortress here in 854. Magerit or Mayrit, as it came to be known, was one of a string of such forts across the so-called Middle March, a frontier land between the core of Al-Andalus in the south and the small Christian kingdoms north of rivers Ebro and Duero. Middle March's capital was Toledo.

The forts were originally built as part of a defensive line against Christian incursion, but medieval Spain was a complex animal. Most of the people living in the Middle March were *muladíes* (or *muwallads*), locals converted to Islam. All that separated them from their Christian neighbours to the north was religion, and it seems local rulers

Introduction

'Throughout the 19th century, Madrid was a dark and dirty city with narrow, unhealthy streets and mean little houses, without any services or police; a city that amounted to nothing in the world.' So wrote one caustic observer of the capital of Spain.

A Johnny-come-lately in the community of European capitals, Madrid was little more than a squalid, petty-minded town when Felipe II chose to make his imperial capital here in 1561. It grew in uneven and unplanned leaps, attracting aristocrats, layabouts, artists, writers, beggars and swindlers from all over the country. The rapid decline of the empire from the time of Felipe's death, and centuries of stagnation and poverty, left Madrid in a parlous state. Bereft of a navigable river, decent road communications or the slightest hint of entrepreneurial spirit, Madrid seemed no more than a large grubby leech, bleeding the surrounding provinces and creating little.

Seen from the air today, this city of 3.1 million inhabitants appears to rise out of nothing upon an unforgiving dry plateau around 700m above sea level. Ugly dormitory suburbs spread inexorably away from the city, swallowing up villages in their stultifying sameness.

Not an auspicious introduction, one might say. Yet how different is the Madrid of 2000 from the depressed Villa of centuries gone by? True, it lacks the historical richness and sophistication of Rome or Paris and, moving closer to home, the physical beauty of Barcelona, but it oozes a life and character that, given the opportunity to work its magic (it doesn't take long), cannot leave you indifferent.

And Madrid is not without charm: the compact old city, with its dignified Habsburg mansions and squares, and narrow winding streets; the splendid tree-lined boulevards; the grand Palacio Real and elegant Parque del Buen Retiro; the wonderful art galleries (among them the Prado). All

this cannot fail to capture the imagination of the newcomer.

But the essence of Madrid is in the life pulsing through its streets. In no other European capital will you find the city centre so thronged so late into the night as here. Living the Madrid 'experience' is to explore its restaurants and eateries, prop up its countless bars, and be swept up in the nocturnal madness of its music scene and clubs.

The longer you stay, the more you become hooked. Madrid has always been a city of immigrants and transients. Until the past few decades they were mostly from other parts of Spain, but the result is an unusually open and accessible city. You may or may not make lasting friendships here, but it probably won't take long to find new drinking pals! Everyone seems to stay out late, as though some unwritten law forbade sleeping before dawn. In this sense it is a city more to be lived in than seen.

This can work out fine, as Madrid makes an ideal base for day trips. Toledo, Segovia, El Escorial, Ávila, Aranjuez, the Sierra de Guadarrama and even Córdoba are all within easy striking distance and make up for the capital's paucity of grand monuments.

The city has had a long way to come and is making giants' strides. In the coming years a high-speed AVE train will connect it with Barcelona and ultimately France. Ambitious programs to renew the central city *barrios* (districts) are converting what were once miserable slums into prime real estate. The metro system is being expanded at a rate that would leave the London Underground's bosses gasping for breath. Madrid is humming. Not all the locals (or expat residents) are completely happy. With growing frequency you'll hear it said that Madrid is becoming more like 'any other European city', more harried and less friendly. There may be truth in this, but the *gatos* (locals) of Madrid can rest assured that their town remains as refreshingly unlike Paris, London or Rome as ever.

HOW TO USE A LONELY PLANET GUIDEBOOK

The best way to use a Lonely Planet guidebook is any way you choose. At Lonely Planet we believe the most memorable travel experiences are often those that are unexpected, and the finest discoveries are those you make yourself. Guidebooks are not intended to be used as if they provide a detailed set of infallible instructions!

Contents All Lonely Planet guidebooks follow roughly the same format. The Facts about the Destination chapter or section gives background information ranging from history to weather. Facts for the Visitor gives practical information on issues like visas and health. Getting There & Away gives a brief starting point for researching travel to and from the destination. Getting Around gives an overview of the transport options when you arrive.

The peculiar demands of each destination determine how subsequent chapters are broken up, but some things remain constant. We always start with background, then proceed to sights, places to stay, places to eat, entertainment, getting there and away, and getting around information – in that order.

Heading Hierarchy Lonely Planet headings are used in a strict hierarchical structure that can be visualised as a set of Russian dolls. Each heading (and its following text) is encompassed by any preceding heading that is higher on the hierarchical ladder.

Entry Points We do not assume guidebooks will be read from beginning to end, but that people will dip into them. The traditional entry points are the list of contents and the index. In addition, however, some books have a complete list of maps and an index map illustrating map coverage.

There may also be a colour map that shows highlights. These highlights are dealt with in greater detail in the Facts for the Visitor chapter, along with planning questions and suggested itineraries. Each chapter covering a geographical region usually begins with a locator map and another list of highlights. Once you find something of interest in a list of highlights, turn to the index.

Maps Maps play a crucial role in Lonely Planet guidebooks and include a huge amount of information. A legend is printed on the back page. We seek to have complete consistency between maps and text, and to have every important place in the text captured on a map. Map key numbers usually start in the top left corner.

Although inclusion in a guidebook usually implies a recommendation we cannot list every good place. Exclusion does not necessarily imply criticism. In fact there are a number of reasons why we might exclude a place – sometimes it is simply inappropriate to encourage an influx of travellers.

Research Authors aim to gather sufficient practical information to enable travellers to make informed choices and to make the mechanics of a journey run smoothly. They also research historical and cultural background to help enrich the travel experience and allow travellers to understand and respond appropriately to cultural and environmental issues.

Authors don't stay in every hotel because that would mean spending a couple of months in each medium-sized city and, no, they don't eat at every restaurant because that would mean stretching belts beyond capacity. They do visit hotels and restaurants to check standards and prices, but feedback based on readers' direct experiences can be very helpful.

Many of our authors work undercover, others aren't so secretive. None of them accept freebies in exchange for positive write-ups. And none of our guidebooks contain any advertising.

Production Authors submit their raw manuscripts and maps to offices in Australia, USA, UK or France. Editors and cartographers – all experienced travellers themselves – then begin the process of assembling the pieces. When the book finally hits the shops some things are already out of date, we start getting feedback from readers, and the process begins again …

WARNING & REQUEST

Things change – prices go up, schedules change, good places go bad and bad places go bankrupt – nothing stays the same. So, if you find things better or worse, recently opened or long since closed, please tell us and help make the next edition even more accurate and useful. We genuinely value all the feedback we receive. Julie Young coordinates a well-travelled team that reads and acknowledges every letter, postcard and email and ensures that every morsel of information finds its way to the appropriate authors, editors and cartographers for verification.

Everyone who writes to us will find their name in the next edition of the appropriate guidebook. They will also receive the latest issue of *Planet Talk*, our quarterly printed newsletter, or *Comet*, our monthly email newsletter. Subscriptions to both newsletters are free. The very best contributions will be rewarded with a free guidebook.

Excerpts from your correspondence may appear in new editions of Lonely Planet guidebooks, the Lonely Planet Web site, *Planet Talk* or *Comet*, so please let us know if you *don't* want your letter published or your name acknowledged.

Send all correspondence to the Lonely Planet office closest to you:

Australia: Locked Bag 1, Footscray, Victoria 3011
UK: 10A Spring Place, London NW5 3BH
USA: 150 Linden St, Oakland CA 94607
France: 1 rue du Dahomey, Paris 75011

Or email us at: talk2us@lonelyplanet.com.au

For news, views and updates see our Web site: www.lonelyplanet.com

Foreword

ABOUT LONELY PLANET GUIDEBOOKS

The story begins with a classic travel adventure: Tony and Maureen Wheeler's 1972 journey across Europe and Asia to Australia. Useful information about the overland trail did not exist at that time, so Tony and Maureen published the first Lonely Planet guidebook to meet a growing need.

From a kitchen table, then from a tiny office in Melbourne (Australia), Lonely Planet has become the largest independent travel publisher in the world, an international company with offices in Melbourne, Oakland (USA), London (UK) and Paris (France).

Today Lonely Planet guidebooks cover the globe. There is an ever-growing list of books and there's information in a variety of forms and media. Some things haven't changed. The main aim is still to help make it possible for adventurous travellers to get out there – to explore and better understand the world.

At Lonely Planet we believe travellers can make a positive contribution to the countries they visit – if they respect their host communities and spend their money wisely. Since 1986 a percentage of the income from each book has been donated to aid projects and human rights campaigns.

Updates Lonely Planet thoroughly updates each guidebook as often as possible. This usually means there are around two years between editions, although for more unusual or more stable destinations the gap can be longer. Check the imprint page (following the colour map at the beginning of the book) for publication dates.

Between editions up-to-date information is available in two free newsletters – the paper *Planet Talk* and email *Comet* (to subscribe, contact any Lonely Planet office) – and on our Web site at www.lonelyplanet.com. The *Upgrades* section of the Web site covers a number of important and volatile destinations and is regularly updated by Lonely Planet authors. *Scoop* covers news and current affairs relevant to travellers. And, lastly, the *Thorn Tree* bulletin board and *Postcards* section of the site carry unverified, but fascinating, reports from travellers.

Correspondence The process of creating new editions begins with the letters, postcards and emails received from travellers. This correspondence often includes suggestions, criticisms and comments about the current editions. Interesting excerpts are immediately passed on via newsletters and the Web site, and everything goes to our authors to be verified when they're researching on the road. We're keen to get more feedback from organisations or individuals who represent communities visited by travellers.

> Lonely Planet gathers information for everyone who's curious about the planet – and especially for those who explore it first-hand. Through guidebooks, phrasebooks, activity guides, maps, literature, newsletters, image library, TV series and Web site we act as an information exchange for a worldwide community of travellers.

This Book

This 1st edition of *Madrid* was researched and written by Damien Simonis, expanding his material from the relevant chapter of Lonely Planet's *Spain* guide.

From the Publisher

This edition of Madrid was produced in Lonely Planet's London office. Sam Trafford coordinated the editing and proofing, with invaluable assistance from Claire Hornshaw, Amanda Canning, Claudia Martin and Christine Stroyan. Ed Pickard coordinated the mapping and design, and produced the colour pages, assisted by David Wenk, Angie Watts and Jimi Ellis. Adam McCrow designed the cover, Jim Miller produced the back-cover map, Sara Yorke produced the climate charts and Claudia helped with the index. The illustrations were drawn by Jane Smith, Mick Weldon, Rachel Imeson, Ann Jeffree, Jenny Jones and Helen Rowley, and the photographs were provided by Lonely Planet Images. Quentin Frayne used his expertise to give the Language chapter a final polish, and Imogen Franks chipped in with some extra research. Big thanks to Tim Ryder for his wise words and encouragement. Thanks also to Damien for turning round proof corrections in record time whilst on the road.

The Author

Damien Simonis

With a degree in languages and several years' reporting and sub-editing on Australian newspapers (including *The Australian* and *The Age*), Sydney-born Damien left the country in 1989. He has since lived, worked and travelled extensively throughout Europe, the Middle East and North Africa. Since 1992, Lonely Planet has kept him busy in *Jordan & Syria*, *Egypt & the Sudan*, *Morocco*, *North Africa*, *Italy*, *Spain*, *The Canary Islands*, *Barcelona*, *Venice*, *Florence* and *Tuscany*. As this book was heading for the bookstores he was busy updating other books on Spain and preparing a new guide to *Catalunya*. He has also written and snapped for other publications in Australia, the UK and North America. When not on the road, Damien resides in splendid Stoke Newington, deep in the heart of north London.

FROM THE AUTHOR

David Ing was foolish enough to roll out the welcome mat on several occasions during my stays in Madrid. Debby, Gary and Alex Luhrman would have done the same, but I finally got my act together!

As usual, a gaggle of friends and acquaintances in Madrid made my time not only productive, but also fun (well, as much as a busy work schedule allowed!). They include: Luis Aguilar-Pryde & Gabriela Contela, Javier Montero, Jean-Marc Simon, Luis Soldevila, Pablo García Tobin, Roberto Fortea, Eril Wiehahn, Nick McCafferty (he of the lists – keep up the good work!) and Dave Ross.

Thanks to Manuel Zafra and Jorge Pérez, in whose home I spent a month researching and writing.

Friends and colleagues David Peevers and Andrea Schulte-Peevers came to town for a few days to assist in bar research. I am still recovering. I also owe a lot to John Noble, comrade-in-arms on the Spanish front, who generously pooled information with me, especially the Córdoba section.

Thanks to Lonely Planet's Jen Loy (US), Leonie Mugavin (Australia) and Didier Buroc (France) for help with airfare information. Thanks also to the London office for their patience during some trying moments early on in the project.

Right: Gaudy posters advertise forthcoming bullfights.

JULIET COOMBE

DAMIEN SIMONIS

DAMIEN SIMONIS

Top: If you want to see a bullfight, Madrid's the place to do it – the Las Ventas bullring is the biggest in the world.

Bottom Left: Horseback-mounted *picadors* try to weaken and anger the bull by stabbing it with a lance.

Bottom Right: The extravagantly dressed *matador* executes his moves.

Then come the horseback-mounted *picadores*. Charged by the bull, which tries to eviscerate the horse, the picador shoves his lance into the withers of the bull – an activity that weakens and angers the bull. Animal-lovers may take some small consolation from the fact that since the 19th century the horses at least have been protected by heavy padding.

The peones then return to the scene to measure their courage against the (hopefully) charging bull. The picador is shortly followed by the *banderilleros*. At a given moment during the fight, one or two banderilleros will race towards the bull and attempt to plunge a pair of colourfully decorated *banderillas* (short prods with harpoon-style ends) into the bull, again aiming for the withers. This has the effect of spurring the animal into action – the matador will then seek to use this to execute more fancy manoeuvres.

Then there is the matador himself. His dress could be that of a fla-menco dancer. At its simplest, in country fiestas, it is generally a straightforward combination of black trousers or tights, white shirt and black vest. At its most extravagant, the *traje de luces* (suit of lights) can be an extraordinary display of bright, spangly colour – the name is apt.

All the toreros, with the occasional exception of the matadors, wear the black *montera* (the Mickey Mouse ears hat). The torero's standard weapons are the *estoque* or *espada* (sword) and the heavy silk and percale *capa* (cape). You will notice, however, that the matador, and the matador alone, employs a different cape with the sword – a

Right: The picador goads and weakens the bull by shoving a lance into its withers.

MICK WELDON

smaller piece of cloth held with a bar of wood called the *muleta* and used for a number of different passes.

La Corrida

To summarise all that takes place on the day of a corrida is no easy task. In many cases, corridas are held over several days, or even weeks, and the whole fiesta is known as the *feria*. The bulls are transported from their farms to a location near the ring, often days in advance. In Madrid, they are kept at an Andalucian-style ranch in the Casa de Campo known as Batán.

In some towns, the bulls are brought to another point in town from where they are let loose on the morning of the corrida to charge to the ring. The *encierro*, as it is known, in Pamplona was made famous by Ernest Hemingway, but scores of towns across the country celebrate it. Barriers are set up along a route to the ring, and some people feel inclined to run with the bulls. It's a dangerous business and people get hurt, sometimes mortally.

When the bulls arrive, the cuadrillas, president and breeders get together to look over the animals and draw lots to see who is going to fight which one. It depends a little on how many breeders are represented, how many matadors and teams there are and so on. The selected bulls are later huddled into darkened corrals, where they await their moment.

The bullfight generally begins at 6 pm, hence the title of Hemingway's manual on the subject, *Death in the Afternoon*. As a rule, six bulls and three matadors are on the day's card. If any bulls are considered not up to scratch, they are booed off (at this point the president will display a green handkerchief) and replacements brought on. Each fight takes about 10 to 15 minutes.

When the fateful moment comes, the corral is opened, light gushes in and the bull charges out, sensing a chance to escape. You wonder if it feels disappointment as it barrels out into the ring to be confronted by the peones, darting about and flashing their rose-and-yellow-coloured capes at the heaving beast. The matador then appears and executes his *faenas* (moves) with the bull. To go into the complexities of what constitutes a fine faena would require a book.

Suffice to say, the more closely and calmly the torero works with the bull, pivoting and dancing before the bull's horns, the greater will be the crowd's approbation. After a little of this, the matador strides off and leaves the stage first to the picadores, then the banderilleros, before returning for another session. At various moments during the fight, the brass band will hit some stirring notes, adding to the air of grand spectacle. The moves must be carried out in certain parts of the ring, which is divided into three parts: the *medios* (centre), *tercios* (an intermediate, chalked-off ring) and *tablas* (the outer ring).

When the bull seems tired out and unlikely to give a lot more, the matador chooses his moment for the kill. Placing himself head-on, he aims to sink the sword cleanly into the animal's neck *(estocada)* for an instant kill. It's easier said than done.

A good performance followed by a clean kill will have the crowd on its feet waving handkerchiefs in the air in clear appeal to the president to award the matador an *oreja* (ear) of the animal. The president usually waits to assess the crowd's enthusiasm before flopping a white handkerchief onto his balcony. If the fight was exceptional, the matador might *cortar dos orejas* – cut two ears off. On rare occasions the matador may be awarded the tail as well. What he does with them when he gets home is anyone's guess.

The sad carcass is meanwhile dragged out by a team of dray-horses and the sand raked about in preparation for the next toro. The meat ends up in the butcher shop.

When & Where

Bullfights are mainly a spring and summer activity, but it is occasionally possible to see them at other times. The season begins more or less officially in the first week of February with the fiestas of Valdemorillo and Ajalvir, near Madrid, to mark the feast day of San Blas. Virtually all encierros and corridas are organised as part of one town or another's fiesta.

Throughout the Comunidad de Madrid there are any number of local fiestas and the encierros can be a wild and unpredictable affair. In addition to the top corridas, which attract 'name' matadors and big crowds, there are plenty of lesser ones in other cities, towns and villages. These are often *novilleras*, in which immature bulls *(novillos)* are fought by junior matadors *(novilleros)*. In small places the Plaza Mayor may serve as a makeshift bullring. Often the small-town fights are amateurish affairs known as *capeas*.

The most prestigious feria in the world is that held in Madrid over four weeks from mid-May as part of the Fiesta de San Isidro (see Public Holidays & Special Events in the Facts for the Visitor chapter).

Right: Bred for conflict, the toro bravo, or fighting bull, is treated like a king until the final, fatal day.

MICK WELDON

The Matadors

If you are spoiling for a fight, look out for the big names. They are no
guarantee you'll see a high-quality corrida, as that depends in no small
measure on the animals themselves, but it is a good sign. The last true
star of the fiesta, Luis Miguel Dominguín, a hero of the 1940s and 50s,
died in 1996. Another maestro was Rafael Ortega (1921–97). Their
present-day successors count among their number some fine performers, but perhaps none of the past stars' stature.

Names to look for include: Jesulín de Ubrique, a true macho whose
attitudes to women don't go down well with everyone; Enrique Ponce,
a serious class act; Joselito (José Miguel Arroyo); Rivera Ordóñez;
Julián 'El Juli' López, a recently arrived teenage sensation; Curro
Romero, born in the 1920s and still fighting; José Tomás; and El Cordobés (Manuel Díaz), one of the biggest names, although for some his
style borders on mocking the animal and is considered unnecessarily
cruel. He is not the only one to go by the name El Cordobés. One of
the older hands to use it is Manuel Benítez. At 63 years of age, he
decided to get back into the ring again in 2000 for the fun of it!

Ethics of the Fight

Is the bullfight 'right'? Passions are frequently inflamed by the subject.
Many people feel ill at the sight of the kill, although this is a merciful
relief and surely no worse than being lined up for the production-line
kill in an abattoir. The preceding 10 or so minutes' torture are cruel.
The animal is frightened and in pain. Let there be no doubt about that.
Aficionados will say, however, that these bulls have been bred for conflict and that their lives before this fateful day are better by far than
those of any other farm animals. Toros bravos are treated like kings.
To other Western cultures – and to many Spaniards too – the bullfight
is 'uncivilised'. Yet there is something about this direct confrontation
with death that invites reflection. As an integral part of Spanish culture,
it deserves to be experienced; there is nothing to say that anyone
should also *like* it.

See Treatment of Animals under Society & Conduct in the Facts
About Madrid chapter for details of organisations that campaign
against bullfighting.

Beyond Spain

La lidia is not merely a Spanish preoccupation. It is a regular, if lower-
profile, part of the calendar of events in southern France and Portugal. The Portuguese specialise in horseback toreros, known in Spanish
as *rejoneadores. Corridas de rejones*, still occasionally seen in Spain,
once served as a kind of cavalry training. The big difference is that in
Portugal it is illegal to kill the bull. That said, in some towns, especially those close to the Spanish frontier, the Portuguese stage corridas *a
la española* regardless.

The bullfight has a big following in Latin America, particularly in Mexico, although Spaniards consider the quality there to be inferior.

Seeing Corridas in Madrid

In spite of the Hemingway-inspired fame of the Pamplona fiesta, connoisseurs would rather get a front seat in Madrid's huge *Plaza de Toros Monumental de Las Ventas* (Map 2; ☎ *91 356 22 00, metro: Ventas*), Calle de Alcalá 237, for a good fight. The ring is the biggest in the bullfighting world. The best fiesta begins in mid-May, marking the holiday for Madrid's patron saint, San Isidro Labrador (see also Public Holidays & Special Events in the Facts for the Visitor chapter), and lasts well into June. It is the most important bullfight season in the world, making or breaking toreros and bull breeders alike. Otherwise, corridas are organised regularly on weekends over the summer. For more information on the season at Las Ventas, and lots of background material too, you can visit the Las Ventas Web page at www.las-ventas.com.

You can also see corridas at the Vista Alegre bullring (which was completely renovated in 2000), near the metro station of the same name.

Tickets *(entradas)* start at 525 ptas for standing room in the sun *(sol)* and a long way from the action. They can rise to about 17,000 ptas for front-row seats in the shade *(sombra)*. Cheaper seats in the shade can come in at anything from 3000 to 7000 ptas, depending on where the seat is in the ring.

You can purchase tickets at the rings, from the ticket offices on Calle de la Victoria (Map 8) or other places selling theatre tickets and the like (see the Entertainment chapter). Note that the ticket offices add 20%. It is wise to buy tickets in advance, although you may be able to get basic seating in the sun on the day. Touts also operate outside the rings and ticket offices. During the San Isidro feria booking is mandatory. Ringside seats in the shade have been known

Right: Love it or hate it, the bullfight's confrontation with death, bravery and performance makes it eternally popular in Spain.

to go for as much as 2000,000 ptas!

Bullfighting magazines such as the weekly *6 Toros 6* carry full details of who's fighting, where and when. When fights are coming up locally, gaudy posters advertise the fact and give ticket information.

If you're interested in knowing more about bullfighting, a good place to start is the Web site Toros Links (www.sol.com/list/toros.htm).

Getting There & Away

Madrid is Spain's biggest international transport hub. It's easy to reach by air from anywhere in Europe and North America. The city is also linked to its European neighbours and Morocco by train and bus, although in general these overland options are more arduous and often no cheaper than flying. From Madrid, railway lines and highways radiate out across the country.

AIR

A number of airlines fly direct to Madrid from the rest of Europe. It pays to shop around for flight deals and, for short stays, it is sometimes more convenient to book a flight-and-hotel package. From North America, the cheaper flights may entail a stopover en route (in another European centre). Travellers coming from more distant locales, such as Asia and Australasia, have fewer choices.

Madrid is not one of the world's great discount ticket centres, although for short hops to the main European capitals you can occasionally dig up cheap deals. See also Travel Agencies in the Facts for the Visitor chapter.

Increasingly travellers are turning to the Internet to look for flight deals and book tickets. Most airlines and many travel agencies now operate interactive Web sites allowing you to do this.

For more detailed information on airport facilities, see Barajas Airport in the Getting Around chapter.

Travellers with Special Needs

If you have a broken leg, are a vegetarian or require a special diet (such as kosher food), are travelling in a wheelchair or have some other special need, let the airline know so they can make arrangements. You should call to remind them of your requirements at least 72 hours before departure and remind them again when you check in at the airport. It may also be worth ringing round the airlines before you make your booking to find out how they can handle your particular needs. Some airlines publish brochures on the subject. Ask your travel agency for details.

Guide dogs for the blind will often have to travel in a specially pressurised baggage compartment and are subject to quarantine laws (six months in isolation and so on) when entering, or returning to, countries currently free of rabies such as the UK and Australia. Quarantine laws in Britain have recently changed; check the current situation with the Ministry of Agriculture, Fisheries and Food on ☎ 0645 335577 or have a look at the Web site at www.maff.gov.uk /animalh/quarantine/index.htm.

Deaf travellers can ask for airport and inflight announcements to be written down for them.

Children aged under two travel for 10% of the standard fare (or free on some airlines), as long as they don't occupy a seat. They don't get a baggage allowance. Skycots, baby food and nappies (diapers) should be provided by the airline if requested in advance. Children aged between two and 12 can usually occupy a seat for half to two-thirds of the full fare and do get a baggage allowance. Pushchairs (strollers) can often be carried as hand luggage.

Departure Tax

Airport taxes are built into the final price of the ticket, although you may see fares quoted without the taxes. At the time of writing, taxes ranged from 3200 ptas for most European destinations to 10,700 ptas for the USA.

Other Parts of Spain

Flying within Spain is generally not an economical affair. Iberia (☎ 902 40 05 00) and the small subsidiaries Iberia Regional-Air Nostrum and Binter Mediterráneo cover all destinations and offer a range of fares. Ask about discounts and special rates. You get 25% off flights departing after 11 pm

Air Travel Glossary

Cancellation Penalties If you have to cancel or change a discounted ticket, there are often heavy penalties involved; insurance can sometimes be taken out against these penalties. Some airlines impose penalties on regular tickets as well, particularly against 'no-show' passengers.

Courier Fares Businesses often need to send urgent documents or freight securely and quickly. Courier companies hire people to accompany the package through customs and, in return, offer a discount ticket which is sometimes a phenomenal bargain. However, you may have to surrender all your baggage allowance and take only carry-on luggage.

Full Fares Airlines traditionally offer 1st-class (coded F), business-class (coded J) and economy-class (coded Y) tickets. These days there are so many promotional and discounted fares available that few passengers pay full economy fare.

Lost Tickets If you lose your airline ticket an airline will usually treat it like a travellers cheque and, after inquiries, issue you with another one. Legally, however, an airline is entitled to treat it like cash and if you lose it then it's gone for ever. Take good care of your tickets.

Onward Tickets An entry requirement for many countries is that you have a ticket out of the country. If you're unsure of your next move, the easiest solution is to buy the cheapest onward ticket to a neighbouring country or a ticket from a reliable airline that can later be refunded if you do not use it.

Open-Jaw Tickets These are return tickets with which you fly out to one place but return from another. If available, this can save you backtracking to your arrival point.

Overbooking Since every flight has some passengers who fail to show up, airlines often book more passengers than they have seats. Usually excess passengers make up for the no-shows, but occasionally somebody gets 'bumped' onto the next available flight. Guess who it is most likely to be? The passengers who check in late.

Promotional Fares These are officially discounted fares, available from travel agencies or direct from the airline.

Reconfirmation If you don't reconfirm your flight at least 72 hours prior to departure, the airline may delete your name from the passenger list. Ring to find out if your airline requires reconfirmation.

Restrictions Discounted tickets often have various restrictions on them – such as needing to be paid for in advance and incurring a penalty for alteration. Others are restrictions on the minimum and maximum period you must be away.

Round-the-World Tickets RTW tickets give you a limited period (usually a year) in which to circumnavigate the globe. You can go anywhere the carrying airlines go, as long as you don't backtrack. The number of stopovers or total number of separate flights is decided before you set off and tickets usually cost a bit more than a basic return flight.

Transferred Tickets Airline tickets cannot be transferred from one person to another. Travellers sometimes try to sell the return half of their ticket, but officials can ask you to prove that you are the person named on the ticket. On an international flight, tickets are compared with passports.

Travel Periods Ticket prices vary with the time of year. There is a low (off-peak) season and a high (peak) season, and often a low-shoulder season and a high-shoulder season as well. Usually the fare depends on your outward flight – if you depart in the high season and return in the low season, you pay the high-season fare.

Panoramic views – the Faro de Madrid

Avoid the queues and zip around by metro.

Watching the world go by in front of the Baroque colossus of the Palacio Real

Escape the hustle and bustle and relax on the lake at the Parque del Retiro.

A view through the fountain of the Centro Cultural de la Villa de Madrid at the Plaza de Colon

The beautiful colour of the Real Jardín Botánico

(admittedly there are few of these). People aged under 22 or over 63 get 25% off all return flights and a further 20% off night flights. A standard one-way fare between Madrid and Barcelona ranges from 12,150 ptas to 16,200 ptas.

Competing with Iberia are Spanair (☎ 902 13 14 15) and Air Europa (☎ 902 40 15 01). Air Europa is the bigger of the two, with regular flights between Madrid and Barcelona, Palma de Mallorca, Málaga and a host of other mainland Spanish destinations.

There are three to eight Air Europa flights daily between Madrid and Barcelona. The cheapest one-way economy *(turista)* fare is 10,400 ptas. The return fare ranges from 12,000 ptas to about 30,000 ptas. What you pay depends on when you fly and the conditions attached. The cheaper tickets are generally non-refundable and allow no changes.

Canary Islands From Madrid, Iberia, Air Europa, Spanair and charters all fly to Tenerife and Las Palmas (Gran Canaria). Tourist-class return flights between Santa Cruz de Tenerife and Madrid average around 28,000 ptas to 35,000 ptas, although return charter fares can be as low as 18,900 ptas.

The UK

Discount air travel is big business in London. Most British travel agencies are registered with ABTA (Association of British Travel Agents). If you have paid for your flight with an ABTA-registered agency which then goes bust, ABTA will guarantee a refund or an alternative. Unregistered travel agencies and bucket shops are riskier, but sometimes cheaper. Advertisements for tickets appear in the travel pages of the weekend broadsheets and – in London – in *Time Out*, the *Evening Standard* and the free magazine *TNT*. Travellers are also increasingly using the Internet to search for good fares.

One of the more reliable, but not necessarily cheapest, agencies is STA (☎ 020-7361 6161 for European flights). STA has

several offices in London, as well as branches on many university campuses and in cities such as Bristol, Cambridge, Leeds, Manchester and Oxford. You can check out its Web site at www.statravel.co.uk.

A similar agency is Trailfinders (☎ 020-7937 5400 for European flights). Its short-haul booking centre is at 215 Kensington High St, London W8, and there are also offices in Bristol, Birmingham, Glasgow, Manchester and Newcastle.

Usit Campus (☎ 0870 2401010), 52 Grosvenor Gardens, London SW1, is in much the same league and has several other branches in London and scattered around the country. You can visit their Web site at www.usitcampus.co.uk.

The two flag airlines linking the UK and Spain are British Airways (BA; ☎ 0845 7733377), 156 Regent St, London W1, and Spain's Iberia (☎ 0870 5341341), Venture House, 27–29 Glasshouse St, London W1. Their Web sites are www.british-airways.com and www.iberia.com respectively. Of the two, BA is more likely to have special deals that are lower than the standard scheduled fares (around UK£200 return in the high season).

Cheaper alternatives abound, however. Air Europa (☎ 0870 2401501) has a flight between London and Madrid daily except Saturday.

EasyJet (☎ 0870 6000000) offers tickets from London's Luton Airport to Madrid for as little as UK£49 each way, plus UK£10 tax. In slow periods (such as winter weekdays), prices one way have been known to drop as low as UK£19 plus tax! Once fares approach the UK£99 mark (one way) it is time to look elsewhere. You can book tickets at www.easyjet.com. In Spain, contact the company on ☎ 902 29 99 92.

Providing direct competition is the BA-owned Go (☎ 0845 6054321). Departures are from London Stansted Airport (a 40-minute train ride from Liverpool St train station). Go offers a variety of fares. If you comply with certain restrictions (easily done if you are planning to spend a week or more in Spain), you are looking at around UK£50 to UK£60 one way (plus taxes) to

Madrid. Go's number in Spain is ☎ 901 33 35 00. You can book through their Web site at www.go-fly.com.

Spanish Travel Services (☎ 020-7387 5337), 138 Eversholt St, London NW1, can get scheduled return flights with Iberia, BA, Air Europa and other airlines for as little as UK£90 in the low season and around UK£150 in the high season (including taxes).

The Charter Flight Centre (☎ 020-7565 6755), 15 Gillingham St, London SW1, has return flights, valid for up to four weeks in the low season, for around UK£130 (including taxes). Remember that, if you miss a charter flight, you lose your money.

Several times a year, usually around Easter and again in autumn (any time from September to November), various charter companies offer special four- or five-day long-weekend fares to Madrid and/or other Spanish destinations for silly prices: UK£49 return is not unheard of.

The budget airlines' fare structure makes it easy to plan open-jaw flights, with which you fly into one destination and leave from another. With other airlines it is also possible, if sometimes a little more complicated, to make such arrangements.

You needn't fly from London, as good deals are easily available from other centres in the UK.

Continental Europe

Short hops can be expensive, but for longer journeys you can often find air fares that beat overland alternatives on cost.

France Standard return flights from Paris to Madrid with Iberia frequently cost under 2000FF. Otherwise, charter and discount flights can come in as low as 1200FF.

From Madrid, low-season offers of around 23,000 ptas are possible, though generally you are looking at closer to 35,000 ptas. In spring 2000 Spanair launched a schedule of six flights daily between Madrid and Paris in conjunction with Lufthansa Airlines.

Regional Airlines (☎ 91 401 21 36) links Madrid (and Barcelona) with Bordeaux in

France, where you can connect with flights to other French destinations. The service is aimed mainly at business travellers. In France you can call them on ☎ 0803 005200. Air Littoral (☎ 0803 834834) operates flights from Nice to Madrid. Neither of these airlines is cheap.

STA Travel's outlet in France is Voyages Wasteels (☎ 08 03 88 70 02), 11 rue Dupuytren, Paris.

Germany In Berlin you could try STA Travel (☎ 030-311 09 50), Goethestrasse 73. STA also has offices in Frankfurt am Main – including at Bockenheimer Landstrasse 133 (☎ 069-70 30 35) – and in 16 other cities across the country. The Web site is www.statravel.de.

High-season return prices from Frankfurt to Madrid range from DM394 with LanChile to DM568 with Sabena and DM687 with Lufthansa Airlines. Taxes range from DM39 to DM53.50.

Italy The best place to look for cheap fares is CTS (Centro Turistico Studentesco), which has branches countrywide. In Rome there's an office at Via Genova 16 (☎ 06 4 67 91).

Virgin Express (☎ 800 097097) offers one flight a day from Rome to Madrid. Fares can range from L167,000 to L269,000 one way.

The Netherlands & Belgium Amsterdam is a popular departure point. The student travel agency NBBS (☎ 0900 235 6227), Rokin 66, offers reliable and reasonably low fares. Compare them with the pickings in the bucket shops along Rokin before deciding. NBBS has several branches throughout the city, as well as in Brussels, Belgium.

Brussels is the main hub for Virgin Express (☎ 02-752 05 05), which has up to seven flights a day between Brussels and Madrid. One-way fares can range from f3300 to f4700. The number in Madrid is ☎ 91 662 52 61.

Portugal In the low season it is possible to get return flights to Lisbon for around

27,000 ptas, including taxes. By the summer, they are more likely to be over 30,000 ptas. The train is a cheaper and fairly painless option.

The USA

Several airlines fly to Madrid (sometimes with a stopover), including Iberia, BA and KLM-Royal Dutch Airlines.

Standard fares can be expensive. Discount and rock-bottom options from the USA include charter flights, stand-by and courier flights.

Stand-by fares are often sold at 60% of the normal price for one-way tickets. Airhitch (☎ 800 3262009 toll free) is a specialist. You will need to give a general idea of where and when you need to go, and a few days before your departure you will be presented with a choice of two or three flights. A one-way flight from the USA to Europe costs from US$159 (east coast) to US$239 (west coast), plus taxes. Airhitch has several offices in the USA, including in New York and Los Angeles. In Europe Airhitch has a central office in France (☎ 01 47 00 16 30), at 5 rue de Crussol, 75001 Paris. Check out their Web site at www .airhitch.org. In summer they have a rep in Madrid on ☎ 91 366 79 27.

Courier flights involve you accompanying a parcel to its destination. A New York–Madrid return on a courier flight can cost under US$300 in the low season (more from the west coast). You may have to be a US resident and apply for an interview first. Most flights depart from New York.

Now Voyager (☎ 212-431 1616), Suite 307, 74 Varrick St, New York, is a courier-flight specialist. You pay an annual membership fee (around US$50), which entitles you to as many courier flights as you like. Check the Web site at www .nowvoyagertravel.com. The Denver-based Air Courier Association (☎ 303-278 8810) also does this kind of thing.

Regular fares fluctuate enormously. Iberia flies nonstop between Madrid and New York, but often you can get better deals with other airlines if you are prepared to fly via other European centres. As a

guide, at the time of writing BA was offering low-season (November–December) return flights to Madrid (via London) for US$499, while Iberia did direct high-season (June–August) flights for US$763. From the west coast you almost always pay a few hundred dollars more, although the occasional amazing deal does crop up. Typically, you are looking at US$650 return in the low season and US$1130 in the high season.

Air Europa (☎ 718-244 6017, 888 2EUR-OPA in the USA) offers direct flights from/to New York. Occasionally they come up with low fares.

One agency that can come up with good, cheap flights is Discount Tickets in New York (☎ 212-391 2313). Otherwise, reliable travel agencies include STA (☎ 800 777 0122) and Council Travel (☎ 800 226 8624). Their Web sites are www.statravel .com and www.counciltravel.com respectively, and both have offices in major cities. Discount travel agencies, known as consolidators, can be found in the weekly travel sections of the *New York Times*, *Los Angeles Times*, *Chicago Tribune* and *San Francisco Examiner*.

At the time of writing no one airline leaving from Madrid could claim to offer unbeatable value. Low-season returns can cost 55,000 ptas to the east coast. To the west coast, you are looking at more like 75,000 ptas. In the high season (15 June to 15 September), about the best you could hope for to the east coast is 85,000 ptas return.

If you can't find a good deal, consider getting an inexpensive transatlantic hop to London and prowling around the discount travel agencies there.

Canada

Scan the travel agencies' advertisements in the *Toronto Globe & Mail*, *Toronto Star* and *Vancouver Sun*. Travel CUTS (☎ 800 667 2887), called Voyages Campus in Quebec, has offices in all major cities in Canada; its Web site is www.travelcuts.com.

For courier flights originating in Canada, contact FB On-Board Courier Services (☎ 514-631 2077), in Toronto.

Iberia offers direct flights to Madrid from Montreal three times a week. Other major European airlines offer competitive fares to most Spanish destinations via other European capitals. Typical round-trip low-season fares hover around the C$620 mark. In the high season they can inflate to as much as C$1400. Round-trip flights from Vancouver cost around C$250 more than from Montreal in the low season, and around C$1000 in the high season.

Australia

STA Travel (☎ 1300 360960 toll free) and Flight Centre (☎ 13 1600 toll free) are major dealers in cheap air fares. Their Web sites are at www.statravel.com.au and www.flightcentre.com.au respectively. Heavily discounted fares can also be obtained through local travel agencies. The Saturday editions of the Melbourne *Age* and the *Sydney Morning Herald* contain advertisements offering cheap fares to Europe.

As a rule, there are no direct flights from Australia to Spain. You will have to fly to Europe via Asia, changing flights (and possibly airlines).

Low-season return fares to Madrid cost from around A$1370 to A$1590 on airlines such as Olympic Airways, Thai Airways International and Lauda Air.

On some flights between Australia and cities such as London, Paris and Frankfurt, a return ticket between that destination and another major European city (such as Madrid) is thrown in. In such flights cost around A$1790 to A$2300 in the low season.

For courier flights, try Jupiter (☎ 02-9317 2230), Unit 3, 55 Kent Rd, Mascot, Sydney 2020.

New Zealand

STA Travel (☎ 09-309 0458) and Flight Centre (☎ 09-309 6171) are popular agencies, with branches throughout the country. Their Web sites are www.statravel.com.au and www.flightcentre.com.au respectively. The *New Zealand Herald* has a travel section in which travel agencies advertise fares.

A round-the-world (RTW) ticket may be cheaper than a normal return. Otherwise,

you can fly from Auckland to pick up a connecting flight in Melbourne or Sydney. Low-season return fares start from around NZ$2015 with Thai Airways International and Air New Zealand.

Asia

Although most Asian countries offer competitive fare deals, Bangkok, Hong Kong and Singapore are still the best places to shop around for discount tickets. Standard return fares to Spain from Bangkok range from 33,000B to 43,700B (US$880 to US$1150). From Hong Kong expect to pay from HK$9800 to HK$10,500 (US$1260 to US$1350) for a return fare.

STA has branches in Bangkok, Hong Kong, Kuala Lumpur, Singapore and Tokyo.

Airline Offices in Madrid

Airlines are listed under Líneas Aéreas in the *Páginas Amarillas* (Yellow Pages). They include:

Aerolíneas Argentinas (Map 4; ☎ 91 590 20 60) Calle de María de Molina 40
Air France (Map 5; ☎ 91 330 04 12, bookings 901 11 22 66) Torre de Madrid, Plaza de España 18
American Airlines (Map 1; ☎ 91 453 14 00) Calle de Orense 4
British Airways (☎ 91 387 43 00, 902 11 13 33) Aeropuerto de Barajas
Iberia (Map 4; ☎ 91 587 75 36, bookings 902 40 05 00) Calle de Velázquez 130
KLM-Royal Dutch Airlines (Map 5; ☎ 91 305 43 47) Gran Vía 59
Lufthansa Airlines (Map 1; ☎ 902 22 01 01) Calle del Cardenal Marcelo Spinola 2
Regional Airlines (Map 2; ☎ 91 401 21 36) Calle del General Pardiñas 62
Sabena (Map 5; ☎ 91 540 18 51) Torre de Madrid, Plaza de España 18
Scandinavian Airlines (SAS) (Map 5; ☎ 91 454 66 00) Edificio de España, Gran Vía 86
Thai Airways International (Map 1; ☎ 91 782 05 21) Calle del Príncipe de Vergara 185
Virgin Express (Map 5; ☎ 91 541 14 94) Torre de Madrid, Plaza de España 18

BUS

The bus is generally cheaper than the train, but less comfortable for long journeys.

There are as many as eight bus stations dotted about Madrid, with companies servicing different parts of the country. The tourist offices can provide detailed information on where you need to go for your destination.

Eurolines is the main international carrier throughout Europe, often working in tandem with national companies such as, in the case of Spain, Enatcar and Alsa. The Web site at www.eurolines.com has links to all national Eurolines Web sites.

Other Parts of Spain

Buses serve all major cities and many minor locations from Madrid.

The Estación Sur de Autobuses (metro: Méndez Álvaro), on Calle de Méndez Álvaro, just south of the M-30 ring road, is the city's principal bus station. It serves most destinations to the south and many in other parts of the country. Most bus companies have a ticket office here, even if their buses depart from elsewhere. You can get information on ☎ 91 468 42 00.

The station is big and operates a *consigna* (left-luggage office), open from 6.30 am to midnight. It's down where the buses are parked (near the exit) and it costs a very strange 174 ptas per bag per 24 hours.

There are cafes, shops, exchange booths, a bank, a police post and direct access to the No 6 metro line and cercanías trains to Atocha and Chamartín train stations (see Public Transport in the Getting Around chapter).

Quite a few companies operate out of other terminals around the city. Of these, some useful ones include:

AutoRes (Map 2; ☎ 91 551 72 00, bookings 902 19 29 39; metro: Conde de Casal) Calle de Fernández Shaw 1. This company operates buses to Extremadura, western Castilla y León (eg Tordesillas, Salamanca and Zamora) and Valencia via eastern Castilla-La Mancha (eg Cuenca).

Continental-Auto (Map 1; ☎ 91 533 04 00, bookings 902 33 04 00; metro: Nuevos Ministerios or Cuatro Caminos) Calle de Alenza 20. This company runs buses north to Burgos, Logroño, Navarra, the País Vasco, Santander and Soria. It also runs buses to Toledo from the Estación Sur and to Alcalá de Henares and Guadalajara from the Intercambiador de Aven-

ida de América (Map 2; metro: Avenida de América or Cartagena), an underground bus station. Note that the station at Calle de Alenza is due to close some time in 2000. The bus routes operating from there will be transferred to the Intercambiador de Avenida de América.

Herranz (☎ 91 890 41 00) Buses to San Lorenzo de El Escorial leave from the Intercambiador de Autobuses, a bus station below ground level at the Moncloa metro station (Map 2). The buses leave from platform 3.

La Sepulvedana (Map 2; ☎ 91 530 48 00; metro: Príncipe Pío) Paseo de la Florida 11. This company operates buses to La Granja de San Ildefonso, Navacerrada and San Rafael (near Cercedilla). Buses for Talavera de la Reina also depart from here.

La Veloz (Map 2; ☎ 91 409 76 02; metro: Conde de Casal) Avenida del Mediterráneo 49. This company offers regular buses to Chinchón.

Some sample one-way fares (in some cases competing companies offer different prices – always check) include:

destination	duration	fare (ptas)
Alicante	5¼ hours	2995
Barcelona	7 or 8 hours	3400
Córdoba	4½ hours	1600
Granada	5 hours	1960
Málaga	6 hours	2625
Oviedo	4¾ hours	3825
San Sebastián	5¾ to 6½ hours	3800
Santiago de Compostela	9 hours	5135
Seville	6 hours	2745

The UK

Eurolines (☎ 0870 5143219), 52 Grosvenor Gardens, Victoria, London SW1 (the terminal is a couple of blocks away), runs buses to Madrid via San Sebastián on Monday and Friday at 9.30 pm, arriving 28 hours later. A third service runs on Saturdays from late June to mid-September. One-way/return fares are around UK£80/140 (UK£70/130 for those aged under 26 and seniors). The standard adult one-way fare going the other way is 15,900 ptas.

France

Eurolines has offices in several French cities, including Paris (☎ 01 49 72 51 51), in the bus station at 28 ave du Générale de Gaulle. It has another, more central office (☎ 01 43 54 11 99) at rue St Jacques 55, off blvd St Michel. UK passengers may have to change buses here. From Paris, you pay FF560 (FF470 for those aged under 26). The standard over-26 fare from Madrid is 12,900 ptas.

Portugal

The Alsa bus company (☎ 91 530 76 00 in Spain) runs buses to Madrid (Estación Sur de Autobuses) from Lisbon (5850 ptas one way, seven hours), Porto (5425 ptas, 8½ hours) and Faro (6500 ptas, 12¼ hours). AutoRes (see Other Parts of Spain earlier in this section) also runs buses between Madrid and Lisbon for around 5800 ptas.

Morocco

Eurolines buses run daily from Madrid to Tangier (8300 ptas; 15 hours) and cities beyond.

Other International Services

Eurolines also runs services at least three times a week to Amsterdam, Brussels, Florence, Geneva, Milan, Montpellier, Nice, Perpignan, Rome, Toulouse, Venice and Zürich.

TRAIN

Madrid is served by two main stations. The bigger of the two is Atocha (Map 9; metro: Atocha RENFE), at the southern end of the city centre. Trains from here fan out right across the country. Chamartín station (Map 1; metro: Chamartín) lies in the north of the city.

The majority of trains for the rest of Spain depart from Atocha, especially those going south. International services arrive at and leave from Chamartín. Several services for northern destinations depart from Chamartín. In some cases trains stop at both stations. Of the two, Atocha is handier for the centre of town, hotels and so on.

Eurail, InterRail, Europass and Flexipass train passes are valid on the national rail network, RENFE (Red Nacional de los Ferrocarriles Españoles), throughout Spain.

Information & Tickets

It's advisable to book at least a day or two ahead for most long-distance trains, domestic or international. The RENFE information and booking office (Map 5; ☎ 91 328 90 20), Calle de Alcalá 44, is open from 9.30 am to 8 pm Monday to Friday. Otherwise, for information on all RENFE train services call ☎ 902 24 02 02 from anywhere in the country.

Information and ticket offices in Atocha station are open from 8 am to 10 pm daily. You will find one for the Grandes Líneas, or long-distance (largo recorrido) services, in the old station (the part now serving as a tropical garden) and another near platforms 9 and 10 (look for the 'Atención al Cliente' sign). Tickets for regional trains can be bought at a separate counter.

The station has a consigna (left-luggage storage), open from 6.30 am to 10.20 pm (300/400/600 ptas for 24 hours, depending on the size of the locker). It's near platform 1, in the AVE and long-distance part of the station, where you'll also find a hotel-reservations office, currency-exchange booths, ATMs and car-rental reps.

At Chamartín station, the information and ticket sales offices (Centro de Viajes) are open from 8.30 am to 10.30 pm daily. They are located between platforms 7 and 10. Exchange booths and ATMs are scattered about the station. The telephone and fax office opposite platform 1 is open from 9.30 am to 10 pm Monday to Friday. You will also find a hotel-reservations desk. Lockers are located outside the main station building (take the exit opposite platform 18) and are available between 7.30 am and 11.30 pm. You pay 300/400/600 ptas per day, depending on the size of the locker.

Arrivals (llegadas) and departures (salidas) appear on big electronic boards and TV screens. In Chamartín station, full timetables are also posted. At Atocha, however, no comprehensive timetable is posted. Instead, you will see separate timetables for cercanías (local trains) and regional trains. For anything else, you need to ask at the information desks. Timetables for specific lines are generally available free of charge.

Other Parts of Spain

Types of Train A host of different train types coasts the wide-gauge lines of the Spanish network. A saving of a couple of hours on a faster train can mean a big hike in the fare.

For short hops, bigger cities have a local network known as *cercanías*. From Madrid, for instance, cercanías trains cover the entire Comunidad de Madrid region and some destinations beyond.

Most long-distance *(largo recorrido)* trains have 1st- and 2nd-class sections. The cheapest and slowest of these trains are the *regionales*, generally all-stops services between provinces within one region (although a few travel between regions). If your train is a *regional exprés* it will make fewer stops. The Tren Regional Diesel (TRD) is a new train that has been put into service to speed up regional travel in some areas.

All trains that do journeys of more than 400km are denominated Grandes Líneas services – really just a fancy way of saying long distance. Among these are *diurnos* and *estrellas*, the standard inter-regional trains. The latter is the night-time version of the former.

Faster, more comfortable and more expensive are the Talgos (Tren Articulado Ligero Goicoechea Oriol). They make few stops and have such extras as TVs in the carriages. The Talgo Pendular is a sleeker, faster version of the same thing; it picks up speed by leaning into curves.

Some Talgos and other modern trains are used for limited-stop trips between major cities. These services are known as InterCity (and, when they're really good, as InterCity Plus).

A classier derivative is the Talgo 200, a Talgo Pendular that uses the standard-gauge, high-speed Tren de Alta Velocidad Española (AVE) line between Madrid and Seville on part of the journey to such southern destinations as Málaga, Cádiz and Algeciras. The trip from Madrid to Cádiz takes five hours (and to Málaga a little less).

The most expensive way to go is to take the high-speed AVE train itself along the Madrid–Seville line (another line, between Madrid and Barcelona, which would link up with the French TGV, is planned).

Other new, fast services include the Alaris service between Madrid and Castelló (via Albacete and Valencia).

Waiting for a train isn't so bad in the tropical garden of Atocha old station.

Autoexpreso and Motoexpreso carriages are sometimes attached to long-distance services for the transport of cars and motorbikes respectively.

A *trenhotel* is an expensive sleeping-car train. There can be up to three classes on these trains, ranging from *turista* (for those sitting or in a couchette), *preferente* (sleeping car) and *gran clase* (sleeping in sheer luxury).

Fares Trains run from Madrid to most large Spanish cities. These trains offer a huge range of seat and sleeper accommodation (see the previous section); there are day and night trains and a mind-boggling array of fares.

The trip to Barcelona can take 6½ to 9½ hours; a basic 2nd-class fare for the longer trip is 5100 ptas one way. The Talgo (which is quickest) costs 6600 ptas. If you buy a return ticket, you get 20% off the return run (25% for a same-day return). The cheapest one-way fare to Seville from Madrid on the high speed AVE is 8200 ptas. Other examples of 2nd-class one-way travel in diurno and estrella trains from Madrid (remember that fares and travel times vary considerably depending on the kind of train you take) include:

destination	duration	fare (ptas)
Granada	6¼ to 8¾ hours	3600
León	4¼ to 5¼ hours	3400
Málaga	5 to 6¾ hours	5000
San Sebastián	6½ to 8¾ hours	4600
Valencia	5 to 5½ hours	3000
Zaragoza	3 to 3½ hours	3000

See also individual destinations in the Excursions chapter for information on getting out and about by train from Madrid.

The UK

You have various options for getting from London to Paris, where you must change trains.

Trains run from Charing Cross or Victoria stations to Paris (via ferry or hovercraft from Dover to Calais or Folkestone to Boulogne), or direct from Waterloo to Paris

(Eurostar). You arrive at the Gare du Nord, from where you must get to the Gare d'Austerlitz (take the RER B to St Michel and change there for the RER C to Austerlitz), Gare de Montparnasse (metro line 4) or Gare de Lyon (RER B to Châtelet, then RER A for Gare de Lyon). See the following section on France for details of trains from Paris.

One-way/return fares to Madrid are UK£100/170 (more if you take the Eurostar), and tickets are valid for two months. Those aged under 26 can get Wasteels or BIJ (Billet International de Jeunesse) tickets costing UK£80/140.

Children qualify for discounts and those aged over 60 can get a Rail Europe Senior card (valid for a year only for trips that cross at least one border). You pay UK£5 for the card, but you must already have a Senior Citizens Rail Card (UK£18), available to anyone who can prove they are aged over 60 (you are not required to be a UK resident). The pass entitles you to roughly 30% off standard fares.

For information on all international train travel (including Eurostar services), call European Rail (☎ 020-7387 0444) or go to the Wasteels office opposite platform 2 at Victoria station. You can also get information on Eurostar and train passes from the Rail Europe Travel Centre (☎ 0870 584 8848) at 179 Piccadilly, London W1V. There's a Web site, where you can make bookings, at www.raileurope.com. For Eurostar, you can also make inquiries and buy tickets at Waterloo station, from where the trains depart.

France

The only truly direct train to Madrid is the *trenhotel* sleeper-only service. It leaves Gare d'Austerlitz at 7.37 pm daily and arrives at 8.58 am (stopping at Poitiers, Vitoria, Burgos and Valladolid). The standard one-way fare in a couchette is 809FF. Going the other way, the trenhotel leaves Madrid Chamartín at 7 pm and arrives in Paris at 8.29 am. A bed costs upwards of 30,400 ptas, or you can get a couchette for 17,800 ptas.

Otherwise, the cheapest and most convenient option to Madrid is the 11.14 pm from Gare d'Austerlitz via Irún. A 2nd-class couchette costs 715FF one way. First-class couchettes cost considerably more – the difference is four people to a compartment rather than six. Those aged under 26 get a 25% reduction. Note also that fares rise in July and August.

There are several other possibilities. Two or three TGV trains daily leave Paris Montparnasse for Irún, where you change to a normal train for the onward trip to Madrid.

Other International Services

To get to most other international destinations from Spain you need to go to Barcelona first. Direct overnight trains from Estació Sants in Barcelona run to Milan (12¾ hours) and Zürich (13 hours), from three to seven times a week, depending on the season. These trains meet connections for numerous other cities. The cheapest beds from Milan cost L207,100, or it's L166,400 for a seat. You need to add on the cost of a train between Barcelona and Madrid.

A daily train runs between Madrid and Lisbon, in Portugal. It leaves Chamartín station at 10.45 pm and arrives at 8.40 am. Going the other way it leaves at 9.56 pm and arrives at 8.35 am. The one-way fare is 6585 ptas if you choose to sit. Otherwise, the cheapest couchette solution costs 9240 ptas.

CAR & MOTORCYCLE

To give you an idea of how many clicks you'll put behind you if travelling with your own wheels, Madrid is 2622km from Berlin, 2245km from London, 1889km from Milan, 1836km from Paris, 1470km from Geneva, 690km from Barcelona and 610km from Lisbon.

Coming from the UK, you can take your car across to France by ferry or the Channel Tunnel car train, Eurotunnel (☎ 0870 535 3535). The latter runs round the clock, with up to four crossings (35 minutes) an hour between Folkestone and Calais in the high season. You pay for the vehicle only and

Warning

The information in this chapter is particularly vulnerable to change: prices for international travel are volatile, routes are introduced and cancelled, schedules change, special deals come and go, and rules and visa requirements are amended. Airlines and governments seem to take a perverse pleasure in making price structures and regulations as complicated as possible. You should check directly with the airline or a travel agency to make sure you understand how a fare (and ticket you may buy) works. In addition, the travel industry is highly competitive and there are many lurks and perks.

The upshot of this is that you should get opinions, quotes and advice from as many airlines and travel agencies as possible before you part with your hard-earned cash. The details given in this chapter should be regarded as pointers and are not a substitute for your own careful, up-to-date research.

fares vary according to time of day and season. The cheapest economy fare (January to May) is around UK£200 return (valid for one year) and the most expensive (May to late September) around UK£290, if you depart during the day Friday to Sunday. Check out the Web site at www.eurotunnel.com.

An interesting Web site loaded with advice for people planning to drive in Europe is www.ideamerge.com/motoeuropa. If you want help with route planning, try out www.shell.com/euroshell.

Paperwork & Preparations

Vehicles must be roadworthy, registered and insured (third party at least). The Green Card, an internationally recognised proof of insurance obtainable from your insurer, is compulsory. Also ask your insurer for a European Accident Statement form, which can simplify matters in the event of an accident.

A European breakdown-assistance policy, such as the AA Five Star Service or the RAC Eurocover Motoring Assistance in the UK, is a good investment.

euro currency converter € 1 = 166 ptas

For information on driving licences, see Documents in the Facts for the Visitor chapter.

In the UK, further information can be obtained from the RAC (☎ 0870 5722722) or the AA (☎ 0870 5500600).

For details of driving conditions in Madrid and renting or purchase, see Car & Motorcycle in the Getting Around chapter.

Access Roads

Madrid is the centre point in Spain from which most of the country's major highways radiate out to the coast. The N-I heads north to Burgos and ultimately Santander (for the UK ferry), the N-II wends its way north-east to Barcelona and ultimately on into France (as the A-7). The N-IV takes you south to Andalucía, while the N-V and N-VI respectively take you west towards Portugal via Cáceres and north-west to Galicia. The N-402 goes south to Toledo.

The city is surrounded by two ring roads, the outermost M-40 and the inner M-30. Both these and the approach roads can become clogged on Sunday and holiday evenings as *madrileños* (natives of Madrid) stream back from vacations and weekend getaways.

Driving in Spain

Road Rules In general, standard European road rules apply. In built-up areas the speed limit is usually 50km/h, rising to 100km/h on major roads and 120km/h on *autopistas* and *autovías* (toll and toll-free motorways). Motorcyclists must use headlights at all times. Crash helmets are obligatory on bikes of 125cc or more. Vehicles already on roundabouts have right of way. The wearing of seatbelts is compulsory in the front seats.

The blood-alcohol limit is 0.05%. Fines for various traffic offences range from 50,000 to 100,000 ptas. Nonresident foreigners can be fined up to 50,000 ptas on the spot. Pleading linguistic ignorance will not help – your traffic cop will produce a list of infringements and fines in as many languages as you like.

Petrol Prices vary (by up to 4 ptas a litre) between service stations *(gasolineras)* and fluctuate with oil tariffs and tax policy. Super (due to be phased out in January 2002 in compliance with EU rules) costs 150 ptas/litre and diesel (or *gasóleo*) 114 ptas/litre. Lead-free (*sin plomo*; 95 octane) costs 140 ptas/litre and a 98 octane variant (also lead free) that goes by various names costs up to 154 ptas/litre.

Road Assistance The Real Automóvil Club de España's head office (RACE; Map 3; ☎ 900 20 00 93) is at Calle de José Abascal 10, in Madrid. For its 24-hour, countrywide emergency breakdown assistance you can try calling ☎ 91 593 33 33 in Madrid or ☎ 900 11 22 22 from elsewhere in Spain. As a rule, however, these numbers are for RACE members. Your own national motoring organisation, which like the RAC and AA may have a mutual agreement with the RACE, will generally provide you with a special emergency-assistance number for use when in Spain. If you plan on a long stay in Madrid, you may want to take out local insurance with the RACE; this is possible for foreign-registered cars.

BICYCLE

If you plan to bring your own bike, check with the airline about additional costs. The bike will have to be disassembled and packed for the journey.

UK-based cyclists planning to do some bike touring to destinations outside Madrid might want to contact the Cyclists' Touring Club (☎ 01483-417217), Cotterell House, 69 Meadrow, Godalming, Surrey GU7 3HS. It has a Web site at www.ctc.org.uk and can supply information to members on cycling conditions, itineraries and cheap insurance. Membership costs UK£25 per annum (UK£15 for those aged under 26).

HITCHING

Hitching is never entirely safe and we don't recommend it. Travellers who decide to hitch should understand that they are taking a small but potentially serious risk. If you do plan to hitch, to get out of Madrid you

GETTING THERE & AWAY

need to start well out of the city centre. The chances of anyone stopping for you on auto-pistas or autovías are low – try the smaller highways.

BOAT
Funnily enough, you can't get anywhere near Madrid by boat. If you are thinking of coming to Spain by sea and then making your way overland, you have several choices. Ferries from the UK, Italy, Morocco, Algeria, the Canary Islands and the Balearic Islands all converge on ports around the country. For more information, get hold of Lonely Planet's *Spain* guide.

ORGANISED TOURS
If you prefer to opt for a package trip to Madrid, perhaps including some day trips to some of the destinations beyond the capital suggested in the Excursions chapter, you'll find a host of tour operators willing to separate you from your money. You should first approach your nearest Spanish tourist office for a list of tour operators in your country. In the UK they list about 100 firms that offer trips to Madrid. You can do it all with comparatively little difficulty yourself, but a package can save you hassle – at a price.

The UK
Cresta Holidays (☎ 0161-927 7000), Tabley Court, Victoria St, Altrincham, Cheshire WA14 1EZ, offers a range of city tours, fly-drive trips and other holidays to Spain. An-other Spain specialist is The Individual Traveller's Spain (☎ 01798-869485), Manor Court Yard, Bignor, Pulborough RH20 1QD. City Escapades (☎ 020-8563 8959, fax 8748 3731), 227 Shepherd's Bush Rd, London W6 7AS, offers long-weekend breaks.

Kirker Travel Ltd (☎ 020-7231 3333, fax 7231 4771), 3 New Concordia Wharf, Mill St, London SE1 2BB, offers a range of more expensive quality city breaks.

Mundi Color Travel (☎ 020-7828 6021), 276 Vauxhall Bridge Rd, London SW1V 1BE, has a one-week coach tour taking in Madrid and parts of Castile as well. The all-in price hovers around UK£800, including flights, tour, accommodation and half-board, but rises in the high season.

The USA
In the USA, Spanish Heritage Tours (☎ 800 2212250), 47 Queens Blvd, Forest Hills, NY 11375, is a reliable operator offering a range of tours. Saranjan Tours (☎ 800 858 9594), PO Box 292, Kirkland, WA 98033, does city-break packages.

Australia
You can organise tours of Spain, taking in Madrid, through Ibertours Travel (☎ 03-9670 8388), 1st Floor, 84 William St, Melbourne 3000, Victoria (www.ibertours.com .au), and Spanish Tourism Promotions (☎ 03-9650 7377, ✉ sales@spanishtravels .com.au), Level 1, 178 Collins St, Melbourne 3000, Victoria.

GETTING THERE & AWAY

Getting Around

BARAJAS AIRPORT

Scheuled and charter flights from all over the world arrive at Madrid's Aeropuerto de Barajas (☎ 91 393 60 00, flight information 902 35 35 70), 13km north-east of the city. You can also get flight information for all Spanish airports at www.aena.es. The site is in Spanish only.

Rapidly increasing air traffic at Barajas has caused no end of headaches for local authorities, who are now rushing headlong into a process of expansion. A third runway went into operation in the late 1990s. A new terminal and additional runways are in the pipeline (see the boxed text 'A New Gateway' later in this chapter). The old terminal buildings meanwhile have been revamped – and work remains to be done, so the information that follows is subject to change.

The main airport complex contains three terminals: T1, T2 and T3. The first deals mainly with intercontinental and some European flights. T2 handles predominantly domestic flights and Schengen-area (see Visas under Documents in the Facts for the Visitor chapter) flights with Spanish airlines. T3 is dedicated to Iberia's Puente Aereo (air shuttle) between Madrid and Barcelona, along with what are referred to as 'regional' flights, which can mean domestic as well as short hops to destinations in France or even Italy. In short, make sure you know from which terminal you are departing to save time.

The arrivals halls are on the ground floor and departures are upstairs. Check-in *(facturación)* is mostly done on the upstairs level.

The tourist office (☎ 91 305 86 56) at the airport is on the ground floor in the T1 area. It opens from 8 am to 8 pm Monday to Friday and 8 am to 1 pm on Saturday.

You will find ATMs on all levels of all terminals. Argentaria and Caja de Madrid banks have branches in T1 and T2. You'll also find American Express branches on the first and ground floors of T1 and T2. Those in T1 are open 24 hours (as are the Argentaria branches in the same terminal).

You'll find a post office *(correos)* in the arrivals lounge of T1. It opens 8.30 am to 8.30 pm Monday to Friday (to 1 pm on Saturday). There is a hotel-reservation desk in T2. Five international car rental companies operate desks in the arrivals area of the ground floor of terminals T1 and T2 (see Rental under Car & Motorcycle later in this chapter for details).

If you have small kids and you'd like to dispose of them for a bit, you can deposit them at the nursery *(guardería)* in T2 (Zona C). It's open from 8 am to 8 pm daily (for children aged six or under).

Newspaper stands and bookshops, a smattering of bars and restaurants and duty-free gift shops provide all the essentials for airport survival.

When you arrive inside the terminals building, follow the Baggage Claim *(Recogida de Equipajes)* signs that will take you through passport control (there is usually no passport control for arrivals from other Schengen countries).

Transit

If you are making a connecting flight in Madrid, a shuttle bus runs between Gate A (T1) and Gate E (T3). It operates from 6 am to 11 pm and is free to passengers with a boarding card for their connecting flight. A shuttle train will ferry passengers between the old and new terminals when the latter is completed.

Left Luggage & Porters

There are two left-luggage offices *(consignas)* in the airport, one in T1 (near the bus stop and taxi stand) and the other in T2 (near the metro entrance). In either you pay 425 ptas for the first 24-hour period (or fraction thereof). Thereafter it costs 740 ptas a day (up until 15 days) in a big locker or 530 ptas in a small one. If you still haven't picked it up the bag will then be moved into storage, which costs 210 ptas a day plus a 5300 ptas transfer fee. The offices are open 24 hours.

Porters operate inside T1 and T2. If you have mountains of luggage, they will ferry it from your taxi, bus or train to the check-in counter, or from the arrivals gate to transport. You pay 175 ptas per person. If you can't see a porter, you can call the service on ☎ 91 305 58 32.

TO/FROM THE AIRPORT

You have several choices on how to get into the city centre from the airport. The metro is probably the most comfortable, although it involves a change of train. Some may find that the direct bus is preferable for this reason, although traffic can be a problem. For fare options see Tickets under Public Transport later in this chapter.

Train

As yet no RENFE (Red Nacionale los Ferrocarriles Españoles) train reaches the airport, but a *cercanías* (see that section under Public Transport later in this chapter) service to the new terminal building (due to open in late 2003) is planned.

Metro

Since 1999 it has been possible to get the metro right at the airport. To get into town from the airport get line 8 to Mar de Cristal, where you change to line 4 to head into the city. Depending on where you want to end up, you may well have to change again. Note that Colón metro stop is on line 4, which is where you would have to go to reach the terminus for the airport bus (see Bus later in this section).

On balance, the metro is probably the best option. It is fast, frequent and gets you around traffic hassles. The only inconvenience is the initial change of line, but at the bus terminus you have a painful walk to the nearest metro stop anyway. Within the next few years line 8 will be extended to the Nuevos Ministerios stop.

The entrance to the metro at the airport is from the upper level of T2. Trains run from about 6 am to about 1.30 am. All up, it

A New Gateway

By the end of 2003, the new terminal building at Barajas airport is supposed to be ready. Originally estimated at 30 billion ptas, it is thought that the project, which began in May 2000, will come in at 90 billion ptas. The airport has been under siege from all directions for years now. Air traffic has exploded in recent years and local residents are up in arms about noisy night flights. Moves to restrict these have met with coughs of disapproval from Brussels, more concerned that the wheels of business and transport in Europe turn smoothly than with people's shuteye.

Transport ministers have regularly tripped up over themselves in arguments over whether to expand Barajas or build another airport. The third runway, now in operation, is itself a bit of a misnomer – its placement means that only two out of three runways are ever operational. The new terminal has been plagued with difficulties – even during the planning stage. Enormous amounts of planning money and time were lost when airlines pointed out to designers that the original site chosen would have been at the end of a future fourth runway – a plane in difficulty could conceivably end up ploughing into the building! Oops, back to the drawing board. Now they have decided to build it close to the third runway. Again airlines have protested (this time in vain), saying that it will be too far away from planned fourth and fifth runways!

The designers paint a rosier picture, claiming the project is the most ambitious of its kind in Europe and that it promises to be the most innovative airport in design and efficiency on the Old Continent. All this remains to be seen.

should not take much more than half an hour to reach the middle of town (for example, Colón station).

Bus

You can get the local No 101 bus (135 ptas for a single ticket, but see Public Transport later in this chapter for other fare options) to Canillejas from the airport and then walk to the metro station of the same name there. There is little to be gained by this however, and the service is really for locals living in the area.

Alternatively, you can take the airport bus. It arrives/departs from an underground terminus on Plaza de Colón (Map 6; metro: Serrano or Colón, both on line 4). When heading out to the airport, you could opt to pick it up at a stop next to the Avenida de América metro station. Using a combination of this stop and the metro you can dodge much of the city-centre traffic. Frankly, if you are considering such complicated manoeuvres you may as well stay on the same metro line and change at Mar de Cristal station for the line 8 (two stops) metro to the airport. If, for whatever reason, you want to catch the bus, the fare is 385 ptas and buses leave every 12 to 15 minutes. Allow about half an hour in average traffic conditions.

Taxi

A taxi to/from the centre will cost you about 2000 ptas, depending on traffic and how much luggage you have (see Taxi later in this chapter for contact details). To the Chamartín train station you might pay about 1500 ptas, or 1900 ptas to Atocha. There are cab ranks outside all three terminals.

Those in a real hurry can use the Aero-CITY service (☎ 91 571 96 96), Calle de Orense 69. They will take you door-to-door from central Madrid to the airport and vice versa. Depending on how many passengers book this minibus, the fare can range from 600 ptas to 1500 ptas per person. It operates 24 hours.

Parking

There are two main parking areas. The P1 zone is best for those with flights departing from T1. P2 is for those with flights from T2 and T3. The first half-hour is free. Otherwise you pay 210 ptas per hour or 1855 ptas per day.

A new 'Express' parking area on the doorstep of T2 arrivals hall is designed for quick pit stops for those with lots of luggage and little desire to walk from the main parking areas. You pay 200 ptas for the first half-hour, after which the price rises each half-hour until you reach 500 ptas per half-hour. As you can calculate, it ain't designed for loitering.

PUBLIC TRANSPORT

The metro is the easiest way of getting around and reaches most places you're likely to visit. Several cercanías can also be handy. The train system is supplemented by a comprehensive bus network (including nightbuses), so between the two you have the city well covered.

You can pick up a map of the bus and metro routes from the main tourist office. For public transport information call ☎ 010 (or see individual numbers later in this section). For information on disabled facilities call ☎ 91 580 19 80.

Tickets

Single-journey bus tickets can be obtained on buses or at most tobacconists (estancos). They are not valid on trains. Single-journey metro and cercanías tickets are available at stations and tobacconists. The two systems are separate and tickets for one are not valid for the other. In most cases, a single ride throughout the city area costs 135 ptas, except on the cercanías, which cost 140 ptas. A Metrobus ticket valid for 10 rides costs 705 ptas. It entitles you to use the buses and metro (but not cercanías), and you can share tickets.

Monthly or season passes (abonos) only make sense if you are staying long term and use local transport frequently. You need to get an ID card (carnet) from metro stations or tobacconists. Take a passport-sized photo and your passport. A monthly ticket for central Madrid (Zoná A) costs 4620 ptas and is valid for unlimited travel on bus, metro and cercanías.

Bus

Buses run by EMT (Empresa Municipal de Transportes de Madrid; ☎ 91 406 88 10) travel along most city routes regularly between about 6.30 am and 11 pm.

Twenty night bus routes *(búhos)* operate from midnight to 6 am. They run from Puerta del Sol and Plaza de la Cibeles.

The single-deck *piso bajo* buses have no steps inside and in some cases have ramps that can be used by people in wheelchairs. About half EMT's 170 lines use some piso bajo buses. In the long run, EMT plans to make at least 50% of its buses on all routes accessible to the disabled.

Information booths can be found on Puerta del Sol, Plaza de Callao and Plaza de la Cibeles.

Metro

The metro (☎ 91 552 59 09) is a fast, efficient and safe way to navigate Madrid and generally easier than getting to grips with bus routes. It has 11 colour-coded lines and operates from about 6 am to 1.30 am. You can buy tickets from staffed booths or machines at most stations. Fares are the same as for buses.

This book contains a colour map of the entire metro system – although stay tuned for changes, as the metro has been in a state of continued expansion since the mid-1990s. Indeed, since 1995 a total of 39 new stations and 57km of track have been opened. The next four-year plan (1999–2003) should see the tentacles of the system spreading even further beyond the city, although most of these developments will probably be of little interest to the average traveller in Madrid.

If you've been to London, you'll notice an odd point of convergence: people take their standing to the right on escalators surprisingly seriously here!

Few lines make concessions to the disabled. A handful of stations are equipped with lifts.

Cercanías

These short-range regional trains operated by RENFE, the national railways, go as far afield as El Escorial, Alcalá de Henares, Aranjuez and other points in the Comunidad de Madrid.

In Madrid itself, they are handy for making a quick north–south hop between Chamartín and Atocha main-line train stations (with stops at Nuevos Ministerios and in front of the Biblioteca Nacional on Paseo de los Recoletos only).

A direct link between Chamartín, Atocha and Príncipe Pío stations, the so-called Pasillo Verde (Green Corridor), is also useful. Single tickets cost 140 ptas and are *not* valid for the metro or buses.

Fines

The fine for being caught without a ticket on public transport is 2700 ptas.

CAR & MOTORCYCLE

As Latin cities go, Madrid is not the most hair-raising to drive in, although there is a fair amount of horn-honking, nippy manoeuvring, sloppy lane recognition and general 'madness' to get used to. Avoid peak hours, when the whole city heaves with the masses struggling to and from work. From about 2 to 4 pm the streets are dead. Once in the city, search for a car park or, if you are not fazed by the likelihood of getting a fine, the nearest likely-looking parking space. Driving from sight to sight within Madrid is pointless.

Parking

Most of central Madrid is governed by the Operación de Regulación de Aparcamiento (ORA) parking system. This means that, apart from designated loading zones, no-parking areas and the like, all parking positions that appear legitimate are only so for people with yearly permits, or coupons obtainable from tobacconists.

In spite of this, many people park without permits or coupons and collect the fines. The authorities are at a loss on what to do about central Madrid's parking congestion – double-parking is as common as the wheel itself – so you can get away with quite a lot.

However, if you park in a designated no-parking area, you risk being towed. Double-parking is also risky in this way if you wander far from your vehicle. Should your car disappear, call the Grúa Municipal (city towing service) on ☎ 91 345 00 50. Getting it back costs around 16,000 ptas.

Obviously, the parking of motorbikes and

GETTING AROUND

scooters is easier. On occasion you'll see spaces marked out especially for bikes.

If you wish to play it safe, there are plenty of car parks across the city, starting at about 200 ptas an hour and a little less for each subsequent hour.

Rental

You obviously wouldn't want to rent a car to cruise around Madrid, but one could come in handy for touring the surrounding countryside. It won't pay if you only intend to make a few simple day trips however.

If you haven't organised a rental car from abroad, be aware that the international companies charge fairly hefty rates in Madrid. Avis' cheapest per-day rate is 8800 ptas with unlimited kilometres (dropping to 5200 ptas a day for seven days or more). On top of this you need to calculate 1900 ptas a day in collision-damage waiver, as well as 950 ptas a day in theft and third-party insurance. Add 16% IVA (VAT) and you have the total daily cost.

Local firms such as Julià Car are generally cheaper than the big international names. From a local firm a typical small car such as a Ford Ka or Fiat Punto, with minimum compulsory insurance, should cost around 2800 ptas a day plus 25 ptas per kilometre, plus IVA. For unlimited kilometres, they cost around 18,000 ptas for three days or 35,000 ptas a week, plus IVA. You pay collision-damage waiver and insurance on top, which can come to around 1500 ptas a day. Special low weekend rates (from Friday to Monday morning) are worth looking into.

The big-name car rental agencies have offices all over Madrid. Avis, Budget, Europcar, Hertz and National/Atesa have booths at the airport. Some of them also operate branches at Atocha and Chamartín train stations. The smaller operators often have one reservation phone number and an out-of-the-way office – ask if they can deliver the car to a convenient location. Some addresses include:

Avis (Map 5; ☎ 902 13 55 31, 91 547 20 48) Gran Vía 60

Budget (☎ 902 20 12 12, 91 577 63 63) Aeropuerto de Barajas

Euro Rental (Map 2; ☎ 91 356 65 78) Avenida de los Toreros 12

Europcar (Map 5; ☎ 91 541 88 92) Calle de San Leonardo 8

Hertz (Map 5; ☎ 902 40 24 05 for reservations, 91 542 58 03) Edificio de España, Plaza de España

Julià Car (☎ 91 779 18 60) Puerto de Used 20. Either call this number or book through travel agencies where you see the Julià Car sign.

National/Atesa (Map 5; ☎ 902 10 01 01, 91 542 50 15) Gran Vía 80

You can rent motorbikes from Moto Alquiler (Map 5; ☎ 91 542 06 57), Calle del Conde Duque 13, but it's a pricey business. Something like a Yamaha 650 will cost you 16,000 ptas a day plus tax, and the deposit is 175,000 ptas on your credit card. Rental is from 8 am to 8 pm if you just take the bike for a day.

Warning If you have a rental car in Madrid, take extra care. Groups of delinquents are known to occasionally zero in on them, puncturing a tyre and then robbing the driver when s/he acts to change it. This is reportedly a particular problem on the road from the airport to the centre of town.

Purchase

Only legal residents in Spain may buy vehicles there. One way round this is to have a friend who is a resident put the ownership papers in their name.

Car-hunters need a reasonable knowledge of Spanish to get through paperwork and understand dealers' patter. Trawling around showrooms or looking through classifieds can turn up second-hand Seats (for example, Ibiza) and Renaults (4 or 5) in good condition costing around 300,000 ptas. The annual cost of third-party insurance on such a car, with theft and fire cover and national breakdown assistance, comes in at between 40,000 and 50,000 ptas (with annual reductions if you make no claims).

Vehicles of five years and older must be submitted for roadworthiness checks,

GETTING AROUND

Statue on the front of Ministerio de Agricultura

A striking fountain in the Parque del Retiro

The Puerta da Alcalá was moved from its original spot on Plaza de la Cibes in 1778.

A sundial painted on a wall, Lavapiés.

A steeple on Carrera de San Jeromino

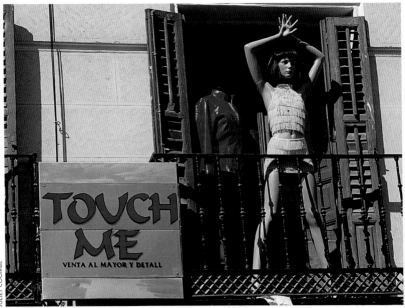

Clothes shopping in Madrid isn't all Armani and Gucci – there's plenty of clubwear too.

known as Inspección Técnica de Vehículos (ITV). If you pass, you get a sticker for two years. Check that this has been done when buying: the test costs about 4000 ptas.

You can get second-hand 50cc motorbikes for anything from 40,000 to 100,000 ptas.

TAXI

By European standards, taxis are inexpensive and well regulated. You can pick up a cab at ranks throughout town or simply flag one down. Flag fall is 190 ptas and you should make sure the driver turns the meter on. You pay 90 ptas per kilometre (120 ptas between 10 pm and 6 am). The fare from Barajas airport to Plaza de Colón should be around 2000 ptas, while the trip from Chamartín train station to the same square will be no more than 1000 ptas. There are several supplementary charges, usually posted up inside the taxi. They include 400 ptas for going to the airport, 150 ptas for running to train or bus stations, 150 ptas between 11 pm and 6 am and also on public holidays, as well as 50 ptas for each piece of luggage.

You can call a cab on: ☎ 91 445 90 08, ☎ 91 547 82 00, ☎ 547 85 00, ☎ 91 371 21 31 or ☎ 91 371 37 11.

Radio-Teléfono Taxi (☎ 91 547 82 00, 91 547 86 00) runs taxis for the disabled. Generally, if you call any taxi company and ask for a *eurotaxi* you should be sent one that is adapted for wheelchair users.

A green light on the roof means the taxi is available *(libre)*. Generally a sign to this effect is also placed in the lower passenger side of the windscreen.

BICYCLE & MOPED

Lots of people zip around town on mopeds *(motos)* but brave souls willing to risk life and limb on bicycles are rather thin on the ground (no pun intended). Indeed, very little has been done to encourage cyclists in Madrid. Bike lanes are virtually unheard of. Madrid's city councillor in charge of traffic issues, Fernando Martínez-Vidal, commented drily in 2000, 'Madrid is not a city for bicycles.'

Bicycle Rental

Karacol Sports (Map 9; ☎ 91 539 96 33), Calle de Tortosa 8, rents out mountain bikes. The best offer is 4000 ptas from Friday to Monday. There's a refundable deposit of 5000 ptas and you also need to leave an original document (passport, driving licence or the like).

Moped Rental

You can rent a moped from Moto Alquiler (see Rental under Car & Motorcycle earlier in this chapter). Rates start at 4500 ptas plus 16% IVA per day for a 50cc Honda Sky. Rental is from 8 am to 8 pm and you have to leave a refundable deposit of 50,000 ptas on your credit card.

WALKING

The centre of Madrid is fairly compact and, day or night, the best way to get around is on your own two feet. Judicious use of the metro and buses will allow you to move around to more far-flung corners of the city (only true lovers of the smell of burning shoe leather will want to walk all the way from, say, Lavapiés up to Malasaña).

Pay attention when crossing roads. A pedestrian crossing and even red lights showing for oncoming traffic are no guarantee that anyone will stop for you. Generally the car (or motorbike) is king. Jay walking is as common as muck here, and basically the same rules apply as at crossings – make absolutely sure no vehicle is headed in your general direction before hitting the asphalt. Once you've made your move, it's a bit like driving – you have to act swiftly and decisively!

ORGANISED TOURS
Central Circuit

You can pick up a special Madrid Vision bus around the centre of Madrid 10 times a day (five daily from November to March). A full round trip costs 1700 ptas and you can board the bus at any of 14 clearly marked stops. Taped commentaries in eight languages, including English, are available, and the bus stops at several major monuments, including the Prado and near Plaza Mayor. If you buy

GETTING AROUND

the 2200 ptas ticket, you can use the buses all day to get around (2900 ptas buys you the same right for two days running). You can get more information at tourist offices or in most travel agencies.

Similar is Sol Open Tours (☎ 902 30 39 03). Buses follow a circuit, calling at 15 stops en route, every half-hour or so from 10 am to 6.30 pm. You buy a ticket for 1600 ptas and can hop on and off at will. Tickets are available at Atocha and Chamartín train stations, the Estación Sur de Autobuses and at the Sol Telecom phone and internet centre (Map 8) at Puerta del Sol 6. A couple of other bus-tour companies doing much the same thing appeared in the course of 2000.

Frankly, you're better off investing in 10-trip Metrobus tickets and getting about by yourself.

Descubre Madrid

The Patronato Municipal de Turismo has chosen more than 120 itineraries around the capital. Tours are free and are conducted in Spanish. You can pick up calendars detailing when and where the walks are held at any branch of the Caja de Madrid bank, which co-sponsors the Descubre Madrid program.

Paseos por el Madrid de los Austrias

The Patronato Municipal de Turismo organises Saturday-morning walks around the centre of old Madrid (500 ptas). They start at 10 am (English) and noon (Spanish). Meet outside the Patronato office (Map 7), at Plaza Mayor 3, half an hour before.

Other Tours

Several companies organise city tours, including Pullmantur (Map 5; ☎ 91 541 18 05), whose office is at Plaza de Oriente 8. These range from half-day jaunts around Madrid for a costly 5250 ptas through to an evening of flamenco flouncing with a meal for up to 12,000 ptas. Most central Madrid travel agencies can fill you in on the details of these and similar trips.

Things to See & Do

For many, the main attraction in Madrid is the Big Three art galleries, locally dubbed the Art Triangle: Prado, Reina Sofía and Thyssen-Bornemisza. No doubt art lovers would be foolish to miss these, but don't ignore the rest of the city. The small centre of Habsburg Madrid repays exploration, with the grand Plaza Mayor at its heart and the haughty Palacio Real at its western flank. Take time for a stroll in the parks, especially the Retiro, and try to catch the Sunday flea market, El Rastro. And don't forget to break up sightseeing with numerous food and drink stops along the way – for the bars, restaurants and other establishments are part of the Madrid experience.

MUSEO DEL PRADO (MAP 9)
Completed in 1785 in the Prado (meadow) de los Jerónimos, the neoclassical Palacio de Villanueva was originally conceived as a house of science, incorporating a natural history museum and laboratories. Events overtook the noble enterprise and during the Napoleonic occupation (1808–13) the building was converted ignominiously into cavalry barracks.

Perhaps inspired by the ideas of the French Revolution and Napoleon's short-lived administration, King Fernando VII resolved in 1814 to create a museum in the Palacio de Villanueva to put on public display a representative chunk of the country's artistic wealth. Five years later the Museo del Prado opened with 311 Spanish paintings.

Of the more than 7000 works in the Prado collection today, fewer than half are on view at any given time. This will eventually change due to the plans afoot for the creation of a Gran Prado. Since 1819, the museum has undergone numerous minor alterations but has rarely received the financial attention it deserves. Architect Rafael Moneo's project for the Gran Prado was approved in 1999, though not without causing some consternation.

> ## Highlights
>
> - The Big Three art galleries: the Prado, the Thyssen-Bornemisza and the Reina Sofía
> - A Sunday-morning stroll in the Parque del Buen Retiro
> - Touring the endless halls of the magnificent Palacio Real
> - Summertime beers and magnificent views to the Sierra de Guadarrama at Las Vistillas
> - Beholding a hidden stronghold of centuries of religious faith in the Convento de las Descalzas Reales
> - Bargain-hunting in El Rastro flea market
> - Admiring Goya's masterpiece in the Ermita de San Antonio de la Florida
> - Coffee and a paper on Plaza Mayor

Moneo's plan involves building a new section of the museum in the cloisters of the Iglesia de San Jerónimo El Real and connecting it to the main building via a subterranean passage. All the administration will move to the new building, and a new library, drawings gallery and temporary exhibition space and seminar centre will be set up there.

Further down the line, it has been mooted that the nearby Museo del Ejército (see Plaza de Colón to the Prado later in this chapter) will be shifted from its present location to Toledo to make room for still more gallery space, allowing more of the Prado's collection to go on show. This is unlikely to happen before 2005 and, judging by the outcry the proposal has unleashed in Madrid and Toledo, it may take still longer.

The Collection
One of the beauties of the collection is the generous coverage given to certain masters. Strings of rooms are devoted to the works of three of Spain's greatest – Velázquez,

Goya and El Greco. This is the cream of the Prado's collection, but there is plenty of good stuff by other major Spanish artists (such as José de Ribera, Murillo and Zurbarán), as well as a fair serving of Flemish and Italian masters. A sprinkling of artists of other nationalities completes the picture.

To have a hope of fully digesting the collection, you really need to consider making more than one visit.

The bulk of the collection as it is set out at present is held on the ground and 1st floors. The ground floor is dominated by Italian and Flemish painters (including the likes of Titian, Tintoretto and Bosch). Three rooms are dedicated to El Greco. A handful of Spanish artists is also represented here.

Head for the 1st floor to see the main body of Spanish art. With the exception of five small rooms given over to the Italian and French artists, and a section mostly devoted to Flemish art, this is an all-Spanish show, with big sections on Velázquez and Goya. The latter extends up into the south wing of the 2nd floor. Also on the 2nd floor, in the north wing, is a mixed collection of 18th-century European painters.

Parts of the collection are moved about as improvements and maintenance of the museum are carried out. This may become more apparent still when work on the extension gets under way.

Velázquez

Of this 17th-century old master's works, *Las Meninas* is what most people come to see, and rightly so. Executed in 1656, it is more properly known as *La Familia de Felipe IV*. It depicts Velázquez himself on the left and, in the centre, the Infanta Margarita. There is more to it than that, though: the artist in fact portrays himself painting the king and queen, whose images appear, according to some experts, in mirrors behind Velázquez. His mastery of light and colour are never more apparent than here. The painting takes pride of place in Room 12, the focal point of the Velázquez collection on the 1st floor.

The bulk of Velázquez's works are in Rooms 12, 14, 15, 15A and 16. Among some of his outstanding portraits are *La Infanta Doña Margarita de Austria* (who stars in *Las Meninas*) and *Baltasar Carlos a Caballo*. *Cristo Crucificado* manages to convey the agony of the Crucifixion with great dignity. *La Rendición de Breda* (The Surrender of Breda) is another classic.

Museum & Gallery Admission

You can take advantage of several options to reduce the cost of admission to Madrid's museums and galleries. In the case of the three big art galleries – the Prado (standard admission charge 500 ptas), Centro de Arte Reina Sofía (500 ptas) and Museo Thyssen-Bornemisza (700 ptas) – you can get a Paseo del Arte ticket which covers all three for 1275 ptas. It's valid for a year.

Better still for one-off visitors, admission to the first two is free on Saturday afternoon (from 2.30 pm) and Sunday. People aged under 18 or over 65 get into the Prado free any time. Students and seniors aged over 65 pay 400 ptas for the Thyssen-Bornemisza, and children aged under 12 get in free.

A year's ticket for unlimited visits to either the Prado or the Reina Sofía costs 4000 ptas. A yearly ticket to both galleries and nine other museums throughout the country costs 6000 ptas.

Admission to many other galleries, museums and other sights is free at least one day a week. In a few cases this is restricted to EU citizens, but others may be able to sneak through too. Saturday afternoon, Sunday and Wednesday are the most common free times.

Most, but not all, museums and monuments close on Monday. Just about everything is closed on Sunday afternoon. In July and August, some close parts of their displays for want of staff, most of whom take annual leave around this time. A few minor museums even close entirely throughout August.

El Greco

Domenikos Theotokopoulos (1541–1614), Velázquez's senior by 58 years, is represented on the ground floor, in Rooms 60A, 61A and 62A. The long, slender figures characteristic of this singular Cretan artist, who lived and worked in Toledo, are hard to mistake. Particularly striking are *La Crucifixión* and *San Andrés y San Francisco*, finished towards the end of the 16th century.

Goya

Francisco José de Goya y Lucientes (1746–1828) is the most extensively represented of the Spanish masters in the Prado. Late to reach the heights of his grandeur, Goya, more than anyone, captured the extremes of hope and misery his country experienced before, during and after the Napoleonic invasion. In Room 89, on the 2nd floor, hang what are probably his best-known and most intriguing oils, *La Maja Vestida* and *La Maja Desnuda*. These portraits of an unknown woman, the Duquesa de Alba (who may have been Goya's lover), are identical save for the lack of clothing in the latter.

The horrors of war had a profound effect on Goya's view of the world. *El Dos de Mayo* and, still more dramatically, *El Tres de Mayo* bring to life the 1808 anti-French revolt and subsequent execution of insurgents in Madrid. They're in Room 39.

The whole southern wing of the 2nd floor is devoted to Goya and includes many of his preparatory paintings for tapestries, his religious paintings and drawings. On the 1st floor, Rooms 32 and 34 to 39 contain more of his work, including his *Pinturas Negras* (Black Paintings), so-called because of the dark browns and black that dominate. Among the most disturbing of these works is *Saturno Devorando a Su Hijo* (Saturn Devouring His Son).

Other Spanish Artists

In the shadow of these greats come a small contingent of important artists and a gaggle of minor ones. Of the former, there are substantial collections of work by Bartolomé Esteban Murillo and José de Ribera (dominating Rooms 25 to 29), Francisco de Zurbarán (Room 18A), Alonso Cano (Room 17A) and Claudio Coello (along with others of the Spanish Baroque period; Room 16A). All these are on the 1st floor.

On the ground floor just four rooms (55B, 56, 57 and 57B) contain various paintings by 16th-century Spanish artists, including Berruguete and Navarrete (el Mudo).

Some medieval Spanish works can be seen in Room 50 (ground floor). In the adjoining Room 51 are the re-creation of a Romanesque church apse and some intriguing murals taken from the Mozarabic Ermita de San Baudelio, an enchanting little chapel in Soria province, north-east of Madrid.

Flemish Artists

The 17th-century works are the backbone of the collection and, although for most visitors the Spanish contribution is paramount, there is a wealth of Flemish art here that should not be missed.

The pick of the work of Hieronymus Bosch (c1450–1516) lives in Room 56A, on the ground floor. Among these paintings is *The Garden of Earthly Delights*, for which no-one has yet been able to provide a definitive explanation, although many have tried. While it is, without doubt, the star attraction of this fantastical painter's collection, all reward inspection. The closer you look, the harder it is to escape the feeling that he must have been doing some extraordinary drugs. Around this room, five others are filled with Flemish works from the 15th and 16th centuries. Artists featured include Roger van der Weyden (1399–1464) and Hans Memling (1433–94).

Up on the 1st floor, Peter Paul Rubens (1577–1640) gets a big run. His works are concentrated mainly in Rooms 9 and 11. He is joined by Anton van Dyck (Room 10A), Jacob Jordaens, David Teniers and others of the same epoch in the surrounding rooms (Rooms 7A through to 11).

Italian Artists

The Italians haven't been left out either. They fully occupy Rooms 49, 56B, 60, 61,

61B, 62, 62B, 63, 63B and 75, on the ground floor. They count among their number Sandro Botticelli (1445–1510), Andrea Mantegna (1431–1506), Raphael (1483–1520), Tintoretto (1518–94), Il Veronese (1528–88), Jacopo Bassano (1517–92) and, in particular, Titian (Tiziano Vecelli; 1487–1576), who fills Rooms 61 and 61B. Felipe II was in fact very partial to Titian, and Venetian artists in general. The Venetian contingent is by far in the majority.

Elsewhere (in Rooms 4 to 6 on the 1st floor) there are some works by Tiepolo (1692–1770) and Caravaggio (1571–1610).

Dutch & German Artists
In one small room on the ground floor containing German works (Room 54), you can see a couple of small pieces by Albrecht Dürer (1471–1528) and Lucas Cranach the Elder (1472–1553). Rembrandt scrapes in for Holland in Room 7 (1st floor), along with Carlos III's court painter, Anton Rafael Mengs (1728–79). Otherwise, there is not much to speak of from the Protestant strongholds of Germany and independent Holland.

French Artists
A small collection of paintings from Spain's eternal enemy, France, huddles together in Rooms 2 to 4 on the 1st floor. Artists include Nicolas Poussin (1594–1665), Louis Michel Van Loo (1707–71) and Jean-Antoine Watteau (1684–1721).

Tesoro del Delfín
Down in the basement, this collection of extraordinary *objets d'art* from the 16th and 17th centuries belonged to the Grand Dauphin, the eldest son of Louis XIV of France.

Cason del Buen Retiro (Map 9)
A short walk east of the Prado, this one-time ballroom of the now non-existent Palacio del Buen Retiro (the only other surviving structure from the former palace is the Salón del Reino, which houses – for now at least – the Museo del Ejército) is home to a selection of lesser-known 19th-

century works. Artists include Joaquín Sorolla, Aureliano de Beruete and Vicente López. The latter's portrait of Goya hangs here. The facility was closed at the time of writing for major refurbishment, particularly in the basement floors, as part of the grand plans for the Prado extension. No doubt the collection will take on a new aspect when the building finally reopens, which could be some time in 2002.

Admission
The Prado (metro: Banco de España or Atocha) is open from 9 am to 7 pm Tuesday to Saturday, and 9 am to 2 pm on Sunday and holidays. You can enter the museum by either the northern Puerta de Goya or the southern Puerta de Murillo. The latter leads you into the ground floor, while you can access the ground and 1st floors from the former.

One ticket covers the Prado and Casón del Buen Retiro (500 ptas; half-price for students). Admission is free on Sunday and Saturday afternoon (from 2.30 to 7 pm), as well as on selected national holidays. It is also free at any time for those aged under 18 and over 65. See the boxed text 'Museum & Gallery Admission' for details of special tickets.

Guides & Information
There is little free printed information. The hand-out map guides you to the main schools and major artists. Otherwise, attractive little booklets in several languages can be extracted from machines located in a couple of the rooms. You'll find one on Goya in the rooms devoted to him on the 2nd floor. Another on Bosch and Flemish painting is available in the room dedicated to Bosch. They cost 200 ptas.

MUSEO THYSSEN-BORNEMISZA (MAP 7)
This is one of the most wide-ranging private collections of predominantly European art in the world. It has been accumulated over two generations by the Thyssen-Bornemiszas, a family of German-Hungarian magnates. Spain managed to acquire the prestigious

collection when it offered to overhaul the neoclassical Palacio de Villahermosa specifically to house most of it. Almost 800 works have hung here since October 1992, with a further 80 at the Monestir de Pedralbes (Barcelona).

In early 2000 the museum acquired two adjoining buildings, which are being prepared to house approximately half of the collection of Carmen Thyssen-Bornemisza. This collection, which ranges from the 15th to the 20th centuries in much the same eclectic style as the permanent exhibition, numbers about 600 works. The emphasis is on 19th-century works and Spanish American, impressionist and expressionist art. The museum hopes to have the new exhibition, which is expected to be on continuous display for 11 years, ready by October 2002. At the moment it is on a long-haul world tour.

The original collection is spread out over three floors, so you could do worse than follow the museum pamphlet's advice to start on the 2nd floor (there is a lift) and work your way down chronologically from 13th- and 14th-century religious paintings to the avant-garde and pop art on the ground floor. The eclectic nature of the collection is such that many artists of a great number of epochs and schools are represented – if only by one or two samples.

Second Floor

The first three rooms are dedicated to medieval art, with a series of remarkable triptychs and paintings (predominantly Italian and Flemish) to get the ball rolling. They include some by Duccio di Buoninsegna (c1255–1318), who led the Sienese school into a gentle break from Byzantine forms in the late 13th and early 14th centuries.

In Room 4, the move away from Gothic painting in Italy is illustrated with works by Paolo Uccello (1397–1475), Benozzo Gozzoli (1420–97) and others from Milan, Venice, Perugia and Ferrara.

Room 5 contains, among others, some works by Italy's Piero della Francesca (1410–92) and a *Henry VIII* by Holbein the Younger (1497–1543). Room 6 (the long

Galería Villahermosa) hosts a sampling of Italian masters, such as Raphael, Lorenzo Lotto (c1480–1556), Il Veronese and Tintoretto. Here and in Room 4 you can also see a couple of examples of the glazed terracotta sculptures for which Florence's Della Robbia family became famous.

In Room 7 are some exemplary works by the brothers Gentile (1429–1507) and Giovanni Bellini (1430–1516), who together with their father, Jacopo (1400–70), launched the Venetian Renaissance in painting. Rooms 8, 9 and 10 are given over to German and Dutch 16th-century masters. Among them are a few works by Cranach the Elder, Hans Holbein the Elder and Dürer.

Room 11 is dedicated to El Greco (with four pieces) and Venetian contemporaries Tintoretto, Titian and Jacopo Bassano.

Caravaggio and José de Ribera, who was much influenced by the former, dominate the next room, while Rooms 13 to 15 mainly contain works by comparatively minor Italians of the 17th century, along with a painting each by Murillo and Zurbarán and a couple of French artists.

Look out for the fine views of Venice by Canaletto (1697–1768), accompanied by some of the best works of Francesco Guardi (1712–93), in Room 17. Indeed, Rooms 16 to 18 are dominated by Venetians.

Rubens leads the way in the last rooms (19 to 21) on this floor, which are devoted to 17th-century Dutch and Flemish masters. Anton van Dyck and Rembrandt also get a showing.

First Floor

The Dutch theme continues on the next floor, with interiors and landscapes (including some Vermeers). They are followed (in Room 27) by a still-life series.

In Room 28 you'll find a Gainsborough (1727–88) – one of the few British works in the collection – along with a few paintings by Watteau and Jean-Honoré Fragonard (1732–1806).

Next (Rooms 29 and 30) comes a representative look at North American art of the 19th century, including pieces by John Singer

Sargent (1856–1925) and James Whistler (1834–1903). In Room 31 John Constable (1776–1837), Gustave Courbet (1819–77) and even Goya (with a bust of Fernando VII) get a run. The images of Palermo and Venice by Robert Salmon (1775–1845) are rather striking.

All the great impressionist and post-impressionist names get a mention in Rooms 32 and 33, with works by Camille Pissarro (1830–1903), Pierre-Auguste Renoir (1841–1919), Edgar Degas (1834–1917), Claude Monet (1840–1926), Edouard Manet (1832–83), Henri de Toulouse-Lautrec (1864–1901), Paul Cézanne (1839–1906), Paul Gauguin (1848–1903) and Vincent Van Gogh (1853–90).

Expressionism rules the remainder of the floor. In Room 35 you'll find canvases by Egon Schiele (1890–1918), Henri Matisse (1869–1954), Edvard Munch (1863–1944) and Oskar Kokoschka (1886–1980). Ernst Ludwig Kirchner (1880–1938), August Macke (1887–1914) and George Grosz (1893–1959) are also all represented. The latter's *Metropolis* is a nightmare vision of a city if ever there was one.

Ground Floor

Here you move firmly into the 20th century, from cubism through to pop art. In Room 41 you'll see a nice mix of Picasso, Juan Gris and Georges Braque (1882–1963). More Picasso beyond cubism follows in Room 45, accompanied by works by Marc Chagall (1887–1985), Vassily Kandinsky (1866–1944) and Joan Miró. In Room 46 the leap is made back across the Atlantic, with Jackson Pollock (1912–56) and Willem de Kooning (1904–97) the stars. Lucian Freud (born 1922), Sigmund's Berlin-born grandson, is joined by David Hockney (born 1937) and Roy Lichtenstein (1923–97) in Rooms 47 and 48.

Admission

The gallery is at Paseo del Prado 8 (metro: Banco de España) and is open from 10 am to 7 pm Tuesday to Sunday. Admission costs 700 ptas (400 ptas for students and seniors). Children aged 12 and under get in free. Separate temporary exhibitions usually cost more: generally 500 ptas (300 ptas for students and seniors).

CENTRO DE ARTE REINA SOFÍA (MAP 7)

Adapted from the remains of an 18th-century hospital, the Centro de Arte Reina Sofía is home to the best Madrid has to offer in modern Spanish art, principally spanning the 20th century up to the 1980s. The occasional non-Spaniard makes an appearance, but the bulk of the collection is strictly peninsular.

The organisation of the permanent display has been greatly improved and expanded over the past couple of years. It is on the 1st floor (Rooms 1 to 17) and top floor (Rooms 18 to 45). In each room you will find explanatory sheets in Spanish and English – please do as asked and return them when you have finished. The ground floor houses a cafe, an excellent art bookshop and a temporary exhibition space. There is more exhibition space on the 2nd floor too.

The big attraction for most visitors is Picasso's *Guernica*. Don't just rush straight for it, though, as there is plenty of other good material.

First Floor

The first room serves as an ice-breaker, taking you through late-19th-century movements in painting that were to some extent dominated by what was happening in Barcelona. Modernistas such as Ramón Casas (1866–1932) and Santiago Rusiñol (1861–1931) are mixed together with their successors – Noucentistas such as Isidro Nonell – and a string of other painters from around the country.

The following room concentrates on the madrileño José Gutiérrez Solana (1886–1945). He depicts himself in typically gloomy fashion in *La Tertulia del Café de Pombo* (1920). Room 3 presents a mix of Spanish and foreign painters whose work presaged what was to come, such as the cubism of Juan Gris, which you can admire in Room 4. Among the bronzes of Pablo Gargallo (1881–1934) in Room 5 is a head of

Picasso. Speaking of whom, the genius takes up all of the long hall that is Room 6.

Guernica fully dominates the hall and is surrounded by a plethora of the artist's preparatory sketches. Already associated with the Republicans when the Civil War broke out in 1936, Picasso was commissioned by Madrid to do the painting for the Paris Exposition Universelle in 1937. He incorporated features of others of his works into this, an eloquent condemnation of the horrors of war – more precisely, of the German bombing of Gernika (Guernica), in the Basque Country, in April of the same year. It has been surrounded by controversy from the beginning and was at the time viewed by many as a work more of propaganda than of art. The 3.5m by 7.8m painting subsequently migrated to the USA and only returned to Spain in 1981, to languish in the Casón del Buen Retiro until its transfer to the Reina Sofía. Calls to have it moved to the Basque Country continue unabated.

Joan Miró takes up a parallel corridor (Room 7) to the Picasso collection. In Room 9 you can see a canvas by Vassily Kandinsky, one of the few foreigners on show here. Some 20 canvases by Salvador Dalí hang in Room 10, including a portrait of the filmmaker Luis Buñuel (1924) and the surrealist extravaganza *El Gran Masturbador* (1929). In the next room is a strange bust of a certain *Joelle* done by Dalí and his pal Man Ray.

Room 12 contains a display dedicated to Buñuel, while Room 13 hosts a long list of artists active in the turbulent decades of the 1920s and 1930s. Particular artists are singled out for attention in Room 14 (Luis Fernández) and Room 15 (Benjamin Palencia and the Toledan sculptor Alberto Sánchez). The latter two formed part of the so-called Escuela de Vallecas and the similarity between Palencia's paintings and Sánchez's sculptures is striking. More sculpture follows in Room 16, including some by madrileño Ángel Ferrant.

Second Floor
The collection on the top floor takes up the baton and continues from the 1940s until the 1980s. A new approach to landscapes evolved in the wake of the Civil War, perhaps best exemplified by the work of Juan Manuel Díaz Caneja (1905–88) in Room 18. In the following room you can study works by two important groups to emerge after WWII, Pórtico and Dau al Set. Among artists of the latter group was Barcelona's Antoni Tàpies (born 1923), some of whose later pieces also appear in Rooms 34 and 35.

Rooms 20 to 23 offer a representative look at abstract painting in Spain. Among the more significant contributors are Eusebio Sempere and members of the Equipo 57 group, such as Pablo Palazuelo.

Rooms 24 to 35 lead us through Spanish art of the 1960s and into the 1970s. Some external reference points – such as works by Francis Bacon and Henry Moore (both in Room 24) – are thrown in to broaden the context.

Coming down to the present day, Room 38 is given over to work by Eduardo Arroyo, while works of the sculptor Eduardo Chillida fill Rooms 41 and 42.

Admission
The gallery is at Calle de Santa Isabel 52 (metro: Atocha) and is open from 10 am to 9 pm on Monday and Wednesday to Saturday (closed Tuesday), and 10 am to 2.30 pm on Sunday. Admission costs 500 ptas (half-price for students). It is free for seniors, and for everyone else on Saturday from 2.30 pm and Sunday.

HABSBURG MADRID
Under Carlos I and Felipe II, the first two kings in the Habsburg dynasty (1517–1700), Spain reached the apogee of imperial greatness, its possessions spreading from Vienna to the Low Countries, from Seville to the Americas. Felipe's immediate Habsburg successors were largely responsible for expressing that glory in the centre of Madrid, at least to the extent that they were prepared to invest in their unassuming new capital.

Puerta del Sol (Map 7)
Once the site of a city gate in the third circuit of walls, the Puerta del Sol (Sun Gate)

A Little Walking Tour of Madrid

What follows aims to suggest a general route through 'essential Madrid'. If you plan to spend time in any of the monuments and museums, or prefer simply meandering at will and stopping in at the many enticing bars and cafes, you will need several days to do justice to such a circuit. You will find more details on the sights mentioned here in the rest of this chapter, and the route is marked on the maps at the end of the book.

Unless you want to head for the big art galleries first, the most fitting place to begin exploring the city is the **Puerta del Sol**, the official centre of Madrid. Walk up Calle de Preciados and take the second street on the left, which will bring you out onto Plaza de las Descalzas. Look at the **baroque doorway** in the Caja de Madrid building – it was built for King Felipe V in 1733 and faces the **Convento de las Descalzas Reales**. Moving south down Calle de San Martín, you come to the **Iglesia de San Ginés**, built on the site of one of Madrid's oldest places of Christian worship. Behind it is the wonderful **Chocolatería de San Ginés**, generally open from 7 to 10 pm and 1 to 7 am.

Continue down to and cross Calle Mayor and then walk onto Madrid's grandest square, **Plaza Mayor**. After a coffee on the square, head west along Calle Mayor until you come to the historic **Plaza de la Villa**, home of Madrid's 17th-century Ayuntamiento (town hall). On the same square stand the 16th-century **Casa de Cisneros** and the Gothic-mudéjar **Torre de los Lujanes**, dating from the Middle Ages and one of the city's oldest surviving buildings.

Take the street down the left side of the Casa de Cisneros, cross the road at the end, go down the stairs and follow the cobbled Calle del Cordón out onto Calle de Segovia. Almost directly in front of you is the mudéjar tower of the 15th-century **Iglesia de San Pedro El Viejo**. Proceeding down Costanilla de San Pedro, you reach the **Iglesia de San Andrés**, where the city's patron saint, San Isidro Labrador, was long interred.

From here you cross Plaza de la Puerta de Moros and head south-west to the **Basílica de San Francisco el Grande**, or you can head east past the market along Plaza de la Cebada – once a popular spot for public executions – to head into the Sunday flea market of **El Rastro**.

From San Francisco el Grande, you can plunge into the small tangle of lanes that forms what was once the **morería** and emerge back onto Calle de Bailén and the wonderful **terrazas** of Las Vistillas – great for drinking in the views. If you can't be bothered with tangled lanes, you can opt to head straight up Calle de Bailén.

After a soothing *cerveza* (beer) follow the viaduct north to the **Catedral de Nuestra Señora de la Almudena**, the **Palacio Real** (Royal Palace) and Plaza de Oriente, with its statues, fountains and hedge mazes. The eastern side of the plaza is closed off by the **Teatro Real**.

At its northern end, Calle de Bailén runs into **Plaza de España**. By continuing up Calle de Ferraz, you could visit the **Museo de Cerralbo** and the **Templo de Debod**. Those with more energy might

is Madrid's most central point. On the southern side, a small plaque marks km 0, the point from where distances along the country's highways are measured. It is hard to imagine that in the late medieval period this was the easternmost extent of the city. From here a road passed through the peasant hovels of the outer 'suburbs' en route to Guadalajara, to the north-east.

The name of the gate appears to date from the 1520s, when Madrid joined the re-volt of the Comuneros against Carlos I and erected a fortress, in the east-facing arch of which the sun was depicted. The fort, which stood about where the metro station is today, was demolished in around 1570.

Just outside the gate, where Calle de Alcalá and Carrera de San Jerónimo meet, stood the Iglesia del Buen Suceso, in front of which, in 1616, was raised a fountain topped by a statue of Diana (or, according to some, Venus). Locals (the area at the time

A Little Walking Tour of Madrid

head west down towards the Río Manzanares to see the **Ermita de San Antonio de Florida**, which contains a masterpiece by Goya. If you were to continue north from the square, you would pass through the *barrio* of Argüelles, with some pleasant summer terrazas, and be heading towards the main centre of Madrid's Universidad Complutense.

The eastern flank of Plaza de España marks the beginning of **Gran Vía**. This Haussmannesque boulevard was slammed through the tumbledown slums to the north of Sol in the 1910s and 1920s.

At the eastern end of Gran Vía, note the superb dome of the **Metropolis** building. Continue east along Calle de Alcalá until you reach **Plaza de la Cibeles**, Madrid's favourite roundabout.

If you head north up the tree-lined promenade of Paseo de los Recoletos, on the left you'll pass some of the city's best-known cafes, including Gran Café de Gijón, Café-Restaurante El Espejo and El Gran Pabellón del Espejo. On your right is the enormous **Biblioteca Nacional** (National Library) and, a little farther on, a statue of Columbus in Plaza de Colón.

From here walk round the back of the National Library, where the **Museo Arqueológico Nacional** is housed. Southwards along Calle de Serrano (which is the backbone of Madrid's most chic shopping district) is Plaza de la Independencia, in the middle of which stands the **Puerta de Alcalá**.

Turn right and then left when you reach Plaza de la Cibeles to head south down Paseo del Prado, an extension of the city's main tree-lined boulevard, and you'll soon reach the art gallery with which it shares its name. On the other side of the boulevard, the **Museo Thyssen-Bornemisza** is, along with the **Prado**, a must.

The area around and north of the Prado is laced with museums, while stretching out behind it to the east are the wonderful gardens of the **Parque del Buen Retiro**. Immediately south of the Prado is the **Real Jardín Botánico**. Past this, looking onto the manic multilane roundabout that is Plaza del Emperador Carlos V, are the city's main train station, **Atocha**, and the third in Madrid's big league of art galleries, the **Centro de Arte Reina Sofía**.

Head a few blocks north along Paseo del Prado again, and west up Calle de las Huertas (through the tiny Plaza de Platería Martínez). The 17th-century **Convento de las Trinitarias** (closed to the public), which backs onto this street, is where Cervantes lies buried. Turn right up Costanilla de las Trinitarias and continue north along Calle de San Agustín until you come to Calle de Cervantes, then turn left. On your right you will pass the **Casa de Lope de Vega** at No 11.

A left turn at the end of Calle de Cervantes into Calle de León will bring you back onto Calle de las Huertas, which, you may have already noticed, is one of Madrid's happening streets. Anywhere along here or up on Plaza de Santa Ana will make a great place to take the weight off your feet at the end of this gruelling tour! For specific tips, consult the special section Into the Night. From Plaza de Santa Ana it's a brief stroll north and then west back to our starting point at the Puerta del Sol.

was a pestilent mire made worse by the presence of a rambling produce market) dubbed her Mariblanca (White Maria), and the statue became something of a symbol of the city. The church, like so many others in Madrid, was demolished in 1854 and the statue moved to Plaza de las Descalzas and then to Paseo de los Recoletos. It finally ended up inside the Ayuntamiento and a copy was erected in the Puerta del Sol – this you can see today.

The main building on the square houses the regional government of the Comunidad de Madrid. (The Asamblea de Madrid, or regional parliament, meets in a new building in the suburb of Vallecas.) The Casa de Correos, as it is called, was built as the city's main post office in 1768. The clock, which marks a classic meeting place for madrileños, was added in 1856. On New Year's Eve, people thronging the square wait impatiently for the clock to strike 12, and at each gong swallow a grape – not as easy to do as it sounds! The semicircular junction owes its present appearance in part to the Bourbon king Carlos III (1759–88), whose equestrian statue (the nose is unmistakable) stands proudly in the middle. In the 1860s the square was further broadened and the housing around it built.

Just to the north of Carlos, the statue of a bear nuzzling a *madroño* (strawberry tree) is not only the city's symbol but also another favourite meeting place for locals.

The square was the central stage for the popular rising against Napoleon's troops on 2 May 1808 – or rather, its repression.

Plaza Mayor (Map 7)

The heart of imperial Madrid beats in the 17th-century Plaza Mayor, a short stroll west of Puerta del Sol. Designed in 1619 by Juan Gómez de Mora and built in typical Herrerian style, of which the slate spires are the most obvious expression, it was long a popular stage for royal festivities, *autos-de-fe* (the burnings of people condemned by the Inquisition) and bullfights. In 1790 a fire largely destroyed the square, which was subsequently resurrected more or less in faithful reproduction of the original under the supervision of Juan de Villanueva.

In the Middle Ages, the site was known as Plaza del Arrabal, since it lay beyond the then city walls (*arrabal*, an Arabic word, signified extramural suburbs). It was a favourite haunt of traders, who could carry on their business here without fear of the taxation to which they would have been subjected within the city walls.

The *alhóndiga del pan*, where the wheat and flour needed to make bread was sold, was located here (to be replaced in the 17th century by the Real Casa de la Panadería, or royal bakery), along with butchers' stalls, fishmongers, wine stores and other shops. These day-to-day activities continued in one form or another for much of the life of

JULIET COOMBE

Take your bearings from this statue of the city's symbol, a she-bear nuzzling a strawberry tree.

Skeletons out of the Closet

In the good old days, from the 15th to the 17th centuries at least, it was not uncommon for serious crimes (which at that time might include something as banal as robbery) to be punished with rather horrible forms of torture and blood-curdling executions. Nobles were decapitated, while common criminals were either hanged or drawn and quartered. Afterwards, the various bits and pieces of their bodies were put on display along city streets, and their heads, where appropriate, were nailed up outside the houses of their victims. The Cofradía de la Caridad, a charitable confraternity, would later collect the remains and inter them in unconsecrated ground just outside one of three Madrid churches, San Ginés, San Miguel or Santa Cruz.

In early 2000, as work was carried out to build a car park on the site of the Iglesia de Santa Cruz (which was destroyed in 1869), one of these mass graves was discovered, with as many as 100 corpses, many quartered, of such unfortunates.

Plaza de Santa Cruz (Map 7)

Just off the south-eastern corner of Plaza Mayor is the Baroque edifice, also known as the Palacio de Santa Cruz, housing the **Ministerio de Asuntos Exteriores** (Ministry of Foreign Affairs), formerly the court prison and something of a landmark with its grey slate spires. It dominates Plaza de Santa Cruz.

Basílica de San Isidro (Map 7)

Calle de Toledo, which runs south from Plaza Major, is no longer the main road to Madrid's one-time competitor for the title of national capital. It's an interesting boulevard, though, and you might want to have a quick look at the imposing church that for some time served as the city's de facto cathedral, until Nuestra Señora de la Almudena was completed in 1992. In fact, Madrid was only granted status as an archdiocese independent of Toledo in 1851, which explains why the city went for so long without a cathedral at all.

The basilica is an austere Baroque edifice that is home to the remains of the city's patron saint, San Isidro (in the third chapel on your left after you walk in). It is open from 8 am to noon and 6 to 8.30 pm.

Next door, the **Instituto de San Isidro** once went by the name of Colegio Imperial and, from the 16th century on, was where many of the country's leading figures were schooled. You can wander in and look at the elegant courtyard.

At this point the road forks. Calle de Toledo leads down to the triumphal arch at the **Puerta de Toledo**, built in 1817 to celebrate the defeat of Napoleon several years earlier. Beyond, the 18th-century bridge of the same name, which was completed in 1729, spans the Río Manzanares. The left fork, Calle de los Estudios, leads into the heart of **El Rastro**, the crowded Sunday flea market. Although increasingly bereft of objects of real interest and busy with tourists, it is worth wandering around just for the atmosphere (see also the Shopping chapter).

the square, which today is still lined with shops.

In 1673, King Carlos II issued an edict allowing food stall-holders to raise tarpaulins above their stalls to protect their wares and themselves from the refuse that people habitually tossed out of the windows above! For some reason such tarpaulins had been banned since the days of the Catholic Monarchs (Isabel and Fernando).

In the middle of the present-day square stands an equestrian statue of Felipe III by the Italian sculptors Giambologna and Pietro Tacca. It was Felipe who ordered construction of the square. The colourful frescoes on the **Real Casa de la Panadería** were painted in 1992, replacing earlier ones.

On a sunny day the plaza's cafes do a roaring trade, with some 500 busy tables groaning under the weight of the rather expensive drinks.

Iglesia de San Ginés (Map 7)

Between Calle Mayor and Calle del Arenal, directly north of Plaza Mayor, San Ginés is one of Madrid's oldest churches: it has been here in one form or another since at least the 14th century. In fact, it is speculated that, prior to the arrival of the Christians in 1085, a Mozarabic community (Christians in Muslim territory) lived around the stream that later became Calle del Arenal and that their parish church stood on this site. Be that as it may, it has suffered various disasters, and what you see today was largely built after a fire in 1824. The church houses some fine paintings, including an El Greco, but is open only for services.

Plaza de la Villa (Map 7)

Back on Calle Mayor and heading west, you pass the 19th-century **mercado** (central produce market) in Plaza de San Miguel before entering Plaza de la Villa. It is thought that the town fathers chose this square for the permanent seat of city government as early as the late Middle Ages.

The 17th-century **Ayuntamiento** (town hall), on the western side of the square, is a typical Habsburg edifice with Herrerian slate-tile spires. When originally planned in 1644 by Juan Gómez de Mora, it was to be used as a prison, but in the end it was used for both functions. The style is said to be Madrid Baroque. It's built of granite and brick and is a fairly sober affair due, in large part, to the scarcity of funds for municipal buildings. In fact, the town council *(consejo)* had for three centuries since 1346 met in the Iglesia de San Salvador, facing the square on Calle Mayor. The church no longer exists.

The final touches to the Casa de la Villa (as the town hall was also known) were only made to the building in 1693, and Juan de Villanueva made some alterations a century later.

You can join a free tour (in Spanish) of the Ayuntamiento at 5 pm and 6 pm on Monday (turn up at least 10 minutes before and join the queue). You are led through various reception halls and finally into the council chambers. The latter were restored in 1870 and again in 1986. Just outside the chambers you can see a ceramic copy of

Bronze Medallions

Since the mid-1990s, a barely perceptible homage to Madrid's past has spread across the city. On more than 80 buildings you can now read a pleasing bronze plaque that gives you the specs and a little historical low-down on the edifice you are admiring (or, indeed, on one you might simply have passed by had you not seen the plaque). It is planned to have 450 of these put up within the next few years. The Colegio de Arquitectos de Madrid decides which buildings, old and new, to flatter in this way.

Pedro Teixera's landmark 1656 map of Madrid.

Leaning more to the Gothic style, on the opposite side of the square is the 15th-century **Casa de los Lujanes**, the brickwork tower of which is said to have been 'home' to the imprisoned French monarch François I and his sons after their capture in the Battle of Pavia (1525). The **Casa de Cisneros**, built in 1537 by the nephew of Cardinal Cisneros, who was a key adviser to Queen Isabel, is plateresque in inspiration, although it was much restored and altered at the beginning of the 20th century. The main door and window above are what remains of the Renaissance-era building. It was acquired by the town council in 1917 and now houses the *alcalde*'s (mayor's) offices.

One block south-east looms the 18th-century Baroque remake of the **Iglesia del Sacramento**. It is the central church of Spain's army. Along Calle Mayor, as you approach Calle de Bailén, stands the Renaissance **Palacio del Duque de Uceda**, identifiable by the soldiers milling around outside as it is now used as a military headquarters (the Capitanía General).

If you duck down behind this massive mansion, you will end up in Calle de la Villa. At No 2 is the site of what was once the Estudio Público de Humanidades. This was one of Madrid's more important schools in the 16th century. Cervantes studied here for a while.

Convento de las Descalzas Reales (Map 5)

Halfway between Calle del Arenal and Plaza del Callao, the grim walls of this one-time palace serve as a mighty buttress to protect the otherworldly interior from the modern-day chaos outside. Behind the sober plateresque facade lies a sumptuous stronghold of the faith.

Doña Juana, daughter of Carlos I and mother of Portugal's ill-fated Dom Sebastian, commandeered the palace for conversion into a convent in the 16th century. She was followed by the Descalzas Reales (the Barefooted Royals), a group of illustrious women who became Franciscan nuns. A maximum of 33 nuns can live here, perhaps because Christ is said to have been 33 when he died. The 26 nuns in residence still live according to the rules of the closed order.

The compulsory guided tour (in Spanish) takes you up a gaudily frescoed Renaissance stairway to the upper level of the cloister. The vault was painted by Claudio Coello and at the top of the stairs is a portrait of Felipe II and family members on the royal balcony.

You then pass several of the convent's 33 chapels. The first contains a remarkable carved figure of a dead Christ recumbent. This is paraded in a moving Good Friday procession every year. At the end of the passage you are led into the antechoir and then the choir stalls themselves, where Doña Juana is buried and a *Virgen la Dolorosa* by Pedro de la Mena is seated in one of the 33 oak stalls.

The former sleeping quarters of the nuns house a museum with some of the most extraordinary tapestries you are likely to see. Woven in the 17th century in Brussels, they include four based on drawings by Rubens. Four or five artisans could take as long as a year to weave a square metre of premium-quality tapestry, so imagine how many years must have gone into these! While on the subject of impressive numbers, Spain and the Vatican were the biggest patrons of the tapestry business: Spain alone is said to have collected four million of them.

The convent is open from 10.30 am to 12.45 pm and 4 to 5.30 pm Tuesday to Saturday (closed Friday afternoon), and 11 am to 1.45 pm on Sunday and holidays. Admission costs 700 ptas (300 ptas for students and EU seniors). All EU citizens get in free on Wednesday.

Plaza de Santo Domingo (Map 5)

There is nothing much to indicate it now, but this square is named after a huge Dominican monastery that once stood here. That nothing remains but the name would seem in itself a telling indication of the power of anticlericalism in 19th-century Spain.

Convento de la Encarnación (Map 5)

After the Convento de las Descalzas Reales, you could also drop into this less well-known monastery. Founded by Empress Margarita de Austria, this 17th-century mansion built in the Madrid style of Baroque is still inhabited by nuns of the Augustine order (Agustinas Recoletas). Inside you'll find a large art collection, mostly from the 17th century, and a host of gold and silver reliquaries. The most famous of these contains the blood of San Pantaleón, which purportedly liquefies every year on 28 June.

The convent is open the same hours as the Convento de las Descalzas Reales. Admission costs 475 ptas (275 ptas for students and EU seniors). All EU citizens get in free on Wednesday.

PALACIO REAL & AROUND
Palacio Real (Map 7)

When the Alcázar, the oft-altered forerunner of the Palacio Real, burned down in 1734, few mourned its demise. Felipe V, the first of the Bourbon kings, took the opportunity to indulge in a little architectural magnificence, planning to build a palace that would dwarf all its European counterparts. He drafted in the Italian architect Filippo Juvara (1678–1736), who had made a name for himself with his works in Turin, such as the Basilica di Superga and the

Palazzo di Stupinigi. On his death, another Italian, Giovan Battista Sacchetti, took over, finishing the job in 1764.

The result, which Felipe did not live to see completed, was the Palacio Real, an Italianate Baroque colossus with some 2800 rooms – of which you are allowed to visit around 50. It is occasionally closed for state ceremonies of pomp and circumstance, but the present king is rarely in residence, preferring to live elsewhere.

The **Farmacia Real** is the first set of rooms you reach after buying your tickets at the southern end of the patio known as the Plaza de Armas (or Plaza de la Armería). The pharmacy is a seemingly endless parade of medicine jars and stills for mixing royal concoctions. Westwards across the plaza is the **Armería Real** (Royal Armoury), a shiny collection of weapons and armour, mostly dating from the 16th and 17th centuries. The full suits of armour, such as those of Felipe III, are among the most striking items on show.

Access to the **apartments** lies at the northern end of the Plaza de Armas. The main stairway, a grand statement of imperial power, leads first to the Halberdiers' rooms and eventually to the Salón del Trono (Throne Room). The latter is sumptuous to the point of making you giddy, its crimson-velvet wall coverings complemented by a Tiepolo ceiling. Shortly after, you'll encounter the Salón de Gasparini, with its exquisite stucco ceiling and walls resplendent with embroidered silks. The Sala de Porcelana is a heady setting, with myriad pieces from the one-time Retiro porcelain factory screwed into the walls. As you progress from one room to another through the palace, the decorative themes change. In the midst of it all comes the spacious Comedor de Gala (Gala Dining Room).

The **Biblioteca Real** (Royal Library) has been closed since the late 1980s. Only students with appropriate permission may enter.

The palace is open from 9.30 am to 6 pm (5 pm October to April) Monday to Saturday, and 9 am to 2.30 pm (2 pm October to April) on Sunday and holidays. It closes on

days when official receptions are held. Admission costs 900 ptas (400 ptas for students and EU seniors) or 1000 ptas if you join a guided tour. All EU citizens get in free on Wednesday (bring your passport).

If you're lucky, you may catch the colourful changing of the guard in full parade dress. This takes place at noon on the first Wednesday of every month (except in July and August) between the palace and the Catedral de Nuestra Señora de la Almudena.

Jardines de Sabatini (Map 5)
Several entrances give access to this somewhat neglected, French-inspired garden on the northern flank of the Palacio Real.

Campo del Moro (Map 2)
Much more inspired are the wonderful gardens of the Campo del Moro (Moor's Field), so-called because an Almoravid army drew up here beneath the walls of Madrid in 1110 in the hope of retaking the town for the Muslims. They succeeded in occupying all but the fortress, whose Christian garrison managed to hold on until the Almoravid fury abated and their forces retired south.

The only entrance to the gardens is on the western side, from Paseo de la Virgen del Puerto.

Acquired by Felipe II, the partly English-style gardens were not laid out as they are now until 1844, with alterations in 1890. The fountain known as Fuente de las Conchas, between the visitors entrance and the palace, was designed by Ventura Rodríguez. At the time of writing, it had been removed for restoration. Inside the grounds is the Museo de los Carruajes, in which royal carriages could be seen until it was closed for restoration some years ago.

The gardens are open from 10 am (9 am on Sunday and holidays) to 8 pm.

Plaza de Oriente (Map 5)
Eastwards across Calle de Bailén from the Palacio Real is the majestic Plaza de Oriente, once partly occupied by dependencies of the Alcázar and given its present form under French occupation in the early 1800s. The square is dominated by an equestrian

JULIET COOMBE

Washday at the crowded district of Lavapiés

JULIET COOMBE

Figures watching the crowds on the Paseo del Prado.

OLIVER STREWE

A statue silently guards the Palacio Real.

The neoclassical portal of the Congresso de los Diputados

Made you look twice?

Murals painted on Casa de la Panadería.

statue of Felipe IV and littered with 20 statues of mostly ancient monarchs, many of which had been destined to adorn the Palacio Real until it was found that they were too heavy. They say that at night the statues get down off their pedestals and stretch their legs a bit – a likely story. And if you were wondering how a heavy bronze statue of a rider and his horse rearing up can actually maintain that stance, the answer is simple – the hind legs are solid while the front ones are hollow.

Since the late 1990s, the stretch of Calle de Bailén between the palace and the square has been a pedestrian zone (a tunnel now takes traffic below it), forming an elegant, car-free space.

Backing onto the eastern side of the square is the city's premier, and unhappiest, opera house, the **Teatro Real**. Started in 1818, it was several decades in the making and has since been burned down, blown up in the Civil War and shut several times for restoration. It finally reopened in October 1997 after nine years of restoration that cost a staggering 21 million ptas.

Organised visits to the theatre (☎ 91 516 06 60) are possible at 1 pm from Tuesday to Friday, and from 11.30 am to 1.30 pm at the weekend and on holidays.

Plaza de Ramales (Map 7)

Just a quick hop south of Plaza de Oriente, the ayuntamiento is busy cleaning up this pleasant little square. That the square exists is due to Joseph Bonaparte, as one of the churches he ordered demolished, the Iglesia de San Juan, previously occupied most of this space. It is believed that Velázquez was buried in the church, but his remains have been lost. Excavations during the course of 2000 revealed the crypt of the former church and the remains of various people buried in it centuries ago. When the research is finished, all will be replaced by an underground car park.

Catedral de Nuestra Señora de la Almudena (Map 7)

South of the Palacio Real, this stark and cavernous church, Madrid's neo-Gothic cathedral, was completed in mid-1992 after more than 110 years of construction. The church is relatively new, but a place of worship has existed here or nearby since the city's earliest settlement.

When the Christians moved into the city in the 11th century, they converted the grand mosque into a church in the name of Santa María. It soon came to be known as Santa María de la Almudena, an allusion to the Muslim name for this part of the town of Magerit. Situated on the corner of what are now Calle Mayor (No 88 – a plaque marks the spot) and Calle de Bailén, the ex-mosque was soon torn down and replaced by a new church that lasted until the 18th century, when town planners demolished it to widen Calle Mayor.

Since Madrid had, until 1851, been considered part of the archdiocese of Toledo, it had never had its own cathedral. The church of Santa María de la Almudena had more or less fulfilled the roll unofficially, after which the baton was passed on to the Basílica de San Isidro, on Calle de Toledo.

The cathedral is open from 10 am to 2 pm and 6 to 8 pm.

Between the cathedral and the Palacio Real you can normally get expansive views of the Casa de Campo, to the west, but access has been blocked while excavation work is carried out on what appear to be remains of the Palacio's predecessor, the Alcázar.

Muralla Árabe (Map 2)

Behind the cathedral apse and down Cuesta de la Vega is a short stretch of the so-called Arab Wall, the city wall built by Madrid's early-medieval Muslim rulers. Some of it dates as far back as the 9th century, when the initial Muslim fort was raised. Other bits date from the 12th and 13th centuries, by which time the city was in Christian hands. The Muslims had been quite crafty. Money was apparently a little scarce so, while the outside of the walls was made to look as sturdy as any mighty wall protecting the most important of cities, on the inside it was done with rather cheap materials. Generally it seems to have worked, as the town was rarely taken by force.

In summer, the city council organises open-air theatre and music performances here.

Iglesia de San Nicolás de los Servitas (Map 7)

Considered to be the oldest surviving church in Madrid, the Iglesia de San Nicolás de los Servitas may well have been built on the site of Muslim Magerit's second mosque – if such a mosque existed.

Apart from the restored 12th-century mudéjar bell tower, the present church dates in part from the 15th century – the vaulting is late Gothic and the fine timber ceiling, which survived a fire in 1936, dates from about the same period. Other elements inside this small house of worship include plateresque and Baroque touches. The architect Juan de Herrera was buried in the crypt in 1597.

LA LATINA

Named after a remarkable 15th-century noblewoman (see Iglesia de San Andrés & Around later in this section), this area includes the one-time Moorish quarter of medieval Christian Madrid and some of the earliest 'suburban' expansion of the original town nucleus. A lively and in places rather gritty part of town, La Latina is a kind of crossroads between the evidently desirable Habsburg Madrid and working-class *barrios* such as Lavapiés.

Viaduct & Calle de Segovia (Maps 2 & 7)

The leafy area around and beneath the southern end of the viaduct that crosses over Calle de Segovia (Jardines de las Vistillas) is an ideal spot to take a break from the hubbub.

The viaduct is also a popular spot for suicides – or at least it was until they put up the plastic barriers in the late 1990s. The original viaduct was built in the late 19th century, but the present one went up in the 1940s. Before its existence, anyone wanting to cross over was obliged to make their way down to Calle de Segovia and back up the other side. In the town's earliest days, a punt ferried people across what had been a

trickling tributary of the Manzanares. Later a bridge was put in place.

While you're here, head down to Calle de Segovia and cross to the southern side. Just east of the viaduct, on a characterless apartment block (No 21) wall, is one of the oldest coats-of-arms of the city. The site once belonged to Madrid's ayuntamiento.

Calle de Segovia itself runs west to a nine-arched bridge, the **Puente de Segovia**, which Juan de Herrera built in 1584.

Climb up the southern side from Calle de Segovia and you reach Calle de la Morería. The area from here south to the Basílica de San Francisco el Grande and south-east to the Iglesia de San Andrés was the heart of the **morería**, or Moorish quarter. Strain the imagination a little and the maze of winding and hilly lanes even now retains a whiff of the North African medina. This is where the Muslim population of Magerit was concentrated following the 11th-century Christian takeover of the town.

Across Calle de Bailén, the terrazas of Las Vistillas offer one of the best vantage points in Madrid for a drink, with views to the Sierra de Guadarrama (see Terrazas in the special section Into the Night). During the Civil War, Las Vistillas was heavily bombarded by Nationalist troops from the Casa de Campo, who in turn were shelled from a Republican bunker here.

Basílica de San Francisco el Grande (Map 2)

Completed under the guidance of Francesco Sabatini, the Baroque basilica has some outstanding features, including frescoed cupolas and chapel ceilings by Francisco Bayeu.

Raised on the site where legend claims St Francis of Assisi built a chapel in 1217, it is one of the biggest churches in the city and has a curious ground plan. When you enter, the building arcs off to the left and right in a flurry of columns. Unfortunately, at the time of writing most of the interior was obscured by restorers' scaffolding.

A 19th-century plan to create a grand linking square supported by a viaduct between this church and the Palacio Real

A Humble Saint

Towards the end of the 11th century, a farm labourer by the name of Isidro travelled from northern Spain to the newly reconquered Madrid to seek his fortune. He was one of many Christian Spaniards encouraged by the Castilian Crown to repopulate territories wrested from Muslim control.

Isidro entered the service of the Vargas family. The story goes that one day, out in the fields just beyond the town walls, Isidro's boss, Iván de Vargas, was feeling so thirsty that Isidro called forth spring water where before there had been none. Iván was no doubt impressed, but not as much as the rest of town as word got around. 'It's a miracle!' they cried. And others followed. Successive generations maintained the memory of this and other miraculous deeds and by the 13th century Isidro had become something of a cult figure.

It was perhaps only natural, then, that such fervour should be repaid with further spectacles. Isidro had been buried in the cemetery of the Iglesia de San Andrés. In the late 13th century, his body was 'discovered' there and, more incredibly, the rot had not yet begun to set in. King Alfonso XI ordered the construction in the church of an ark to hold his remains and a chapel in which to venerate his memory.

Later, the chapel was replaced by a Baroque version at the back of the church, erected by the Vargas family in an effort to bask in the reflected saintly glory of their one-time family servant. His remains were moved in 1535, but only lasted 25 years here. After an argument between the parish priest of San Andrés and the chaplain of the new chapel (the Capilla del Obispo), his body was moved back to the church. In 1669 (47 years after the saint was canonised) yet another chapel was built for him there (it can be seen, in its restored form, today). A dividing wall went up between the church and the Capilla del Obispo, just in case anyone had any doubts about the severity of the tiff.

San Isidro Labrador (St Isidro the Farm Labourer), as he is officially known, made his last move, to the Basílica de San Isidro, about 100 years later. His bones still rest there today (except on those occasions when, as in 1896 and 1947, he is paraded about town in the hope he will intercede with divine forces and bring rain). Another curious thing about San Isidro is that his whole family was canonised. His wife was Santa María de la Cabeza and his son San Millán. Another holy family.

never left the drawing board – you can see a model in the Museo Municipal.

The church is open from 11 am to 1 pm and 4 to 7 pm Tuesday to Saturday. Admission is supposedly by guided visit at 100 ptas per person, although at the time of researching there seemed precious little to stop you just wandering in and taking a look around.

Iglesia de San Andrés & Around (Map 7)

This proud church was largely gutted during the Civil War. Restoration work still continues to this day. Like a good many of Madrid's churches, it looks its best when lit up at night as a backdrop for the local cafe life.

That said, it is worth taking a peek inside. You enter from Plaza de San Andrés and as you turn left inside the church to face the altar you are confronted by a quite extraordinary work of Baroque decoration. Stern, dark columns with gold-leaf capitals against the rear wall lead your eyes up into the dome, all rose, yellow and green, and rich with sculpted floral fantasies and cherubs poking out of every nook and cranny.

Around the back, on Plaza de la Paja, is the **Capilla del Obispo**, a fine and (for Madrid) rare example of the transitional style between Gothic and Renaissance – look at the (largely Gothic) vaulting in the ceilings and the fine Renaissance reredos (screen). The Vargas family had the chapel built to house San Isidro's remains, which it did for a short while. For more on the story, see the boxed text 'A Humble Saint'.

The church and chapel open from 8 am to 1.30 pm and 5.30 to 8 pm daily, although the chapel is often closed – you may only be able to get in if there is a temporary exhibition on at the time.

They say Plaza de la Paja, by the way, got its name (Straw Square) because it was medieval Madrid's main grain store.

Next door to the church, in Plaza de San Andrés, is a modest building on the spot where they say San Isidro ended his days in around 1172. Here is also the 'miraculous well', in which popular tradition says the saint saved his son from drowning. A small museum containing assorted archaeological finds from old Madrid reopened here in mid-May 2000. The largely new building has a 16th-century courtyard and a 17th-century chapel. It opens from 9.30 am to 8 pm Tuesday to Friday, and 10 am to 2 pm at the weekend.

Just south-east of the church, you wind up in an ill-defined square, Plaza de la Cebada (Barley Square), where in medieval times city-dwellers came to purchase barley – an important staple – from local farmers. In the wake of the Christian conquest the square was, for a time, the site of the Muslim cemetery. The nearby **Plaza de la Puerta de Moros** (Moors Gate) underscores that this area was long home to the city's Muslim (or mudéjar) population. The square eventually became a popular spot for public executions. Until well into the 19th century, the condemned would be paraded along Calle de Toledo, before turning into the square and there mounting the gallows. In an era when good entertainment was hard to come by, it appears that madrileños rather enjoyed the spectacle of a fine execution.

The **Teatro de la Latina**, on Plaza de la Cebada, stands where one of Queen Isabel's closest advisers, Beatriz Galindo, built a hospital in the 15th century. Her aims were twofold – to provide the city with a charitable institution for the sick and the poor (as her deceased husband had ordered in his will), and to provide herself with decent digs for her coming years as a widow. A noted humanist, Galindo was known as 'La Latina' for her prodigious knowledge of Latin. In its heyday, the hospital occupied a large chunk of land between Calle de Toledo and Calle de San Francisco (the former Islamic cemetery had been taken over after the order of 1492 imposing the conversion or expulsion from Spain of Muslims and Jews). All that remains of the late-Gothic building is a fine stone doorway, which was moved to the gardens of the Escuela de Arquitectura, in the Ciudad Universitaria in the north of the city. Only Galindo's nickname reminds us of what once stood here.

Not far off, the narrow streets of Calle de la Cava Alta and Calle de la Cava Baja delineate where the second line of medieval Christian city walls ran. They continued up along what is now Calle del los Cuchilleros (Knifemakers St) and along the Cava de San Miguel, and were superseded by the third circuit of walls, which was raised in the 15th century. The *cavas* were initially ditches dug in front of the walls, later used as refuse dumps and finally given over to housing when the walls clearly no longer served any defensive purpose.

Iglesia de San Pedro El Viejo (Map 7)

The outstanding feature of this church is its clearly mudéjar bell tower. Along with the fine brick bell tower of the Iglesia de San Nicolás de los Servitas, a little way to the north, it is one of the few surviving testaments to the industriousness of mudéjar (Muslim) builders. Both towers have been carefully restored, but all other traces of mudéjar Madrid have disappeared. To get an idea of what you might have expected to see had Madrid's Muslim heritage been better respected, head down to Toledo.

Basílica de San Miguel (Map 7)

A short way north of the San Pedro, this basilica stands on the site of an earlier Romanesque church. This version, with a curved, late-Baroque facade and rococo interior, was completed in 1745. You can get in from 11 am to 12.15 pm and 5.30 to 7 pm Monday to Saturday (admission free).

LAVAPIÉS (MAP 7)

With the exception of **La Corrala**, an intriguing traditional tenement block built round a central courtyard, which functions now as a makeshift stage for (mainly summertime) theatre, there are no specific sights in this lively quarter. La Corrala is at Calle de Mesón de Paredes 65, opposite the ruins of a church.

The real attraction of Lavapiés is the gritty feel of what is one of the city's last true barrios. Thought to be where the bulk of the city's Jewish population once lived (the existence centuries ago of at least one synagogue in the area is documented), it is now the residence of an interesting mix of working-class *gatos* (native madrileños), *gitanos* (Romany people) and predominantly North African immigrants.

PLAZA DE ESPAÑA & AROUND

A curiously unprepossessing square given its grand title, Plaza de España is flanked to the east by the Edificio de España, reminiscent of some of the larger efforts of Soviet monumentalism but somehow not unpleas-

ing to the eye, and to the north by the rather ugly Torre de Madrid. Taking centre stage in the square is a statue of Cervantes. At the writer's feet is a bronze of his most famous characters, Don Quixote and Sancho Panza.

Museo de Cerralbo (Map 5)

You could walk past this noble mansion and barely notice it amid the bustle in the tight, narrow streets just north-west of Plaza de España. Inside is a haven of 19th-century opulence. The 17th Marqués de Cerralbo – politician, poet and archaeologist – was also an inveterate collector. You can see the results of his efforts in what were once his Madrid lodgings, at Calle de Ventura Rodríguez 17.

The upper floor boasts a gala dining hall and a grand ballroom. The mansion is jammed with the fruits of the collector's eclectic meanderings – from religious paintings to Oriental pieces, to suits of armour and clocks. Occasionally there's a gem, such as El Greco's *Éxtasis de San Francisco*.

The museum is open from 9.30 am to 2.30 pm Tuesday to Saturday, and 10 am to

Portrait of the Bandit as a Young Man

In 1806 one of Spain's most legendary bandits was born in the highly *castizo* (working-class madrileño) barrio of Lavapiés. Son of a well-off carpenter who hoped for big things for him, Luis Candelas was already dabbling in the gentle art of gang warfare at the tender age of 13. He showed an early talent with sharp instruments.

His sharpest instrument was, however, between his ears. By the age of 18 he had a respectable job in the Madrid public service, which he used to tap into information that could be of use to the liberals, with whom he sympathised. At the same time, he led a third existence as head of a successful gang of thieves.

Denounced as a liberal at the age of 20, Candelas was transferred to La Coruña. His parents set him up with a nice middle-class girl from Zamora. All to no avail. Candelas re-created himself as a respectable businessman with 'interests' in Peru by day, and became one of the most audacious *bandoleros* by night, pulling off increasingly daring heists in and around Madrid. He was captured several times, but always managed to escape with ease and maintain his double identity. As the years went by, he became something of a hero to working-class madrileños. By day, in his other persona, he cut a dashing figure in the court and was something of a lady killer.

All good things come to an end, however, and Candelas was finally caught in July 1837. This time there was no getting away and he was sentenced to death after being found guilty of more than forty counts of robbery, armed and otherwise. Candelas observed that the sentence was fair, if a little late in coming! He was executed just outside the Puerta de Toledo on 4 November 1837.

2 pm on Sunday. It is closed on Monday and public holidays. Admission costs 400 ptas (200 ptas for students). It's free on Wednesday and Sunday.

Templo de Debod (Map 2)

Looking out of place in the Parque de la Montaña, in the Jardines del Paseo del Pintor Rosales, this 4th-century BC Egyptian temple was saved from the rising waters of Lake Nasser, formed by the Aswan High Dam, and sent block by block to Spain in 1970.

The temple is open from 10 am to 2 pm and 6 to 8 pm (9.45 am to 1.45 pm and 4.15 to 6.15 pm from 1 October to 31 March) Tuesday to Friday, and 10 am to 2 pm at the weekend. Admission costs 300 ptas (half-price for seniors or those aged under 18). It is free for all on Wednesday and Sunday.

Ermita de San Antonio de la Florida (Map 2)

Some of the finest works produced by Goya are in this small hermitage, aka the Panteón de Goya, about 10 minutes' walk north from the Campo del Moro (metro: Príncipe Pío). You'll see two small chapels. In the southern one, the ceiling and dome are covered in frescoes by the master (restored in 1993). Those on the dome depict the miracle of St Anthony, who is calling on a young man to rise from the grave and absolve his father, unjustly accused of his murder. Around them swarms a typical Madrid crowd. Usually in this kind of scene the angels and cherubs appear in the cupola, above all terrestrial activity. But Goya places the human above the divine.

The painter is buried in front of the altar. His remains were transferred in 1919 from France, where he died in self-imposed exile.

The chapel is open from 10 am to 2 pm and 4 to 8 pm Tuesday to Friday, and 10 am to 2 pm at the weekend (and in the hot summer months of July and August). Admission costs 300 ptas (half-price for seniors and children aged under 14). It is free for everyone on Wednesday and Sunday.

Just across the road is one of Madrid's great eating institutions – the chicken and cider house Casa Mingo (see Río Manzanares Area under Budget in the Places to Eat chapter).

Across the train tracks, on Calle de Francisco, is the **Cementerio de la Florida**, where 43 rebels executed by Napoleon's troops lie buried; they were killed on the nearby Montaña del Príncipe Pío in the predawn of 3 May 1808, after the Dos de Mayo rising. The event was immortalised by Goya and a plaque was placed here in 1981. The forlorn cemetery, established in 1796, is generally closed.

Antiguo Cuartel del Conde Duque & Palacio de Liria (Map 5)

Over Calle de la Princesa, on the western edge of the Malasaña district (see Malasaña & Chueca later in this chapter), is the grand barracks known as the Antiguo Cuartel del Conde Duque. This has a day job housing government archives and as an occasional art exposition centre, and now and then does a night gig as a music venue.

Virtually next door, the 18th-century Palacio de Liria, rebuilt after a fire in 1936 and surrounded by an enviably green oasis, holds an impressive collection of art, period furniture and *objets d'art*. To organise a visit, send a formal request with your personal details to Palacio de Liria, Atención Don Miguel, Calle de la Princesa 20, 28008 Madrid. The waiting list is long and most mortals content themselves with staring through the gates into the grounds.

GRAN VÍA (MAP 5)

Gran Vía arches south-eastwards from Plaza de España. It is a chokingly busy boulevard, with more energy than elegance, although it gains some of the latter in the approach to Calle de Alcalá. From luxury hotels to cheap *hostales*, pinball parlours and dark old cinemas to jewellery stores and high fashion, from fast food and sex shops to banks, Gran Vía has it all. It's a good place to take the city's pulse. Behind the grand facades lie some of the tackier scenes of madrileño life.

The street was pushed through here in the first decades of the 20th century, sweeping away entire neighbourhoods. In the following years, grand if bland buildings were raised along much of its length. Among the more interesting ones is the **Edificio Metropolis** (finished in 1910), which marks the southern end of Gran Vía. The winged victory statue atop its dome was added in 1975. A little way up the boulevard is the **Edificio Grassy** (with the Piaget sign), another of the more interesting piles raised in the early decades of the 20th century.

On a rise about one-third of the way along Gran Vía stands the **Telefónica** building. The national phone company was formed in the 1920s, when this colossus was constructed. It was for years the highest building in the city and even today can be seen from various points in central Madrid. Farther along you see another eyecatching, if neglected, construction, the **Carrión** building, on the corner of Gran Vía and Calle de Jacometrezo. This was the city's first tower-block apartment hotel and caused quite a stir when it was put up in the pre-WWI years.

MALASAÑA & CHUECA

Just north of Gran Vía is one of Madrid's sleazier red-light zones, populated by an interesting, if not entirely savoury, collection of pimps, junkies and wasted-looking hookers. This warren of long, narrow streets intersected by even narrower lanes is known officially as the Barrio de Universidad, but more generally as Malasaña. For the purposes of this guide, that definition extends some blocks west across Calle de San Bernardo into the area bounded by Gran Vía, Calle de la Princesa and Calle de Alberto Aguilera. Chueca is a small area around the square and metro station of the same name.

Long one of Madrid's slummiest areas, the heart of Malasaña retains an atmosphere of decay, but mostly in a charming sort of way. Away from the seedy red-light zone around Calle de la Luna, it is, for the most part, a lively haven of bars, restaurants and other drinking dens.

It is also laced with contrasts. The north-eastern corner is dominated by the Palacio de Justicia, the country's supreme law courts. Calle de Génova, which forms part of its

northern boundary, is home to the headquarters of Spain's ruling Partido Popular. To the south-east, Malasaña butts against the walls of the national army headquarters. On its western edge are the Antiguo Cuartel del Conde Duque and the Palacio de Liria (see Plaza de España & Around earlier in this chapter).

Museo Municipal (Map 5)

The main attraction here is the restored Baroque entrance, raised in 1721 by Pedro de Ribera. Until its conversion into a museum in 1929, the building served as a hospice. Of the original building, founded in 1673, only the chapel remains. It lies dead ahead when you walk into the building and is dominated by a grand canvas, *San Fernando Ante La Virgen* (St Ferdinand Before the Virgin Mary), by the Neapolitan Baroque artist Luca Giordano (1634–1705). Before you step into the chapel proper, you will see two sculpted sepulchres. The one on the right is of Beatriz Galindo (see Iglesia de San Andrés & Around under La Latina earlier in this chapter) and the other of her husband, Francisco Ramírez.

Inside the museum, you are taken on an interesting but hardly masterful tour through the history of Madrid. In the basement (closed at the time of writing) you can see various Iron and Bronze Age artefacts dug up around the Manzanares, along with a few Roman mosaics and odds and ends from the Visigoths and Muslims.

On the ground floor, Madrid de los Austrias (in other words Habsburg Madrid) is brought to life, up to a point, through paintings and models. The theme continues on the floor above, where the various rooms take you from Bourbon Madrid through to the final years of the 19th century. Of interest are a couple of Goyas and, possibly more than anything else, a huge model of Madrid made in 1830 by a military engineer called León Gil de Palacios (1778–1849). It took him the best part of two years to complete. The top floor is set aside for temporary exhibits and a room devoted to the satirist and artist Enrique Herreros (1903–77). The selected drawings take an ironic look at the Madrid of the 1950s and 1960s.

At Calle de Fuencarral 78, the museum (metro: Tribunal) is open from 9.30 am to 8 pm (to 2.30 pm in July and August) Tuesday to Friday, and 10 am to 2 pm at the weekend. It closes on Monday and public holidays. Admission costs 300 ptas (half-price for seniors and people aged under 18). It's free for all on Wednesday and Sunday.

Museo Romántico (Map 5)

The late-18th-century building in which this curious little museum is housed was rented back in 1920 by the Marqués de la Vega-Inclán to house the tourism body he himself had founded, the Comisaría Regia de Turismo. Vega-Inclán was at the forefront of initiatives to promote Spain as a tourist destination, although perhaps a little ahead of his time. He was involved in the creation of the chain of luxury hotels known as the Paradores, and was also behind the creation of such museums as the Casa y Museo de El Greco in Toledo.

In 1924 Vega-Inclán turned the building into the Museo Romántico, a minor treasure trove of mostly 19th-century paintings, furniture, porcelain and other bits and bobs from a bygone age. The downstairs rooms contain books, photos and documents relating to the life of Vega-Inclán, while his collection is upstairs. It is interesting, above all, as an insight into what upper-class houses were like in the 19th century.

The museum is at Calle de San Mateo 13, just east of the Museo Municipal. It is open from 9 am to 2.45 pm Tuesday to Saturday, and 10 am to 1.15 pm on Sunday. It is closed on Monday, holidays and throughout August. Admission costs 400 ptas (half-price for students). Seniors get in free, as does everyone else on Sunday.

Sociedad General de Autores y Editores (Map 5)

A couple of blocks east of the Museo Romántico, on Calle de Pelayo, this joyously self-indulgent ode to Modernismo looks akin to a huge ice-cream cake half-melted by the summer sun. It is virtually one of a kind in Madrid, although a couple of other, much more modest examples of the genre are scattered about.

PLAZA DE COLÓN TO THE PRADO

The modern Plaza de Colón (metro: Colón; cercanías: Recoletos), with the almost surreal Edificio de Colón on its western side,

---

St Valentine's Bones

Nobody much thinks about poor old St Valentine on what in Spain is called 'Lovers' Day' (El Día de los Enamorados) – 14 February. This 3rd-century bishop and academic was born in Terni, Italy, and according to the legend had quite a thing about young people. Apparently, he was so enchanted by the blossoming of young love that he'd help to write love letters, hand out flowers to young newlyweds and even send a little money to struggling lovers in difficult financial circumstances. Whether for this or some other reason, Bishop Valentine was not popular with the Roman administration – and Christianity had yet to become Rome's official faith. So the authorities had Valentine arrested and executed on 14 February 269. Make of all that what you will.

Valentine seems then to have disappeared from sight and mind until the 18th century, when his bones, along with those said to belong to hundreds of other saints, were dug up during excavations in Rome. Since the Eternal City had insufficient churches to each host one of these venerable skeletons, the Church decided to send some of them on a trip to other good Catholic countries.

And so it was that St Valentine's bits landed in the crypt of the Iglesia de San Antón (more properly known as San Antonio Abad), in central Madrid (several other churches around Europe also claim to have been the lucky recipients). In 1986 it was decided to put this skull-and-crossbones arrangement on public view in the church proper, at Calle de Hortaleza 65, just north-west of Chueca metro station. The church is open for visits from 5 to 6.30 pm.

---

is at first glance a rather uninspired affair. Its physical aspect, although softened by the fountains of the Centro Cultural de la Villa, is certainly nothing to write home about. The statue of Colón (Columbus) seems neglected and the **Monumento al Descubrimiento** (Monument to the Discovery – of America, that is), for all its cleverness, does not leave a lasting impression. It was cobbled together in the 1970s.

Still, the area is an artistic nerve centre. The Centro Cultural plays host to theatrical and musical events, and just south of the square loom the Biblioteca Nacional and two museums. These can be looked upon as the beginning of museum row – the walk from Colón to the Prado is laced with them.

Biblioteca Nacional & Museo del Libro (Map 6)

Perhaps one of the most outstanding of the many grand edifices erected in the 19th century on the avenues of Madrid, the Biblioteca Nacional was commissioned by Isabel II in 1865 and completed in 1892.

Some of the library's collections have been imaginatively arranged in displays recounting the history of writing and the storage of knowledge. The Museo del Libro, which opened in 1995, is a worthwhile stop for any bibliophile yearning to see a variety of Arabic texts, illuminated manuscripts, centuries-old books of the Torah and still more. If your Spanish is up to it, the displays come to life with interactive video commentaries.

The museum is usually open from 10 am to 9 pm Tuesday to Saturday, and 10 am to 2 pm on Sunday. Admission is free. At the time of writing, the museum was closed due to renovation work in the library, but was due to open late in 2000.

Museo Arqueológico Nacional (Map 6)

Out the back of the same building, at Calle de Serrano 13, the forbidding entrance to this museum of archaeology may seem just a little too heavy for your liking. Inside, you will find a delightfully varied collection spanning everything from prehistory to the Iberian tribes, Imperial Rome, Visigothic Spain, the Muslim conquest and specimens of Romanesque, Gothic and mudéjar handiwork. There is a lot in here and those passing through Madrid more than once could well benefit from a second visit.

The basement contains displays on prehistoric man and spans the Neolithic period to the Iron Age. Modest collections from ancient Egypt, Etruscan civilisation in Italy, classical Greece and southern Italy under Imperial Rome can also be seen. There are also some Spanish specialities: ancient civilisation in the Balearic and Canary Islands.

The ground floor is the most interesting. Sculpted figures such as the *Dama de Ibiza* and *Dama de Elche* reveal a flourishing artistic tradition among the Iberian tribes – no doubt influenced by contact with Greek, Phoenician and Carthaginian civilisation. The latter must continues, a century after it was found near the Valencian town, to attract controversy over its authenticity.

The arrival of Imperial Rome brought predictable changes. Some of the mosaics here are splendid, particularly the incomplete *Triumph of Bacchus* in Room 22. The display on Visigothic Spain, and especially material from Toledo, marks a clear break, but only previous experience with Muslim Spain (for example, the great cities of Andalucía) or other Muslim countries can prepare you for the wonders of Islamic art. The arches taken from Zaragoza's Aljafería are a centrepiece.

The influences of pure Islamic precepts persist in the later mudéjar style of re-Christianised Spain, which stands in remarkable contrast with Romanesque and later Gothic developments – all of which can be easily appreciated by soaking up the best of this eclectic collection.

Outside, stairs lead down to a partial copy of the prehistoric cave paintings of Altamira (Cantabria), which will be as close to the paintings as many people get.

The museum is open from 9.30 am to 8.30 pm Tuesday to Saturday, and 9.30 am to 2 pm on Sunday. It's closed on Monday and national holidays. Admission costs 500 ptas, except on Sunday and from 2.30 pm on Saturday, when it's free. Seniors always get in free.

Museo de Cera (Map 6)

This is a rather pathetic version of a wax museum. Still, 450 characters have been captured in the sticky stuff – you'll need a good dose of imagination to recognise some of them. In addition, you can board the Tren del Terror (500 ptas) or the Simulador (400 ptas) – the latter shakes you up a bit, as though you were inside a washing machine. Another side show is the Multivisión animated 'experience' (200 ptas). All a bit dire really, although it might amuse pesky small people.

Next to Colón metro station, the museum is open from 10 am to 2.30 pm and 4.30 to 8.30 pm Monday to Friday, and 10 am to 8.30 pm at the weekend and on holidays. Admission costs 1500 ptas to the lot or 1000 ptas to the wax museum alone (600 ptas for children aged 10 and under). You can pay separately for any of the other attractions.

Palacio de Linares (Map 6)

Walk southwards down Paseo de los Recoletos and you reach this 19th-century pleasure dome (metro: Banco de España), built in 1873 and a worthy member of the line-up of grand facades on Plaza de la Cibeles. Its innards are notable particularly for the copious decoration in Carrara marble. The problem is that you don't get to see very much of it. In compensation, you can visit the **Casa de América**, a modern exposition centre in the palace's grounds. It is open from 11 am to 8 pm (to 2 pm on Sunday and holidays), and admission is free.

Plaza de la Cibeles (Maps 5 & 6)

The fountain of the Cybele is one of Madrid's most beautiful. Ever since it was erected in 1780 by Ventura Rodríguez, this assessment has remained much the same. Carlos III thought it so nice that he wanted to have it moved to the gardens of the Granja de San Ildefonso, on the road to Segovia, but the madrileños were so in-

censed that he was persuaded by leading figures of the day to let it be.

The goddess Cybele had Atalanta and Hippomenes, recently paired off thanks to the intervention of Aphrodite, converted into lions and shackled to her chariot for having profaned her temple. They had been put up to this by Aphrodite, irritated by the apparent ingratitude of the newlyweds for her good work.

One might expect a degree of respect for ancient mythology and centuries-old public art. Football, however, seems more sacred still. Ever since the Spanish national competition got under way at the beginning of the last century, the Cibeles fountain has been the object of a kind of ritual rape by the players and supporters of Real Madrid when the side has won anything of note. Down through the years, these people have celebrated by clambering all over the fountain in a frenzy and chipping bits off as souvenirs. Oddly, the club itself has never done anything to stop this. The city council now occasionally boards up the statue on the eve of important matches.

The building you are least likely to miss on the square is the sickly-sweet **Palacio de Comunicaciones** – newcomers find it hard to accept that this is only the central post office. Diametrically opposite this is the **Palacio Buenavista**, which now belongs to the army. A block behind it to the west, on the tiny Plaza del Rey, is the **Casa de las Siete Chimeneas**, a 16th-century mansion that takes its name from the seven chimneys it still boasts. Nowadays, it is home to the Ministry of Culture. They say that the ghost of one of Felipe II's lovers still runs about here in distress on certain evenings, although the fact is that the place was built for a senior government official. From the Plaza del Rey you can see the rear of the **Iglesia de San José**, whose facade is actually on Calle de Alcalá but is easily missed.

Museo Naval (Map 6)

A block south, seafaring folk may well find this museum interesting. It is jammed with quite extraordinary models of ships from the earliest days of Spain's maritime history to the 20th century. Accompanying them is a plethora of maps, arms, uniforms, flags (including a Nazi flag from the German warship *Deutschland*, which was bombed by Republican planes off Ibiza in 1937) and other naval paraphernalia.

Of greatest historical interest is Juan de la Cosa's parchment map of the known world, put together in 1500. The accuracy of Europe is quite astounding, and it is supposedly the first map to show the Americas (albeit with considerably greater fantasy than fact).

The museum is open from 10.30 am to 1.30 pm Tuesday to Sunday. Admission is free.

Museo de Artes Decorativos (Map 6)
At Calle de Montalbán 12, this museum is full of sumptuous period furniture, ceramics, carpets, tapestries and the like, spanning the 15th to the late 19th centuries. It is actually quite a bit more interesting than it sounds. Spread over five floors, it presents the visitor with an enormous variety of objects.

Ceramics from around the country and dating from different periods are on display throughout the building. The re-creations of kitchens from several regions are curious – it is surprising how much the kind of utensils used and layout of a well-stocked kitchen varied! Reconstructions of regal bedrooms, women's drawing rooms and 19th-century salons all help shed a little light on how the privileged classes of Spain have lived through the centuries.

It is open from 9.30 am to 3 pm Tuesday to Friday, and 10 am to 2 pm at the weekend and on holidays. Admission costs 400 ptas (half-price for students). Seniors get in free, as does everyone else on Sunday.

Museo del Ejército (Map 9)
In 1803 the chief minister, Manuel Godoy, ordered the establishment of an army museum in one of the few remaining parts of the one-time Palacio del Buen Retiro. Filled with weapons, flags, uniforms and other remnants of Spanish military glory, the mu-

seum is housed in what was the Salón de Reinos del Buen Retiro (metro: Banco de España or Retiro), at Calle de Méndez Núñez 1.

An interesting room containing portraits of Franco is devoted to the glorious Nationalist campaign in the Civil War, while the Sala Árabe (decorated Alhambra-style) holds various curios, including the sword of Boabdil, the last Muslim ruler of Granada. He signed the instrument of surrender to the Catholic monarchs that marked the end of the Reconquista in 1492.

Just what the immediate future holds in store for the museum is not entirely clear. The plan is to shift it to the Alcázar in Toledo and so make room for the expansion of the Prado gallery (see Museo del Prado at the beginning of this chapter). The idea has raised protests in Madrid and Toledo, in the latter case because it is claimed the Alcázar cannot house such a large collection on top of what it already contains. Judging by the size of the Alcázar, that seems rather unlikely, but there you go.

For the time being, the museum is open from 10 am to 2 pm Tuesday to Sunday. Admission costs 100 ptas (half-price for students). Seniors get in free, and everyone else does too on Saturday.

Iglesia de San Jerónimo el Real (Map 9)
The church was the nucleus of one of the most powerful monastic groups in Madrid. The Isabelline style inside is actually a 19th-century reconstruction that took its cues from San Juan de los Reyes in Toledo. The original had been largely destroyed during the Peninsular War, and suffered more with the subsequent expropriations. King Juan Carlos I was crowned here in 1975.

Next door, what remains of the 17th-century cloisters looks set to disappear as it becomes part of the extension of the Prado. The plan caused some uproar and neighbours' balconies sport placards demanding the cloister (or what's left of it) be saved.

A block east of the roundabout on Calle de Felipe IV is the custodian of the Spanish language, the **Real Academia Española de la Lengua** (Map 9).

Plaza de Neptuno (Map 7)

Officially known as Plaza de Cánovas del Castillo, the next roundabout south of Cibeles is commanded by an 18th-century sculpture of the sea god by Juan Pascual de Mena. It is a haughty focal point, flanked not only by the Thyssen-Bornemisza gallery and the Prado, but also by the city's famous competitors in the hotel business, the Ritz and the Palace.

The Neptune fountain is to the fans of Atlético Madrid what the Cibeles is to Real Madrid's mob. The results are equally painful.

Parque del Buen Retiro (Map 9)

After a heavy round of the art galleries, a stroll in Madrid's loveliest public gardens might be the best way to end the day. The gardens are at their busiest at the weekend, when street performers appear.

Once the preserve of kings, queens and their intimates, the park is now open to all. You can hire boats to paddle about on the artificial lake *(estanque)*, watched over by the massive structure of Alfonso XII's mausoleum. On the western side of the lake, you may notice an odd structure decorated with sphinxes. It is the Fuente Egipcia (Egyptian Fountain) and legend has it that an enormous fortune buried in the park by Felipe IV in the mid-18th century is here. Park authorities assure us the legend is rot, but it is hard not to dream of what treasure might be buried somewhere in the waterless fountain.

Weekend buskers and tarot readers ply their trade around the same lake, while art and photo exhibitions take place at a couple of places, in particular the Palacio de Exposiciones. Puppet shows for the kids are a summertime feature (look for Tiritilandia, or Puppet Land).

The Palacio de Cristal, a charming metal and glass structure to the south of the lake, was built in 1887 as a winter garden for exotic flowers. It is also the scene of occasional exhibitions.

At the southern end of the park, near the

rose gardens (La Rosaleda), a statue of El Ángel Caído (the Fallen Angel, aka Lucifer) brings a slightly sinister note to the place. The south-western end of the park is a popular cruising ground for young gay men.

Real Jardín Botánico (Map 9)

Ask most madrileños about the city's botanical gardens and they won't know what you are talking about. All the worse for them, as the Real Jardín Botánico is a refuge more beautiful than El Retiro, although not nearly as extensive. Created in 1755 under Fernando VI at El Huerto de Migas Calientes, on the banks of the Río Manzanares, the original gardens consisted of some 2000 plants collected by the botanist José Quer in his travels and through exchanges with European colleagues.

Carlos III ordered the transfer of the gardens to their present location, which was completed in 1781. His proud statue presides over the centre of the gardens. The rather bombastic Ministerio de Agricultura building, which was built in 1882, robbed the gardens of two precious hectares, leaving a total of eight. Over the more than two centuries of their existence the gardens have gone through highs and lows, and were closed for regeneration from 1974 to 1981.

In the Pabellón Villanueva, on the northern flank of the gardens, art exhibitions are frequently staged – opening hours are the same as for the park and usually the exhibitions are free.

The gardens open daily at 10 am and close at anything from 6 to 9 pm, depending on the time of year. Admission costs 250 ptas.

Antigua Estación de Atocha (Map 9)

The old train station at Atocha has become something of a botanical sight in itself. The interior of the old terminal, which is the departure point for the high-speed AVE to Seville, has been converted into a tropical garden – certainly a pleasant, if slightly sweaty, departure or arrival point. Just across the road is the Centro de Arte Reina Sofía (see that section earlier in this chapter).

Museo del Ferrocarril

Train buffs might want to head a little farther south for this railway museum, housed in the otherwise now disused 1880s Estación de Delicias. Along the platforms are lined up about 30 pieces of rolling stock, from the earliest steam locomotives through to a sleeping car from the late 1920s and the Talgo II, which ran on the country's long-distance routes until 1971. Several rooms off the platforms are set aside for dioramas of train stations, memorabilia, station clocks and the like. This is one for the kids, who will probably beg you to buy them model trains and track at the shop on the way out.

The museum is open from 10 am to 2.30 pm Tuesday to Sunday (it's closed throughout August). Admission costs 500 ptas, but is free on Saturday.

Real Fábrica de Tapices (Map 9)

Founded in the 18th century to provide the royal family and other bigwigs with tapestries befitting their grandeur, this workshop is still producing today. If you like tapestries and carpets of a high quality and price, a visit is well worth your while. With luck you will get to see how they are made, and have been made over the centuries. The factory (metro: Menéndez Pelayo), at Calle de Fuenterrabía 2, is open from 10 am to 2 pm Monday to Friday (except holidays). Admission costs 300 ptas.

THE PRADO TO SOL

The main reason for heading into the area known to locals as Huertas, roughly contained in the triangle west of Paseo del Prado and between Calle de Atocha and Carrera de San Jerónimo, is to eat and drink. It is a smaller, brighter and perhaps more touristy version of Malasaña.

Mention has already been made, in the boxed text 'A Little Walking Tour of Madrid' earlier in this chapter, of Cervantes' burial place and the **Casa de Lope de Vega**. The latter, at Calle de Cervantes 11 (Map 8; metro: Antón Martín), is open from 9.30 am to 2 pm Tuesday to Friday, and 10 am to noon on Saturday. Admission costs 200 ptas. The

playwright lived here for 25 years until his death in 1635, and the place is filled with memorabilia related to his life and times.

A block to the north along Calle de León is the **Ateneo de Madrid**, a venerable club of learned types founded in the 19th century. It is also home to a library. You can probably manage to wander into the foyer, which is lined with portraits of terribly serious-looking fellows.

Where Carrera de San Jerónimo runs into Plaza de las Cortes stands the **Congreso de los Diputados** (lower house of parliament). Originally a Renaissance building stood here, but it was completely revamped in 1843 and given a facade with a neoclassical portal. The modern extension tacked onto it seems a rather odd afterthought. It is possible to visit the Congreso de los Diputados between 10 am and 12.45 pm on Saturday. Make sure you have your passport. A guided visit (in Spanish) starts every 45 minutes.

Real Academia de Bellas Artes de San Fernando (Map 5)

If you need another art injection, try this somewhat fusty old institution at Calle de Alcalá 13. Fernando VI founded it in the 18th century as a centre to train promising artists. Little seems to have changed since then. Picasso and Dalí were both sent here to study in their younger days, but neither seemed particularly to appreciate the academic atmosphere.

The gallery is not without interest, however. The 1st floor, mainly devoted to a mix of 16th- to 19th-century paintings, is the most noteworthy. If you follow the museum's convoluted route map, you will visit rooms that contain, in the following order: a set of canvases by José de Ribera and Alonso Cano; works by Zurbarán (especially arresting is the series of full-length portraits of white-cloaked friars); one El Greco; a couple of minor portraits by Velázquez; a couple of Rubens and a handful of minor paintings by Italian masters such as Tintoretto and Giovanni Bellini; a roomful of Bravo Murillo; and last, but perhaps most captivating, a set of 20 or so

euro currency converter € 1 = 166 ptas

pieces by Goya (Room 20). These Goyas include self-portraits, portraits of King Fernando VII and the infamous minister Manuel Godoy, and a take on bullfighting.

Upstairs, with the exception of a room given over to drawings by Picasso (one assumes they were done well after his young school days here), the pickings are slimmer. Among artists represented are Sorolla, Juan Gris, Eduardo Chillida and Ignacio Zuloaga – in most cases with only one or two items.

The museum is open from 9 am to 7 pm Tuesday to Friday, and 9 am to 2.30 pm the rest of the week. Admission costs 400 ptas. Seniors get in free, as does everyone at the weekend. Since the commentaries are poor, you may find it worthwhile investing 100 ptas in a small booklet (it comes in several languages).

SALAMANCA & AROUND

Madrid's most chichi quarter, the Salamanca area to the north-east of the city centre, is lined with elegant apartments and smart department stores. Named after the Marqués de Salamanca, a 19th-century aristocrat with a penchant for property development (he went broke in the effort), it was always meant to end up as it did. As Madrid slowly came to grips with the need to extend the city in the course of the 19th century, one of the few areas to be developed initially was this barrio.

The snappy dressers wandering the grid-pattern boulevards around here seem to be on a different planet from the people of inner-city districts such as Lavapiés. Apart from shopping, you can take in a little culture.

Puerta de Alcalá (Map 6)

The gate was begun under the supervision of Francesco Sabatini at Plaza de la Cibeles to celebrate the arrival of Carlos III in Madrid in 1769. Completed in 1778, it was later moved to its present spot on Plaza de la Independencia as the city grew.

Museo Sorolla (Map 4)

If you liked Sorolla's paintings in the Casón del Buen Retiro, don't miss this museum.

Housed in the artist's former residence, it contains the most comprehensive collection of his work in Spain, mostly the sunny Valencian beach scenes for which he is best known. The museum (metro: Rubén Darío) is set amid cool gardens at Paseo del General Martínez Campos 37.

The museum is open from 10 am to 3 pm Monday to Saturday, and 10 am to 2 pm on Sunday and holidays. Admission costs 400 ptas (half-price for students). Seniors pay nothing, and nor does anyone else on Sunday.

Museo Lázaro Galdiano (Map 4)

A surprisingly rich, formerly private collection awaits you in this museum at Calle de Serrano 122 (metro: República Argentina). Aside from some fine works by artists such as Van Eyck, Bosch, Zurbarán, Ribera, Goya, Gainsborough and Constable, this is a rather odd-ball assembly of all sorts of collectibles. The ceilings were all painted according to their room's function. The exception is Room 14, where the artist created a collage from some of Goya's more famous works, including *La Maja* and the frescoes of the Ermita de San Antonio de la Florida, in honour of the genius.

The museum is open from 10 am to 2 pm Tuesday to Sunday (plus 7 to 11 pm from July to September). Admission costs 500 ptas (half-price for students). It's free on Saturday.

Museo de la Escultura Abstracta (Map 4)

This interesting open-air collection of 17 abstracts includes works by Eduardo Chillida, Joan Miró, Eusebio Sempere and Alberto Sánchez. The sculptures are beneath the overpass where Paseo de Eduardo Dato crosses Paseo de la Castellana (metro: Rubén Darío). All but one are on the eastern side of Paseo de la Castellana.

OUTSIDE THE CENTRE
Museums

Madrid seems to have more museums and art galleries than the Costa del Sol has high-rise apartment blocks. The following are a sample:

Museo de América (Map 2) For centuries, Spanish vessels plied the Atlantic between the mother country and the newly won colonies in Latin America. Most carried adventurers one way and gold the other, but the odd curio from the indigenous cultures found its way back.

The two levels of the museum show off a representative display of ceramics, statuary, jewellery and instruments of hunting, fishing and war, along with some of the paraphernalia of the colonisers. The Colombian gold collection, dating as far back as the 2nd century AD, and a couple of shrunken heads are eye-catching. Temporary exhibitions with various Latin American themes are regularly held.

The museum (metro: Moncloa), Avenida de los Reyes Católicos 6, is open from 10 am to 3 pm Tuesday to Saturday (to 2.30 pm on Sunday and holidays). Admission costs 500 ptas (half-price for students), but is free on Sunday.

Faro de Madrid (Map 2) The odd tower (or 'lighthouse') just in front of the Museo de América is designed not to control air traffic but to transport visitors up for panoramic views of Madrid. There is no cafe up here, so be warned. The observatory is open from 10 am to 1.45 pm and 5 to 6.45 pm (as late as 8.45 pm in high summer) Tuesday to Sunday. The ride in the elevator costs 200 ptas.

If you look south-east towards the city centre you will hardly fail to notice the nearby **Arco de la Victoria**, a rather bombastic memorial celebrating the end of Napoleon's control of Spain.

Museo de la Ciudad (Map 1) Described perfectly by one traveller as 'a must for the infrastructure buff', this rather dry technical museum traces the growth and spread of Madrid, with abundant information on municipal services and the like. Established in 1992, it's at Calle del Príncipe de Vergara 140 (metro: Cruz del Rayo) and is open from 10 am to 2 pm and 4 to 7 pm Tuesday to Friday. At the weekend it opens in the morning only. Admission is free.

Museo de la Moneda (Map 2) If you like coins, this is the place for you: the national mint. Collections in the slightly dingy museum range from ancient Greek to the present day. The museum (metro: O'Donnell), Calle del Doctor Esquerdo 36, is open from 10 am to 2.30 pm and 5 to 7.30 pm Tuesday to Friday, and 10 am to 2.30 pm at the weekend and on holidays. Admission is free.

Museo Taurino The Plaza de Toros Monumental de las Ventas, the most important bullring in the world, is, typically for this kind of structure, a classic example of the neomudéjar style. The area in which it stands is known as Las Ventas because, in times gone by, several of these wayside taverns, along with houses of ill repute, were to be found here. In those days, a fairly pungent stream flowed by, which was a deterrent to more clean-living folk moving into the area.

Aficionados might like to wander into the Museo Taurino, right by the bullring. It's open from 9.30 am to 2.30 pm Monday to Friday. During the bullfighting season it also opens at the weekend. In summer (June to September), it opens Sunday (from 10 am to 1 pm) instead of Monday.

Art Galleries

The city is sprinkled with small private galleries and there are a couple of important foundations where you can check out the latest trends in contemporary work. There are numerous exhibition spaces, so the best advice is to keep an eye on newspapers and gig guides such as the *Guía del Ocio*.

Among the most important centres is the **Fundación Juan March** (Map 2; metro: Núñez de Balboa), Calle de Castelló 77. The foundation has its own collection and is responsible for organising some of the better temporary exhibitions each year. The **Fundación La Caixa** (Map 6), Calle de Serrano 60, is another busy place, putting on regular contemporary-art exhibitions.

For some commercial galleries, see Art Galleries in the Shopping chapter.

The Battle of Madrid

When Franco's Nationalists rose in revolt in July 1936, the army planned a lightning assault on the capital. General Mola quickly moved several thousand troops south from Pamplona and east from Valladolid, with the aim of crossing the Somosierra and other passes and descending rapidly on Madrid before the Republicans could get organised. They never made it over the passes, which were held tenaciously by Republican militia who knew their failure would mean the loss of Madrid.

With Mola stopped in his tracks, the element of surprise was lost, but soon the capital faced a new threat as Franco's columns advanced rapidly from Seville through Extremadura and halted in the Casa de Campo, at the western gates of the city. In November the government fled to Valencia, but Madrid was not abandoned. A medley of Spanish Republican forces of all political persuasions was joined by Soviet advisers and the International Brigades. The latter would bear the brunt of Franco's assaults directed at the university part of town. Although these attacks had some success – at the cost of a great many lives – the Nationalists never made it much beyond the barrio of Argüelles.

As fortunes seesawed and then declined for the Republicans, Madrid remained out of Nationalist hands. Fighting continued on the Madrid front but, even when communist forces clashed with other Republicans in early 1939, the Nationalists failed to move. Of course, by that time they did not really need to. The writing was on the wall and the Republicans' days were numbered. As their forces in the centre crumbled and Franco's columns advancing from Toledo linked up with others, the few commanders who had not already fled surrendered Madrid on 27 March. Four days later the war was over.

Paseo de la Castellana

This boulevard almost makes a sight in its own right. It follows the course of a one-time stream and carves its way right up to the north of the city, where it runs into **Plaza de Castilla** (Map 1). This busy roundabout is remarkable above all for the leaning **Torres Puerta Europa**, designed by John Burgee. At 115m high and with a 15° tilt, they have become a symbol of modern Madrid.

To the right (east) of the plaza, the huge squat tower is a water tank used as part of the Canal de Isabel II.

Parque del Oeste (Map 2)

Spread out between the university and Moncloa metro station, this is a tranquil and, in parts, quite beautiful park for a wander or shady laze in the heat of the day.

By night it undergoes a transformation, when the city's transsexual prostitute population and their clients come out to play. Part of the beat is reserved for female prostitutes too. Most of the activity takes place in cars, which become remarkably numerous as the night wears on. Although you are

unlikely to be bothered – police keep an eye out for anything more untoward than the routinely untoward – the area is not the ideal choice for a late-evening family stroll.

Casa de Campo (Map 2)

This huge and rather unkempt semiwilderness stretching west of the Río Manzanares undergoes similar metamorphoses to the Parque del Oeste. It was in royal hands until 1931, when the recently proclaimed Republic threw open its 1200 hectares to the people.

By day, cyclists and walkers eager for something resembling nature, but with no time or desire to leave Madrid, clog the byways and low roads that crisscross the park. There are also tennis courts and Madrid's most central swimming pool (see the following Swimming section), as well as an amusement park for the kids (see Amusement Parks in the Entertainment chapter).

Madrid's **zoo** (metro: Batán), also in the park, contains some 3000 animals and a respectable aquarium. It is open from 10.30 am to sunset Monday to Friday. The best part is the dolphin section and the aquarium. Admission costs 1655 ptas.

On a different note, the Andalucian-style ranch known as Batán is used to house the bulls destined to do bloody battle in the Fiestas de San Isidro (see Public Holidays & Special Events in the Facts for the Visitor chapter).

Finally, the none-too-exciting **teleférico** (cable car) from Paseo del Pintor Rosales (on the corner of Calle del Marqués de Urquijo) ends at a high point in the middle of the park. From 1 April to the last weekend in September it runs between 11 am and 10 pm; the rest of the year it runs from noon to 10 pm at the weekend and on holidays. The trip costs 365 ptas one way, 520 ptas return.

Many people just come to sip a drink by the small artificial lake (metro: Lago).

As night sets in, the scene takes on other hues. The occasional junkie, prostitute or pimp you may have espied in the area around the lake during the day turns into something of an avalanche. As the girls (and on occasion the boys who want to be girls) jockey for position, not a few punters keep their places around the lakeside *chiringuitos* (open-air bars or kiosks) as though nothing out of the ordinary were happening. The traffic in the middle of the night here is akin to rush hour in the city centre!

SWIMMING

Outdoor municipal pools open from June to September in several locations around the city. During the rest of the year, municipal indoor pools open their doors. There are also various private pools. For information on pools and other municipal sporting installations around town, call the Oficina de Información Deportiva (☎ 91 540 39 39).

One handy location is the Instituto Municipal de Deportes (metro: Lago), in the Casa de Campo. It is open from 10 am to 8 pm daily from June to September. During the rest of the year, the indoor pool is open from 11 am to 6 pm Monday to Friday. A swim costs 520 ptas or you can buy a *bono*, good for 20 visits, for 7800 ptas. The same bono is valid in other municipal pools, such as the indoor one at the Instalación Deportiva Municipal Chamartín (☎ 91 350 12 23), Plaza de Perú s/n. This is an Olympic-size pool, open from 8.30 am to 9 pm Monday to Friday, and 10 am to 8 pm at the weekend.

LANGUAGE COURSES

The Universidad Complutense offers a range of language and cultural courses throughout the year. Contact the Secretaría de los Cursos para Extranjeros (☎ 91 394 53 25, fax 91 394 52 98), Facultad de Filología (Edificio A), Universidad Complutense, Ciudad Universitaria, 28040 Madrid.

You could also sign up at the overworked and chaotic Escuela Oficial de Idiomas (Map 3; ☎ 91 533 00 88, 91 554 99 77), Calle de Jesús Maestro s/n. It offers courses in Spanish for foreigners (Español para Extranjeros) at most levels.

International House (Map 5; ☎ 91 310 13 14, fax 91 308 53 21) is at Calle de Zurbano 8. Intensive courses start at around 50,000 ptas a week. Staff here are happy to organise accommodation with families or in *pensiones*.

Many of the language schools aimed at teaching locals English and other foreign tongues also run courses in Spanish for foreign visitors.

Places to Stay

Madrid is crawling with *pensiones* (guesthouses), *hostales* (cheap hotels) and hotels, so there should rarely be trouble finding a place to stay. However, since 1998 Madrid's hoteliers have been enjoying a boom. This means that at peak holiday periods (for instance Christmas and Easter) you should try to book ahead. Many of the budget places will not, however, accept reservations – they want to see your mug and the colour of your money first hand. This also means that, sooner or later, you should always be able to come up with something!

You will find virtually every type of accommodation: youth hostels; hidden-away pensiones; good mid-range hostales and hotels with character (faded or spruced up); as well as the usual five-star crowd – a few with a good deal of charm, and others of the this-could-be-anywhere-in-the-world variety.

Prices have shot up in the past couple of years, at a rate well ahead of inflation. A room in a better budget hostal with own bathroom and maybe extras such as a phone, TV and air-con or heating costs about 4000/6000 ptas for singles/doubles. It is still possible to get simpler rooms, usually with a washbasin only (shared shower and loo in the corridor) for as little as 2000/3500 ptas.

Seasons & Reservations
The price of any type of accommodation may vary with the season. Some places have separate price structures for high season (*temporada alta*), mid-season (*temporada media*) or low season (*temporada baja*), all usually displayed on a notice in reception or close by. (Hoteliers are not actually bound by these displayed prices. They are free to charge less, which they quite often do, or more, which happens fairly rarely.)

The prices for accommodation in this book are a guide only (based on high-season prices). Always check room charges before putting down your bags.

Taxes
Virtually all accommodation prices are subject to IVA, the Spanish version of value-added tax, which is 7%. This is often included in the quoted price at cheaper places, but less often at more expensive ones. To check, ask: *'Está incluido el IVA?'* (Is IVA included?). In some cases you will be charged the IVA only if you ask for a receipt.

PLACES TO STAY – BUDGET
Camping
The camp site within easiest striking distance is *Camping Osuna* (☎ 91 741 05 10), on Avenida de Logroño near the airport. Take metro No 5 to Canillejas (the end of the line), from where it's about 500m. It charges 660 ptas per person, per car and per tent.

Another option is *Camping Madrid* (☎ 91 302 28 35), on the N-I highway north of town. Take the Alcobendas bus from Plaza de Castilla (Map 1), from where it's a fairly short ride. It costs 600 ptas per person, car and tent.

Youth Hostels
An HI membership card is necessary for both hostels. For information on obtaining a card see Hostel Cards under Documents in the Facts for the Visitor chapter.

There are two HI youth hostels in Madrid. *Albergue Richard Schirrman* (☎ 91 463 56 99; metro: El Lago; bus No 33 from Plaza Ópera) is in the Casa de Campo. B&B in a room for four costs 1200/1700 ptas for those aged under/over 26.

Albergue Santa Cruz de Marcenado (Map 5; ☎ 91 547 45 32, Calle de Santa Cruz de Marcenado; metro: Argüelles; bus Nos 1, 61 and Circular) offers rooms for four, six and eight people. B&B costs 1200/1700 ptas for those aged under/over 26.

Hostales & Hotels
Around Sol If you don't mind traffic, *Hostal Cosmopolitan* (Map 7; ☎ 91 522 66 51,

3rd Floor, Puerta del Sol 9) offers basic singles/doubles with washbasin costing just 1800/3300 ptas.

A much more attractive deal is the characterful *Hostal Riesco (Map 7; ☎ 91 522 26 92, fax 91 532 90 88, Calle del Correo 2)*, which has comfortable rooms looking right onto Puerta del Sol. Rooms with bathroom cost 4000/5800 ptas.

Hostal Tineo (Map 8; ☎ 91 521 49 43, Calle de la Victoria 6) charges a standard 3500/5500 ptas for singles/doubles with washbasin only. Rooms with bathrooms cost up to 5000/6500 ptas. In the same building, *Hostal Gibert (Map 8; ☎ 91 522 42 14)* offers rooms with their own bathroom costing 3000/4000 ptas.

A pretty decent place is *Hostal Esmeralda (Map 8; ☎ 91 521 00 77, fax 91 521 07 58, Calle de la Victoria 1)*. Bright, clean rooms with bath, TV and phone cost 4800/6300 ptas.

Busting the low-budget bank a little is *Hostal Madrid (Map 7; ☎ 91 522 00 60, fax 91 532 35 10, ✉ hsmadrid@teleline .es, Calle de Esparteros 6)*. It offers good, clean secure rooms with TV, air-con/heating, phone and even a safe in each room. But you pay 6000/9000 ptas for singles/doubles.

Hostal Centro Sol (Map 7; ☎ 91 522 15 82, fax 91 522 57 78, Carrera de San Jerónimo 5) is a funny place with long corridors, but the smallish rooms (on the 2nd and 4th floors) are secure and in top order, with their own bath, TV, phone, heating/air-con and minibar. They are good value, costing 6000/7500/9500 ptas for singles/doubles/triples.

Around Plaza Mayor South-west of Puerta del Sol towards Plaza Mayor, *Hostal Santa Cruz (Map 7; ☎/fax 91 522 24 41, Plaza de Santa Cruz 6)* is in a prime location. Single/double rooms with bathroom here start from 3600/5200 ptas. Two of the rooms look out over the square. A better option, still in the same building, is the revamped *Hostal Cruz Sol (Map 7; ☎ 91 532 71 97)*. Rooms cost upwards of 3700/5700 ptas and have bath, TV and air-con.

Overlooking the same square is the characterful *Hostal La Perla Asturiana (Map 7; ☎ 91 366 46 00, fax 91 366 46 08, Plaza de Santa Cruz 3)*. Here you can reckon on paying 2700 ptas per person. Rooms have bath, TV, phone and air-con, and most of them look out onto one of the two squares by which the hostal is surrounded.

Closer to Plaza Mayor is another good deal. At *Hostal Montalvo (Map 7; ☎ 91 365 59 10, Calle de Zaragoza 6)* you can expect to pay up to 6500 ptas for a double with bath, TV, phone and air-con. It takes approximately two minutes to be seated on Plaza Mayor for your morning coffee.

Hostal Arcos (Map 7; ☎ 91 522 59 76, fax 91 532 78 96, Calle del Marqués Viudo de Pontejos 3) is one of several oldish hostales on this little street. The location is handy and fairly quiet, and rooms with their own bath and TV cost 3000/4000 ptas.

The pick of the group around Plaza Mayor is *Hostal La Macarena (Map 7; ☎ 91 365 92 21, fax 91 366 61 11, Cava de San Miguel 8)*. It is the only place to stay on the west side of the square and is in a fine, well-manicured building. Rooms are kept immaculately clean and are secure. They all have bathroom, TV and air-con/heating. Singles/doubles/triples cost 6500/8500/10,500 ptas and are worth every peseta.

Plaza de Santa Ana, Huertas & Atocha
Atocha train station is close to the city centre, so it is worth making the effort to walk north up Calle de Atocha towards Plaza de Santa Ana if you arrive here. All the places listed below are marked on Map 8.

Roughly halfway between the station and Santa Ana, *Hostal López (☎/fax 91 429 43 49, Calle de las Huertas 54)* is a good choice. Singles/doubles start at 3600/4500 ptas without their own bath, or 4200/5200 ptas with. It's on a quiet part of an otherwise lively street.

There are a few places along the noisy Calle de Atocha itself and, if you can't be bothered tramping around and looking, you could do worse than *Hostal Castilla I (☎ 91 429 00 95)*, at No 43. Small, spotless rooms with bathroom and TV cost 5000/6000 ptas.

In its range there are better-value places around – it's merely convenient if you have just arrived at Atocha train station and need to drop your stuff *now*.

Hostal Casanova (☎ *91 429 56 91, Calle de Lope de Vega 8*) offers small single rooms without their own bath costing 2000 ptas. Roomier doubles with en suite bathroom cost 4500 ptas.

Hostal Castro (☎ *91 429 51 47, Calle de León 13*) is an attractive place with good, clean doubles with bathroom costing up to 5300 ptas. Staff are not always marvellously helpful. **Hostal Gonzalo** (☎ *91 429 27 14, Calle de Cervantes 34*) is in sparkling nick. Singles/doubles with shower and TV cost 5000/6200 ptas. You can get a few hundred pesetas off if you stay at least three days.

Better than either of these is **Hostal Dulcinea** (☎ *91 429 93 09, fax 91 369 25 69,* 🖂 *donato@teleline.es, Calle de Cervantes 19*), across the road. It offers immaculate rooms and is often full. You pay 5500/6000 ptas. If you are alone you will usually get a double to yourself. The owners have some apartments in the same street.

Hostal Matute (☎ *91 429 55 85, fax 91 429 55 85, Plaza de Matute 11*) offers spacious if somewhat musty singles/doubles costing 3500/5000 ptas with shower and loo. These mainly look onto the street and can be noisy. Others, at 4500/6000 ptas, look onto an internal patio (nothing special in itself), are quiet and have full bathroom.

Hostal Vetusta (☎ *91 429 64 04, Calle de las Huertas 3*) has admittedly small, but cute, rooms with their own shower starting at 3000/4500 ptas. A couple out the back look onto Plaza de Santa Ana.

Hostal Delvi (☎ *91 522 59 98, 3rd Floor, Plaza de Santa Ana 15*) is a friendly enough place with reasonable rooms, some having glimpses of the square. The singles are tiny. You will pay upwards of 2000/2500 ptas for rooms without their own bath, or 4000 ptas for a double with. **Hostal Santa Ana** (☎ *91 521 30 58, Plaza de Santa Ana 1*) has average singles with shower for 2500 ptas, and doubles with bathroom for 4500 ptas.

North-east of Plaza de Santa Ana, **Hostal**

Mondragón (☎ *91 429 68 16, Carrera de San Jerónimo 32*) is pretty good value at 1900/3100 ptas for a biggish room without bathroom. This building is a paradise of basic, cheap accommodation. **Hostal León** (☎ *91 429 67 78*) is not bad and has heating. It charges around 2000 ptas per person. **Hostal Universal** (☎ *91 429 67 79*) comes in at 2400/4800 ptas. A cut above the rest in this building is **Hostal Aguilar** (☎ *91 429 36 61*), which charges 4000/6000 ptas for rooms with bathroom, TV, phone and heating/air-con.

Hostal Sardinero (☎ *91 429 57 56, Calle del Prado 16*) is a good choice. Rooms with bath, heating/air-con, safe and satellite TV come in at 5500/7000 ptas.

Hostal San Isidro (☎ *91 429 15 91, Calle de Príncipe 17*) offers clean single/double rooms with bathroom, TV, phone, air-con and safe that cost 5350/7000 ptas. **Hostal Persal** (☎ *91 369 46 43, fax 91 369 19 52, Plaza del Ángel 12*) is another hostal that is edging out of budgeteers' range. Comfortable rooms with bath, TV and phone cost 5800/8700 ptas, which includes breakfast.

Around Ópera Calle del Arenal is a good hunting ground, although it's a noisy thoroughfare. **Hostal Ivor** (*Map 5;* ☎ *91 547 10 54, Calle del Arenal 24*) has singles/doubles with bath, phone and TV costing 3800/5500 ptas. The rooms are quite OK but showing their age. Beds are a little lumpy.

The tiny **Hostal Paz** (*Map 5;* ☎ *91 547 30 47, Calle de la Priora Flora 4*) looks horrible from the outside, but the cheap rooms inside are reasonable value, if a little cramped, at 2600/4000 ptas. All rooms have TV and air-con/heating but, except for a couple of doubles with their own shower, bathrooms are in the corridor.

Quietly tucked away, **Hostal Mairu** (*Map 7;* ☎ *91 547 30 88, Calle del Espejo 2*) is a simple place with singles/doubles costing 2600/4200 ptas. Doubles with their own bath cost 4400 ptas.

Nearby, **Hostal Pinariega** (*Map 7;* ☎/*fax 91 548 08 19, Calle de Santiago 1*) is a sunnier alternative with rooms starting at

3500/4800 ptas. Rooms have shower and washbasin. If you want a bathroom, you pay 4000/5800 ptas.

Paseo del Prado & Retiro If you want to be a stone's throw from the Prado, you have a couple of choices on the grand boulevard. *Hostal Sudamericano (Map 7; ☎ 91 429 25 64, Paseo del Prado 12)* is not bad, with singles/doubles starting at 3800/5000 ptas. Rooms are simple and bathrooms are in the corridor. There are a few tiny singles that cost 2600 ptas. In the same building, *Hostal La Coruña (Map 7; ☎ 91 429 25 43, Paseo del Prado 12)* has similar rooms (with TV) for 3000/5000 ptas.

Hotel Mora (Map 9; ☎ 91 420 15 69, fax 91 420 05 64, Paseo del Prado 32) is an affordable place along this leafy boulevard for those with a budget that can stretch to lower middle. Rooms with satellite TV, own bath and phone cost 6772/8875 ptas.

Right around the other side of the Parque del Buen Retiro, *Hostal Retiro (Map 2; ☎ 91 576 00 37, Calle de O'Donnell 27)* offers about the only opportunity to hang out in one of the more exclusive parts of town for modest money. The place is unspectacular but at 3200/4500 ptas for rooms with washbasin and shower it's not bad for this end of town. Doubles at about 6000 ptas have full bathroom. The only problem is that you are a little far from the action.

Gran Vía, Malasaña & Chueca Gran Vía is laden with accommodation, but it's a noisy area. The following can be found on Map 5.

Hostal Lamalonga (☎ 91 547 26 31, Gran Vía 56) is reliable. Singles/doubles with bath start at 4500/6500 ptas.

Hostal Alcázar Regis (☎ 91 547 93 17, fax 91 559 07 85, Gran Vía 61) is not a bad choice at the cheaper end of the scale along this heaving boulevard. Singles/doubles cost 4000/6000 ptas.

Hostal Andorra (☎ 91 532 31 16, fax 91 521 79 31, ✉ andorra@arrakis.es, Gran Vía 33) is on the 7th floor but has fine rooms with bath, TV and phone for 4700/6600 ptas.

The stylish *Hostal Besaya (☎ 91 541 32*

07, Calle de San Bernardo 13) offers good rooms costing up to 5900/8000 ptas with bath. It's a little overpriced.

Calle de Fuencarral is choked with hostales and pensiones, especially at the southern end of Gran Vía. *Hostal Ginebra (☎ 91 532 10 35, Calle de Fuencarral 17)* is a reliable choice not far from Gran Vía. All rooms have TV and phone; singles with washbasin start at 3200 ptas, while singles/doubles with bathroom cost 4200/5000 ptas. *Hostal Palacios (☎ 91 531 48 47, Calle de Fuencarral 25)* is a safe choice, with singles/doubles costing upwards of 2500/4000 ptas. Rooms with bath cost 3500/5000 ptas.

Hotel Laris (☎ 91 521 46 80, fax 91 521 46 85, Calle del Barco 3) is nudging mid-range but has decent rooms with all the extras for 5800/8700 ptas.

Hostal Medieval (☎ 91 522 25 49, Calle de Fuencarral 46) has spacious and bright singles/doubles with shower for 3000/4500 ptas. Doubles with full bathroom cost 5500/6000 ptas. *Hostal Serranos (☎ 91 448 89 87, Calle de Fuencarral 95)* is spick and span; rooms with bath and TV cost 4000/6000 ptas. In the same building and a floor up, *Hostal Sil (☎ 91 448 89 72, fax 91 447 48 29)* has better rooms still and charges 5500/7500 ptas for rooms with bath, TV, phone and air-con/heating.

Hostal Delfina (☎ 91 522 64 23, Gran Vía 12) is up on the 4th floor, putting some distance between you and the traffic noise. Doubles with bath start at 5500 ptas. They have no singles. *Hostal Senegal (☎ 91 319 07 71, Plaza de Santa Bárbara 8)* is in a pretty spot and offers decent rooms with bath for 5000/6600 ptas.

PLACES TO STAY – MID-RANGE

Around Sol For a hint of faded elegance, *Hotel Inglés (Map 8; ☎ 91 429 65 51, fax 91 420 24 23, Calle de Echegaray 8)* is reasonable at 8500/12,000 ptas plus IVA for singles/doubles. You get the feeling everything could do with some freshening up, but the hotel has some curious rooms that seem almost like small apartments.

Just off Puerta del Sol, *Hotel Moderno (Map 7; ☎ 91 531 09 00, fax 91 531 35 50,*

@ info@hotel-moderno.com, Calle del Arenal 2) has comfortable enough rooms costing 10,400/13,000 ptas plus IVA, but you are really paying for the position more than anything else.

A better option is **Hotel Regina** *(Map 5; ☎/fax 91 521 47 25, Calle de Alcalá 19)*. Singles/doubles with bath, phone and TV cost 9750/13,500 ptas plus IVA.

Hotel París *(Map 7; ☎ 91 521 64 96, fax 91 531 01 88, Calle de Alcalá 2)* is an old stalwart around here and reasonable value. Rooms with all the usual extras come in at 9000/12,000 ptas plus IVA (which includes breakfast). This was one of the first luxury hotels in Madrid – indeed at the turn of the century it was the only one of any class at all. It was only overshadowed in 1910 by the arrival of the Ritz.

Gran Vía, Malasaña & Chueca The following are all on Map 5. **Hotel Regente** *(☎ 91 521 29 41, fax 91 532 30 14, @ info@ hotelregente.com, Calle de los Mesoneros Romanos 9)* has decent mid-range single/ double rooms with bath, TV, air-con and telephone for 6500/10,000 ptas plus IVA.

Hotel Los Condes *(☎ 91 521 54 55, fax 91 521 78 82, @ hcondes@verial.es, Calle de los Libreros 7)* is a comfortable, modern option with rooms starting at 9000/ 12,500 ptas plus IVA. **Hotel California** *(☎ 91 522 47 03, fax 91 531 61 01, Gran Vía 38)* is a smart choice, with attractive rooms going for 8525/10,900 ptas plus IVA.

Hotel Mónaco *(☎ 91 522 46 30, fax 91 521 16 01, Calle de Barbieri 5)* is one of Madrid's rare truly quirky places, in the most likeable sense of the word. Just wandering into the foyer is a trip. Rooms are olde worlde camp (try for room 123, with mirror above the bed!) and cost 7490/ 10,700 ptas.

Salamanca, Goya & Beyond Those wanting to mix in the smarter parts of town could try **Hostal Don Diego** *(Map 6; ☎ 91 435 07 60, fax 91 431 42 63, Calle de Velázquez 45)* for size. It has comfortable singles/doubles with bath, TV, minibar and phone for 7600/10,500 ptas plus IVA.

In the Chamberí area north of Malasaña, another perfectly good mid-range possibility is **Hotel Trafalgar** *(Map 3; ☎ 91 445 62 00, fax 91 446 64 56, Calle de Trafalgar 35)*. It's in a quiet part of town but close to several metro stops and a short stroll from the Malasaña area. It has increased its prices to 10,400/14,900 ptas plus IVA and in so doing has almost, but not quite, lost the moral right to a mention.

Hotel Ramón de la Cruz *(Map 2; ☎ 91 401 72 00, fax 91 402 21 26, Calle de Don Ramón de la Cruz 94)* offers good, comfortable rooms costing 7000/10,000 ptas plus IVA. It's a little out of the way.

PLACES TO STAY – TOP END

Note first that stated prices can often be negotiated down, especially on slow weekends, in August or if you are travelling in groups. Savings can nudge 50% in some places when your luck is in. When booking ahead always look into this.

There is no shortage of bland, four- and five-star hotels with all the mod cons scattered across Madrid, particularly along the main drags such as Paseo de la Castellana. An attractive alternative to these and just off the Castellana is **Hotel Emperatriz** *(Map 4; ☎ 91 563 80 88, fax 91 563 98 04, @ em peratriz@mad.servicom.es, Calle de López de Hoyos 4)*. Its tranquil singles/doubles generally cost 23,000/28,000 ptas plus IVA.

One of the better addresses in Madrid and an excellent choice in terms of price is **Hotel Arosa** *(Map 5; ☎ 91 532 16 00, fax 91 531 31 27, @ arosa@hotelarosa.com, Calle de la Salud 21)*, just off Gran Vía. It has charming rooms and comes highly recommended. Rooms start at 14,295/ 22,295 ptas plus IVA.

A popular choice is **Hotel de Santo Domingo** *(Map 5; ☎ 91 547 98 00, fax 91 547 59 95, Plaza de Santo Domingo 13)*. It is so popular they have doubled their prices in the past couple of years! Rooms here are fine but cost a hefty 22,625/26,625 ptas plus IVA in the high season.

Hotel Tryp Ambassador *(Map 5; ☎ 91 541 67 00, fax 91 559 10 40, @ ambassador@ trypnet.com, Cuesta de Santo Domingo)*, just down the hill, has been given the thumbs-up from some of our better-heeled readers. It costs 24,000/30,000 ptas plus IVA to stay the night.

Among those with a touch of (faded) charm is *Gran Hotel Reina Victoria (Map 8; ☎ 91 531 45 00, fax 91 522 03 07, Plaza de Santa Ana 14)*. For 100 years it has been a classic haunt of bullfighters. If there's a *feria* (bullfight) in town you can be sure it will be full of *toreros* (bullfighters). It has a hint of class from days gone by but could do with a thorough overhaul. Bit by bit they seem to be addressing the problem but many of the rooms are looking a shade shabby. You pay 24,000/30,000 ptas plus IVA (but they often do cheap weekend offers).

Hotel Villa Real (Map 8; ☎ 91 420 37 67, fax 91 420 25 47, ✉ villareal@derbyhotels .es, Plaza de las Cortes 10) is right by the parliament. The standard price is 37,700/ 41,600 ptas plus IVA for singles/doubles that are kept in top condition. Some are split level and many have a balcony overlooking the little square. Suites on two floors cost 75,000 ptas.

Heading to the top of the league is one of Madrid's old classics, the former palace of the Duque de Lerma which this century became the *Hotel Palace (Map 7; ☎ 91 360 80 00, fax 91 360 81 00, ✉ palace1@ mol.es, Plaza de las Cortes 7)*. Elegant suites come in at 56,000/63,000 ptas plus IVA. Not far away is its old rival, *Hotel Ritz (Map 7; ☎ 91 521 28 57, fax 91 532 87 76, Plaza de la Lealtad 5)*. At 49,000/64,000 ptas plus IVA, this is Madrid's priciest location. Suites can cost up to 84,000 ptas. It opened its doors in 1910. Depending on whose story you prefer, Mata Hari stayed in one of the two hotels during WWI before heading to France and a firing squad in 1917.

LONG-TERM RENTALS

For longer stays in Madrid, you can usually make a deal in the pensiones and smaller hostales to include meals, laundry and so on.

For flatshares and rental, check the notice boards at cultural centres, university campuses (see those sections in the Facts for the Visitor chapter) and the Escuela Oficial de Idiomas (see Language Courses in the Things to See & Do chapter), as well as in the *Segundamano* magazine.

At the Mercado Fuencarral (see Clothing and Fashion in the Shopping chapter) you can also occasionally find ads or put up your own. Another possible source is Room Madrid (Map 5; ☎ 91 548 03 35), Calle del Conde Duque 7. You fill in a form and are matched with potential flatshares. They charge 15,000 ptas for the service.

Finding a room in shared flats is not too difficult, but look around, as you can be offered some pretty dismal mouse holes for big money. Indeed, since early 1999 rents have been soaring in Madrid after a year in which house prices rose enormously. With luck and persistence you can find good-quality rooms in central locations for around 40,000 ptas a month. Your bills will include electricity *(luz)*, water, gas (most older places still use bottled butane gas, which sells for around 1000 ptas per orange *bombona*), phone and *comunidad*. The latter is a fixed bimonthly charge for building maintenance, sometimes included in the rent.

Places to Eat

Madrid is riddled with restaurants, snack bars and fast-food outlets, so rumbling tummies need not suffer for long.

FOOD

While it does not reach the elegant heights of French cuisine or the regional variety and careful attention of the best of Italian cooking, the fun of the food is definitely part of the attraction of Madrid. Spain is a little rougher and readier at the table than its closest Mediterranean neighbours. That said, only the most demanding of foodies will be disappointed by what's on offer. Whether you stand at a bar nonchalantly chomping away on seafood tapas over a beer or sit down for a full meal at one of the city's better restaurants, the experience is generally pleasant (for the palate *and* wallet) and sometimes delightful.

When to Eat

You may not arrive in Madrid with jet lag but, due to the different Spanish eating habits, your tummy will think it has abandoned all known time zones. Breakfast *(desayuno)* is generally a no-nonsense affair taken at a bar on the way to work. Lunchtime *(comida, almuerzo)* is basically from 2 to 4 pm and is the main meal of the day. No local would contemplate dinner *(cena)* before 9.30 pm. Most (but not all) kitchens close by 1 am.

Don't panic! If your gastric juices can't hold out, you can easily track down bar snacks or fast food (local and international) outside these times. And, anxious to ring up every tourist dollar possible, plenty of restaurants cater for northern European stomach habits – although you often pay for this with mediocre food and the almost exclusive company of other tourists.

Where to Eat

Many bars and some cafes offer some form of solid sustenance. This can range from *bocadillos* (filled rolls) and *tapas* (bar snacks) through to more substantial *raciones*

(basically bigger versions of a *tapa*) and full meals in *comedores* (sit-down restaurants) out the back. *Cervezerías* (beer bars), *tabernas* (taverns), *tascas* (snack bars) and *bodegas* (cellars) are just some of the kinds of establishment in this category.

For a full meal you will most frequently end up in a *restaurante*, but other names will pop out at you. A *marisquería* specialises in seafood, while a *mesón* (a 'big table') might indicate (but not necessarily!) a more modest eatery.

What to Eat

Breakfast A coffee with some sort of pastry *(bollo)* is the typical breakfast. You may get a croissant or some cream-filled number. Some people prefer a savoury start – you could go for a *sandwich mixto*, a toasted ham and cheese. A Spanish *tostada* is simply buttered toast (you might order something to go with it). Some people, especially party animals headed home at dawn after a night out on the tiles, go for an all-Spanish favourite, *churros y chocolate*, a lightly deep-fried stick of plain pastry immersed in thick, gooey hot chocolate. They are sold at stands around town.

Lunch & Dinner Many straightforward Spanish dishes are available here, as elsewhere in the country. The traveller's friend is the *menú del día*, a set-price meal comprising three or more courses, with a drink usually thrown in. This is often available at lunch only and can range in price from around 800 ptas at simple establishments to 3500 ptas at posher places. A *plato combinado* is a simpler version still: a one-course meal consisting of basic nutrients – the 'meat-and-three-veg' style of cooking. You'll see pictures of this stuff everywhere. It's filling and cheap but has little to recommend it in culinary terms.

You'll pay more for your meals if you order a la carte but the food will be better. The menu *(la carta)* begins with starters such as *ensaladas* (salads), *sopas* (soups) and *entremeses* (hors d'oeuvres). The latter can range from a mound of potato salad with olives, asparagus, anchovies and a selection of cold meats – almost a meal in itself – to simpler cold meats, slices of cheese and olives.

Later courses on the menu are often listed under headings such as *pollo* (chicken), *carne* (meat), *mariscos* (seafood), *pescado* (fish), *arroz* (rice), *huevos* (eggs) and *verduras* (vegetables). Meat may be subdivided into *cerdo* (pork), *ternera* (beef) and *cordero* (lamb).

Desserts have a lower profile. *Helados* (ice cream), fruit and *flans* (a kind of creme caramel) are often the only choices in cheaper places. Sugar addicts should look out for a couple of local specialities where possible.

Madrid's Cuisine

Capital for more than 400 years, Madrid has attracted as many cuisines from the provinces as hopefuls to royal, liberal, republican and dictatorial courts. To speak of a distinctly madrileño cuisine is a trifle difficult as, here more than anywhere else in the country, a national hodge podge rules. This is of course one of the beauties of the place. Here you can sample some of the nation's best culinary traditions, from the imaginative cooking of the Basques to delicious Valencian paella.

Good thing too really, because the city's history is hardly one of culinary richness. Medieval Madrid was a simple place and the bulk of its inhabitants scraped by on a limited diet, the staple of which was cereals (often barley). Meat was a rarity and seafood (unlike today) unheard of. Fruit and vegetables, typically grown along the Manzanares, were by no means available to all. Olive oil, a standard element of much Mediterranean cooking and an integral part of the Muslim diet, was an expensive luxury to madrileños. In such a calorie-poor diet, wine (bad wine) played an important nutritional role, but even it was in chronic short supply.

Thankfully, times changed and Madrid is now a culinary melting pot. In spite of the rather harsh history of inland Spain, the nation's cuisine as a whole is typically Mediterranean, liberal in its use of olive oil, garlic, onions, tomatoes and peppers. A particular spin comes from the country's long history of Muslim occupation, reflected in the use of such spices as saffron and cumin, and for dessert the predominance of honeyed sweets. The high place accorded to almonds and fruit also reflects the Muslim influence.

The regions of Spain all have their own peculiarities and specialities. The Catalans and, perhaps even more so, the Basques are the most serious and inventive about their food. Their tables are replete with seafood and meat and in both cases various sauces play an important role. Farther west along the coast, fish and seafood rule, especially in Galicia. Valencia brought us probably the country's single most famous dish, paella. At its best it is a huge wok-like pan of saffron-coloured rice dripping with seafood bits. There are many variations on this theme, some better than others.

Inland, meat (especially roasts) and game dominate – simple and heavy fare but when it's good it's very good. From the south comes the intense obsession with ham (*jamón*) as well as the tapa, a little snack to accompany your drink at the bar. The tapa has become a phenomenon of its own and can range from a few free olives with your tipple through to the elaborate (and sometimes rather expensive) concoctions the Basques come up with.

It may come as a surprise that landlocked Madrid is one of the biggest fish- and seafood-consuming cities in the world. Tons and tons of the stuff are daily trucked and trained into town from the distant coasts of north-western Galicia and Andalucía in the south. Spain's fishing fleet is the European Union's biggest and they cast their nets far and wide to keep madrileños (among others) happily munching on the catch of the day.

This is no recent phenomenon either. Laurie Lee mentions it in his *As I Walked Out One Summer Morning*, a delightful tale

PLACES TO EAT

of his pre-Civil War rambles across Spain, and the tradition goes back a couple of centuries now. Just how fresh the fish transported from the coast by horse-drawn cart can have been is a moot point. Maragatos from the north-west of Castile, who dominated much of the Spanish carrying trade, had the best idea when they began buying up and salting cod in the ports, then sending it on to Madrid. This *bacalao* was prepared in various ways, and one local version that has remained is bite-sized fried portions with a thin strip of red capsicum on top, colourfully known as *soldaditos de Pavía*. What bits of cod have to do with little soldiers from Pavia (Italy) is anyone's guess. Other favoured fish in Madrid are *merluza* (hake) and *besugo* (sea bream).

Of the truly local dishes, *cocido a la madrileña* is probably the best known. It is a kind of hotpot or stew. In the broth are tossed various vegetables, chick peas, chicken, beef, lard and possibly other sausage meats too. In the poor man's version you were lucky to find any meat at all. A real favourite with madrileños but something of an acquired taste is *callos* – tripe. A typical Castilian opener is *sopa de ajo* (garlic soup) or *sopa castellana*, basically broth with an egg floating about in it. All this stuff, as you may have guessed, is pretty basic. A good deal of Castilian cooking reflects the poverty in which many of its people lived for centuries, indeed until the last 40 years or so.

A general food glossary appears in the Language chapter to help you through your standard Spanish menus.

Foreign Cuisines

Local food, even at its best, can become tiresome if you hang around for any length of time. Madrid is no centre of international cuisine, but a smattering of foreign restaurants, including Middle Eastern, Italian, Chinese, Indian, Japanese, Cuban and Thai, provide the palate with a variety of non-Spanish alternatives. A few of the better addresses have been sprinkled in among the recommendations below. Various fast-food options, from McDonald's to home-grown

versions offering bocadillos with various fillings, also abound.

Vegetarian

Vegetarians, and especially vegans, can make heavy weather of it in Spain, but a few vegetarian restaurants offer welcome relief to meat-loathers in Madrid.

DRINKS
Nonalcoholic

Clear, cold water from a public fountain or tap is a Spanish favourite – but check that it's *potable* (fit to drink). For tap water in restaurants, ask for *agua de grifo*. *Agua mineral* (bottled water) comes in innumerable brands, either *con gas* (fizzy) or *sin gas* (still).

Coffee Coffee in Spain is strong and slightly bitter. A *café con leche* (generally drunk at breakfast only) is about half coffee, half hot milk. Ask for *grande* or *doble* if you want a large cup, *en vaso* if you want a smaller shot in a glass, or *sombra* if you want lots of milk. A *café solo* is a short black; *café cortado* is a short black with a little milk. For iced coffee, ask for *café con hielo*; you'll get a glass of ice and a hot cup of coffee, to be poured over the ice – which, surprisingly, doesn't all melt straight away!

Tea Like most Spaniards, madrileños prefer coffee, but increasingly it is possible to get hold of many different styles of tea and *infusiones* (herbal concoctions). Locals tend to drink tea black. If you want tea, ask for it to come separately *(a parte)* to avoid ending up with a cup of tea-flavoured watery milk. You will find some inspiring *teterías* (tea houses) around town and some appear under Cafes & Tea Houses later in this chapter.

Soft Drinks Orange juice *(zumo de naranja)* is the main freshly squeezed juice available. It's often served with sugar. To make sure you are getting the real thing, ask for the juice to be *natural*, otherwise you run the risk of getting a puny little bottle of runny concentrate.

PLACES TO EAT

Refrescos (cool drinks) include the usual international brands of soft drinks, local brands such as Kas, and *granizado* (iced fruit crush).

A *batido* is a flavoured milk drink or milk shake. *Horchata* is a Valencian drink of Islamic origin. Made from the juice of *chufa* (tiger nuts), sugar and water, it is sweet and tastes like soya milk with a hint of cinnamon. You'll come across it both fresh and bottled: Chufi is a delicious brand. A naughtier version is called a *cubanito* and involves sticking in a blob of chocolate ice cream.

Alcoholic

Wine Spain is a wine-drinking country and *vino* (wine) accompanies almost every meal. Spanish wine is strong because of the sunny climate. It comes *blanco* (white), *tinto* (red), or *rosado* (rosé). In general it is cheap, although there is no shortage of expensive wines. A 500 ptas bottle of wine, bought from a supermarket or wine merchant, will be quite drinkable. The same money in a restaurant will get you a very mediocre drop. The cheapest *vino de mesa* (table wine) sells for less than 200 ptas a litre, but wines at that price can be pretty rank.

You can order wine by the glass *(copa)* in bars and restaurants. At lunch or dinner it is common to order a *vino de la casa* (house wine) – usually by the litre or half-litre.

The production of quality wines in Spain is a comparatively recent phenomenon. Until the 1960s, the emphasis throughout most of the country was on quantity and cheapness. Flavour was a secondary consideration. That is changing fast.

A complicated system of wine classification is in place. As in the other major wine-producing countries of the EU, there are two broad categories: table wine and quality wine. The former ranges from the straightforward *vino de mesa* (table wine) to *vino de la tierra*, which is a wine from an officially recognised wine-making area. Such wines showing promise can be awarded DOP status *(denominación de origen provisional)*. If they meet certain strict standards for a given period, they receive DO

status. An outstanding wine might get the DOC *(denominación de origen calificada)*. The number of DO regions is growing, although some may cover little more than a few vineyards. The only DOC wines come from the Rioja region in northern Spain, which was demarcated in 1926.

Classifications are not always a guarantee of quality, unfortunately, and many drinkers of Spanish wine put more faith in the name and reputation of certain producers or areas than in the denomination labels. Most of the best wine is produced in the north of the country, the Penedès area in Catalunya (whites and sparkling wine), Rioja, Navarra, Ribera del Duero (reds) and Galicia (whites). Sherry rules in Andalucía, while the Valdepeñas area of southern Castilla-La Mancha produces some interesting wines.

Locals may try to sell you on some of the young, light *vinos de Madrid* from the surrounding region. They have DO standing and some aren't bad at all, but it is fair to say the Comunidad is not renowned for its quality wine production. Traditionally, the Valdepeñas area has long been the capital's principal wine supplier. The thing about Madrid today, however, is that you can get your hands on wines from across the country, giving you a chance to sample the best Spain has to offer without leaving the city.

Beer If Madrid could be said to have a flagship drink, apart from the strange animal that is *licor de madroño* (see Other Drinks, next), it would be beer. The most widespread local draft and bottle brand is Mahou, followed by Cruzcampo. See the boxed text 'Frothing at the Mouth' over the page.

Otherwise, two Catalan companies, Damm and San Miguel, each produce about 15% of all Spain's beer. San Miguel is common; Damm's main brand, Estrella, a little harder to come by. If you can get hold of beers by Galicia's Estrella you'll be pleased. Plenty of foreign beers are also widely available.

Other Drinks Sangria *(sangría)* is a wine and fruit punch, sometimes laced with brandy. It's refreshing going down but can

Frothing at the Mouth

Of course, to slake your thirst at the bar you can just ask for a *cerveza* (beer). But what you get will then depend on whomever is behind the bar. It's better to be a little more specific.

The most common thing to order is a *caña*, a small glass *(vaso)* of draught beer *(cerveza de barril)*. In the heat of the summer, this is the best way to make sure they keep coming cold. A larger beer (about 300ml), more common in the hipper bars and clubs, comes in a *tubo* (a long, straight glass).

The equivalent of a pint is a *jarra*, unless of course you're in a pseudo-Irish pub, in which case you can also ask for a *pinta*.

If you do just ask for a cerveza you may get bottled beer, which is more expensive. A small bottle of beer is called a *botellín*. A larger one (330ml) is often referred to as a *tercio* (as in a third of a litre).

A *clara* is a shandy, a beer cut with lemonade *(gaseosa)*.

Who said the Spaniards don't have a sense of humour? Many bars also provide extremely large plastic beakers of beer (usually for the youngsters). The beer is not always great (almost definitely cut with a little water at times), but is cheap and abundant. These huge containers are called...*minis*.

JANE SMITH

---

leave you with a sore head. *Tinto de verano* is a mix of wine and Casera, a brand of lemonade, or sweet, bubbly water.

There is no shortage of imported and Spanish-produced top-shelf stuff – *coñac* (brandy) is popular. Larios is a common brand of gin but it doesn't get too many rave reviews from resident Brits!

Madrid's emblematic drink, but one few locals actually bother with, is *licor de madroño*, a clear, high-octane drop extracted from the fruit of Madrid's symbolic tree, the strawberry tree. A couple of madroño bars exist in Madrid (one is listed under La Latina Bars in the Nightlife special section).

Anisado de Chinchón is a very popular aniseed-based drink produced in the town of the same name south of Madrid (see also Chinchón under South of Madrid in the Excursions chapter).

PLACES TO EAT – BUDGET

One traveller's budget restaurant may be another's splurge, so these categories are a little arbitrary. Those hoping to satisfy their hunger for around 1000 ptas to 1500 ptas could try the following places (in a few cases you can opt to spend a little more – say up to around 2000 ptas – and broaden your range of choices).

The line dividing bar and restaurant is often blurred and some of the places in the Nightlife special section also serve food. They are listed as bars because the food can be regarded as an adjunct to the drink.

Asking a madrileño where to find a 'tapas bar' may cause a moment of perplexity. In one sense there is no such thing, since virtually all bars will serve up some kind of tapa with a drink. True, in some cases the bar staff must be prompted and in others the tapa is nothing to write home about. But it is equally true that certain places have a justly good reputation for fine bar snacks.

Around Sol & Plaza Mayor

Plaza Mayor and the immediate area offer plenty of possibilities, but a good number are tourist traps, serving up average food at not-so-average prices. They huddle together especially along Calle de la Cava de San Miguel and Calle de los Cuchilleros.

A wonderful old tapas bar is **Casa Labra** *(Map 7; Calle de Tetuán 11)*. It has been going in much the same style since 1860. Locals pile in here after a day's work or shopping, but more than one hundred years ago Pablo Iglesias and pals founded the Spanish socialist party while sipping on wine here.

If you feel like snuggling into a northern Spanish environment, head for **Casa Parrondo** *(Map 5; ☎ 91 522 62 34, Calle de Trujillos 9)*. This Asturian cider tavern and restaurant offers hearty tapas (lots of chorizo sausage and cheese) and well-prepared food. The restaurant out the back is like an Asturian house in the mountains and, if the photos of the owner killing pigs and turning them into sausages (strange taste in decor) don't put you off, you will eat well. The lunchtime menú del día is good value at 1400 ptas. It's closed on Sunday evening.

Heading closer to the Teatro Real you'll find **La Cruzada** *(Map 7; ☎ 91 548 01 31, Calle de la Amnistía 8)*. Actually founded a couple of blocks away in 1827, the tavern was shifted (complete with the remarkable sculpted wooden bar) to its present address in 1972, from which point the rot gradually set in. It has recently been tarted up as a bar and restaurant, and the raciones coming out of the kitchen at the hands of a skilled Basque chef are original and tasty. The tavern gets a combination of local and passing theatre trade; it closes Sunday evening.

La Latina

After more than 10 years well shut, **Oliveros** *(Map 7; Calle de San Millán 4)* opened up in early 2000. The Oliveros family has done everything to maintain the style and atmosphere of the place their family took over in 1921. It had been serving up food since 1857 and locals in particular seem pleased with the 1750 ptas set meal.

Plaza de Santa Ana, Huertas & Atocha

Aside from the bars, the area around Plaza de Santa Ana is busy with eating options. In and around Calle de la Cruz, Calle de Espoz y Mina and Calle de la Victoria is a cluster of restaurants and bars, many specialising in seafood with a more or less legitimate *gallego* (Galician) touch. All the following are on Map 8 unless indicated otherwise.

At **Maceira** *(Map 7; Calle de Jesús 7)* you can splash your *pulpo a la gallega* (Galician-style octopus) down with a crisp white Ribeiro. It closes at lunchtime on Monday.

In **La Casa del Abuelo** *(Calle de la Victoria 14)*, on a backstreet south-east of Puerta del Sol, you can sip a *chato* (small glass) of the heavy, sweet El Abuelo red wine, made in Toledo province, while munching on heavenly prawns, grilled or with garlic. Across the road are two other good tapas options: at No 4, **La Oreja de Oro**, and next door the recently spiffed-up, Andalucian-style **Taberna Alhambra** *(☎ 91 521 07 08, Calle de la Victoria 9)*. After these, duck round the corner to **Las Bravas** on Callejón de Álvarez Gato for a *caña* (small glass of beer) and the best *patatas bravas* (spicy fried potatoes) in town. The antics of the bar staff are enough to merit a pit stop, and the distorting mirrors are a minor Madrid landmark.

La Trucha *(☎ 91 532 08 90, Calle de Núñez de Arce 6)* is one of Madrid's great tapas bars. It closes on Sunday and Monday. It's just off Plaza de Santa Ana, and there's another *(☎ 91 429 58 33, Calle de Manuel Fernández y González 3)* nearby. You can eat your fill at the bar or sit down in the restaurant.

Something of an institution is the **Museo del Jamón** *(☎ 91 521 03 46, Carrera de San Jerónimo 6)*. Walk in here or one of several branches around town and you'll understand the name. Huge clumps of every conceivable type of ham dangle all over the place. You can eat plates and plates of ham – the Spaniards' single most favoured source of nutrition.

The unassuming **Mesón La Casolera** *(Calle de Echegaray 3)* is a popular hangout with madrileños. Ask for a *fritura*, a mixed platter of deep-fried seafood.

If it's just plain cheap food you want, **Restaurante Pasadero** *(Calle de Lope de Vega 9)* has a solid set-lunch menu for

1150 ptas. It closes in the evening from Sunday to Wednesday. Cheaper still and good is **Restaurante La Sanabresa** (☎ *91 429 03 38, Calle del Amor de Dios 12*), where the menú del día is 900 ptas.

La Finca de Susana (☎ *91 369 35 57, Calle de Arlabán 4*) is a great new spot in Madrid. Soft lighting and a veritable jungle of greenery create a soothing atmosphere for a meal that need not cost more than about 2000 ptas. Try the salads, grilled vegetables and variations on the carpaccio theme.

Vegetarian A good vegetarian place which also offers a non-vegetarian menu is **Restaurante Al Natural** (☎ *91 369 47 09, Calle de Zorrilla 11*). It's closed on Sunday evening.

Near Atocha station, **Restaurante La Mazorca** *(Map 9; ☎ 91 501 70 13, Paseo de la Infanta Isabel 21)* has mains for around 1000 ptas. The *crep de espinacas en salsa de queso* (spinach crepe in a cheese sauce) is good. It closes Sunday evening and Monday.

Elqui (Map 7; ☎ 91 468 04 62, Calle de Buenavista 18) is a handy self-service vegetarian buffet-style place. It opens daily but only for lunch on Monday (until 4 pm) and for dinner on Friday and Saturday (a la carte).

International Cuisine The Middle Eastern and North African eateries and *salones de té* popping up around Lavapiés are fun. They are often simple, with tasty Arab food and, often at the weekend, a little belly dancing. **Babilonya** *(Map 7; Calle del Ave María)*, opposite the Nuevo Café Barbieri off Plaza de Lavapiés, is a perfect example.

El Basha (☎ *91 39 06 57, Calle de los Relatores 18*) is not a bad spot if you are in the mood for Lebanese food. It's closed on Tuesday. *Beirut (Map 7; Calle de Miguel Servet 12)* is another, with a set lunch for 900 ptas.

Early Morning Just by the Centro de Arte Reina Sofía, *El Brillante (Map 7; Calle del Doctor Drumén 7)* is a Madrid classic for bocadillos and other snacks in the wee hours after a hard night on the tiles.

A funny little place is **La Farfalla** (☎ *91 369 46 91, Calle de Santa María 17*). They serve an odd mix of salads, vegetarian,

pseudo-Italian and other dishes. The big news is they do this until 4 am! Expect to pay about 2000 ptas per head for a full meal with wine and coffee.

Gran Vía, Malasaña & Chueca
Plunge into the labyrinth of narrow streets and alleys north of Gran Vía to satisfy your taste buds. The following are marked on Map 5 unless stated otherwise.

For a cheap pizza and beer outdoors, **Restaurante Sandos** *(Plaza del Dos de Mayo 8)* is fine. They also offer a decent set menu for 850 ptas. Better still is the crowded **Pizzeria Mastropiero** *(Calle de San Vicente Ferrer 34)* on the corner of Calle del Dos de Mayo, a justifiably popular Argentine-run joint where you can get pizza by the slice. They also do a *tarta de chocolate con dulce de leche* (chocolate tart with a thick caramel sauce) to die for.

Vegetarian Just off Plaza del Dos de Mayo, **Restaurante La Granja** (☎ *91 532 87 93, Calle de San Andrés 11*) has a set vegetarian lunch costing 1100 ptas.

Early Morning Madrid taxi drivers and other early-morning persons congregate at **Restaurante Iberia** *(Map 3; Plaza de Ruiz Jiménez 4)* for the best tortilla and callos you'll find in town at 5 am. A little further north is a branch of **El Brillante** *(Map 3; Calle de Eloy Gonzalo 14)*, also good for pre-dawn munchies.

Chamberí
El Doble (Map 3; ☎ 91 441 47 18, Calle de Ponzano 58) is a busy little tapas bar run, judging by all the photos on the wall, by rather intense bullfighting aficionados. The raciones, such as the gambas and ventresca are good if a bit pricey at around 1000 ptas. There are two bars with the same name on this street and both serve good food. They close early – expect to be out by midnight.

Río Manzanares Area
Head down past the Príncipe Pío train station towards the Río Manzanares and turn north. Here is a great old place for chicken

and cider. A full roast bird, salad and bottle of cider – plenty for two – at *Casa Mingo* (Map 2; ☎ 91 547 79 18, *Paseo de la Florida 34*) will cost less than 2000 ptas. They've been pouring cider here since 1888.

Prada a Tope (Map 2; ☎ 91 559 39 53, Cuesta de San Vicente 32) is another atmospheric place. Señor Prada, from the El Bierzo region in north-western Castilla y León, doesn't often make an appearance here anymore, but the food from his home region is as good as ever. Specialities include *cecina* (a kind of beef jerky), *empanada* (pie) and various chorizos. There's a brand-spanking-new branch at Calle del Príncipe 11 (Map 8), off Plaza de Santa Ana.

Around Plaza de España
You can get a set menu (including a bottle of wine) for 950 ptas at *Restaurante Veracruz (Map 5; ☎ 91 247 11 50, Calle de San Leonardo de Dios 5)*. The menu is topped off by wonderful homemade desserts. Manuel García López has been welcoming locals here since 1961. He takes a break on Sunday.

Salamanca, Goya & Beyond
A great lunch stop just north of El Retiro is *Alfredo's Barbacoa (Map 6; ☎ 91 576 62 71, Calle de Lagasca 5)*. On the menu are lightly spiced spare ribs for 1035 ptas and good steaks. You can eat in or take away. It closes on Sunday evening and Monday.

For midday tapas, *Taberna de Daniela (Map 2; ☎ 91 575 23 29, Calle del General Pardiñas 21)* is one of the best-known places in the snootier Goya area. The tile decor is great, but service can be patchy and you're probably better off at the bar.

International Cuisine A sparky little Italian restaurant is *Il Pastaio (Map 3; ☎ 91 554 29 25, Calle de Ríos Rosas 49)*, which concentrates on pasta dishes alone. The results are not bad and, at less than 900 ptas a dish, you're doing quite well. It's closed on Sunday evening and Monday.

Self-Catering
The *mercado (Map 7)* on Plaza de San Miguel, off Plaza Mayor, is the main fresh-produce market. Self-caterers can also try *Marks & Spencer's food department* for foodstuffs generally unavailable in Spanish shops. The food departments in the *Corte Inglés* stores are also good.

PLACES TO EAT – MID-RANGE
Opening your purse wider will improve your options greatly. At the places listed below you can expect to pay anything from 2000 to 3500 ptas for a full meal with all the trimmings.

Around Sol & Plaza Mayor
A classic spot to enjoy madrileño cooking at reasonable prices is *Casa Paco (Map 7; ☎ 91 366 31 66, Plaza de la Puerta Cerrada 11)*. They specialise in steaks except on Sundays, when they sleep instead.

More of an institution is *Casa Ciríaco (Map 7; ☎ 91 548 06 20, Calle Mayor 84)*, a bar and restaurant with loads of character. It was founded in 1917 in a building previously popular with would-be assassins: one threw a bomb from a balcony at Alfonso XIII as he passed by with his queen, Victoria Eugenia, on their wedding day in 1906. The attack failed, but 24 people died. On the subject of eating, mains cost anything from 1000 ptas to 2700 ptas. Closing day is Wednesday.

If it's paella your heart desires, the best advice is to head for Valencia. Failing that, you could try *Restaurante La Paella Real (Map 5; ☎ 91 542 09 42, Calle de Arrieta 2)*. This place does a whole range of rice-based dishes costing from 1840 ptas to 2425 ptas per head. It's not cheap, but halfway decent paella never is in Madrid. It's shut on Sunday evening.

International Cuisine Try *El Locro (Map 5; ☎ 91 522 43 82, Calle de Trujillos 2)* for a fine Argentinean restaurant whose speciality, predictably enough, is succulent slabs of grilled meat. It closes on Wednesday. Mains cost up to around 2300 ptas, but the lunch set menu comes in at 1200 ptas. Friday and Saturday nights they throw in some tango music.

Fado (Map 5; ☎ 91 532 21 02, Plaza de San Martín 2) is a good Portuguese eatery and something of a Madrid stalwart. Come for the seafood dishes in particular. It closes on Monday.

Marechiaro (Map 7; ☎ *91 547 00 42, Calle del Conde de Lemos 3)* is a cheap and cheerful Italian restaurant. It is closed on Sunday.

La Latina
You'll be met with a pleasingly simple brick-and-timber decor and a limited menu at *Restaurante Julián de Tolosa (Map 7;* ☎ *91 365 82 10, Calle de la Cava Baja 8).* If you feel like a *chuletón* (huge chop) it will cost upwards of 2500 ptas per head. It's closed on Sunday.

Upstairs at *Casa Víctor (Map 7;* ☎ *91 366 13 36, Calle de la Cava Baja 26)* seems like any other good-old-boys bar, where you can snack, slurp and burp. Downstairs is a small but attractive dining area, where you can eat well from a good if rather limited menu. You can expect to spend from 3500 ptas up. The *revuelto* (omelette with beans, prawns and ham) is great. It is closed on Monday.

A few doors down, *Casa Pepa (Map 7;* ☎ *91 366 72 12, Calle de la Cava Baja 38)* is an altogether different style of place, with low lighting and a hushed feel. It's been getting quite a few accolades. Their mains of fish or meat cost around 2500 ptas.

An excellent Asturian place in La Latina, *La Burbuja Que Ríe ('Laughing Bubble'; Map 7;* ☎ *91 366 51 67, Calle del Ángel 16),* serves up a tempting array of hearty dishes (try the *setas con almejas* – mushrooms and clams) that you can wash down with cider.

Vegetarian You should be able to get away with 2500 ptas for a full meal at *El Estragón (Map 7;* ☎ *91 365 89 82, Plaza de la Paja 10),* a delightfully atmospheric restaurant that has become something of a hit in Madrid.

Plaza de Santa Ana, Huertas & Atocha
In the gaudily decorated *Champagnería Gala (Map 8;* ☎ *91 429 25 62, Calle de*

Moratín 22), named after Dalí's odd Russian consort, you can tuck into Catalan rice dishes and *fideuá,* the noodle version.

La Vaca Verónica (Map 7; ☎ *91 429 78 27, Calle de Moratín 38)* is a refreshing locale offering Mediterranean cuisine with a little fantasy. Expect to pay about 2000 ptas. It closes at Saturday lunchtime and on Sunday.

At the rather camp *Gula Gula (Map 8;* ☎ *91 420 29 19, Calle del Infante 5)* the thing to do is dig into their amazing salad buffet for 2000 ptas. It closes on Monday.

Vegetarian A full meal at the excellent *Restaurante Integral Artemisa* (☎ *91 429 50 92, Calle de Ventura de la Vega 4)* will cost around 2000 ptas. There is another branch (☎ 91 521 87 21) off Gran Vía at Calle de las Tres Cruces 4 (Map 5).

International Cuisine The following are all marked on Map 8.

A pleasant place for a cocktail and some fairly authentic Cuban fare is *El Tocororo* (☎ *91 369 40 00, Calle del Prado 3).* You can snack at the bar or sit down to eat, in which case you will probably part with about 3000 ptas. It closes on Monday.

Los Gabrieles Restaurant (☎ *91 429 38 10, Calle de Ventura de la Vega 13)* is odd if only for the mix of dishes they offer, ranging from couscous through French-Argentinean-style meat platters.

Aki (☎ *91 420 10 49, Calle de Echegaray 9)* is a cheerful Japanese spot. You can sit at the bar and nibble at sushi or a wide variety of other specialities. The sushi special mix for 3000 ptas is enough for a main meal.

For quality Peruvian nosh check out *El Inti de Oro* (☎ *91 429 67 03, Calle de Ventura de la Vega 12).* Try the melt-in-your-mouth *merluza con salsa de camarones* (hake done in a light prawn sauce and served with rice). Wash it down with imported Peruvian beer (Cristal). For a full meal expect to shell out around 3500 ptas per head.

Lavapiés
Vegetarian You can pick up some good vegetarian food as well as a couple of nice

JULIET COOMBE

Keep your strength up for more galleries with platefuls of paella from street-side cafes.

OLIVER STREWE

Relax, have a drink, chat with friends – ah, this is the life...

Taverna sign opposite Opera Metro

Ham, ham and more ham – the Museo del Jamón

La Torre del Oro, Plaza Mayor – excellent bar, cheap beer and menacing bulls' heads non-vegetarian dishes at *El Granero de Lavapiés (Map 7;* ☎ *91 467 76 11, Calle de Argumosa 10)*. Expect to pay around 2000 ptas per person. They open daily for lunch but only Friday and Saturday for dinner as well.

International Cuisine The Argentine *Restaurante La Pampa (Map 7;* ☎ *91 528 04 49, Calle del Amparo 61)* is good for grilled meats. At the weekend you can experience live tangos. After all that excitement, the owners close for a rest on Monday.

Gran Vía, Malasaña & Chueca

Everything in this section is on Map 5 unless otherwise indicated.

For excellent *extremeño* food, make for *Restaurante Extremadura (*☎ *91 531 89 58, Calle de la Libertad 13)*. A meal with wine can come to around 3000 ptas per person. It shuts on Sunday night and Monday. There is a more modern and less enticing branch at No 31, which closes on Tuesday night and Wednesday.

One of the better places for paella is *Restaurante de Cañas y Barro (*☎ *91 542 47 98, Calle de Amaniel 23)*. Expect to pay around 2000 ptas per head for the paella alone. It is closed on Monday.

Expect about the same prices at the Valencian *Restaurante La Barraca (*☎ *91 532 71 54, Calle de la Reina 29)*, which does a fair paella for around 2000 ptas.

Restaurante Momo (☎ *91 532 71 62, Calle de Augusto Figueroa 41)* has an above-average set evening menu costing 1500 ptas, including wine. The cuisine tends to be inventive, steering well clear of standard Spanish stuff.

Undata (☎ *91 523 33 63, Calle de Clavel 5)* is a cool place to dine if the minimalist, shiny-chrome deal is your thing. They offer what could be described as international Mediterranean cuisine, a bit of a pastiche. Prices are moderate. It is closed Sunday lunchtime and Monday evening.

Divina la Cocina (☎ *91 531 37 65, Calle de Colmenares 13)* does 'modern' Spanish, whatever that means. On the menu is leg of ostrich. The place has a cheerily camp feel

to it and the food is not bad at all, if a little pricey. It is closed on Sunday and Monday evening.

International Cuisine For mouthwatering steak tartare and other French temptations, head for *Restaurante Dame Noire (*☎ *91 531 04 76, Calle de Pérez Galdós 3)*. It's open for dinner only from Tuesday to Sunday.

For decent Italian cooking try *La Dolce Vita (Map 3;* ☎ *91 445 04 36, Calle de Cardenal Cisneros 58)*. The desserts are sublime. Count on paying about 3500 ptas per person.

Good Mexican food and excellent margaritas can be had at the *Taquería de Birrä (*☎ *91 522 80 49, Plaza de las Comendadoras 2)*, which has a lovely summertime *terraza* (terrace). Otherwise, head for their other branch *(Map 7;* ☎ *91 366 45 39, Calle de Don Pedro 11)*, just off Calle de Bailén.

Not only can you eat good, meaty Argentine food at *La Carreta (*☎ *91 532 70 42, Calle de Barbieri 10)* but you can do so until about 4 am at the weekend.

Around Plaza de España

The restaurants below are all on Map 5.

La Dama Duende (☎ *91 532 54 41, Calle de la Palma 63)* is a tastefully simple little eatery with a touch of class. Try the *pez espada con salsa de puerros* (swordfish in leek sauce) and be sure to follow with one of the delicious desserts. You will probably pay around 3000 ptas.

International Cuisine The *Adrish (*☎ *91 542 94 98, Calle de San Bernardino 1)* is about Madrid's best attempt at Indian and does pretty convincing dishes, so you can expect to pay a minimum of 2500 ptas per person.

Restaurante Bali (☎ *91 541 91 22, Calle de San Bernardino 6)* is Madrid's only Indonesian restaurant. The authentic cooking is a welcome alternative to Iberian fare. A good meal should come in at 5000 ptas or less for two. It closes on Sunday night and Monday lunchtime.

PLACES TO EAT

Salamanca, Goya & Beyond

For this part of town, *Casa Julián (Map 6;* ☎ *91 431 35 35, Calle de Don Ramón de la Cruz 10)* is a no-nonsense and atmospheric place, specialising in grilled meats. Expect to pay around 1500 ptas per person for grilled flesh of various red varieties. It closes on Sunday evening.

Restaurante El Pescador (Map 2; ☎ *91 402 12 90, Calle de José Ortega y Gasset 75)* is a seafood specialist that's been around forever. It closes on Sunday.

You can dig into a limited variety of roast meats at the sumptuous *Asador La Tahona (Map 1;* ☎ *91 555 04 41, Calle del Capitán Haya 21).* A full meal will cost you around 3000 ptas with wine. Sunday nights they pull down the shutters.

International Cuisine All of the best Chinese restaurants (and none match those you may be used to in your respective Chinatowns, from London to Sydney) seem to be scattered about the north of the city. One of them is *China Crown (Map 1;* ☎ *91 572 14 64, Calle de la Infanta Mercedes 62).* Expect to pay about 2000 ptas. They do an acceptable dim-sum.

Every city's got one. The *Hard Rock Café (Map 6;* ☎ *91 436 43 40, Paseo de la Castellana 2)* serves up American-style club sandwiches, nachos and cocktails. It's lively and the food is generally good value; helpings are of the American jumbo persuasion. You can eat large for around 2500 ptas.

PLACES TO EAT – TOP END

Clearly, eating in Madrid is considerably cheaper than in many other Western European capitals. But it is possible to part company with reasonable sums of money if you wish. Eating at the restaurants listed below will see your wallet lightened by sums from about 4000 ptas up. In some cases, if you choose carefully, you could bring the bill down below that mark, but not by much.

Around Sol & Plaza Mayor

At *Restaurante Sobrino de Botín (Map 7;* ☎ *91 366 42 17, Calle de los Cuchilleros 17)* the set menu costs 4050 ptas. The restaurant is popular with those who can afford it and featured in Benito Pérez Galdós' novel *Fortunata y Jacinta.*

The *Taberna del Alabardero (Map 5;* ☎ *91 547 25 77, Calle de Felipe V 6)* is fine for a splurge – expect little change per person from 6000 ptas. Or just try a few tapas at the bar.

La Latina

A fine Basque eatery, *Restaurante Gure-Etxea (Map 7;* ☎ *91 365 61 49, Plaza de la Paja 12)* is typically expensive. The *menú de degustación,* which allows you to sample a range of excellent Basque dishes, costs 3650 ptas per head.

Plaza de Santa Ana, Huertas & Atocha

All of the restaurants mentioned in this section are marked on Map 8.

Lhardy (☎ *91 521 33 85, Carrera de San Jerónimo 8)* has been serving up gourmet tapas since 1839. Mr Lhardy, a Frenchman, was convinced to come to Madrid by his pal Prosper Merimée, who assured him he would have no competition. As befits its long history of attracting an illustrious local clientele, the prices are not exactly rock bottom. You can also sit down to full meals (the house specialities are Madrid dishes such as callos and cocido). It is closed on Sunday and holidays.

El Cenador del Prado (☎ *91 429 15 61, Calle del Prado 4).* For elegant dining and mixed modern cuisine, you could do worse than this place. You will emerge at least 4000 ptas lighter. It closes Saturday lunchtime and Sunday.

International Cuisine One of Madrid's popular Japanese places is the *Restaurante Donzoko (*☎ *91 429 57 20, Calle de Echegaray 3).* A cheap meal will start at about 3500 ptas but could easily go considerably higher. It is closed on Sunday.

Gran Vía, Malasaña & Chueca

Tucked away off Plaza de las Salesa is one of Madrid's quality secrets, *El Mentidero de la Villa (Map 5;* ☎ *91 308 12 85, Calle de Santo Tomé 6).* It recently changed hands and the jury is still out on the new owners. The Spanish nouvelle cuisine is worth a try but you'll get little change from 5000 ptas. It's closed Saturday lunchtime and Sunday.

International Cuisine If you're after a good restaurant with a French leaning, try *La Gastroteca de Stéphane y Arturo (Map 5;* ☎ *91 532 25 64, Plaza de Chueca 8).* Expect to part with at least 4000 ptas. They close at lunchtime on Saturday, all day Sunday and on public holidays.

Restaurante Robata (☎ *91 521 85 28, Calle de la Reina 31)* is reputedly one of Madrid's best Japanese eating houses. You'll end up spending about 6000 ptas per person for a set dinner. It is closed on Wednesday.

Around Plaza de España

Since 1880 *Taberna La Bola (Map 5;* ☎ *91 547 69 30, Calle de la Bola 5)* has been stirring up a storm with its traditional cocido a la madrileña. The atmosphere reflects the years, making this a worthwhile once-off in spite of the prices. It's closed on Sunday evening.

International Cuisine The Thai *Restaurante Siam (Map 5;* ☎ *91 559 83 15, Calle de San Bernardino 8),* next door to Restaurante Bali (see Places to Eat – Mid-Range) and run by the same woman, is not as good as its neighbour, although the food is quite all right. The menú de degustación for 3000 ptas includes a cross-section of dishes. It is closed on Sunday.

Salamanca, Goya & Beyond

The following restaurants can be found on Map 6 unless stated otherwise.

Restaurante Oter (☎ *91 431 67 71, Calle de Claudio Coello 73)* is a rather upmarket spot for Navarran cuisine. Expect to free 6000 ptas from your wallet. It closes on Sunday.

Teatriz (☎ *91 577 53 79, Calle de la Hermosilla 15)* is a stylish hangout with a difference. The former Teatro Beatriz has an

eerily lit bar right on the stage. The food is ostensibly Italian and not bad.

At *El Amparo (*☎ *91 431 64 56, Calle de Puigcerdà 8)* the food is variously described as Basque and *nueva cocina madrileña* ('nouvelle Madrid cuisine'). Whichever, it is good inventive food that has won the admiration of Michelin. It closes Saturday lunchtime and Sunday.

La Trainera (☎ *91 576 05 75, Calle de Lagasca 60)* is an old favourite among lovers of good seafood. The decor is simple, the ingredients fresh and the prices high.

International Cuisine Madrid's top Thai alternative is the lavish *Thai Gardens (*☎ *91 577 88 84, Calle de Jorge Juan 5).* The best time to enjoy this place without committing a financial crime is for the weekday set lunch at 2900 ptas. Otherwise each dish comes in at around 2000 ptas.

For the city's only shot at Filipino cuisine (mixed with some Japanese dishes just to keep you on your toes), try *Restaurante Sulú (Map 1;* ☎ *91 359 10 40, Paseo de la Castellana 172).* A full meal will come to around 4500 ptas. It closes all day Sunday.

CAFES & TEA HOUSES

There is no shortage of places to get a drink in Madrid – some areas consist of wall-to-wall bars.

A feature of many that can take a little getting used to is the habit of dropping all rubbish – from napkins and uneaten bits of tapas to cigarette ash and coffee dregs – onto the floor by the bar. At one point or another it all gets swept out and there is some logic to it. If one or two people do it, you have to sweep it up, so you may as well let everyone do it! At tables or outside on the terrazas the habit does not apply.

Unlike, say, in Italy, the price difference between drinking at the bar and at a table is not always rigidly enforced, but in some places the price of sitting down may be quite high. Table prices on the terrazas, especially in summer, are always higher than bar prices.

The neat Anglo-Saxon division between cafes (for coffee or tea and scones) and pubs

PLACES TO EAT

or bars (for getting plastered) is a feature absent from the madrileño approach to drinking in society. Nevertheless, some bars are fairly evidently *not* intended for a leisurely café con leche and a read of the paper; these are dealt with in the Nightlife special section. Others clearly do lean this way. Following are some suggestions for the latter.

Around Plaza Mayor

On Plaza de Isabel II, *Café del Real* (*Map 7; ☎ 91 547 21 24*) is an atmospheric place with a touch of elegance. It gets busy at night but also makes a pleasant spot for breakfast. Head for the low-ceilinged upstairs section.

Up Calle de Vergara to Plaza de Ramales is a series of fine cafes. *Café Vergara (Map 7; ☎ 91 559 11 72, Calle de Vergara 1)* is good, and the rather stiff *Café de los Austrias (Map 7; ☎ 91 435 78 65, Plaza de Ramales 1)* seems as imperial as its name implies.

Café de Oriente (Map 5; ☎ 91 541 39 74, Plaza de Oriente 2) feels like a set out of Mitteleuropa – it's well worth stopping by. If you are feeling peckish they have some very expensive food.

From Plaza de Colón to the Prado

Just near Plaza de Colón, *Café-Restaurante El Espejo (Map 6; ☎ 91 308 23 47, Paseo de los Recoletos 31)* doubles as one of Madrid's most elegant cafes. You could also sit in the turn-of-the-century-style *Pabellón del Espejo* outside. Despite appearances, it was opened only in 1990. Both are a little pricey and the latter also forms the nucleus of one of Madrid's more expensive summer terrazas.

Just down the road is the equally graceful *Gran Café de Gijón (Map 6; ☎ 91 521 54 25, Paseo de los Recoletos 21)*, which has been serving coffee and meals since 1888.

If you're strolling around here but want something a little more down to earth, *Café de la Villa (Map 6)*, in the cultural centre of the same name on Plaza de Colón, is a cheery den for arty types.

Another wonderful old place with chandeliers and an atmosphere belonging to another era is the cafe at the *Círculo de Bellas Artes (Map 5; ☎ 91 531 85 03, Calle de Alcalá 42)*. You have to buy a temporary club membership (100 ptas) to drink in here, but it's worth it.

Malasaña

The following cafes are marked on Map 5. For an old Madrid cafe with a good whiff of its castizo past, track down *Café Comercial (☎ 91 521 56 55, Glorieta de Bilbao 7)*. The odd foreigner stops in, but it's just far enough off the usual tourist trail to be reasonably genuine.

Café Manuela (☎ 91 531 70 37, Calle de San Vicente Ferrer 29) lies on that borderline between cafe and bar. It is a young, hip place with a vaguely alternative flavour. *Café Isadora (☎ 91 445 71 54, Calle del Divino Pastor 14)* is great for chatting away the early evening over a coffee or cocktail.

An enchanting tea house with a hint of the 1960s is *Tetería de la Abuela (Calle del Espíritu Santo 19)*. Along with the great range of teas you can indulge in scrummy crepes.

For a somewhat camp but pleasant ambience, and a great cup of coffee and cheesecake, try *Café La Sastrería (☎ 91 532 07 71, Calle de Hortaleza 74)*. In keeping with the tailor theme, the black-clad waiters wear measuring tapes for ties.

Huertas & Lavapiés

Calle de las Huertas has a string of cafes and bars to choose from. On Plaza de Canalejas, you'll strike a fine, old madrileño bar, *Café del Príncipe (Map 8)*. It serves good food if you're peckish and the people-watching is an attraction in itself.

A wonderful old place, once the haunt of the artistic and hopefully artistic, *Nuevo Café Barbieri (Map 7; ☎ 91 527 36 58, Calle del Ave María 45)* provides newspapers to browse through while you sip your cortado.

If you'd prefer tea, there are several teterías in the Granada fashion dotted about the place. *Damasco Salón de Te (Map 8;*

Calle del Infante) and ***El Café de Sherazade*** *(Map 8; Calle de Santa María 18)* are equally good.

Around Plaza de España

A few steps away from several of Madrid's better cinemas, off Plaza de España, is the perfectly appropriate ***Café de las Extrellas*** *(Map 5; Calle de Martín de los Heros 5)*. It attracts a film-going crowd and is plastered with portrait photos of screen greats. A block away, at ***Café Macaluca*** *(Map 5; Calle de Juan Álvarez Mendizábal 4)*, you can nosh up on fabulous crepes and cheesecake, washed down with one of any number of teas and infusions.

PASTRY SHOPS

Central Madrid is riddled with pastry shops. A particularly good one is the ***Antigua Pastelería del Pozo*** *(Map 8; ☎ 91 522 38 94, Calle del Pozo 8)*, near the Puerta del Sol. In operation since 1830 (and for 20 years before that as a bread bakery), it is the city's oldest dealer in tooth-rotting items.

Entertainment

What Madrid may lack in grand sights, it makes up for in the life of its bars and clubs, its cinemas, theatres and cafes. Madrileños take their enjoyment seriously and there is every opportunity to join them.

The busiest time of year on Madrid's cultural calendar – from theatre to rock concerts – runs from late September to early December in the Fiesta de Otoño (see Arts & Music Festivals under Public Holidays & Special Events in the Facts for the Visitor chapter).

You'll want to get some tips. *El País* has a daily listings section *(cartelera)*, good for cinema and theatre. Original-language films and cinemas are clearly indicated (look for movies in *versión original*, or *v.o. subtitulada*). Also listed are museums, galleries, music venues and the like. *El Mundo* publishes a weekly magazine supplement, *Metropoli*, on Friday. Rival newspaper *ABC* brings out *Guía de Madrid* on the same day. The latter is better organised and strong on cinema and where to eat. The weekly entertainment bible is, however, the *Guía del Ocio*, available at newsstands for 125 ptas. You can sometimes find a free listings guide, *En Cartel*, in bars and bookshops around town.

You can generally get tickets for plays, concerts and other performances at the theatre concerned, but there are centralised ticketing offices too. Quite a few lottery ticket booths also sell tickets for theatre, football and bullfights. Try the Localidades La Alicantina (Map 5), on Plaza de Santo Domingo, or Localidades Galicia (Map 5; ☎ 91 531 27 32) on Plaza del Carmen 1.

For bands and popular-music acts you can often get tickets at the Madrid Rock record store, at Calle Mayor 38 (Map 7), Gran Vía 25 and Calle de San Martín 3 (both Map 5). You can pay for tickets in cash only. The FNAC store (Map 5), on Calle de Preciados, also sells tickets to major concerts in and beyond Madrid.

Telephone booking is also possible. The Caixa de Catalunya operates the Tel-Entrada system, which covers many shows of all kinds. You call ☎ 902 10 12 12, pay for tickets by credit card and pick them up at the theatre before the show starts.

For tips on where to go to drink, dance and degenerate, see the Nightlife special section at the end of the chapter. Here follow some less exacting entertainment possibilities in the city. After all, there's more to Madrid than simply bar-hopping and dancing beyond dawn!

FLAMENCO

There are several *tablaos* (flamenco performance spots) in central Madrid, but most are designed for the tourist crowd. They generally feature dinner and flamenco shows of indifferent quality, much avoided by locals. The best of this poor lot appears to be *Café de Chinitas (Map 5; ☎ 91 559 51 35, Calle de Torija 7)*. You will almost certainly need to book ahead. Another is *Corral de la Morería (Map 7; ☎ 91 365 84 46, Calle de la Morería 17)*. Look in local entertainment guides for more information.

To get a feel for the more genuine article, you have several options. You can try the handful of *peñas flamencas*, bars where flamenco music is often played, although not necessarily live. For some, *La Soleá (Map 7; ☎ 91 365 52 64, Calle de la Cava Baja 34)* is the last real flamenco bar in Madrid, where aficionados enjoy performers who know it all. At *Candela (Map 7; ☎ 91 467 33 82, Calle del Olmo 3)* the *gitanos* (Romany people) practise their music and dance out the back (you probably won't be allowed to watch), but the bar is charged with an Andalucían flamenco atmosphere. Occasionally you'll get lucky and witness impromptu jam sessions.

Casa Patas (Map 8; ☎ 91 369 04 96, Calle de Cañizares 10) is a little more organised and hosts recognised masters of flamenco guitar, song and dance.

Teatro Lara (Map 5; ☎ 91 521 05 52, Calle de la Corredera Baja de San Pablo

15) occasionally puts on some flamenco performances.

Not infrequently the bigger names play to packed houses in various of Madrid's theatres; check the papers. For more information on this passionate musical and dance phenomenon, see Music & Dance under Arts in the Facts about Madrid chapter.

CLASSICAL MUSIC & OPERA

At the city's grandest stage, the *Teatro Real (Map 5; ☎ 91 516 06 06, Plaza de Isabel II; bookings through the Caja de Madrid bank 902 48 84 88)*, tickets for the opera or ballet can range in price from 1000 ptas, for a spot so far away you will need a telescope, to around 20,000 ptas.

The *Auditorio Nacional de Música (Map 1; ☎ 91 337 01 40, Calle del Príncipe de Vergara 146; metro: Cruz de Rayo)* is the main venue for classical music. On a smaller scale, the *Fundación Juan March (Map 2; ☎ 91 435 42 40, Calle de Castelló 77; metro: Núñez de Balboa)* holds regular Sunday concerts.

If you can't get into the Teatro Real, the *Teatro Calderón (Map 7; ☎ 91 369 14 34, Calle de Atocha 18)* plays second fiddle for opera. The *Teatro de la Zarzuela (Map 8; ☎ 91 524 54 00, Calle de Jovellanos 4; metro: Banco de España)* is the place for that very Spanish genre of classical dance and music, the zarzuela. The theatre was built in 1856 in vague imitation of Milan's La Scala.

For other musical and operatic performances, the Centro Cultural de la Villa (see Theatre later in this chapter) and the *Teatro Monumental (Map 8; ☎ 91 429 81 19, Calle de Atocha 65)* are the main venues to check out.

CINEMAS

Standard cinema tickets cost around 850 ptas, but many cinemas have at least one day set aside as the *día del espectador* (viewer's day) with cut-price tickets (usually about 200 ptas off).

One of the best concentrations of cinemas for original-language films is on and around Calle de Martín de los Heros and

Calle de la Princesa (Map 5). The *Renoir* and *Princesa (both ☎ 91 541 41 00)* and *Alphaville (☎ 91 559 38 36)* cinema complexes around this area all screen such movies.

The *Cine Doré (Map 8; ☎ 91 549 60 11, Calle de Santa Isabel 3; metro: Antón Martín)*, which houses the Filmoteca Nacional, is a wonderful old cinema that shows classics past and present, all in the original language. It has a cheap restaurant attached. If you're in Madrid for any length of time, consider getting their *bono*, which gives you cut-price tickets.

You can also see subtitled movies at *Multicines Ideal (Map 7; ☎ 91 369 25 18, Calle del Doctor Cortezo 6)*, the *Renoir (Map 1; ☎ 91 541 41 00, Calle de Raimundo Fernández Villaverde 10; metro: Cuatro Caminos)* and *Real Cinema (Map 5; ☎ 91 547 45 77, Plaza de Isabel II)*.

The huge-screen *Cine Imax (☎ 91 467 48 00; metro: Méndez Álvaro)* is in the Parque Enrique Tierno Galván at Camino de Meneses s/n, south of Atocha train station. For this 3D-cinema experience you pay between 900 ptas and 1400 ptas, depending on what's showing.

THEATRE

After the torpor of summer, autumn is a busy season for theatre. Although the theatre, music and dance scene is not as diverse or of as high a quality as in some other European capitals, there is plenty happening and a plethora of venues large and small, of which the following are a representative selection.

The beautiful old *Teatro de la Comedia (Map 8; ☎ 91 521 49 31, Calle del Príncipe 14)* is home to the Compañía Nacional de Teatro Clásico and often stages gems of classic Spanish and European theatre. The *Teatro de Bellas Artes (Map 5; ☎ 91 532 44 38, Calle del Marqués de Casa Riera 2)* also leans towards the classics.

You can see mainstream drama at the *Teatro Español (Map 8; ☎ 91 429 62 97, Calle del Príncipe 25)*. A theatre has stood on this spot since 1583, when it was known as the Corral del Príncipe. It later became

ENTERTAINMENT

Right Royal Footballers

JANE SMITH

In the closing years of the 19th century, an odd sport imported from the UK began to attract the attention of young lads in Madrid and elsewhere in Spain. It involved two teams of chaps booting a spherical object around a pitch, and by all accounts it quickly caught on.

Like any traditional invasion, the first landings took place on the coast, where the Brits already had a presence. The game was first played in Barcelona, the Basque Country, Vigo (Galicia) and Huelva (Andalucía). Nevertheless, young madrileños could soon be seen bounding about, booting balls across open fields along the Manzanares and parks around the city.

The first clubs sprang up at the turn of the century. Among them was Madrid Foot-Ball, which came into being on 8 March 1902. It would later become Real Madrid, voted team of the century in 1998 by the international football association, FIFA. In April of the following year, Atlético ('Atléti' in the madrileño drawl) Madrid was formed as a kind of protege of the Athletic de Bilbao club, which won the first ever Spanish championship cup, the Campeonato de Copa de España (later known as the Copa del Rey, Spain's equivalent of the English FA Cup), staged in 1902 to celebrate the arrival on the throne of Alfonso XIII.

In those early days, Madrid Foot-Ball team members wore white shirts, long trousers and blue berets. Later on, the blue berets went and a splash of purple was added to the team colours. Nowadays, depending on the day, they don anything from all white to light-blue jerseys with navy-blue trousers. Atlético chose red and white, with blue trousers, as its colours. Of course, as time went by the trousers got shorter.

Teams from the Basque Country dominated the first few years of the sport at a national level but in 1905 Madrid took its first national cup against Athletic de Bilbao.

In 1920, King Alfonso XII conceded the title of 'royal' to the Madrid club, which henceforth would be known as the Real Madrid Football Club.

The national league, or Liga, got into full swing in 1928, but it was not until 1931 that *los blancos* (whites) or *merengues* (meringues), as Real Madrid were known, came out on top for the first time. It was hardly the last. Indeed, with 27 victories since then Real Madrid has dominated the Spanish Primera División (First Division) with almost alarming consistency. Fans of arch-rival FC

known as the Teatro del Príncipe and in 1849 was renamed the Teatro Español.

At the **Centro Cultural de la Villa** (Map 6; ☎ 91 575 60 80), under the waterfall at Plaza de Colón, you can see anything from classical-music concerts to comic theatre, opera and quality flamenco.

Teatro Alfil (Map 5; ☎ 91 521 58 27, Calle del Pez 10) is a good little alternative theatre. At **Teatro Albéniz** (Map 7; ☎ 91 531 83 11, Calle de la Paz 11) they put on every-

thing from *Who's Afraid of Virginia Woolf?* to flamenco festivals. Another venue to keep an eye on is the **Teatro Olimpia** (Map 7; ☎ 91 527 46 22, Plaza de Lavapiés).

AMUSEMENT PARKS

Travellers with kids on the leash can let them loose at the **Parque de Atracciones**, full of rides, shows and all the usual diversions you would expect of an amusement park, including several new attractions

Right Royal Footballers

Barcelona will tell you that in the years of Primo de Rivera's dictatorship, and then again under Franco, their team was frequently the victim of dodgy decisions at the national level.

Meanwhile, as the rest of Europe was playing at WWII, Spain kept playing football. In September 1943 Santiago Bernabéu took the helm as president of Real Madrid, a post he retained for 32 years. A year later work started on the stadium along the Paseo de la Castellana that would bear his name and remains to this day a mecca of Spanish football. That year was a remarkable one for the side too. Among the feats of 1943 was Madrid's astonishing 11–1 victory over FC Barcelona in the Copa del Rey.

Bernabéu's time at the helm was the club's golden age. With hefty backing from Franco during the 1950s and 60s, the side swept from one victory to the next at national and international level. Skill was involved too. In 1951 Miguel Muñoz started a 25-year career as coach. In that time his team took nine Ligas and two Copas. Alfredo di Stefano, possibly the best player of all time in Spain, seemed to spend all his time at the opponents' goal mouth. From 1953 to 1958 he was consistently the side's top goal-scorer. He shot 31 goals in the 1956–7 season alone, and he remains to this day (he bowed out of competition in 1967) Real Madrid's most prolific scorer in the Champions League, with 50 goals.

Real Madrid has dominated not only the Liga, but just about every other available competition. The Copa del Rey has fallen into the whites' hands on 17 occasions.

The introduction of the Copa de Europa (Champions League) in 1956 only gave the side more space to display its bravura. Real Madrid managed to take the cup five times in a row. In all, the side has taken this cup eight times (the last in 2000), a record unequalled by any other European club. The side has been equally keen to lay its hands on the Spanish Supercopa (Super Cup), the UEFA and Cup Winners' Cup trophies. The latter has eluded the team, but Real Madrid have managed to grab two UEFA cups and four Super Cups.

In 1998, as Real Madrid took its seventh Champions League cup, the FIFA solemnly declared the side the all-time greatest team in the history of the game. This was not good enough for some, and coach Jupp Heynkes was sacked for the heinous crime of guiding the team to a humiliating fourth place in the Liga that year.

And what of the 'rojiblancos' (white-and-reds) of Atlético de Madrid? Although well and truly overshadowed by the merengues, the side has a creditable record, with nine Ligas, nine Copas del Rey, one Super Cup and one Champions League victory. That's the good news. The bad news is that the side, debt-ridden and playing awfully at the time of writing, were relegated to the Segunda División after the 1999–2000 season for the first time in 64 years.

Rayo Vallecano, a suburban Madrid team based in Vallecas, was performing much better and even proved a match on occasion for the faltering Real Madrid.

added in 2000. The park is in the Casa de Campo area west of the city centre (metro: Batán). It is open daily, except some Mondays, from May to mid-September. Opening times vary considerably (usually from noon until midnight or later, but generally from 6 pm in late July and August). It tends to open from noon to 7 pm at the weekend and on holidays only in winter. The cheapest ticket (600 ptas) allows you admission only. An unlimited all-rides stamp costs 2675 ptas for adults and 1500 ptas for children aged seven and under. Single-ride tickets are available too (most rides cost adults the price of two such tickets).

SPECTATOR SPORTS
Football

Even if football (or soccer as it is known to some) doesn't interest you, a good match in Spain provides an insight into an essential side of Spanish leisure.

euro currency converter € 1 = 166 ptas

Real Madrid Football Club is one of Europe's best teams and has a fine stadium, *Estadio Santiago Bernabéu (Map 1; ☎ 91 398 43 00; metro: Santiago Bernabéu)*, which has a capacity of 85,000. Games are quite an occasion as long as the opposition is good enough to fire up the home team and the crowd. Check the daily press for upcoming games.

Tickets generally cost from 2500 ptas to 9000 ptas. They can be bought on the day or in advance at the stadium or from ticket offices (more expensive) on Calle de la Victoria, near Puerta del Sol. You can also try Localidades La Alicantina and Localidades Galicia (see the beginning of this chapter), or book them over the phone through the Servi-Caixa (☎ 902 33 22 11).

The city's other main club (recently relegated to the second division as we write), Atlético de Madrid, is based at the *Estadio Vicente Calderón (☎ 91 366 47 07; metro: Pirámides)*, south-west of the centre on Calle de la Virgen del Puerto. Tickets cost the same and are available at the stadium or through the offices mentioned above. See also the boxed text 'Right Royal Footballers'.

A local derby, or better still a match between Real Madrid and arch-rivals Barcelona, is a guarantee that sparks will fly – although getting tickets can be difficult.

Bullfighting

For information on when and where to see bullfights in Madrid, see the special section on that subject earlier in the book.

NIGHTLIFE

Madrid can justly think of itself as one of the most frenetic nightlife capitals of Europe. It may not have the cachet of the London clubbing scene or perhaps the reputation of some of the Continent's summer resorts (Spain's own Ibiza springs to mind). But for sheer density of locals and out-of-towners rubbing shoulders in a seemingly effortless desire to have a good time almost round the clock, Madrid is hard to beat. Where else will you see bumper-to-bumper traffic at 4 am?

Since the heyday of the *movida* in the years after Franco's death, Madrid has gone through some ups and downs, but as never before it seems bursting with nocturnal activity and an almost religious devotion to having a good time.

For tips on how to get plugged into the scene (local gig guides and the like) turn to the introductory paragraphs to the Entertainment chapter. Below we take a trip into just a few of the pubs, bars and clubs that keep Madrid hopping all year round.

BARS
Plaza de Santa Ana, Huertas & Atocha

Plaza de Santa Ana is lined with interesting bars, although clearly they have been much 'discovered' by locals and out-of-towners alike. The plaza was created when Joseph Bonaparte ordered the destruction of a convent that previously occupied the whole square.

Madrileños increasingly refer to the whole area as *guirilandia* on account of the high percentage of *guiris* (foreigners) that hang out here. Nevertheless, the atmosphere in the places on the square is buzzy, and in the streets radiating off it there is a lifetime supply of bars new and old to suit most tastes. Thursday night is the best, as the place is full to bursting with guiris and *gatos* (natives of Madrid) Friday and Saturday. All the following are on Map 8.

Cervecería Alemana (☎ 91 429 70 33, Plaza de Santa Ana 6) is a century-old meeting place and a traditional haunt of bullfighters who stay at the Gran Hotel Reina Victoria on the same square. It closes on Tuesday. A few doors up, *La Moderna* has been going since 1994 and attracts a mixed, 30-something crowd. Any of the bars along here makes for a pleasant watering stop, especially when you can sit outside in the warmer months.

La Fontana de Oro (☎ 91 531 04 20, Calle de la Victoria 2) is a reasonable 'Irish-style' pub with rather a longer history than most. Before occupation of the city by Napoleon's troops early in the last century, it was a hotbed of political dissent, as wine and antigovernment talk flowed freely.

Right: Swig sangria in a crowded cocktail joint or sip sherry in a cosy corner – Madrid's bar scene has something for all palates.

Although it gets hellishly crowded at the weekend, you should at least poke your head

JANE SMITH

into **Viva Madrid** (☎ 91 429 36 40, Calle de Manuel Fernández y González 7). The tiles and heavy timber ceilings make a distinctive setting for drinks earlier in the evening. Equally beautiful, but even more cheekily expensive, is **Los Gabrieles** (☎ 91 429 62 61, Calle de Echegaray 17), just a few steps away. If tiles are your thing, another good choice is **España Cañí** (Plaza del Ángel 14), west off Plaza de Santa Ana. The staff do a nice sangria.

To step into a space/time warp, slip into **La Venencia** (Calle de Echegaray 7) for a sherry. This place is the real thing: it looks as though nothing has been done to clean it in many a long year. Ill-lit and woody, it is the perfect place to sample one of six varieties of sherry – from the almost sweet amontillado to the rather biting fino.

Across the road, **El Margai** (Calle de Echegaray 10) is a classy little bar with a long drinks menu – and the drinks are very good. All Madrid seems to be raving about their cocktails.

At **Cardamomo** (☎ 91 369 07 57, Calle de Echegaray 15) there's flamenco and related music, although nothing live. Virtually around the corner, **Carbones** (Calle de Manuel Fernández y González) is busy, open until about 4 am and features a good selection of mainstream music on the jukebox.

Cuevas de Sésamo (☎ 91 429 65 24, Calle del Príncipe 7) is a wonderful old cellar bar that specialises in sangria. The walls are plastered with meaningful aphorisms and the air is heavy with smoke – just the way bars used to be.

All They Do Is Talk, Talk

Back in the 1830s, when writers, politicians, dilettantes and liberals were busily engaged in endless tertulias (get-togethers for serious chats), a series of cafes popped up to accommodate them. Dissident voices against the absolutist King Fernando VII started to grow louder in the late 1820s and the French occupation of 1824–29 did not help pacify spirits. Disquiet continued after the king's death in 1833.

In 1830, a group of writers and liberal politicians started meeting in the Café del Príncipe and there plunged into endless heated debates on what should be done in Spain. The tertulia here came to be known as El Parnasillo and dominated the intellectual life and debates about Madrid throughout the 1830s. The Café del Príncipe was a handy meeting place. Right on Plaza de Santa Ana was the city's oldest theatre, now known as the Teatro Español, and in 1835 some learned fellows opened the Ateneo Científico, Literario y Artístico down the road on Calle del Prado.

The Café del Príncipe, which to some was a rather dingy place for learned discussion but no doubt livened up by throaty Valdepeñas wine, still exists albeit in an altered guise. **El Parnasillo** (Map 8; Calle del Príncipe 33) didn't just change its name. One hundred and seventy years later it now trades as yet another Guinness-dispensing 'Irish pub', which seems rather a shame.

Bar Matador (☎ *91 531 89 81, Calle de la Cruz 39*), opposite the Torero disco, is a popular spot for a few drinks before crossing the road for some dance action (see Plaza de Santa Ana, Sol & La Latina under Discos & Clubs later in this special section). **Casa Alberto** (☎ *91 429 93 56, Calle de las Huertas 18*) was founded in 1827 in a building where Cervantes did a spot of writing. It's a fine old place for vermouth on tap and you can also get a meal. It closes Sunday night and Monday.

Café Populart (☎ *91 429 84 07, Calle de las Huertas 22*) often has music, generally jazz or Celtic. For more jazz with your drinks, **Café Central** (☎ *91 369 41 43, Plaza del Ángel 10*) is another good choice.

Just beyond the hubbub of Huertas is **El Parnaso** (☎ *91 420 19 75, Calle de Moratín 25*), a quirky but engaging spot. The area around the bar is jammed with an odd assortment of decorative paraphernalia, while out the back you get the feeling you're sitting in an ancient tramcar.

El Hecho (*Calle de las Huertas 56*) is a cosy cocktail bar generally open until 3 am. They do great daiquiris and *mojitos* (a delicious popular Cuban-rum-based concoction), for which they have quite a name around town. **Begin the Beguine** (*Calle de Moratín 27*) is a quiet haven, where discreet couples smooch in the barely lit corners.

Bet you never realised they make *cava* in Extremadura? Well they do, and it's not bad. Enjoy a bottle in the **Taberna de los Conspiradores** (☎ *91 369 47 41, Calle de Moratín 33*) while chomping Extremaduran snacks, such as *migas* (fried bread chunks). It closes on Monday.

Around Sol & Plaza Mayor

Although there is no shortage of bars immediately around Madrid's main square, few stand out.

Casa Antonio (*Map 7; Calle de Latrones 10*) is a wonderful old Madrid watering hole with loads of character and vermouth on tap.

El Templo del Gato (*Map 5;* ☎ *91 547 83 75, Calle de Trujillos 7*) is a Madrid classic. The music has a west coast tendency (which explains the alternative name, California Music Bar) and the atmosphere is of a gutsy rock bar. Cute young things let their hair down in this utterly unpretentious place where wire-mesh enclaves and pinball machines are part of the scenery. They finish around 4 am.

La Latina

Calle de la Cava Baja in particular is full of taverns and eating houses. The places listed here are on Map 7.

La Chata (*Calle de la Cava Baja 24*) has a spectacular tiled frontage and is nice for a quick *caña* (small glass of beer) or two. Don't spend all your time here though. **Taberna Tempranillo** at No 38 has plenty of character and an endless selection of Spanish wines that you'll be encouraged to sample. You can get a beer anywhere, so take a look at the wine list here instead.

Taberna Almendro 13 (☎ *91 365 42 52, Calle del Almendro 13*) has become a popular watering hole with locals. You can also get a bite to eat here. It used to be a spit-and-sawdust sherry bar but has been tastefully overhauled to attract a 'better' kind of clientele. Loiter about upstairs or head underground for seating. **Taberna Cien Vinos** (☎ 91 365 47 04, Calle del Nuncio 17) is a pleasant little locale to sit back in and wrap your taste buds around a broad selection of Spanish wines.

Back in Franco's heyday, the **Berlin Cabaret** (☎ 91 366 20 34, Costanilla de San Pedro 11) was a haven of late-night entertainment. Since the great dictator went on to Jesus, the place has transformed itself into a dance bar. With its endless different and interlocking levels, it has the feel of a cross between a theatre and an Escher drawing. The bar still puts on some kind of a show most nights, starting around 1 am. Come during the week as it's crammed on Friday and Saturday. It closes on Sunday.

There is a handful of intriguing places near the summertime *terrazas* of Las Vistillas (see Terrazas later in this special section). The gaudily coloured **Travesía** (☎ 91 366 87 92, Travesía de las Vistillas 8) attracts a diverse crowd with its cocktails and South American music.

Café del Nuncio (Calle del Nuncio 12) straggles down a stairway passage to Calle de Segovia. You can drink on one of several cosy levels inside or, better still in summer, tipple outdoors.

One of the few bars specialising in Madrid's *licor de madroño* (strawberry-tree liqueur) is **El Madroño** (Plaza de la Puerta Cerrada 7). It recently moved from a much more genuine and historical location in Lavapiés. Still, it's something of a unique experience. If a glass of the liqueur doesn't appeal, try the little *pasteles* (pastries), which are made of the firewater but can be eaten with more conventional beverages.

Lavapiés

This district is one of the last worker-*gitano* quarters in central Madrid. While the bars are often *cutre* (basic, spit-and-sawdust style), they brim with a raw energy. All these spots are on Map 7.

Taberna de Antonio Sánchez (☎ 91 539 78 26, Calle de Mesón de Paredes 13) is an old-time drinking place with a slightly conspiratorial air; it serves beer, wine and snacks, and that's about it.

An excellent place for cañas and seafood *pinchos* (snacks) is **El Boquerón** (Calle de Valencia 14), which has a rough-around-the-edges feel and is popular with people in the area. Round the corner you can hang out in **La Mancha de Madrid** (Calle de Miguel Servet), which attracts a colourful array of local tipplers earlier in the evening.

Just round the corner from the Teatro Olimpia is **Eucalipto** (Calle de Argumosa 4), something of a local hub and a great place for daiquiris.

Gran Vía, Malasaña & Chueca

Along with the Santa Ana and Huertas area, the web of streets and lanes stretching northwards off Gran Vía is Madrid's other great party paradise, with more bars, pubs, dance places and general drinking potential than you can shake a stick at. The atmosphere of the area is decidedly different, no doubt shaped by the lowlife element that is an essential part of it. Prostitutes, pimps, dealers and a general mix of down-and-outs mix with revellers of all types, ages and sexual persua-sions. In particular, damsels of the night haunt Calle de la Ballesta (lined with tacky escort bars and the like), Calle de la Luna and the immedi-ate area. All these places are on Map 5.

If you really want to get basic, the place marked **Vinos** *(Calle de Sagasta 2)* is for you; it serves wine and various cheeses. Round the corner you can get an Asturian cider and an *empanada* (pie) for 185 ptas at **Corripio** *(Calle de Fuencarral 102)*.

Cervecería de Santa Bárbara *(☎ 91 319 04 49, Plaza de Santa Bárbara 8; metro: Alonso Martínez)* is a classic old Madrid drinking house and is generally packed early on in the night. It is a good place to kick off a night in Malasaña. Nearby, **Cervecería Bulevar** *(☎ 91 308 34 17, Calle de Santa Teresa 2)* is another fun and busy meeting place. Even on a Saturday night it's possible to reach the bar. It opens until 2 am (4 am on Friday and Saturday).

Big Bamboo *(☎ 91 562 88 38, Calle de Barquillo 42)* is a smoky lit-tle joint where punters sway to the reggae rhythms until at least 6 am. You pay 500 ptas (including a beer) to get in, which ain't bad at all. Another nearby reggae place currying favour at the moment is **Kingston's** *(☎ 91 521 15 68, Calle de Barquillo 29)*.

Café Belén *(☎ 91 308 27 47, Calle de Belén 5)* is a good spot to retire for a quiet romantic cocktail. The music is low key and eclectic and the punters are intent on enjoying each other's company rather than being raucous and rowdy.

Bodega de la Ardosa *(☎ 91 521 49 79, Calle de Colón 13)* is a won-derful, dimly lit bar where you can sip vermouth drawn from the barrel.

If it really must be a Guinness, step round the corner to **The Quiet Man** *(☎ 91 523 46 89, Calle de Valverde 44)*. On the Irish theme, **Finnegan's** *(☎ 91 310 05 21, Plaza de las Salesas 9)* has become an obligatory stop for aficionados of the dark fluids. Calle de San Vicente Ferrer has a fair quota of bars, and on the corner of Corradera Alta de San Pablo is **Triskel** *(☎ 91 523 27 83, Calle de San Vicente Ferrer 3)*, yet another jolly Irish joint.

The **Maderfaker** *(Calle de San Vicente Ferrer 17)* rock bar (pro-nounce the name out loud with a Spanish accent and see what you get) is one of the most satisfying of the watering holes along this street. The music is good, the crowd mixed and the barman has the most im-pressive moustache in Madrid. It closes on Sunday and Monday but otherwise serves libations until 3.30 am.

La Vía Láctea *(☎ 91 446 75 81, Calle de Velarde 18)* is a bright, thumping sort of place with a young, *macarra* ('rough-and-ready') crowd. It's an old classic that has somehow managed to survive from the days of the movida.

In **Café del Foro** *(☎ 91 445 37 52, Calle de San Andrés 38)* the decor of traditional Madrid shopfronts surrounds an intimate stage where you can often hear good live music.

For one of the best mojitos (a rum-based drink) in the area, pop into the **Café Magerit** *(Calle del Divino Pastor 21)*.

Partying in the Park

Ever wonder as you wander the streets of Madrid at night what's going on with all those bright young adolescents partying in the parks and squares? They don't get together simply because the bars are too full. Often these kids have barely two brass pesetas to rub together, so they bring their own booze and party al fresco.

Don't be at all surprised to see young 'uns lurching around with huge bottles of beer. In case they run out of supplies, they usually make sure they are near a bar that sells *minis* – outsize plastic tumblers often filled with beer but sometimes with another favourite among young Spaniards: *calimocho*. This has to be one of the most awful concoctions conceivable: cheap red wine (Tetrapaks of Don Simón are particularly favoured) and coke!

Plaza del Dos de Mayo can seem like a scene from a young alcoholic *Ben Hur*, with madrileños careering around in all directions clutching large cups and bottles of various beverages.

Up on Plaza de las Comendadoras, the lightly Art Deco *Café Moderno* (☎ 91 522 48 35) is a cosy place in winter, especially if you're there on a Thursday night for the belly dancing!

Chueca (see also Gay & Lesbian Venues later in this special section) is not exclusively gay. Everyone can enjoy this pleasingly seedy district. Watch out for the wonderful, gloomy old vermouth bar *Sierra Ángel* (*Calle de Gravina 11*), overlooking Plaza de Chueca.

Heading towards Gran Vía, *Bar La Carmencita* (☎ 91 531 66 12, *Calle de la Libertad 16*) is a pleasant place with tiled walls and a cosy feel. *Libertad 8* (☎ 91 532 11 50, *Calle de la Libertad 8*) was a favoured haunt of the Left around the time of Franco's demise. It still gets an animated crowd to see singer-songwriters or sit in on the odd poetry reading.

Star's Dance Café (☎ 91 522 27 12, *Calle del Marqués del Valdeiglesias 5*) is a bright place especially popular with the gay community where you can eat, drink and even be merry. It bills itself as the only cafe in Madrid where you can dance in the late evening. A beer costs 250 ptas until midnight – after that it's double the price.

The simply decorated *Del Diego Bar* (☎ 91 523 31 06, *Calle de la Reina 12*) does great cocktails for around 900 ptas. The music and atmosphere are good and it fills up pretty quickly.

Museo Chicote (☎ 91 532 67 37, *Gran Vía 12*) is an Art Deco special (founded in 1931) and long the haunt of Madrid's chic and well connected. Hemingway and other swells used to hang out here and in the 1940s and 50s it was *the* place to be seen. The decor reflects the era but the music often jars. Drinks are average and pricey – you are paying for the tradition rather than the quality. The bar used to be directly connected with *Cock Bar* (☎ 91 532 28 26, *Calle de la Reina 16*), which once served as a discreet salon for a higher class of prostitution. The ladies in question have gone, but this popular bar retains plenty of atmosphere – even if the name is a little startling.

ELLIOT DANIEL

ELLIOT DANIEL

Top: Getting down to the serious business of DJing, Midnight nightclub, Calle Amaniel

Bottom: Partying 'till the wee hours at Midnight

Top: Eat, drink and be merry at Star's Dance Café, Malasaña district.

Middle: Midnight, and things are only just hotting up.

Bottom: Sweaty dance fun at Joy Eslava, Sol district

ELLIOT DANIEL

Chamberí

This area north of Malasaña is a rather more upmarket residential district, characterised by leafy, grid-pattern streets and a slightly more refined local fauna. A few bars around here can be fun, and it's unlikely you'll come across too many other *guiris*. These spots are on Map 3.

Strock *(Calle de Fernández de la Hoz 42)* is a basement bar that attracts a youngish 30-something crowd. The music is a little loud but it's not bad. Down on Paseo del General Marti\'nez Campos are a few similar places that tend to be full to bursting. Among there are **Valmont**, at No 17, and **La Siesta**, next door at No 19.

One of Madrid's happy little secrets is simply called **The Bar** *(Calle de Viriato 17)*. What's so good about it? It seems to be always open. If you want to stay out all night but not get stuck in a club, it's the ideal solution.

Around Plaza de España

Good for cocktails after the movies is **Ambigú 16** *(Map 5; Calle de Martín de los Heros 16)*. They do a mean caipirinha (a Brazilian cocktail) and have all sorts of wonderful hard stuff, including Colombian rum.

La Viuda de Cuenllas *(Map 2; ☎ 91 547 31 33, Calle de Ferraz 3)* is a good place to relax and taste quality wines.

Salamanca, Goya & Beyond

There's usually some kind of show or open buffet at **Garamond** *(Map 6; ☎ 91 578 19 74, Calle de Claudio Coello 10)*, which has the air of a medieval *parador* (inn) and serves expensive drinks. It's definitely for the jacket-and-tie yuppie brigade.

Playing to a younger crowd is **Terraza de Serrano** *(Map 6; Calle de Serrano 41)*. This cavernous drinking hall heaves with one of the greatest concentrations of adolescent hormones in the city.

Teatriz *(Map 6; ☎ 91 577 53 79, Calle de la Hermosilla 15)* is a stylish hangout with a difference. The former Teatro Beatriz, decorated by French designer Philippe Starck, has an eerily lit bar right on the stage. Drinks are for heavily lined wallets only, as is the food (see also Salamanca, Goya & Beyond under Top End in the Places to Eat chapter). It sounds like odd advice, but check out the loos.

Moving north, Avenida del Brasil (Map 1) hosts half a dozen bars that keep a faithful crowd occupied until around 6 am. The best is the immense and hugely popular **Irish Rover** *(☎ 91 556 09 83)* at No 7.

LIVE MUSIC

Bands don't usually appear on stage before 10 pm and often wait until midnight. You can dance at some of these venues.

Rock Concerts

Several venues are used for major concerts, whether Spanish groups or international acts. A common one is the **Plaza de Toros Monumental** *de Las Ventas (Map 2; see The Bullfight special section earlier in the book)*. Others include the former **Antiguo Cuartel del Conde Duque** *(Map 5, Calle del Conde Duque)* and the **Teatro Monumental** *(Map 8; ☎ 91 429 81 19, Calle de Atocha 65)*. A smaller venue but one that regularly features acts from Spain and abroad is **La Riviera** *(Map 2; ☎ 91 435 85 08, Paseo de la Virgen del Puerto s/n)*, near the Puente de Segovia. **Sala Caracol** *(Map 2; ☎ 91 528 69 77, Calle de Bernardino Obregón 18; metro: Embajadores)* is another long-standing venue for Spanish and foreign acts.

Jazz

One of Madrid's better-known jazz haunts is **Clamores Jazz Club** *(Map 3; ☎ 91 445 79 38, Calle de Alburquerque 14; metro: Bilbao)*. It generally opens all week. Usually there is no cover charge, and the place gets a good selection of acts. You can also catch the occasional jazz performance at **Café Central** and **Café Populart** *(both Map 8)*, listed under Plaza de Santa Ana, Huertas & Atocha under Bars earlier in this section.

Latin

A mix of Hispanic dance groups and vocalists appear at **Galileo Galilei** *(Map 3; ☎ 91 534 75 57, Calle de Galileo 100)*.

A good place to indulge in salsas, merengues and other Latin grooves is **Vaiven** *(Map 5; ☎ 91 319 28 18, Travesía de San Mateo 1; metro: Chueca)*. There is no cover charge, but a beer costs about 600 ptas.

El Son *(Map 8; Calle de la Victoria 6)* rocks away daily from 7 pm to the wee hours. Often they have live Cuban music, and midweek you can get in some saucy salsa lessons with the island's teachers.

Other

A wide variety of acts, from Cuban to African, strut their stuff at **Suristán** *(Map 8; ☎ 91 532 39 09, Calle de la Cruz 7)*. Music usually kicks off at 11.30 pm and there is sometimes a cover charge of up to 1000 ptas (including a drink). At the **Café del Mercado** *(Map 7; ☎ 91 365 87 39, Ronda de Toledo 1)*, in the old Mercado de la Puerta de Toledo, you can get into a whole range of different acts, from Spanish pop to blues, soul and occasionally even a little cabaret. You pay 1200 ptas to get in, which buys you a drink too.

DISCOS & CLUBS

At the weekend in particular, it is quite possible to continue the 'night' well into the day. While most places tend to start edging punters out around dawn, a 9 or 10 am finish is the norm in a few clubs (which in Spain still tend to be called *discotecas*).

Gran Vía, Malasaña & Chueca

All the following are on Map 5. **Morocco** *(☎ 91 531 31 77, Calle del Marqués de Leganés 7)* is still a popular stop on the Madrid dance circuit, although some say it has passed its peak. It usually swings into gear from about 1 am. **Ya'stal** (☎ *91 531 37 20, Calle de Valverde 10*) is another place that doesn't swing into action until the early morning. It has a reputation as a meat market, but is a lot of good sweaty dance fun.

Pachá (☎ *91 447 01 28, Calle de Barceló 11*) is an old favourite that seems to come and go. It is open until 5 am and admission can cost up to 2000 ptas (including your first drink).

Around Plaza de España

All the following are on Map 5. **Arena** (☎ *559 19 43, Calle de la Princesa 1*) offers music for all tastes – funky, house, techno and acid jazz – until 6.30 am from Wednesday to Sunday. This used to be one of the city's 'after-hours', in other words a club that only got started in the morning (see the boxed text 'Sour After Hours' over the page). Since a regional law capped opening hours in 1999, it has had to change its spots.

Midnight (*Calle de Amaniel 13*) is one of the few clubs to steer clear of house, but the punters still manage to have fun. It opens to the wee hours from Thursday to Saturday.

Siroco (☎ *91 593 30 70, Calle de San Dimas 3*) gets in new DJs every week to pump out sounds ranging from hip hop to Spanish pop. It opens until 6 am from Thursday to Saturday.

Plaza de Santa Ana, Sol & La Latina

Remarkable for its decor as much as for anything else, from about 1 am **Villa Rosa** (*Map 8;* ☎ *91 521 36 89, Plaza de Santa Ana 15*) is a mellow place for a drink and some shaking of stuff on the small dance floor. The tile decoration

Right: Madrid wakes up to dance the night away just when the rest of Europe is going to bed.

JANE SMITH

outside (pictures of Seville, Granada and Córdoba) and within, as well as the decorative ceiling, make it a unique spot.

On Calle de la Cruz are a couple of dance spaces. You may have to queue if you have no passes or fliers for them. *Torero* (Map 8; ☎ 91 523 11 29), at No 26, has two floors, featuring Spanish music upstairs and international tunes downstairs. The bouncers can be a real pain, so you could opt instead for the distinctly tacky *La Cartuja* (Map 8), at No 10.

Oui (Map 8; Calle de Cervantes 7) puts on all sorts of music through the week in a build-up to a diet of hip hop, techno and drum 'n' bass at the weekend. *No Se Lo Digas A Nadie* (Map 8; Calle de Ventura de la Vega 7) is a popular dance spot open until 3 am. The real hardcore night-owls can later make their way to *Stella-Wake Club* (Map 8; Calle de Arlabán 7), open until about 10 am at the weekend. Friday and Saturday nights typically heave with house.

The post-modern *Café Club Mad* (Map 5; ☎ 91 532 62 28, Calle de la Virgen de los Peligros 4) starts the evening with easy listening (until about midnight), after which it cranks things up a little with anything from funk to acid jazz on Tuesday, Friday and Saturday. On Thursday the nostalgia strikes with faves from the 60s to the 80s.

El Sol (Map 5; ☎ 91 532 64 90, Calle de los Jardines 3) is another 'in' location with tireless madrileños. Crimson lighting suffuses the basement dance space and music ranges from mainstream tunes to occasionally silly

---

Sour After Hours

Until early 1999, Madrid boasted 30 or more 'after-hours', clubs that throw open their doors to racy dance-addicts at 6 am or later.

Then came a new regional law governing opening times for places of public diversion in the Comunidad de Madrid. The law quite simply rendered these places illegal by not even acknowledging their existence. Reactions to the move were varied. Initially most of these places simply reverted to 'normal' hours – closing by 5.30 or 6 am as the law stipulates. A handful continued to operate illegally. Then in April 2000 around 30 'afters' joined forces and demanded to be legalised; nine mounted a court challenge against the regional government, demanding one billion pesetas' compensation.

Claiming the regional law unconstitutional, the after-hours demanded the application of a 1977 national government ruling under which clubs and discos that closed at 4 am could then open again two hours later – which is how many after-hours in Madrid used to work.

Space of Sound (Map 1; Plaza de la Estación de Chamartín s/n) is one Madrid after-hours that has, at least on occasion, defied the law. If on a Sunday morning you haven't had enough dancing and you're recharged on *churros y chocolate* (or something less conventional) you could try heading to this place in the Chamartín train station building. When it operates it goes from about 9 am to 2 pm.

As for the regional law and the other outraged after-hours, it's a case of watch this (or any other relevant) space.

disco stuff. That aside, it's a fun and friendly spot that will keep you going to 6 am and beyond. You pay 1200 ptas to get in, which includes a drink.

Palacio Gaviria (Map 7; ☎ 91 526 60 69, Calle del Arenal 9) is indeed palatial. It's divided into a series of old-style salons to meet most middle-of-the-road tastes, from waltzes to mainstream disco blah, with a couple of small corners scattered about for a quiet drink or a snog. The place gets going about 2 am and admission can cost up to 2000 ptas. A beer is 900 ptas and a mixed drink is 1500 ptas.

Just next door is one of Madrid's premier nightspots, **Teatro Joy Eslava** (Map 7; ☎ 91 366 37 33 for reservations, Calle del Arenal 11). It started life as a comedy theatre in 1871. It is now deadly serious dance fun and admission costs 2000 ptas at the weekend. When you stumble out of here in the morning, head round the corner to the *Chocolatería de San Ginès* for a breakfast of *churros y chocolate* (sticky chocolate-covered snacks).

El Viajero (Map 7; ☎ 91 366 90 64, Plaza de la Cebada 11) is good for acid jazz, trip hop and funk.

Kapital (Map 7; ☎ 91 420 29 06, Calle de Atocha 125) boasts seven floors of heaving bods, from midnight to dawn, Thursday to Saturday. Expect queues and to pay up to 2000 ptas admission.

GAY & LESBIAN VENUES

Most of Madrid's gay and lesbian life is played out around Chueca. This is the area to head for not only for night-time distraction but also for hotels catering to gays, gay shops, saunas and associations. A heavy concentration of the city's gay population actually lives in the neighbourhood too. Except where specified, all these places are on Map 5.

Bars

A quiet place with a gay arty atmosphere, **Acuarela Café** (☎ 91 522 21 43, Calle de Gravina 10) is a good place for an intimate drink. Right next door, on the corner with the square, is **Truco** (☎ 91 532 89 21), one of the city's few predominantly lesbian bars, although plenty of straights seem to end up here too.

Rimmel (Calle de Luis de Góngora 4) and **Cruising** (☎ 91 521 51 43, Calle de Pérez Galdós 5) are among the more popular gay haunts. The latter has a dark room and puts on occasional shows. The **New Leather** (☎ 91 308 14 62, Calle de Pelayo 42) is just one of the many gay bars towards the southern end of this street. The name describes the theme. All these places stay open until between 3 and 4 am.

Discos & Clubs

At **Truck** (☎ 91 531 18 70, Calle de la Libertad 28) you can get down to popular hits from the 60s onwards – a lively, fun place.

Rick's (Calle de Clavel 8) is a heaving bar that fills to bursting most nights. They open the doors at 11 pm and stay up until the wee hours.

Ales (☎ 91 548 20 22, Calle de Veneras 2) is a classic of the gay night circuit, open from 1.30 am to dawn. Admission costs from 500 ptas to 1500 ptas, depending on the night and whether there is some kind of show – usually of the drag persuasion.

Strong (☎ 91 531 48 27, Calle de Trujillo 7) is a fairly intense gay guys' disco with a particularly active dark room. It opens every night from midnight to dawn and admission costs 1000 ptas.

Refugio (Map 7; Calle del Doctor Cortezo 1) is a popular gay dance club open from midnight to dawn. It's relaxed and a few straights manage to find their way in too. You pay 1000 ptas to get in, which includes a drink.

TERRAZAS

Many of the places listed under Bars, earlier in this special section, have terrazas – tables set up on the footpath or square – most of which spring up like mushrooms in the summer. The season lasts from about April to October and the bars that run them pay for a specific extra licence to operate.

Probably the best located one is **Bar Ventorrillo** (Map 7; Corral de la Morería), near the Jardines de las Vistillas. This is a wonderful spot to relax and drink in the views of the Sierra de Guadarrama, especially at sunset. During the Fiestas de San Isidro (see Public Holidays & Special Events in the Facts for the Visitor chapter) bands play in the gardens.

Some of the terrazas, such as those that emerge along Paseo de la Castellana and Paseo de los Recoletos, are something of a haunt for *la gente guapa* (the beautiful people) – those who want to be seen spending serious money for their libations. A perfect case in point is **Bolero** (Map 4; Paseo de la Castellana 33), where a modest beer costs 600 ptas. **Boulevard 37** (Map 4; Paseo de la Castellana 37) is largely the domain of better-off university students. For a more staid beginning to the evening, **Pabellón del Espejo** (Map 6; Paseo de los Recoletos 31) is hard to beat for elegance (see also From Plaza de Colón to the Prado under Cafes & Tea Houses in the Places to Eat chapter).

Less pretentious and considerably more pleasant are the terrazas that set up in Argüelles – more specifically, on Paseo del Pintor Rosales. With parkland on one side and considerably less traffic than Paseo de la Castellana, these places also exercise a little more control over their prices. **Terraza España** (Map 2) is one of several.

Madrid's squares make perfect locations for outdoor drinking. Several of the bars on Plaza de Santa Ana operate terrazas, as does . **Café de Oriente** (Map 5; ☎ 91 541 39 74, Plaza de Oriente); see also Around Plaza Mayor under Cafes & Tea Houses in the Places to Eat chapter. Bars spread summertime liquid satisfaction across such squares as Plaza del Dos de Mayo and Plaza de las Comendadoras, both in the Malasaña area (Map 5), as well as Plaza del Conde Barajas (just south off Plaza Mayor) and around Plaza de los Carros (both Map 7).

Shopping

Madrid has a way to go before becoming one of Europe's top shopping destinations. Still, there are plenty of interesting nooks and crannies to explore and, although it ain't Milan, you will often turn up interesting stuff at affordable prices.

For the best Madrid has to offer in chichi shopping, Calle de Serrano, in the haughty Salamanca district, is the main address for the city's leading department stores and fashion outlets. If the truth be told, only a handful of local firms produce clothes of interest – but plenty of Italian stylists are represented here. More fun for fashion victims is Calle del Almirante and the immediate area, near Chueca.

Leather is a good buy. Shoes in particular, but also bags and other items, are generally well made. Opinion is divided on ceramics. Madrid itself does not have a tradition of ceramics production, but several stores collect stuff from around the country and it is pleasing to most eyes.

Two classics of Spanish shopping are Lladró porcelain figurines and Majorica pearls. Along Gran Vía, in particular (especially between Plaza de España and Plaza de Callao), you will find a string of shops selling one, the other, or both.

Various markets, above all El Rastro, liven up the city at the weekend.

Department store bargain-hunters should note that the winter sales officially start on or around 10 January, and the summer equivalents on or around 5 July.

If you want a comprehensive guide to shopping here, ask the tourist office for its *Guía de Compras* booklet.

ANTIQUES

The two obvious areas to look for antiques – from porcelain wash basins and faded paintings of hunting scenes to grandfather clocks – are along Calle del Prado, on the southern side of Plaza de Santa Ana, and in the shops scattered about the Rastro area (see Markets later in this chapter). The latter tend to be cheaper and junkier.

Lladró figures are just some of the things you can acquire for your mantelpiece in Madrid.

Of those on Calle del Prado, you might take a look inside Rolle, at No 9; Brunswick, at No 12; and Romero, at No 23. All are on Map 8.

ART GALLERIES

The *Guía del Ocio* has extensive art gallery listings, as does the *ABC* newspaper's Friday pull-out section, *Guía de Madrid*. The city is, in fact, crawling with commercial art galleries of varying styles and quality. More expensive galleries have traditionally been concentrated in the Salamanca district, but there is a busy art scene in Chueca and various galleries are scattered about the rest of the city too. The following is a representative selection:

Elba Benítez
(Map 5; ☎ 91 308 054 68) Calle de San Lorenzo. Here the policy seems to be to mix known foreign artists with rising home-grown talent.

Elvira González
(Map 5; ☎ 91 319 59 00) Calle del General Castaños 9. Here you can often find works by modern masters, and occasionally even the odd Picasso.

Galería Helga de Alvear
(Map 7; ☎ 91 468 05 06) Calle del Doctor Fourquet 12. This gallery has been going since the mid-1990s and concentrates on innovative new artists emerging on the Spanish scene. Several other galleries are clustered along this street behind the Centro de Arte de Reina Sofía.

Galería Juana de Aizpuru
(Map 5; ☎ 91 310 55 61) Calle del Barquillo 44. A mover and shaker in the Spanish art world, this gallery concentrates mainly on local production.

Moriarty
(Map 5; ☎ 91 531 43 65) Calle del Almirante 5. Here you are likely to find more offbeat displays than in some of the other big-name galleries. It's been going since the 1980s and has made quite a name for itself.

ART PRINTS & POSTERS

Fann (Map 6; ☎ 91 435 72 23), at Calle de Velázquez 24, is a bright, cavernous store with all sorts of colourful stationery and a range of prints and posters – it's not a bad place for gift ideas.

At Mexico (Map 8; ☎ 91 429 94 76), Calle de las Huertas 20, you can dig up some wonderful old prints, maps of Spain and other printed curios.

BOOKS

There is no shortage of decent bookshops in Madrid, but the local product is a little pricey, so people used to UK and US prices for English-language titles should hesitate before plunging in. The cost of printing in Spain is high, so books in Spanish will be expensive here and still more so abroad.

Berceo
(Map 7; ☎ 91 559 18 50) Calle de Juan de Herrera 6. Lovers of old books, some rare and others less so, and not exclusively in Spanish, should poke their noses in here.

Berkana
(Map 5; ☎ 91 532 13 93) Calle de Gravina 11. This gay bookshop on Plaza Chueca is a good place for information on the local scene.

El Bosque
(☎ 91 383 11 39) Calle de Añastro 15. This is an outlet for books in French.

La Casa del Libro
(Map 5; ☎ 91 521 21 13) Gran Vía 29–31. This is Madrid's leading bookstore and it stocks a broad selection of books on all subjects. There is a respectable selection of books in English, French and other languages.

La Librería
(Map 7; ☎ 91 541 71 70) Calle Mayor 80. This is *the* place to get books on every imaginable aspect of Madrid's history and life – mostly in Spanish, however.

La Tienda Verde
(Map 1; ☎ 91 533 07 91) Calle de Maudes 38. This is about the best shop in Madrid for hiking and walking literature and maps. The owners have another shop at No 23 dedicated more to general travel and ecology.

Lenguajes
(Map 5; ☎ 91 310 44 02) Calle de Gravina 9. This is an interesting little store with books in and on several languages.

Lesen
(Map 1; ☎ 91 564 97 47) Calle de Serrano 222. This shop's a good place for German literature, as well as general books.

Librería Alemana Auryn
(Map 1; ☎ 91 561 76 55) Calle del Príncipe de Vergara 205. Here is a decent purveyor of books in the Teutonic tongue.

Librería Booksellers
(Map 3; ☎ 91 442 79 59) Calle de José Abascal 48. Here you'll find books in English.

Librería Carmelo Blázquez
(Map 9; ☎ 91 527 76 61) Calle de Alfonso XII 66. Up on the 1st floor, this is Madrid's largest second-hand bookshop. For more pre-loved literature, you could try the row of 30-odd bookstalls along Cuesta de Claudio Moyano, on the southern edge of the botanical gardens.

Librería Henri Avellan
(Map 2; ☎ 91 576 42 44) Calle del Duque de Sesto 5. This is one of the city's leading French-language bookstores.

Librería Italiana
(Map 1; ☎ 91 554 90 73) Calle de Modesto Lafuente 47. Here you can get Italian literature and language-learning materials.

Librería de Mujeres
(Map 7; ☎ 91 523 23 20) Calle de San Cristóbal 17. This is a women's bookshop and well-known feminist meeting place.

Librería del Patrimonio Nacional
(Map 5; ☎ 91 541 80 37) Plaza de Oriente 6. Here you can find all sorts of books on the monuments, palaces and other worthy sights of Madrid and the surrounding area. They have some beautiful coffee-table tomes and some serious, high-brow literature. Most of it's in Spanish, but various volumes are in other languages.

The International Bookshop
(Map 5; ☎ 91 541 72 91) Calle de Campomanes 13. This is not a bad spot to hunt around for cheap second-hand books of all types, predominantly in English.

CERAMICS

The Antigua Casa Talavera (Map 5; ☎ 91 547 34 17), Calle de Isabel la Católica 2, is not a bad little cavern, full of ceramics not only from Talavera, the Castilian town known for little else, but from as far afield as Granada and Seville. Close by, Cántaro (Map 5; ☎ 91 547 95 14), Calle de la Flor Baja 8, is a less fusty sort of place, worth a visit for a representative look at pottery and ceramics from around the country.

CLOTHING & FASHION

Those looking to do some shopping in a more chichi environment should head for Calle de Serrano, the city's premier shopping street, in Salamanca. You'll find many international fashion names on or off this

boulevard, including: Armani (No 8), the successful Gallego fashion house Adolfo Dominguez (No 18), Max Mara (No 38), Gucci (Calle de Don Ramón de la Cruz 6), Kenzo (Calle de José Ortega y Gasset 15) and Louis Vuitton (Calle de José Ortega y Gasset 15). All but the last two (Map 4) are on Map 6.

You can do more fashion shopping, or simply shop fashionably, in the elegant El Jardín de Serrano (Map 6; ☎ 91 577 00 12), a complex of stores at Calle de Goya 6–8. Tea and cakes are available at the Mallorca cafe, which looks onto a garden, on the ground floor.

Also well worth exploring is Calle del Almirante (Map 5), east of Plaza de Chueca, a hipper showcase for younger fashion.

Some specific places you may want to look out for include:

Ararat
(Map 5; ☎ 91 310 34 55) Calle del Almirante 10, 11 & 13. This is one of the more interesting clothing stores along this alternative fashion street. Women go to Nos 10 and 11 and men to No 13. All the latest trends get an airing.

Capas de Seseña
(Map 8; ☎ 91 531 68 40) Calle de la Cruz 23. Need a fashionable cape? This is the place. Hillary Clinton shopped here on the odd occasion she and Bill used to come to town.

Mercado Fuencarral
(Map 5) Calle de Fuencarral 115. Inside this building is clustered a clan of small-scale fashion shops appealing to the young urban set bereft of income – it has become quite a focal point for shopping in the Malasaña district. Apart from clothes (which hover in the young grunge category), you can browse for cheap jewellery and hip CDs, or simply knock back a beer at the downstairs cyberlounge.

Moda Shopping
(Map 1) Avenida del General Perón 40. This glass-domed mall houses enough boutiques to keep most fashion shoppers busy for hours.

Pedro Muñoz
(Map 4; ☎ 91 577 26 53) Calle de Serrano 72. Here you'll find formal and also more casual menswear.

Purificación García
(☎ 91 435 80 13, 91 576 72 76) Calle de Serrano 28 (Map 6) and 92 (Map 4). Young people flock here, attracted by the fresh designs and moderate prices.

CONVENIENCE STORES

For late-night attacks of the munchies and other emergencies, there is a sprinkling of stores across central Madrid. VIPS is the most widespread chain and tends to remain open when everything else but the clubs have shut their doors. Several are marked on the maps. There is also a 24-hour 7-Eleven (Map 5) at Calle del Arenal 28. It is one of several around town.

CRAFTS

Surprisingly, given its location on the most touristy square in town, El Arco Artesanía (☎ 91 365 26 80), Plaza Mayor 9, is a delightful shop, with all sorts of original bits and pieces, from masks to lamps. Since you'll end up in Plaza Mayor sooner or later anyway, it can't hurt to poke your nose in for a quick browse.

Prefer Mexican curios to Spanish ones? Pop into Azteca (Map 8; ☎ 91 429 72 68), at Calle de las Huertas 14, for a quick browse. Mamah Africa (Map 5; ☎ 91 542 40 91), Calle del Conde Duque 34, is a curious little store where you can find a collection of African crafts, ranging from wood figurines to cheerfully coloured clothes, rugs and the like.

CROCKERY & KITCHENWARE

Alambique (Map 5; ☎ 91 547 42 20), at Plaza de la Encarnación 2, sells everything imaginable for the kitchen, from all kinds of glassware through pots and pans to terracotta casserole dishes. It stocks some fine products, and even organises cookery classes.

DECORATION & FURNITURE

For odd furnishings and household decorations, candles and so on, La Maison Folle (Map 5; ☎ 91 521 98 97), Calle de San Marcos 37, is an intriguing shop to browse if nothing else.

Not far away from La Maison Folle, Adamante (Map 5; ☎ 91 522 58 05), Calle de las Infantas 19, is along similar lines. You can pick up crockery and all sorts of nick-nacks to clutter your shelves with when you get home.

DEPARTMENT STORES

Spain's best-known department store is El Corte Inglés. There are branches all over town, including on Calle de Preciados (Map 5), just off Puerta del Sol; Calle de la Princesa (Map 2); and Calle de Serrano (Map 4).

Of interest to those hanging around Madrid for the long haul is Marks & Spencer (Map 6; ☎ 91 431 67 60), at Calle de Serrano 52. Its food department holds all sorts of goodies otherwise unavailable in Madrid.

FILM & PHOTOGRAPHY

If you need camera gear or repairs, a couple of shops are worth checking out. Playmon (Map 2; ☎ 91 573 57 25), Calle de Jorge Juan 133, is a reputable place for camera repairs. Fotocasión (Map 7; ☎ 91 467 64 91), Calle de Carlos Arniches 22, is a good store to start looking for second-hand camera equipment of all sorts. It's near El Rastro.

FLAMENCO

Tienda El Flamenco Vive (Map 7; ☎ 91 542 16 39), Calle del Conde de Lemos 7, is the only store in Madrid dedicated to the subject of flamenco dance and music. Here you can pick up books on the history and styles of flamenco, CDs, instruments and costumes. They also stock the free monthly information magazine *Alma 100*.

FOOD & DRINK

If you're looking for nice gifts of quality Spanish wines and foodstuffs, there are quite a few shops in the Salamanca area.

Bombonería Santa
(Map 6; ☎ 91 576 86 46) Calle de Serrano 56. The chocolates and confectionery in this shop are enough to make your teeth shudder...and they package them to·make fine gifts.
Casa Mira
(Map 8; ☎ 91 429 88 95) Carrera de San Jerónimo 30. This is the best place in Madrid to get a hold of *turrón*, a nutty nougat delicacy that is something of a tradition in great swathes of the country (thanks to the Muslim conquests). Locals queue for it at Christmas. Even if you don't want to buy any, drop into this classic old Madrid pastry shop, in business since 1842 and

still, six generations later, in the same family's hands.

La Oleoteca
(Map 1; ☎ 91 359 18 03) Calle de Juan Ramón Jiménez 37. French chef Jean Pierre Vandelle runs this temple to olive oil, selling more than 60 varieties alongside vinegars and other items (not all of them edible).

Mallorca
(Map 6; ☎ 91 431 99 09) Calle de Velázquez 59. This large store in the heart of Salamanca has a vast range of wines and Spanish delicacies on display. It is part of a chain and a good source of high-quality victuals. They have nine branches around town, including another in Salamanca (Map 6; ☎ 91 577 18 59), at Calle de Serrano 6.

Patrimonio Cultural Olivarero
(Map 5; ☎ 91 308 05 05) Calle de Mejía Lequerica 1. The range at this olive oil outlet is not as great as at La Oleoteca, but you will find good-quality and nicely bottled green liquid here, and it's handier for central Madrid.

LLADRÓ & MAJORICA

Lladró (Map 4; ☎ 91 435 51 12) has an outlet at Calle de Serrano 68. This is a good spot to see the very best porcelain they have to offer. If you can't make it here, shops acting as agents for Lladró abound in Madrid.

You could also try out the Sefarad store (Map 5; ☎ 91 547 07 22), at Gran Vía 43. It has both Lladró and Majorica pearls.

Objetos de Arte Toledano (Map 7; ☎ 91 429 50 00), Paseo del Prado 10, is a rather touristy shop and you can probably live without the Toledan swords and so on. But here and next door, at No 12, you will find a wide range of Lladró and Majorica products.

MARKETS

On Sunday morning, the Embajadores area of Madrid seems to contain half the city's population as all and sundry converge on El Rastro (Map 7), the flea market. Starting from Plaza de Cascorro, its main axes are Calle de Ribera de Curtidores and Calle de los Embajadores. A good deal of what's on sale is rubbish, but the atmosphere alone is worth making the effort for, and you can find interesting items. There are a good many junk and antique stores scattered about the area.

A much less touristed flea market is the Sunday-morning Mercadillo Marqués de Viana (Map 1), held on and around the street of the same name in the Tetúan barrio on Sunday morning. You'll find abundant fresh produce, second-hand-clothes stalls and all sorts of other junk. It has come to be known as El Rastrillo, the little brother of the more famous version mentioned already.

Another Madrid Sunday-morning classic is the Mercadillo de Sellos y Monedas, the stamp- and coin-collectors market held under the arches of Plaza Mayor.

MUSIC

CDs and cassettes are not especially cheap in Spain but, if you're looking for local music difficult to find at home, try the music sections of El Corte Inglés (Map 5) or FNAC (Map 5), on Calle de Preciados. A couple of other places to look are:

Ático Tipo
(Map 5; ☎ 902 10 38 21) Calle de Fuencarral 4. This is a hip, happening music store in Malasaña that not only sells CDs and T-shirts but also regularly hosts appearances by performers to sign CD covers and give a little concert (typically from 6 pm).

Madrid Rock
(Map 5; ☎ 91 521 02 39) Gran Vía 25. This store probably has the broadest general music selection of any, and reasonable prices. There are other branches at Calle Mayor 38 (Map 7; ☎ 91 559 77 60) and Calle de San Martín 3 (Map 5; ☎ 91 522 48 95).

MUSICAL INSTRUMENTS

Hunt around along Calle Mayor, especially towards its western end, for guitars and other instruments.

Contreras
(Map 7; ☎ 91 559 14 48) Calle Mayor 80. This is a good guitar specialist.

Garrido-Bailén
(Map 7; ☎ 91 542 45 01) Calle Mayor 88. You can get just about every kind of instrument imaginable here, along with sheet music and other related bits and bobs.

Real Musical
(Map 7; ☎ 902 10 16 66, 91 541 30 07) Calle de

Carlos III 1. This place has an extensive collection of sheet music, books on all sorts of musical subjects (leaning towards classical) and instruments.

ODDS & ENDS
If you are interested in old postcards and other pre-loved memorabilia, Casa Postales (Map 5; ☎ 91 532 70 37), at Calle de la Libertad 37, is a curious little store to inspect.

SHOES & LEATHER
Shoes are one of the prime good buys in Spain, and Madrid is no exception. The place is swarming with shoe shops, and their styles range from tastefully straight-laced to fairly well-over-the-top.

For chic shoe shopping, you can try out a few stores along Calle de Serrano. Another area to consider looking is along Calle de Fuencarral.

Often shoe shops double as outlets for general leather goods and accessories. Some suggestions to get you started include:

Ana Benjumea
(Map 5; ☎ 91 310 51 98) Calle de Orellana 3. This shop is a little more straight-laced than some places, but with some interesting footwear.
Camper
(Map 5; ☎ 91 547 52 23) Gran Vía 54. Camper is something akin to the Clarke's of Spain. There probably isn't a Spaniard who hasn't worn a pair of Camper shoes at some stage in his/her life. This is not to say that they are boring shoes. Styles change every year and the quality is high. Plenty of other shoe stores stock this brand too.
Farrutx
(Map 6; ☎ 91 576 94 93) Calle de Serrano 7. You can slip into a new set of pumps or sandals at this trendy shoe store.
Gutiérrez
(Map 6; ☎ 91 515 08 46) Calle de Serrano 66. This is part of a chain of shoe stores with branches across the country. The styles are sober and classic.
Los Pequeños Suizos
(Map 4; ☎ 91 435 16 95) Calle de Serrano 68. This is another reasonable store for shoes and leather.
Marquitos
(Map 4; ☎ 91 576 33 84) Calle de Serrrano 70. Parents who have finished worrying about how to clothe their own feet could pop in here to dress up the kids' tootsies.
Piamonte
(Map 5; ☎ 91 522 45 80) Calle de Piamonte 16. This is a fun and imaginative stop for ladies' shoes and leather accessories.

SOUVENIRS
We all succumb at one stage or another to a little kitsch. There's plenty on sale around Plaza Mayor and Puerta del Sol, along Gran Vía and around the Prado. A popular item is a bullfighting poster with your name inscribed as lead torero.

Excursions

One of the attractions of Madrid is what lies around it. A generous helping of fascinating cities rings the capital like satellites in orbit round the sun. In between lie charming Castilian towns, regal palaces and the enticing mountain country of the Sierra de Guadarrama to the north-west.

These trips take you across three regions, the Comunidad de Madrid, Castilla-La Mancha and Castilla y León, but essentially what you experience is the Castilian heartland. The high-speed AVE train permits us to include a fascinating detour into Andalucía, to the one-time caliphal capital of Córdoba.

What appears in this chapter is merely a taste of what is accessible on day trips out of Madrid. Lonely Planet's *Spain* and *Andalucía* contain many more hints on heading farther afield.

This chapter is designed for the daytripper, so no accommodation information has been provided. If you plan to do overnight trips, approach each town's tourist office for accommodation lists. In general, you should have little trouble finding rooms in most of the towns below, although high-season periods such as Easter and Christmas can be tricky. In several towns, including Ávila, Toledo and Chinchón, you'll find a *parador*, particularly attractive hotels arranged in historic buildings. They are worth seeking out if you have some extra cash (up to 18,500 ptas).

NORTH & WEST OF MADRID
Palacio Real de El Pardo
Just north of Madrid is the nearest of several regal retreats. This one ended up as Franco's favoured residence, and the same building served Felipe II in the same fashion as far back as 1558. It has only been open to the public since 1978. Of the art displayed inside, the many tapestries stand out, particularly those based on cartoons by Goya.

The palace is open from 10.30 am to 6 pm (5 pm October to April) Monday to Saturday, and 9.30 am (10 am October to April) to 1.40 pm on Sunday and holidays. Admission costs 700 ptas (students 300 ptas).

The palace and grounds are on the Carretera de El Pardo (main road to El Pardo), about 15km north-west of central Madrid. Bus No 601 (140 ptas) leaves every 15 minutes from a stop on Plaza de la Moncloa (metro: Moncloa) in Madrid.

Alcobendas
postcode 28100 • pop 86,146 • elevation 670m

At Alcobendas, 17km north of Madrid along the N-I to Burgos, the only thing of interest is the **Cosmocaixa** interactive science museum (☎ 91 484 52 00) in the Parque de Andalucía. It was opened in 2000 and replaced an earlier fairly poor attempt. There is a permanent exhibition, *Ciencias del Mundo*, with all sorts of interactive gismos allowing kids (and grown-ups) to push buttons, pull levers and generally get a glimpse of what makes our world work. A digital planetarium and other specialised sections are occasionally complemented with temporary exhibitions on specific themes. It's open from 10 am to 10 pm daily and admission costs 500 ptas.

Bus Nos 151, 153, 154 and 157 provide a frequent service to Alcobendas from Plaza de Castilla. The ticket costs 185 ptas.

San Lorenzo de El Escorial
postcode 28200 • pop 10,995 • elevation 1032m

Sheltering against the protective wall of the Sierra de Guadarrama, the majestic palace-and-monastery complex of San Lorenzo de El Escorial serves today as a place for ordinary madrileños to escape from the pressure-cooker atmosphere of the capital, just as it did for kings and sycophants of old. The site enjoys a mild and exceptionally healthy climate.

Felipe II had the San Lorenzo complex built above the hamlet of El Escorial in the

EXCURSIONS

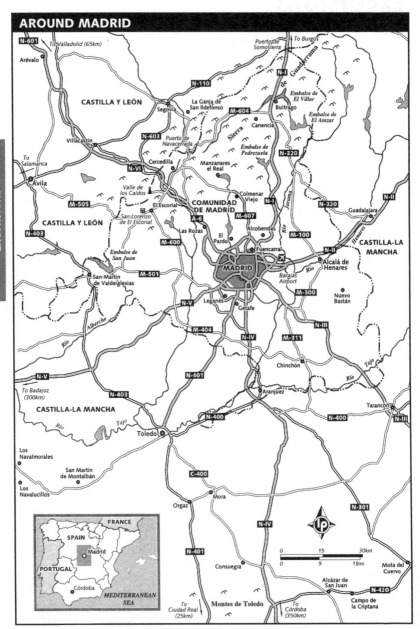

AROUND MADRID

latter half of the 16th century. A huge monastery, royal palace and mausoleum for Felipe's parents, Carlos I and Isabel, were raised under the watchful eye of the architect Juan de Herrera. Not everyone was overjoyed by the project – several villages were emptied and razed to make way for the regal whim. Felipe II died in El Escorial on 13 September 1598.

The tourist office (☎ 91 890 15 54), Calle de Floridablanca 10, is open from 10 am to 2 pm and 3 to 5 pm Monday to Friday, and 10 am to 2 pm on Saturday.

The Monastery The main entrance lies on the western side. Above the gateway a statue of St Lawrence stands watch, holding a symbolic gridiron, the instrument of his martyrdom (he was roasted alive on one). Indeed, the shape of the monastery complex recalls the same object. You then enter the **Patio de los Reyes**, which houses the statues of the six kings of Judah.

Directly ahead lies the sombre **basílica**. As you enter, look up to the unusual flat vaulting below the choir stalls before the main body of the church. Once inside, turn left to view Benvenuto Cellini's white Carrara marble statue of Christ crucified, carved in 1576.

When you exit the church, follow the signs to the ticket office *(taquilla)*, from where arrows guide you through the monastery and palace quarters.

You are led through several rooms containing tapestries and an El Greco and then downstairs to the north-eastern corner of the complex. First you pass through the **Museo de Arquitectura** and, subsequently, the **Museo de Pintura**. The former covers (in Spanish) the story of how the complex was built, while the latter contains a range of Italian, Spanish and Flemish art from the 16th and 17th centuries.

At this point you are obliged to head upstairs again into a gallery around the eastern

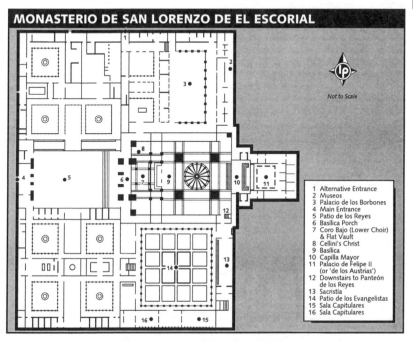

MONASTERIO DE SAN LORENZO DE EL ESCORIAL

Not to Scale

1 Alternative Entrance
2 Museos
3 Palacio de los Borbones
4 Main Entrance
5 Patio de los Reyes
6 Basílica Porch
7 Coro Bajo (Lower Choir)
  & Flat Vault
8 Cellini's Christ
9 Basílica
10 Capilla Mayor
11 Palacio de Felipe II
  (or 'de los Austrias')
12 Downstairs to Panteón
  de los Reyes
13 Sacristía
14 Patio de los Evangelistas
15 Sala Capitulares
16 Sala Capitulares

EXCURSIONS

protuberance of the complex known as the Palacio de Felipe II or **Palacio de los Austrias**. From here you descend to the 17th-century **Panteón de los Reyes**, where almost all Spain's monarchs since Carlos I lie interred with their spouses. Backtracking a little, you find yourself in **Panteón de los Infantes**. Don Juan de Austria (better known to Anglo-Saxons as Don John of Austria), victor over the Turks at the Battle of Lepanto, lies under a memorial in the fifth vault.

Stairs lead up from the Patio de los Evangelistas to the **Salas Capitulares** (chapter-houses) in the south-eastern corner of the monastery. These bright, airy rooms, whose ceilings are richly frescoed, contain a minor treasure chest of works by El Greco, Titian, Tintoretto, José de Ribera and Hieronymus Bosch (El Bosco to the Spaniards).

Grounds & Annexes You can wander around the **Huerta de los Frailes**, the orderly gardens just south of the monastery. In the **Jardín del Príncipe** that leads down to the town of El Escorial (and the train station) is the **Casita del Príncipe** (closed at the time of writing), built under Carlos III for his heir. The **Casita de Arriba**, another 18th-century neoclassical gem, is along the road to Ávila.

Opening Times & Tickets San Lorenzo is open from 10 am to 6 pm (to 5 pm from October to March) Tuesday to Sunday. Only the basilica is free; admission costs 900 ptas (students 400 ptas). For an extra 100 ptas you can tag along for a guided tour of the *panteónes* and the Palacio de los Austrias. It is possible to join a guided tour of the Palacio de los Borbones (quarters laid out by the Bourbon monarchs) on Friday and Saturday. To do so you must book at least a day in advance by calling ☎ 91 890 59 03. It costs 550 ptas person.

The Casita de Arriba and its gardens are open from 10 am to 7 pm in Easter week and in August. Admission costs 375 ptas. The Casita del Príncipe was closed for repairs at the time of writing.

All of the complex is closed on Monday. Admission on Wednesday is free for EU citizens.

You have the option of buying an all-in ticket including all the elements of El Escorial and the Valle de los Caídos (see the following section) for 1500 ptas.

Places to Eat An ample locale is *Restaurante Los Pescaitos* (☎ 91 890 77 20, Calle de Joaquin Costa 8). It boasts some sea-shanty decoration in questionable taste, but the seafood is good and appreciated by locals. The financially challenged can get a decent set lunch for 1100 ptas.

Getting There & Away The Herranz bus company (☎ 91 890 41 00) runs buses every 20 minutes from 7 am to 10.45 pm (18 services at the weekend) from the Intercambiador de Autobuses at the Moncloa metro station in Madrid to San Lorenzo de El Escorial (405 ptas one way; one hour).

Up to 26 sluggish *cercanías* trains (line C-8a) serve El Escorial from Atocha station via Chamartín (430 ptas; 70 minutes).

Valle de los Caídos

Spain's ambivalent attitude to 40 years of Francoism is best demonstrated in this over-sized memorial to 'the Fallen'. Built by prison labour – leftists and other opposition undesirables – it is a crude piece of monumentalism in the awful architectural taste of the great dictators.

The turn-off and ticket booth is 9km north of El Escorial. It's another 6km drive to the shrine. There is something spooky about the subterranean basilica and little, artistically, to recommend it. By the altar lies Franco himself.

The site is open from 9.30 am to 7 pm (10 am to 6 pm from 1 October to 31 March) Tuesday to Sunday. Entry costs 700 ptas.

About the only way there, if you don't have a vehicle, is to get the daily Herranz bus from El Escorial. It leaves from Calle de la Reina Victoria 3 at 3.15 pm, returning at 5.30 pm. The all-in price of the return trip and admission costs 970 ptas.

Sierra de Guadarrama

The hills of the Sierra de Guadarrama form a getaway for madrileños but are seldom

El Rastro flea market – as much a place to hang out as to pick up a bargain.

Kitsch religious icons for sale near Plaza Mayor

El Rastro sells everything from religous icons...

This charcutería statue is popular for photo calls.

...to frilly flamenco frocks.

Spirits, nuts & sweets make perfect gifts.

frequented by foreigners. Longer-term visitors to the capital may care to explore it, popping into the odd *pueblo* (village) and doing a little walking to relieve the big-city stress.

In **Manzanares El Real** stands the charming little 15th-century Castillo de los Mendoza. The castle is open from 10 am to 2 pm and 3 to 6 pm (10 am to 5 pm in winter) Tuesday to Sunday. Admission costs 300 ptas. Several trails lead into the nearby Pedriza park, one of which brings you to freshwater pools. Bus No 724 runs to Manzanares from Plaza de Castilla in Madrid. It costs 310 ptas.

The mountain town of **Cercedilla** and the area surrounding it are popular with hikers and mountain bikers. Several trails are marked out through the Sierra, the main one known as the Cuerda Larga or Cuerda Castellana. This is a forest track that takes in 55 peaks between the Puerto de Somosierra in the north and Puerto de la Cruz Verde in the south-west. It would take days to complete, but shorter walks include day excursions up the Valle de la Fuenfría and a climb up Monte de Siete Picos.

You can get information at the Centro de Información Valle de la Fuenfría (☎ 91 852 22 13), a couple of kilometres from Cercedilla train station. Accommodation in the area is scarce.

When winter snows fall, skiing is possible in the mountains on the pistes of Navacerrada (☎ 91 852 14 35), Cotos (☎ 91 852 08 57) and Valdesqui (☎ 91 852 04 16), just on the border with Segovia province. Snowless years are common and the available pistes are not extensive, but it's a popular business with madrileños at the weekend, when the area should be avoided. Navacerrada is the main centre and there are 13km of mostly easy – and frustratingly short – runs.

You can reach Navacerrada by train from Cercedilla (26 minutes; up to nine a day) or by bus from Madrid (station at Paseo de la Florida 11). During winter a special train service, known as the Tren de la Nieve, operates from Cercedilla to the pistes of Navacerrada and Cotos (from where it's a 20-minute walk to Valdesqui).

Ávila
postcode 05080 • pop 47,650 • elevation 1128m
Huddled behind hefty defensive walls, Ávila must be one of the chilliest cities in Spain. Known for its long and bitter winters, it is a remarkable sight for the visitor and is particularly pleasant in summer.

History According to myth, one of Hercules' sons founded Ávila. The more prosaic truth, however, gives the honour to obscure Iberian tribes, who were soon assimilated into Celtic society and later largely Romanised and Christianised. For almost 300 years, Ávila changed hands regularly between Muslims and Christians, until the fall of Toledo to Alfonso VI in 1085.

In the following centuries, 'Ávila of the Knights' became an important commercial centre. Fray Tomás de Torquemada was busy at the end of the 15th century organising the most brutal phase of the Spanish Inquisition. He ended his days in Ávila. Decades later, Santa Teresa began her difficult mystical journey and the unwelcome campaign to reform the Carmelites in the same city. By the time Teresa died in 1582, Ávila's golden days were over, and the city has only recently begun to shake off the deep slumber of neglect that ensued.

Orientation The old centre is enclosed by a rough quadrangle of robust walls at the western end of town, with the cathedral butting into the walls at their eastern extremity. The RENFE train station is about a 10-minute walk north-east of the cathedral, while the bus station *(estación de autobuses)* is a little closer, just off Avenida de Madrid.

Information The helpful tourist office (☎ 920 21 13 87), Plaza de la Catedral 4, is open from 9 am to 2 pm and 5 to 7 pm Monday to Friday, and 10 am to 2 pm and 5 to 8 pm at the weekend. A municipal tourist

EXCURSIONS

ÁVILA

PLACES TO EAT
8 El Molino de la Losa
12 Hostal Mesón del Rastro
14 Posada de la Fruta
16 Restaurante El Ruedo

OLD CITY GATES
6 Puerta de San Vicente
7 Arco del Mariscal
9 Puerta del Carmen
10 Puerta del Puente
13 Puerta de Santa Teresa
19 Puerta del Rastro
22 Puerta del Alcázar
23 Puerta de los Leales

OTHER
1 Train Station (Renfe)
2 Bus Station (Estación de Autobuses)
3 Basílica de San Vicente
4 Tourist Information Kiosk
11 Convento de Santa Teresa
15 Iglesia de San Juan
17 Tourist Office
18 Monteporquera Ivande
20 Entrance to City Walls
21 Cathedral
22 Entrance to City Walls
24 Covento de San José
25 El Monasterio de Santo Tomás

information kiosk (☎ 920 35 71 26) also operates just outside the Puerta de San Vicente. It opens for the same hours, but only at the weekend, Semana Santa and (maybe) the summer months.

Cathedral The double vocation of Ávila's cathedral is symbolised in its menacing granite apse, which forms the central bulwark in the eastern wall of the town. Around the western side, the main facade betrays the Romanesque origins of what is essentially the earliest Gothic church in Spain. It also betrays some unhappy 18th-century meddling in the main portal. Worth inspecting are the fine walnut choir stalls, while the Capilla Mayor boasts a *retablo* (altarpiece) mainly carried out by Pedro de Berruguete in the mid-15th century.

The cathedral and its museum are open from 10 am to 1 pm and 3.30 to 5 pm. From Easter to the end of September hours are extended to 8.30 am to 2 pm and 4 to 7 pm. Admission costs 250 ptas.

Basílica de San Vicente Lying outside the fortified gate of the same name, the Romanesque–Gothic basilica is striking in its subdued elegance. The Gothic elements were built over and around the much smaller Romanesque original and this remains evident today. The use of granite and sandstone in a seemingly haphazard fashion produces a strange visual effect. The Jardín de San Vicente across the road was, by the way, once the Roman cemetery.

The church is open from 10 am to 2 pm and 4 to 6 pm, and admission costs 200 ptas.

El Monasterio de Santo Tomás A grandiose combination of monastery and royal residence put up in haste by the Reyes Católicos (Catholic Monarchs), Fernando and Isabel, in 1482, this is formed by three interconnecting cloisters and the church. It is thought the Inquisitor Torquemada is buried in the sacristy. The monastery complex, about half a kilometre south-east of the cathedral in the new town, is open from 8 am (10 am from October to Easter) to 1.30 pm and 4 to 8 pm. Admis-

sion costs 100 ptas, plus 200 ptas for the adjoining museum.

In Santa Teresa's Footsteps Santa Teresa, the 16th-century mystic and ascetic, has left her mark all over the city. Born in 1515, she joined the Carmelites 20 years later. Shaken by a vision of hell in 1560, she undertook to reform the Carmelites, an arduous task that led her to found convents of the Carmelitas Descalzas across Spain. She also co-opted San Juan de la Cruz (St John of the Cross) to begin a similar reform in the masculine order, which earned him several stints incarcerated by the mainstream Carmelites.

The **Convento de Santa Teresa** was built over the saint's birthplace in 1636. In the tiny museum next door (through the souvenir shop) are a few bits of memorabilia and relics, including Teresa's ring finger and bone fragments of San Juan de la Cruz. The museum is open from 10 am to 2 pm and 4 to 7 pm daily, and admission costs 300 ptas.

Nearby, the **Iglesia de San Juan** on Plaza de la Victoria contains the font in which Teresa was baptised. A five-minute walk east of the cathedral is the **Convento de San José**, the first convent Teresa founded (1562). Its museum is replete with Teresian memorabilia and is open from 10 am to 2 pm and 4 to 7 pm, with shorter opening hours in winter. Admission costs 150 ptas.

City Walls With its eight monumental gates and 88 towers, Ávila's 2.5km-long *muralla* (city wall) is one of the best-preserved medieval defensive perimeters in the world.

For years it has been possible to walk along only a brief stretch of the eastern wall below the cathedral. It is open from 10 am to 6 pm Tuesday to Sunday, and you pay 200 ptas at a booth near Plaza de Calvo Sotelo. A longer stretch running north of the cathedral was opened in March 2000. You enter from below the arch of the Puerta de San Vicente. It's open from 10 am to 8 pm (7 pm in winter) and admission costs 400 ptas.

EXCURSIONS

Special Events Ávila's principal festival (15 October) takes place, not surprisingly, in memory of Santa Teresa. The early-morning Good Friday procession of *pasos* (sculpted figures depicting the passion of Christ) is equally noteworthy.

Places to Eat A good moderately priced choice is the *Hostal Mesón del Rastro* (☎ *920 21 12 18, Plaza del Rastro 1)*. The set meal is good value and the *comedor* (dining room), with its dark wood beams and wrought-iron work, exudes Castilian charm. Also good and with alfresco dining is the *Posada de la Fruta* (☎ *920 25 47 02, Plaza de Pedro Dávila 8)*. Succulent meat mains come in at around 2000 ptas. *Restaurante El Ruedo* (☎ *920 21 31 98, Calle de Enrique Larreta 7)* is an unassuming place that offers a reasonable set meal for 1490 ptas.

Just outside town in an old mill by the river is the atmospheric *El Molino de la Losa* (☎ *920 21 11 01, Bajada de la Losa 12)*. The food, typical Castilian cooking with roasts at the fore, is good quality and affordable.

Don't miss the local sweet-tooth speciality – *yemas*, a scrummy, sticky business made of egg yolk and sugar. To get a hold of these and other local specialities, head for Mantequerías Irande (☎ 920 21 30 55), Plaza del Teniente Arévalo 8.

Getting There & Away The Larrea bus company (☎ 91 539 00 05) runs three or four services to Ávila from the Estación Sur de Autobuses in Madrid. The one-way trip costs 910 ptas and travel time is about two hours. It's easier to get the train, of which up to 24 run daily to and from Madrid's Chamartín station (800 ptas; 1½ to two hours).

By car from Madrid, you need to get onto the N-VI. You can follow this or the parallel A-6 tollway as far as Villacastín, where you need to bear south-west along the N-110. You could also take the M-505 (which later becomes the C-505) via El Escorial, which branches off the N-VI just before Las Rozas.

Segovia

postcode 40080 • pop 54,012 • elevation 1002m

To some, the ridge-top city of Segovia resembles a warship ploughing through the sea of Castile. The town has a surprising array of monuments, and those contemplating visiting Segovia as a day trip from Madrid will have a full program.

History The Celtic settlement of Segobriga was occupied by the Romans in 80 BC. Later, as Christian Spain recovered from the initial shock of the Muslim attack, Segovia became a front-line city until the invaders were finally evicted from central Spain in 1085. A favourite residence of Castile's roaming royalty, the city backed Isabel and saw her proclaimed queen in the Iglesia de San Miguel in 1474. In 1520, the rebellious Comuneros, who rose against Carlos I, found unequivocal support in Segovia, where they were led by Juan Bravo. From then on it was all downhill for the town until the 1960s, when tourism and the introduction of some light industry helped it pull itself up by the bootstraps.

Orientation The old town of Segovia is strung out along a ridge, peaking in the fanciful towers of the Alcázar to the west. If you arrive by train or bus, the local bus will take you to Plaza Mayor, the heart of the city. The main road leading downhill from Plaza Mayor to the aqueduct *(acueducto)* and the new town is a pedestrian thoroughfare that changes name several times along the way (Calle de Isabel la Católica, Calle de Juan Bravo and Calle de Cervantes); locals know the length of it simply as Calle Real.

Information The main tourist office (☎ 921 43 03 34), Plaza Mayor 10, is open from 9 am to 2 pm and 5 to 7 pm Monday to Friday, and 10 am to 2 pm and 5 to 8 pm at the weekend. The municipal tourist office (☎ 921 44 03 02), Plaza del Azoguejo 1, is open from 10 am to 8 pm daily.

Aqueduct & Around The 894m-long granite-block bridge you see today, made

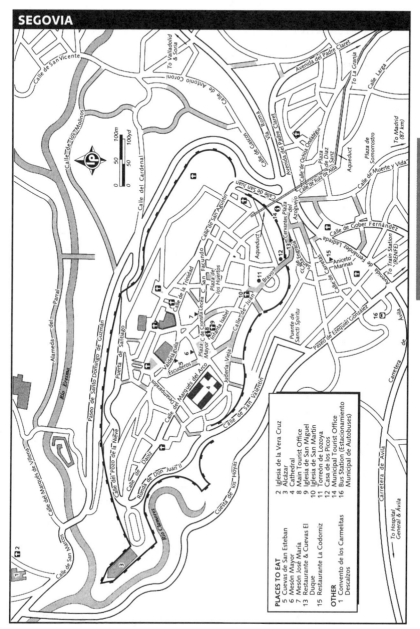

SEGOVIA

PLACES TO EAT
5 Cuevas de San Esteban
6 Mesón Mayor
7 Mesón José María
13 Restaurante & Cuevas El Duque
15 Restaurante La Codorniz

OTHER
1 Convento de los Carmelitas Descalzos
2 Iglesia de la Vera Cruz
3 Alcázar
4 Cathedral
8 Main Tourist Office
9 Iglesia de San Miguel
10 Iglesia de San Martín
11 Torreón de Lozoya
12 Casa de los Picos
14 Municipal Tourist Office
16 Bus Station (Estacionamiento Municipal de Autobuses)

EXCURSIONS

up of 163 arches, is the most extraordinary element of the engineering effort that went into the once 15km-long Roman aqueduct raised here in the 1st century AD. It measures up to 28m high, and not a drop of mortar was used to hold the thing together – just good old Roman know-how. For almost 2000 years it had withstood the elements, but by 1993 experts were predicting it would start falling apart if urgent action were not taken. Seven years and one billion pesetas later, an intensive research and restoration program that should keep it standing a while longer was completed. For the first time in 40 years, water began to flow along the top of the structure in February 2000. Climb the steps up to the old town walls for the best view.

Cathedral From Plaza del Azoguejo, Calle Real climbs into the innards of Segovia. On the way you pass the Renaissance **Casa de los Picos** and later **Plaza de San Martín**. The latter is presided over by a statue of Juan Bravo, the 14th-century **Torreón de Lozoya** and the Romanesque **Iglesia de San Martín**.

The shady **Plaza Mayor** is the nerve centre of old Segovia, lined by an eclectic assortment of buildings, arcades and cafes.

The **Iglesia de San Miguel**, where Isabel was crowned Queen of Castile, recedes humbly into the background before the splendour of the cathedral across the square.

Completed in 1577, 50 years after its Romanesque predecessor had burned to the ground in the revolt of the Comuneros, the **Cathedral** is a last, powerful expression of Gothic art (with some baroque afterthoughts thrown in) in Spain. The cathedral's museum (containing religious art) and cloister are open from 9 am to 7 pm (9.30 am to 6 pm from October to April) daily. Admission costs 300 ptas.

Alcázar Walt Disney liked it so much he made one in California. Blessed with unrestricted views right around, the site of Segovia's Alcázar has been fortified since Roman days. It takes its name from the Arabic *al-qasr* (castle) and was rebuilt and expanded in the 13th and 14th centuries. Felipe II added the touch of the slate witch's hats, but the whole lot burned down in 1862 and was subsequently painstakingly rebuilt, albeit as an over-the-top version of the original. It is open from 10 am to 7 pm (6 pm in winter) daily. Admission costs 400 ptas. It's free for EU citizens on Tuesdays.

JANE SMITH

The 2000-year-old Roman aqueduct in Segovia stands proudly without the aid of mortar.

euro currency converter 1000 ptas = €6.01

Churches & Convents Segovia is blessed by a rich smorgasbord of religious buildings, many of them in a disarmingly attractive Romanesque style, frequently accompanied by mudéjar bell towers and covered verandahs.

Possibly the most interesting of Segovia's churches – and the best preserved of its kind in Europe – is the twelve-sided **Iglesia de la Vera Cruz**, just outside the town in the valley facing the Alcázar. It was built in the 13th century by the legendary Knights Templar on the pattern of the church of the Holy Sepulchre in Jerusalem, and long housed what was said to be a piece of the *Vera Cruz* (True Cross). The church is open from 10.30 am to 1.30 pm and 3.30 to 7 pm (to 6 pm in autumn and winter) from Tuesday to Sunday, and admission costs 200 ptas. Nearby, San Juan de la Cruz is buried in the **Convento de los Carmelitas Descalzos**.

Places to Eat Segovians seem obsessed with roasts. Every second restaurant proudly boasts its *horno de asar* (roasts) and they say that 'pork has 40 flavours – all of them good'. Here the speciality is *cochinillo asado* (roast suckling pig) and there isn't a restaurant, no matter how unlikely, that won't do its best to serve it up.

A good little place for a comparatively cheap bite is the **Cuevas de San Esteban** (☎ *921 46 09 82, Calle de Valdeláguila 15*). It serves a double role as eatery and bar. The set lunch menu is filling and costs 900 ptas.

A widely respected favourite is **Mesón José María** (☎ *921 46 11 11, Calle del Cronista Lecea 11*), where mains cost about 1500 to 2600 ptas.

Pricier is **Mesón Mayor** (☎ *921 46 09 15, Plaza Mayor 3*), which is popular and recommended for traditional dishes. The set menu, bound to include cochinillo, costs 2500 ptas.

At **Restaurante La Codorniz** (☎ *921 46 38 87, Calle de Aniceto Marinas 1*) you can expect to pay close to 3000 ptas for a good main meal. **Restaurante El Duque** (☎ *921 46 24 87, Calle de Cervantes 12*), a short way up from the aqueduct, has been going since 1895 and is Segovia's oldest dining

establishment. For less formality, try its **Cuevas**, in the same building but entered at Calle de Santa Engracia 10. For a full meal you'll be lucky to get much change from 4000 ptas.

Getting There & Away The Estacionamiento Municipal de Autobuses (☎ 921 42 77 07) is just off Paseo de Ezequiel González, near the junction with Avenida de Fernández Ladreda. Up to 16 buses run daily from Madrid (Paseo de la Florida 11). The trip costs 765 ptas and takes 1½ hours.

Up to nine trains run daily from Chamartín and Atocha but they can take more than two hours.

Of the two main roads from the N-VI, which links Madrid and Galicia, the N-603 is the prettier. The alternative N-110 cuts south-west across to Ávila and north-east to the Madrid–Burgos highway.

Around Segovia
La Granja de San Ildefonso It is not hard to see why the Bourbon king Felipe V chose this site, nestling in the western foothills of the Sierra de Guadarrama 12km east of Segovia, to create his version of Versailles, the palace of his French grandfather Louis XIV, the Sun King. In 1720 French architects and gardeners, with some Italian help, began laying out the elaborate gardens. El Real Sitio de la Granja de San Ildefonso remained a favourite summer residence with Spanish royalty for the next couple of centuries – and is now a very popular weekend destination for stressed madrileños.

La Granja's centrepiece is the garden's 28 fountains. Some of them are switched on from about 5 pm on Wednesday, weekends and holidays from April to the end of September and during Semana Santa. Three days a year (30 May, 25 July, 25 August) all the fountains are switched on. The gardens open from 10 am to sunset daily, and admission is free except when the fountains are on, when you have to purchase a 375 ptas ticket.

The 300-room Palacio Real, badly damaged by a fire in 1918 and subsequently restored, is impressive, but perhaps the lesser of La Granja's jewels. You can visit about half of the palace, including its Museo de Tapices (Tapestry Museum). The palace is open from 10 am to 6 pm daily, June to September; and 10 am to 1.30 pm and 3 to 5 pm daily, the rest of the year. Admission costs 700 ptas (students 300 ptas).

The easiest way to get here is by bus from Segovia, Up to a dozen buses run each day.

EAST OF MADRID
Alcalá de Henares
postcode 28801 • pop 163,700
• elevation 587m

A little way north of the Roman town of Complutum (of which nothing remains) and 35km east of Madrid on the N-II to Zaragoza, Alcalá de Henares entered a period of greatness when Cardinal Cisneros founded a university here in 1486. Now centred on a much restored Renaissance building in the centre of what is virtually a satellite of Madrid, the university was long one of the country's main seats of learning.

The town is also dear to the hearts of Spaniards as the birthplace of the country's literary figurehead, Miguel de Cervantes Saavedra (see Literature under Arts in the Facts About Madrid chapter for some more details).

You can wander through parts of the universidad any time. Various faculty buildings, dating mostly from the 17th century, are scattered around the centre of town and you can wander about them from 9 am to 9 pm Monday to Saturday.

The core of the university is the Colegio Mayor de San Ildefonso. You can wander through here too, but to see inside the buildings you need to join a guided tour. The ornate entrance, facing Plaza de San Diego, is in the plateresque style. Of particular interest inside are the Paraninfo (the auditorium where Spain's top literary prize, the Premio Cervantes, is awarded each year), with a fine mudéjar ceiling, and the Capilla de San Ildefonso. The latter contains the tomb of Cardinal Cisneros. Tours take place five times between 11.30 am and 5.30 pm on

weekdays, and 10 times between 11 am and 7 pm at the weekend and during holidays. The visits cost 350 ptas.

It is thought Cervantes was born at Calle de la Imagen 2, on the corner of Calle Mayor. Here the locals have re-created his place of birth in the **Museo Casa Natal de Miguel de Cervantes**. They have filled it with period furniture and bits and pieces relating to his life. It is open from 10.15 am to 1.30 pm and 4 to 6.30 pm Tuesday to Sunday.

Other sights around town worth seeking out are the early-17th-century Cistercian **Monasterio de San Bernardo** (open for infrequent but daily guided tours which cost 350 ptas) and the **Capilla del Oidor**, with some Gothic–mudéjar decoration and a reconstruction of the font in which Cervantes is said to have been baptised.

The *Hostería del Estudiante* (☎ 91 888 03 30, Calle de los Colegios 3) is an expensive but charming restaurant backing onto the Paraninfo in the main university building. You will probably pay around 5000 ptas for fine Castilian cooking in this Renaissance building.

The easiest way to reach Alcalá is by one of the frequent cercanías trains shuttling between Madrid (Chamartín) and Guadalajara. The fare is 350 ptas and the trip takes 33 minutes.

SOUTH OF MADRID
Aranjuez
postcode 28300 • pop 38,680 • elevation 489m

A refreshing patch of green in sun-drenched central Spain, Aranjuez continues to play its centuries-old role as a haven from the capital, 48km to the north. The difference is that it's no longer a royal playground – the privilege has been extended to all and sundry.

The tourist office (☎ 91 891 04 27), Plaza de San Antonio 9, is open from 10 am to 2 pm and 4 to 6 pm Monday to Friday.

Palacio Real When Felipe II built his summer palace here on the lush banks of the Tajo in the 16th century, there had already been a country residence on the site for 200 years. What was in Felipe's day a modest 20-room affair, later destroyed by fire, became under his successors the 18th-century excess that stands today. With more than 300 rooms and inspired by Versailles (an ever-popular model with European monarchs), it is filled with a cornucopia of ornamentation. Of all the rulers who spent time here, Carlos III and Isabel II left the greatest mark.

After touring the palace, take a stroll in the gardens. Within their shady perimeter you'll find two other man-made attractions. The **Casa de Marinos** contains royal pleasure boats from days gone by. Farther away, towards Chinchón, is the **Casa del Labrador**, a tasteless royal jewellery box crammed to the rafters with gold, silver, silk and some second-rate art. The garden itself is a minor miracle, a mix of local and exotic species that have rubbed along nicely since Spanish botanists and explorers started bringing back seeds from all over the world in the 19th century.

The Palacio Real is open from 10 am to 6.30 pm Tuesday to Sunday (to 5.30 pm from October to April). Admission costs 700 ptas, but is free for EU citizens on Wednesday. Admission to the Casa del Labrador costs 700 ptas (you must book ahead on ☎ 91 891 03 05), and the Casa de Marinos costs 350 ptas. The gardens (the palace ticket covers all the gardens) are open from 10 am to sunset, year round.

Places to Eat One of the best deals in town is the *Casa de Comidas Gobernación* (☎ *91 891 65 76, Calle de Gobernación 2)*, just off the central arcaded Plaza de San Antonio. This place is popular and offers a set lunch costing 1100 ptas.

La Rana Verde (☎ 91 891 13 25, Calle de la Reina 1), on the Tajo, is the town's best-known restaurant but rather tired. Still, you may want to shell out 3000 ptas for frogs' legs and the riverside location.

Getting There & Away The Automnibus Urbanos bus company (☎ 91 530 46 06) runs 31 daily services (405 ptas), with 10 on

Sunday, from Estación Sur de Autobuses in Madrid. The trip takes an hour.

Frequent cercanías trains (line C-3) connect with Madrid's Atocha station (430 ptas; 45 minutes), and occasional trains go to/from Toledo.

Chinchón
postcode 28370 • pop 3856 • elevation 753m

Home of a well-known brew of *anís*, the aniseed-based heart-starter favoured by not a few Spaniards, Chinchón is an agreeable little settlement 50km south-east of Madrid.

The focal point is the **Plaza Mayor**, ringed by centuries-old two- and three-tiered balconies, most of which now accommodate dining madrileños. The plaza also doubles as a bullring. Just north of the plaza lies the 16th-century **Iglesia de la Asunción**, containing an *Asunción* attributed to Goya. On a bluff to the south stand the ruins of a late-16th-century **castle**.

You can scout around the several restaurants right on Plaza Mayor, or head away from the centre. A special but pricey option is the *Mesón Cuevas del Vino (☎ 91 894 02 06, Calle de Benito Hortelano 13)*. This cavernous bodega, lined with huge wine barrels and popular with weekenders from Madrid, serves great Castilian food, but you won't get away with less than 3000 ptas per person. It's closed on Tuesday.

If you want to buy a bottle of the local firewater, head for the Alcoholera de Chinchón on Plaza Mayor.

Buses of the La Veloz company (☎ 91 409 76 02) run regularly (405 ptas; 55 minutes) between Chinchón and Madrid (Avenida del Mediterráneo 49). There are four a day (two on Saturday, none on Sunday) to and from Aranjuez (Calle del Almibar, near the Plaza de Toros; 125 ptas).

Toledo
postcode 45080 • pop 66,989 • elevation 529m

They still call it La Ciudad Imperial – and for a while Toledo indeed looked set to become the capital of a united Spain. The Iberian Peninsula's Rome and something of

EXCURSIONS

an army town, this remarkable medieval city bristles with monumental splendour.

Like a creaky museum, spruced up but not without problems, *la ciudad de la tres culturas* (the city of the three cultures) has survived as a unique centre where Romans and Visigoths once ruled and, for a time, Jews, Muslims and Christians lived in comparative harmony. The artistic legacy is a complex cross-breed of European and Oriental values that can be seen elsewhere in Spain, but rarely with such intensity.

History Its strategic position made ancient Toletum an important waystation in the days of Rome's domination of the Iberian Peninsula, and in the 6th century the Visigothic king Atanagild made his capital here.

The city also became the scene of endless feuds between Visigothic nobles which so weakened their state that when the Muslims crossed the Strait of Gibraltar in 711 they had little problem in taking Toledo on their lightning advance north. It remained an important Muslim centre for the next three centuries.

Alfonso VI marched into Toledo in 1085 and shortly thereafter the Vatican recognised it as seat of the Church in Spain. Carlos I toyed with the idea of making Toledo his permanent capital in the 16th century, but his successor, Felipe II, dashed any such ideas with his definitive move to Madrid.

In the early months of the 1936–9 Civil War, Nationalist troops (and some civilians) were kept under siege in the Alcázar, but were eventually relieved by a force from the south.

Orientation Toledo is built upon a hill around which the Río Tajo (Tagus) flows on three sides; modern suburbs spread beyond the river and walls of the old town *(casco)*.

The bus station *(estación de autobuses)* lies just to the north-east of the old town *(casco antiguo)*, and the train station lies a little farther east across the Tajo. Both are connected by local bus to the centre.

Whether you arrive on foot or by bus, you are bound to turn up sooner or later at Plaza de Zocodover (known as Zoco to the locals), the main square of the old town. From it spreads out an at times confusing medieval labyrinth.

Information The main tourist office (☎ 925 22 08 43, fax 925 25 26 48) is just outside Toledo's northern main gate, the Puerta Nueva de Bisagra. It is open from 9 am to 6 pm Monday to Friday, until 7 pm on Saturday and until 3 pm on Sunday. A smaller, more helpful, information office is open in the Ayuntamiento (Town Hall), across from the cathedral, from 10.30 am to 2.30 pm and 4.30 to 7 pm (mornings only on Monday).

Zocodover From 1465 until the 1960s Zocodover was the scene of El Martes, the city's Tuesday market and successor to the Arab *souq ad-dawab* (livestock market) from which the square derives its name.

Alcázar Just south off Zocodover, at the highest point in the city, looms the Alcázar. Abd ar-Rahman III raised a fortress *(al-qasr)* here in the 10th century, and Covarrubias and Herrera rebuilt it as a royal residence for Carlos I. However, the court moved to Madrid and the Alcázar eventually became the Academia de la Infantería (now on the opposite bank of the Tajo).

The Alcázar was largely destroyed during the Republican siege of Franco's forces in 1936, but Franco had it rebuilt and turned into a military museum. Plans are afoot to transfer the Museo del Ejército from Madrid to the Alcázar as well. It is open from 10 am to 2.30 pm Tuesday to Sunday. Admission costs 200 ptas.

Museo de Santa Cruz Just outside what were once the Arab city walls along Zocodover, this 16th-century former hospital on Calle de Cervantes holds several El Grecos and a mixed bag of other items, including war standards from the Battle of Lepanto in 1571. It is open from 10 am to 6.30 pm (until 2 pm on Sunday) but it shuts from 2 pm to 4 pm on Monday. Admission costs 200 ptas (free on Saturday afternoon and Sunday). In 2000, special exhibitions celebrating the birth of the emperor Carlos I were being planned, which meant some of the permanent displays were likely to become inaccessible.

Cathedral From the earliest days of the Visigothic occupation of ancient Roman Toletum, the site of the cathedral has been the centre of worship in the city. For several centuries it was home to the central mosque, replaced in the 13th century by an essentially Gothic structure. Mudéjar, Spanish Renaissance and other elements jostle for attention, and behind the main altar lies a masterpiece of *churrigueresque* baroque, the Transparente.

All the chapels and rooms off the main church body are worth visiting. Among the 'don't misses' are the **Capilla de la Torre** (Tower Chapel), in the north-western corner, and the **sacristía** (sacristy). The latter contains what amounts to a small gallery of El Greco, while the former houses what must be one of the most extraordinary monstrances in existence, the Custodia de Arfe, by the celebrated 16th-century goldsmith Enrique de Arfe. With 18kg of pure gold and 183kg of silver, this conceit bristles with some 260 statuettes.

The cathedral is open to visitors from 10.30 am to 6 pm (7 pm in summer). Admission costs 700 ptas.

El Greco Trail Hordes of tourists pile down Toledo's narrow streets searching out the paintings of El Greco. First stop is the **Iglesia de Santo Tomé** on Plaza del Conde, which contains his masterpiece, *El Entierro del Conde de Orgaz* (The Burial of the Count of Orgaz). The church is open from 10 am to 6.45 pm and admission costs 200 ptas.

In 1910 Marqués de la Vega-Inclán set up the **Casa y Museo de El Greco** in a house on Calle de Samuel Leví, but it is unlikely that El Greco actually ever lived here. Inside you will find *Vista y Plano de Toledo* and about 20 of the Cretan's minor works. It's open from 10 am to 2 pm and 4 to 6 pm (closed Sunday evening and Monday). Admission costs 200 ptas. At the time of writing part of the house was closed.

If you want to develop your own El

El Greco in Toledo

After a long apprenticeship in Crete, where he was born in 1541, Domenikos Theotokopoulos moved to Venice in 1567 to be schooled as a Renaissance artist. Under the influence of masters such as Tintoretto, he learned to extract the maximum effect from few colours, concentrating the observer's interest in the faces of his portraits and leaving the rest in relative obscurity, a characteristic that remained one of his hallmarks. From 1572 he learned from the Mannerists of Rome and the work left behind by Michelangelo.

Theotokopoulos came to Toledo in 1577 hoping to get a job decorating El Escorial. Things didn't quite work out, and Felipe II rejected him as a court artist. In Toledo, itself recently knocked back as permanent seat of the royal court, the man who came to be known simply as El Greco felt sufficiently at home to hang around, painting in a style different from anything local artists were producing. He even managed to cultivate a healthy clientele and command good prices.

His rather high opinion of himself and his work, however, did not endear him to all and sundry. He had to do without the patronage of the cathedral administrators, who were the first of many clients to haul him to court for his obscenely high fees.

El Greco liked the high life and, with things going well in the last decade of the 16th century, he took rooms in a mansion on the Paseo del Tránsito, where he often hired musicians to accompany his meals.

As Toledo's fortunes declined, so did El Greco's personal finances, and, although the works of his final years are among his best, he often found himself unable to pay the rent. He died in 1614, leaving his works scattered about the city, where many have remained to this day.

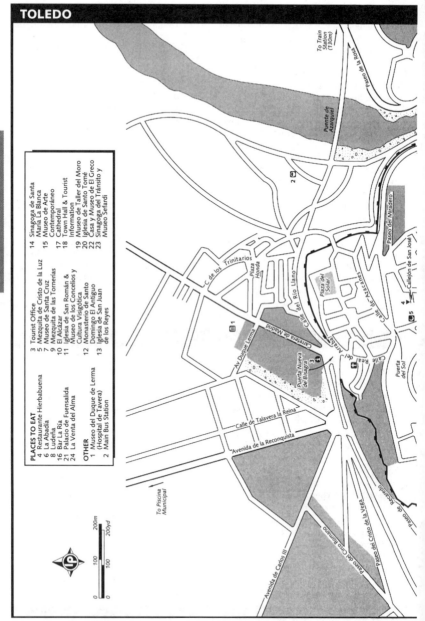

TOLEDO

PLACES TO EAT
4   Restaurante Hierbabuena
6   La Abadía
8   Ludeña
16 Bar La Ria
21 Palacio de Fuensalida
24 La Venta del Alma

OTHER
1   Museo del Duque de Lerma
    (Hospital de Tavera)
2   Main Bus Station
3   Tourist Office
5   Mezquita de Cristo de la Luz
7   Museo de Santa Cruz
9   Mezquita de las Tornerías
10 El Alcázar
11 Iglesia de San Román &
    Museo de los Concelios y
    Cultura Visigótica
12 Monasterio de Santo
    Domingo El Antiguo
13 Iglesia de San Juan
    de los Reyes
14 Sinagoga de Santa
    María La Blanca
15 Museo de Arte
    Contemporáneo
17 Cathedral
18 Town Hall & Tourist
    Information
19 Museo de Taller del Moro
20 Iglesia de Santo Tomé
22 Casa y Museo de El Greco
23 Sinagoga del Tránsito y
    Museo Sefardí

euro currency converter 1000 ptas = €6.01

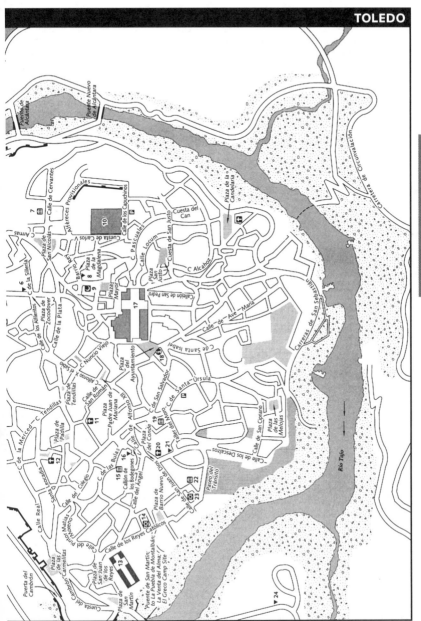

TOLEDO

EXCURSIONS

Greco trail, other places in Toledo where you can see his works include the Museo de Santa Cruz, the sacristy of the cathedral, the Monasterio de Santo Domingo El Antiguo and the Hospital de Tavera (Museo del Duque de Lerma).

Jewish Quarter Near El Greco's supposed house is what was once the *judería*, or Jewish quarter. Of the two synagogues that survive, the 14th-century **Sinagoga del Tránsito** on Calle de los Reyes Católicos is the most interesting. Its main prayer hall has been expertly restored and the mudéjar decoration is striking. The synagogue's **Museo Sefardi** affords insights into the history of Jewish culture in Spain. The complex is open from 10 am to 2 pm and 4 to 6 pm (closed Sunday morning and Monday). Admission costs 400 ptas (free on Saturday afternoon and Sunday).

A short way north along Calle de los Reyes Católicos, the **Sinagoga de Santa María La Blanca** is characterised by the horseshoe arches that delineate the five naves – classic Almohad architecture. It is open from 10 am to 2 pm and 3.30 to 6 pm (7 pm in summer). Admission costs 200 ptas.

San Juan de los Reyes A little farther north lies one of the city's most visible sights. The Franciscan monastery and church were founded by Fernando and Isabel, who had planned to be buried here until they took Granada in 1492 and opted for the brilliance of the southern city's Muslim palace.

Begun by the Breton architect Juan Güas in 1477, the Iglesia de San Juan de los Reyes was finished only in 1606. Throughout the church and two-storey cloister the coat of arms of Fernando and Isabel (in other words of the united Spain) dominates, and the chains of Christian prisoners liberated in Granada hang from the walls. The church and cloister are open from 10 am to 1.45 pm and 3.30 to 6.45 pm. Admission costs 200 ptas.

Muslim Toledo Little that is specifically Muslim remains. On the northern slopes of

town you'll find the **Mezquita de Cristo de la Luz**, a modest mosque built around 1000 AD that suffered the usual fate of being converted into a church. It is now partly covered by researchers' scaffolding and getting in is virtually impossible. You can get into the **Mezquita de las Tornerías**, where some remnants of the mosque can be seen, along with the base of a Roman tower that appears to have been part of an ingenious system for supplying water to ancient Toletum. It is now used for arts and crafts exhibitions and is generally open from 10 am to 2 pm and 5 to 8 pm. Admission is free.

Museums Round the corner from the Iglesia de Santo Tomé is the 14th-century **Taller del Moro**. It houses a modest collection of mudéjar decorative items and is open from 10 am to 2 pm and 4 to 6 pm (closed Sunday afternoon and Monday). Admission costs 100 ptas.

The **Museo de Arte Contemporáneo**, housed in the restored 16th-century mudéjar Casa de las Cadenas, in the lane of the same name, is home to a small collection of Spanish modern art. Opening hours and admission are as for the Taller del Moro.

The Iglesia de San Román, an impressive hybrid of mudéjar and Renaissance styles, houses the **Museo de los Concilios y Cultura Visigótica**. The documents, jewellery and other items are perhaps less interesting than the building itself. Opening hours and admission are also as for Taller del Moro.

Farther north, below Plaza de Padilla, the **Monasterio de Santo Domingo El Antiguo** is one of the oldest convents in Toledo, dating from the 11th century. It houses some of El Greco's early commissions (most are copies). It's open from 11 am to 1.30 pm and 4 to 7 pm (afternoons only on Sunday). Admission costs 150 ptas.

Outside the city walls on the road to Madrid, the **Museo del Duque de Lerma** is in what was the Hospital de Tavera. Built in 1541, it now contains an interesting art collection, including some of El Greco's last works. It is open from 10.30 am to 1.30 pm and 3.30 to 6 pm daily. Admission costs 500 ptas.

Special Events The feast of Corpus Christi falls on the Thursday of the ninth week after Easter and is by far the most extraordinary event on Toledo's religious calendar. Several days of festivities culminate in a procession in which the massive Custodia de Arfe (see Cathedral earlier in this section) is paraded around the city.

Places to Eat The cuisine of Toledo, and indeed of the whole region, is based on simple peasant fare. Partridge, cooked in a variety of fashions, is probably the premier dish and is particularly representative of Toledo. *Carcamusa*, a meat dish, is also typical, as is *cuchifritos*, a kind of potpourri of lamb, tomato and egg cooked in white wine with saffron.

An excellent little place for a full meal (set lunch for 1200 ptas), or simply a beer and tapas, is *Ludeña* (☎ 925 22 33 84, *Plaza de la Magdalena 13*). It's closed on Wednesday. *Palacio de Fuensalida* (☎ 925 22 20 88, *Plaza del Conde 2*), in the palace of the same name and near the Iglesia de Santo Tomé, serves paella under vaulted ceilings. They do a solid set lunch costing 1100 ptas.

As well as being a popular bar, *La Abadía* (☎ 925 25 07 46, *Plaza de San Nicolás 3*) offers excellent downstairs dining with typical Toledan dishes such as *perdiz estofada* (stewed partridge). The set lunch *menú*, at about 1275 ptas, is reliable. For Toledo's best seafood, *Bar La Ría* (☎ 925 25 25 32, *Callejón de los Bodegones 6*) is hard to beat.

Restaurante Hierbabuena (☎ 925 22 39 24, *Callejón de San José 17*) offers costly but imaginatively classy fare. It is closed on Monday.

Just outside Toledo is a charming old roadside hostelry, *La Venta del Alma* (*Carretera de Piedrabuena 25*). Cross the Puente de San Martín and turn left up the hill – it's a couple of hundred metres up on your left.

Getting There & Away Galiano Continental buses run every half-hour between Madrid (Estación Sur) and Toledo from 6.30 am to 10 pm (to 11.30 pm on Sunday

and holidays). Direct buses (585 ptas; 50 minutes) run roughly every hour; the remainder call at all villages.

Although the trains operating from Madrid (Atocha station) are more pleasant than the bus, there are only 10 of them per day (the first at 7.05 am, the last at 8.40 pm). A one-way ticket costs 660 ptas.

The N-401 connects Toledo with Madrid. Heading south, you can take the same road to Ciudad Real, from where it becomes the N-420 to Córdoba.

Córdoba
postcode 14080 • pop 309,961
• elevation 123m

It may seem strange to include Córdoba, a city 400km south of Madrid, among suggestions for day trips from Madrid. But if you take the high-speed AVE train you can be there in 1¾ hours, not much longer than the trip to Segovia.

The main attraction is the magnificent Mezquita, surely the most extraordinary hybrid of grand mosque and Christian church in the world. Around it weave the colourful lanes of the city's old quarter, where the scent of orange trees and foliage-filled patios mingles in the air with the animated hum of sherry-drinking punters in some fine old *bodegas* (wine bars).

History The Roman colony of Corduba, founded in 152 BC, was the capital first of Hispania Ulterior province then, after a reorganisation in the 1st century BC, of Baetica province. In 711 AD it fell to the Islamic invaders and soon became the Muslim capital of the peninsula, under the emir of Al-Andalus, Abd ar-Rahman I.

Córdoba's heyday came under Abd ar-Rahman III (912–61). In 929 he gave himself the title Caliph, setting the seal on Al-Andalus's de facto independence of the Abbasid caliphs in Baghdad. The city flourished and the court of Abd ar-Rahman III was frequented by Jewish, Arab and Christian scholars.

By the 11th century Córdoba was in decline and in 1236 Fernando III took it for the Christians. From then on it sank into

EXCURSIONS

provincial anonymity, although the arrival of industry in the 19th century reversed the downwards spiral.

Orientation Immediately north of the Río Guadalquivir is the old city, a warren of narrow streets focused on the Mezquita. The area north-west of the Mezquita was the Judería (Jewish quarter). The main square of the modern city is Plaza Tendillas, 500m north of the Mezquita.

Information The Junta de Andalucía tourist office (☎ 957 47 12 35) is housed in a 16th-century chapel facing the western side of the Mezquita, at Calle de Torrijos 10. It's open from 9.30 am to 8 pm Monday to Friday, 10 am to 8 pm on Saturday and 10 am to 2 pm on Sunday and holidays. It can close as early as 6 pm in slow periods.

The municipal tourist office (☎ 957 20 05 22), on Plaza de Judá Levi, opens from 8.30 am to 2.30 pm Monday to Friday, sometimes opening for extra hours in summer.

A tourist information kiosk at the train station opens from 10 am to 2 pm and 4.15 to 8 pm Monday to Friday.

Mezquita (Mosque) From 785 AD until well into the 10th century, construction continued on this grand central mosque of Córdoba. It has some truly beautiful architectural features, among them the rows of two-tier arches in mesmerising stripes of red brick and white stone, and the more elaborate arches, domes and decoration around the splendid *mihrab* (prayer niche). The outside of the building has thick stone walls punctuated by ornate gates.

What you see today, however, is not quite the grand mosque where Muslims gathered in the days of the Caliphate. For in the 16th century the Christian rulers of the city undertook a rather strange renovation – they plonked a cathedral smack in the middle of the mosque!

Of the 1300 pillars the mosque once contained, 850 remain. At first the Christians were content to make minimal alterations, but in the 16th century they ripped out the mosque's centre to allow construction of

the **Capilla Mayor** and **coro** (choir). The final result is a bizarre travesty, albeit a fascinating one, but we should be grateful that the Mezquita was not simply torn down, as happened frequently in other cities that fell to the Reconquista.

The main entrance is the Puerta del Perdón, a 14th-century mudéjar gateway on Calle Cardenal Herrero. The Mezquita (☎ 957 47 05 12) is open from 10 am to 7.30 pm Monday to Saturday, and 3.30 to 7.30 pm on Sunday, April to September; and 10 am to 5.30 pm Monday to Saturday, and 2 to 5.30 pm on Sunday and holidays, the rest of the year. Admission costs 800 ptas.

Beside the Puerta del Perdón a 16th-century tower replaces the original minaret. Inside is the pretty **Patio de los Naranjos** (Courtyard of the Orange Trees), from which a door leads into the Mezquita itself.

Judería (Jewish Quarter) The Judería, extending from the Mezquita almost to Avenida del Gran Capitán, is a maze of narrow streets and small plazas, of whitewashed buildings with flowers dripping from window boxes, and wrought-iron doorways giving glimpses of plant-filled patios.

The **Museo Taurino** (Bullfighting Museum) on Plaza de Maimónides celebrates Córdoba's legendary *toreros* (bullfighters). The museum is open from 10 am to 2 pm and 6 to 8 pm Tuesday to Saturday (4.30 to 6.30 pm from October to April), and 9.30 am to 3 pm on Sunday and holidays. Admission costs 450 ptas (free on Friday).

Just up Calle Judíos are the **Zoco**, a crafts centre with fairly up-market silver and leather goods for sale, and artisans at work, and the small 14th-century **Sinagoga** (synagogue). The latter is open from 10 am to 2 pm and 3.30 to 5.30 pm Tuesday to Saturday, and 10 am to 1.30 pm on Sunday and holidays. Admission costs 50 ptas (free for EU citizens).

Just west of the top of Calle Judíos is the **Puerta de Almodóvar**, an Islamic gate in the old city walls.

Alcázar de los Reyes Cristianos Southwest of the Mezquita, the Castle of the

euro currency converter 1000 ptas = €6.01